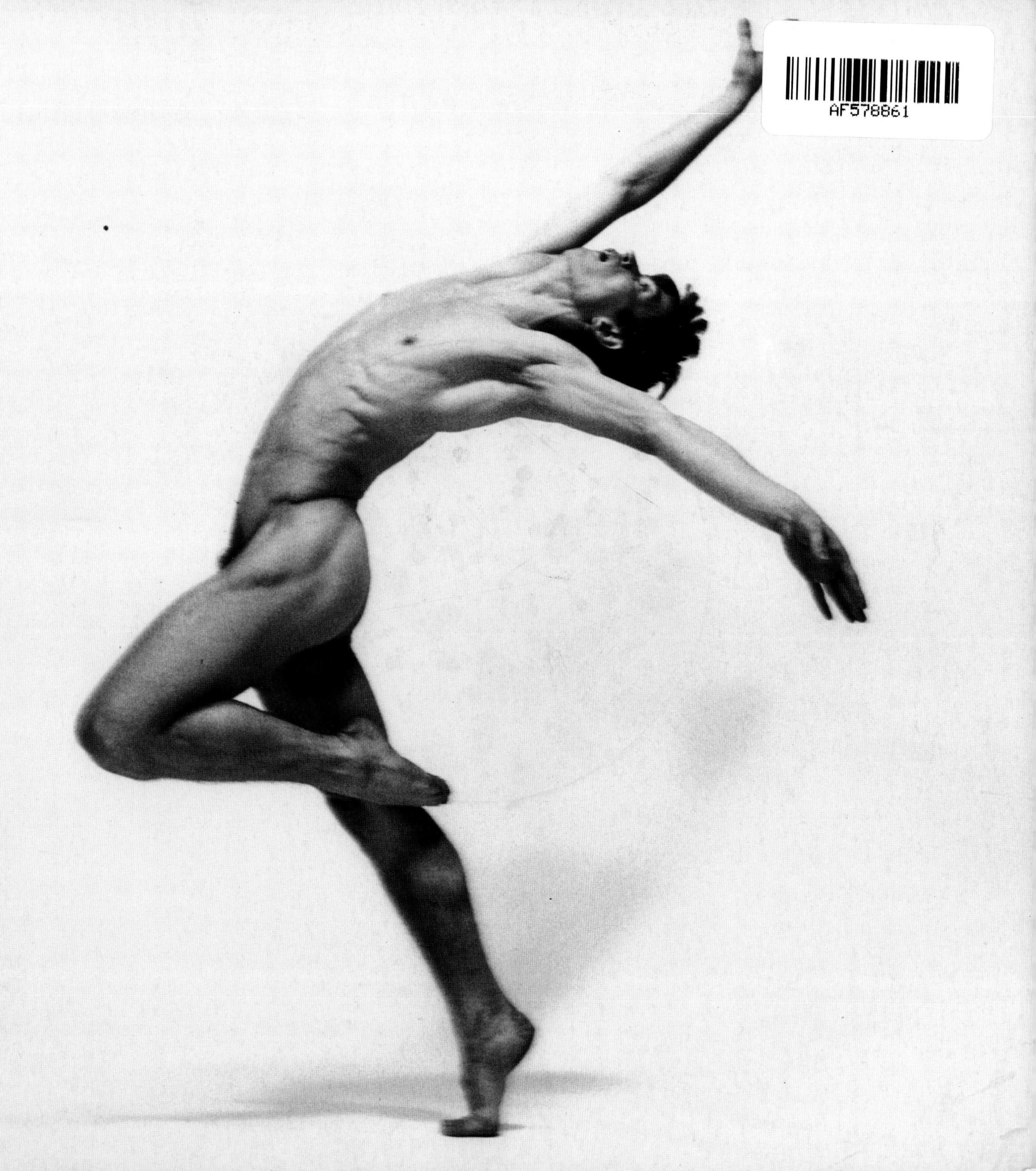

AF578861

THE NAKED

PORTRAIT

1900 to 2007

Martin Hammer

National Galleries of Scotland
Edinburgh
Compton Verney
Warwickshire

Published by the Trustees of the National Galleries of Scotland to accompany the exhibition *The Naked Portrait* held at the Scottish National Portrait Gallery, Edinburgh from 6 June until 2 September 2007 and Compton Verney, Warwickshire from 29 September until 9 December 2007.

Text © Martin Hammer and the Trustees of the National Galleries of Scotland

ISBN 978 1 903278 95 6

Designed and typeset in Haarlemmer and Helvetica by Dalrymple
Printed in Belgium on Chromomat 150gsm by Die Keure

Cover image: Richard Avedon *Rudolf Nureyev, Dancer, 25 July 1961, Paris*
The Richard Avedon Foundation

The proceeds from the sale of this book go
towards supporting the National Galleries of Scotland.
www.nationalgalleries.org

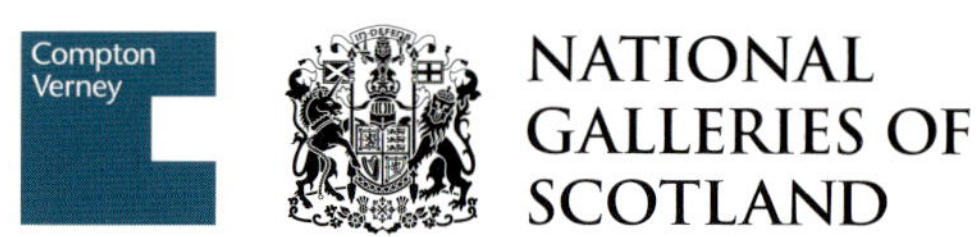

Contents

Foreword 7

Author's Acknowledgements 9

1 What's in a Name? 11

2 Beginnings 31

3 With Love 41

4 Two More Naked Than One 63

5 In the Family 75

6 A Crisis of Masculinity? 83

7 Our Bodies, Our Selves 93

8 Brief Encounters 109

9 Time and Motion 123

10 The Naked Celebrity 129

Exhibition Checklist 139

Bibliography 145

Notes and References 147

Copyright and Photo Credits 151

Index 152

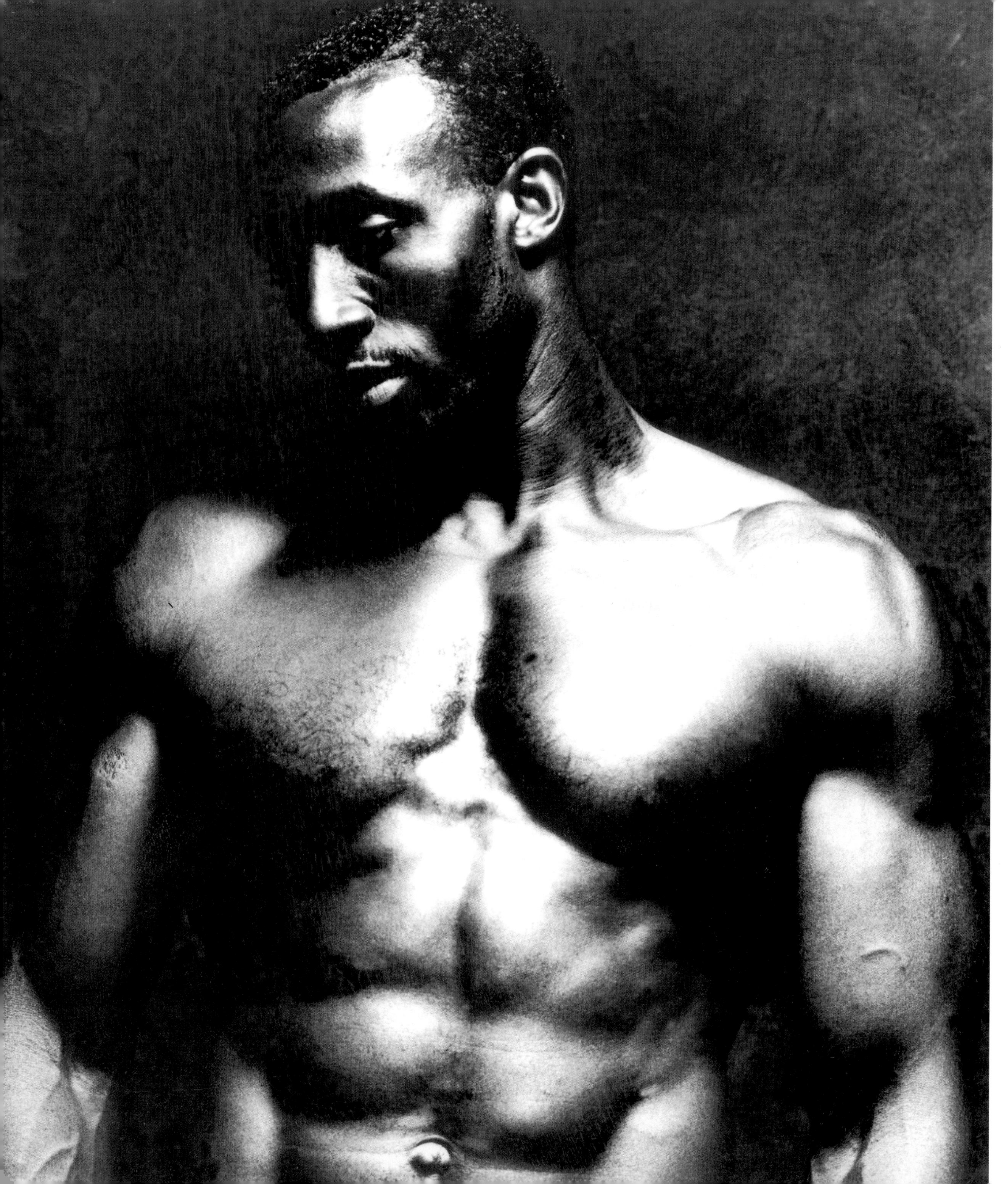

Foreword

The portrait has played a much larger role in the modern period than might be expected, given the gloomy predictions by early twentieth-century commentators that we had seen the demise of portraiture under the combined assault of modern art and photography. That portraiture is alive and well will not come as a surprise to those who have been visiting the Scottish National Portrait Gallery over the last few decades; however, it may come as a surprise to many that it is still possible to discover a category of portraiture – a genre within this genre – that has hitherto been either overlooked or unrecognised. It is to his great credit that Martin Hammer, Reader in History of Art at the University of Edinburgh, has both identified and, in the text of this book, explored the different forms that the naked portrait has taken. In doing so, he provokes new ways of seeing familiar works and insights that reveal the personal meanings for the artists of these works and their sitters. In this he has been ably assisted by Julie Lawson, Chief Curator at the Scottish National Portrait Gallery.

The Naked Portrait marks the second collaboration between Compton Verney and the National Galleries of Scotland and we are both greatly indebted to all those individuals and institutions that have lent so generously to the exhibition and enabled us to bring together so many important works. Finally, we would like to thank Dunard Fund and the Friends of the National Galleries of Scotland for their generous contribution towards the costs of the Edinburgh showing of this ambitious exhibition.

John Leighton
Director-General, National Galleries of Scotland

Kathleen Soriano
Director, Compton Verney, Warwickshire

1 Alastair Morrison
Linford Christie, 1996
National Portrait Gallery, London

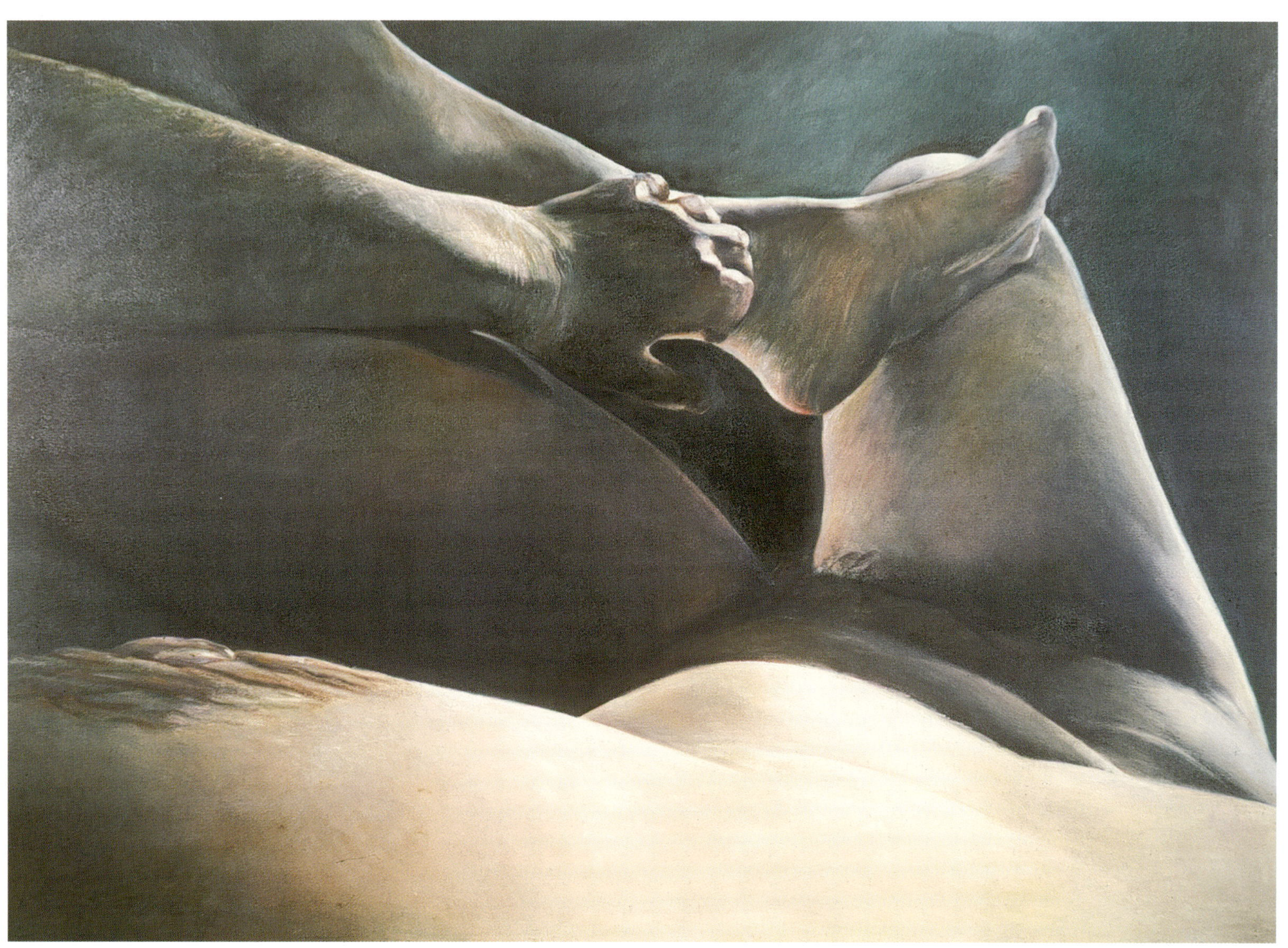

2 Joan Semmel
Out of Darkness, 1977
The Artist

Author's Acknowledgements

The aim of this exhibition and catalogue is to show that naked portraiture has been a widespread, international phenomenon over the past hundred years. The project arose from the very simple observation that this striking and unconventional imagery had been explored by many major artists, a coincidence that nobody had investigated. The theme turned out to be even richer and more complex than I envisaged, and I wish to offer thanks to the many people who helped me construct this account of the naked portrait.

I am especially grateful to the museums, private collectors, dealers and artists who have lent works to the exhibition. It has also been illuminating to talk to several of the artists about their work, including the late John Coplans, Ken Currie, Catriona Grant, Joyce Gunn-Cairns, Melanie Manchot, Joan Semmel, Gary Schneider, Jemima Stehli, Steve Tynan, and David Williams. In galleries and museums, the following individuals were especially helpful in showing me works and discussing or facilitating loans: in Austria, Michael Fuhr, Leopold Museum, Vienna; in London, Phyllis Adams, Saatchi Gallery; Brian Clarke and Liz Beatty, Francis Bacon Estate; Fred Mann, Fred; Sophie Hall, Flowers East; James Hyman, James Hyman Fine Art; Matthew Gale and Chris Stephens, Tate, London; Martin Barnes, Victoria & Albert Museum, London; Tim Marlow, White Cube. In New York, Payal Parekh, Edwynn Houk Gallery; Rose Lord, Marian Goodman Gallery; Kimberley Jones, Pace MacGill Gallery; Martina Batan, Ronald Feldman Fine Arts; in Paris, Quentin Bajac at the Pompidou Centre; and in Switzerland, Thomas Seelig, Fotomuseum, Winterthur. A morning spent with Thomas Koerfer viewing his collection in Zurich was instructive and memorable.

Within the National Galleries of Scotland, John Leighton has been a supportive presence since his arrival as Director-General. At the Scottish National Gallery of Modern Art, Richard Calvocoressi, Patrick Elliott, Keith Hartley, and Fiona Pearson have all given me useful help and advice. Janis Adams, Christine Thompson and David Simpson have nurtured this publication, Duncan Thomson proved a model editor, and Robert Dalrymple has done a splendid job on the design. It has been valuable to work with James Simpson on the installation of the exhibition. My most profound thanks go to James Holloway, Director, Julie Lawson, Chief Curator, and their colleagues at the Scottish National Portrait Gallery. They showed faith in the concept, and enabled it to happen. Julie Lawson, in particular, has contributed immensely, in numerous practical and less tangible ways, to the realisation of the exhibition. It has also been a great pleasure to work with Kathleen Soriano, Director, Antonia Harrison, Curator, and their colleagues at Compton Verney.

Closer to home, my colleagues in History of Art at the University of Edinburgh have provided support and encouragement, notably Michael Bury, Viccy Coltman, Richard Thomson, and above all Elizabeth Cowling. The Research Fund of the School of Arts, Culture and Environment has helped with travel and illustration expenses. Over the years, the many students who have taken courses and written dissertations with me in this area have stimulated my thinking and sustained my enthusiasm. My wife Christina Lodder has been an invaluable inspiration, and a sounding board for ideas. She kindly read through a draft with her usual sharp eye for sloppy prose and incoherent reasoning. My ten-year-old daughter Lucy has put up with my obsessive immersion in this project, even though she thought it gross and disgusting. I can only hope that her response is not too widely shared amongst viewers and readers.

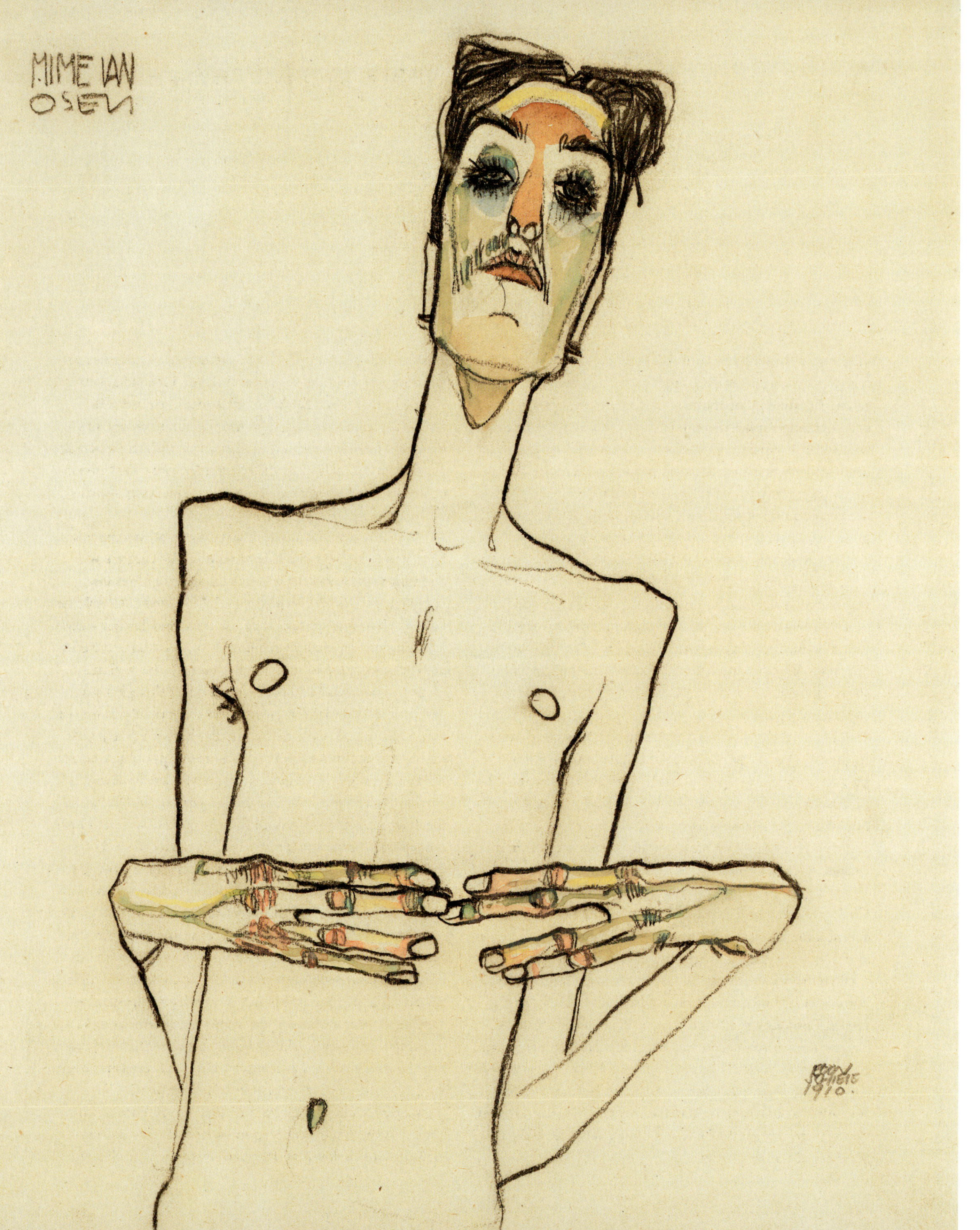
MIME VAN
OSEN
1910

Chapter 1 What's in a Name?

3 Egon Schiele
Erwin Dominik Osen with Fingertips Touching, 1910
Leopold Museum, Vienna

What is a portrait? We assume it is a study of an individual's character and appearance and the way they project themselves. But during the modern period, portraiture has also been extended and reinvented in all manner of ways. Several will become apparent as we focus on one very striking innovation, a tendency towards portraying the sitter in the nude. I want first to consider some general properties of naked portraiture, and then, in subsequent chapters, identify categories of sitter who have been presented in this way. This will open up for scrutiny the varied personal and artistic concerns that have motivated artists.

As images, naked portraits, like any work of art, operate on three broad levels. They invite us to respond to them in terms of our everyday experience; to consider them in the context of art history; and to interpret them as signs of wider currents in society.[1] At a basic level, we encounter representations of people without any clothes, or with very few. We react directly, even viscerally, to such imagery. Depending on the person depicted and the person looking, the experience may involve curiosity, compassion, admiration, desire, shock, or revulsion. Instinctively, we measure the other body against the one we know from the inside, and against those of our acquaintance. In each case our response will combine empathy, since the physical container is in some ways universal, and recognition of difference, given that bodies are also infinitely varied by gender, age, colour, physical type, let alone individual physiognomy and self-presentation. Features and naked body create a very different effect from the more controlled relationship between face and clothing, as the painter William Coldstream remarked: 'one doesn't read the figure in the way that one reads the expression in the face and therefore you have this tremendously concentrated and expressive focal point, yet indissolubly attached to the figure – somehow it's a piquant contrast which I find moving and interesting.'[2] Photographer Melanie Manchot also notes the complexities of our response:

I think the naked human body brings up so many intense and important psychological issues in all of us. It is at times both vulnerable and strangely threatening when stripped of its façade, mask, persona and signs which clothing provides us with. So a lot of my work attempts to explore the complicated feelings that we all have when encountering the naked human body, our feelings of delight, shame, amusement, embarrassment, or indifference.[3]

The next stage involves our knowledge of cultural tradition, with its categories and narratives. The works under discussion most obviously evoke the genre of the nude, going back to classical antiquity.[4] Confronted by a nude, as by any other represented figure, we tend to ask whether he or she depicts a particular individual, and whether we need to know this to make sense of the image. Beyond visual recognition, identification is provided by titles, giving a particular point to the analogy between people's names and pictures' titles. Both serve as introductions, and help us to classify the actual or represented person. We might expect historical images of the nude to conform to a repertoire of figures from classical or Christian mythology – Hercules, the Three Graces, Adam and Eve, St Sebastian. Then there are personifications (nymph, Truth, River God) and types such as bather or heroic warrior. In the modern period, we encounter numerous generic nudes, but a substantial body of work continues to insist upon the specific identity of the figure represented. Yet, these people are from the here and now, and reference to named individuals raises the spectre of portraiture. We are dealing with an apparent synthesis of two longstanding genres in the European tradition. The term naked portraiture captures this hybrid status, with a nod to Lucian Freud, who has often used *Naked Portrait* as a title for his pictures. The imagery, if not the term, has been in circulation since the early twentieth century.

Now is a timely moment to consider naked portraiture, given its ubiquity in contemporary art. Manifestations include Sam Taylor-Wood's video portrait of the sleeping

David Beckham, his body naked to the waist. The vacant Fourth Plinth in Trafalgar Square has acquired Marc Quinn's pseudo-classical statue of Alison Lapper, whose deformed body parodies the perfection of its architectural surroundings, and the notions we have of 'heroism'. Naked portraiture has featured in the work of such widely admired photographers as David Bailey [plate 5], Gary Schneider, Rineke Dijkstra, Wolfgang Tillmans, and Katy Grannan. In painting, Freud is the artist most people would immediately associate with naked portraiture. The widespread regard for his work testifies to our acceptance of a vein of imagery that breaks radically from both traditional portraits and nudes. The work of Jenny Saville likewise finds enthusiasts across the art world. One of her vast painterly celebrations of female flesh marked the culmination of a recent survey of self-portraiture since the Renaissance at London's National Portrait Gallery.[5] In the art of Tracey Emin, Saville's rival as the most celebrated young British female artist, naked self-portraiture has been a constant concern. Moreover, our evident fascination with the theme informs attitudes to the past. Egon Schiele receives huge exposure, and it is taken for granted that some of his most remarkable works are naked portraits of himself or others in his circle. Or we might note the widespread interest in Francesca Woodman, whose photographs often present her naked body in conjunction with bizarre props and sinister interiors.

Nevertheless naked portraiture remains an odd and surprising idea. Portraits have tended to depict their sitters' public selves. They reflect the ways people project themselves, in work, or family and social rituals. They exploit the ways that dress or costume can characterise, flatter, and signify social identity. Yet nakedness seems intrinsically private. Most people would be horrified at the thought of strangers contemplating pictures of them in a state of undress. Nakedness may have cultural connotations of a more 'natural' mode of being, but in virtually all societies it is thought taboo. As Anne Hollander commented in *Seeing through Clothes*:

Surveys of many cultures lead us to conclude that the truly natural state of the adult human is dressed, or decorated, but that his sense of nature demands from him a deep respect for nakedness. This respect may lead him to invent ideas not only of the 'wickedness' of nakedness, to which generations of Protestants became so accustomed, but also of the 'naturalness' of nakedness, which is all the more powerful for being a fiction.[6]

So naked portraiture becomes almost exclusively a category of *artistic* imagery. Identifying the type has been made possible by a convergence of preoccupations with the body in general and portraiture in particular. The portrait fell into disrepute during the early twentieth century, but has been given a new lease of life by artists such as Chuck Close and Thomas Ruff, while books and exhibitions have reconsidered the portrait and self-portrait in the work of a variety of artists, from Van Gogh and Picasso to Bacon and Warhol. A fascination with images of nudity has been current for several years. *The Body* (1994) surveyed such imagery in past and present photography, and enquired: 'Why is it today that the human body is at the centre of so much attention? Why are magazines, newspapers, television and advertisements saturated with images of naked, or virtually naked, bodies? Why are so many writers, artists and photographers so profoundly concerned with the subject?'[7] The continuing obsession amongst artists was registered ten years later by the book *Stripped Bare: The Body Revealed in Contemporary Art*.[8]

I have assumed that naked portraiture is a straightforward classification. Naked is easy, and we all think we know what portraits are. But how *do* we decide when a work of art is a portrait, naked or otherwise? There are two obvious criteria, neither of which relates to visual properties of the object. The first is verbal: the artist can identify a work as a portrait by giving it a title such as *Self-portrait* or *Joanna Smith*. The second relates to the contexts in which the image is encountered. Portraiture is usually understood as func-

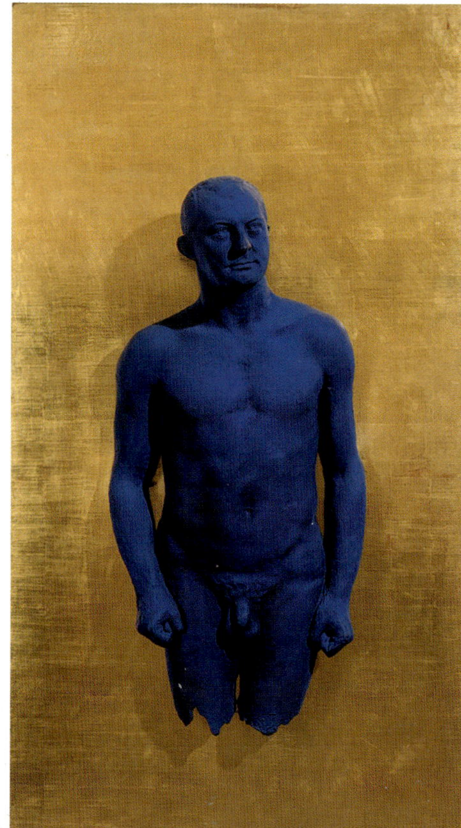

left **4 Yves Klein**
Arman, Portrait-relief, 1962
Pompidou Centre, Paris

right **5 David Bailey**
Belinda Selby, 2002
David Bailey (Camera Eye Ltd)

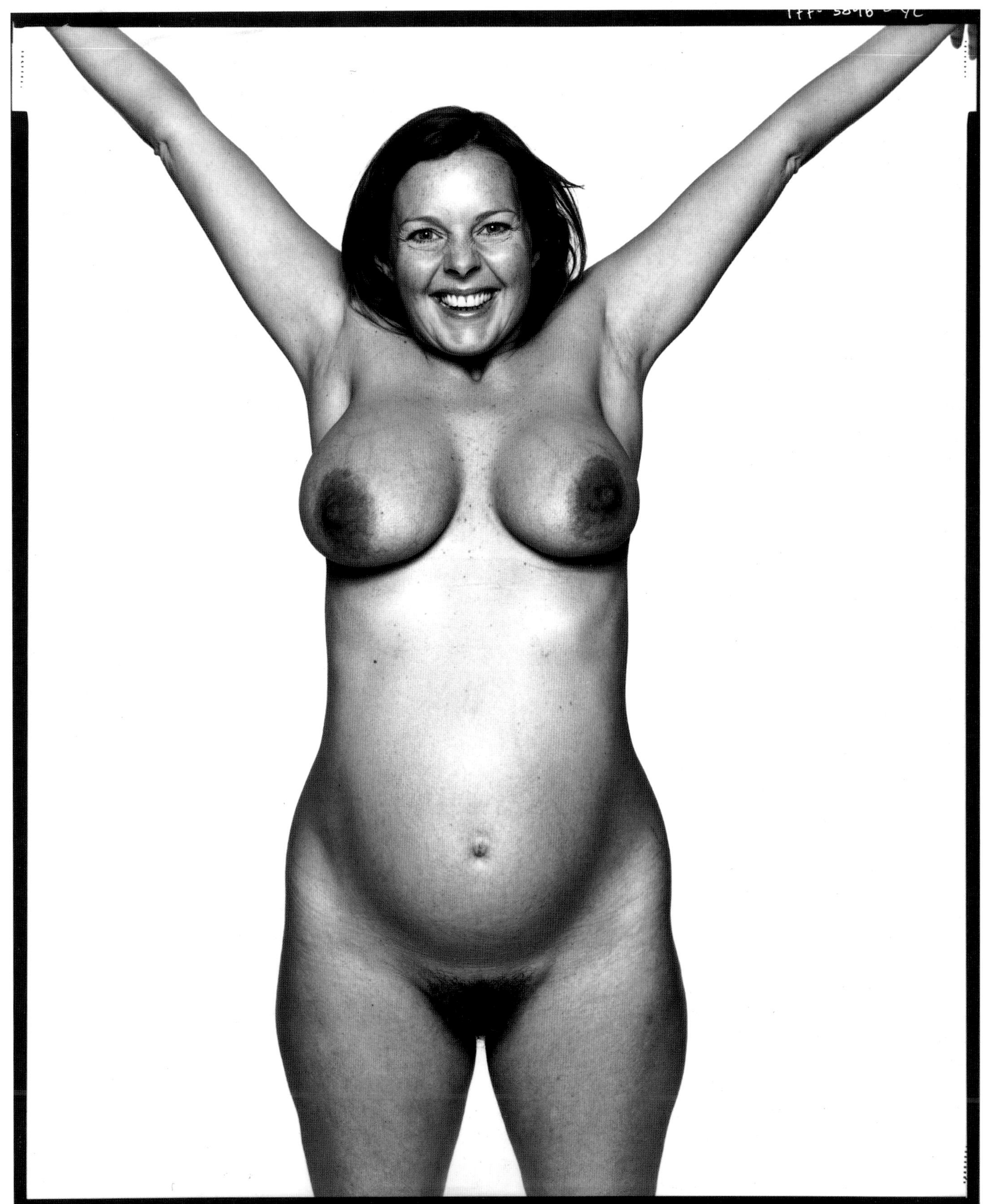

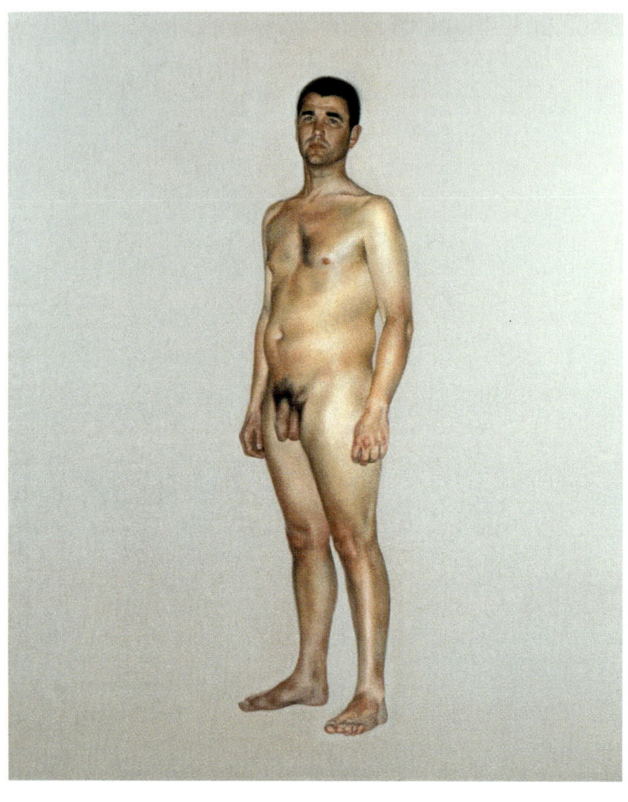

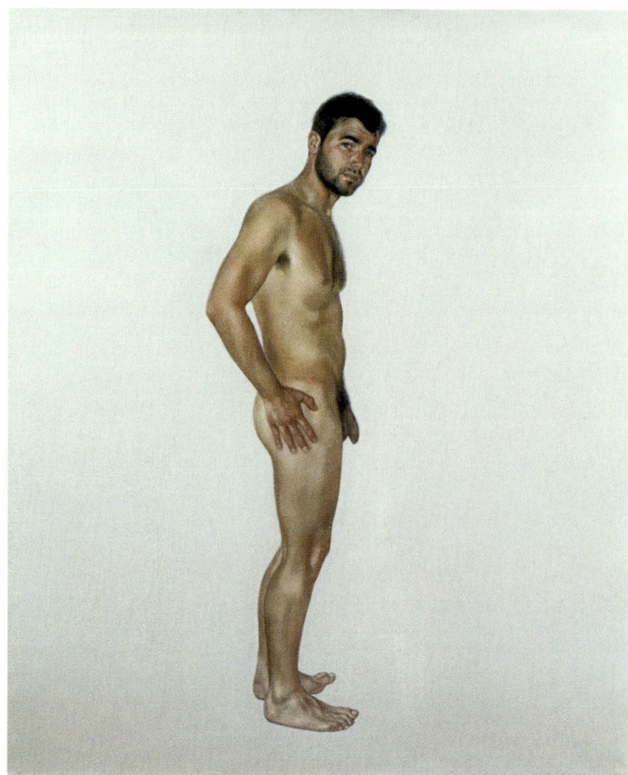

left **6 Jonathan Yeo**
Being Geri Halliwell
(Ivan Massow diptych), 2000–2
Ivan Massow

right **7 Egon Schiele**
Erwin Dominik Osen
with Crossed Arms, 1910
Leopold Museum, Vienna

tional, a representation of an individual that is required for some particular purpose, like hanging in a board room or National Portrait Gallery, sitting on the mantelpiece, or ornamenting a book jacket. Yet in the modern period, the most interesting portraits have generally not been commissioned, but made because artists have wished to explore the format for their own purposes. An exception that proves the rule is Jonathan Yeo's diptych portrait of Ivan Massow [plate 6]. This was commissioned, amongst other portraits of himself, by the wealthy entrepreneur.[9] The two pictures were made eighteen months apart, and the second showing Massow minus three stones and with a beard. Here, portraiture is being used as self-promotion. Generally, though, it is the artist who chooses the sitter, with the result that we often encounter self-portraits, and images of lovers or close friends. Loved ones have a chapter to themselves, but naked examples of friends include Larry Rivers's picture of Frank O'Hara (1955), and Yves Klein's cast portraits of his fellow New Realist artists.[10] [plate 4] Other artists have departed radically from traditional assumptions, such as the need to supply a legible representation. A portrait might not even include facial features, the traditional signifiers of identity, as in Stieglitz's portraits of Georgia O'Keefe or John Coplans's images of his own aged body. We may be given a back rather than a front view. Such works, however unorthodox, require to be understood as some form of portraiture when the artist signals this through their choice of title, but if the artist is using the genre as a vehicle for experiment, unconstrained by expectations of what a portrait should be, they are also free to give pictures whatever titles they like.

If we dispense with title and social function, how do we distinguish portraits from other kinds of image of the human figure? How should we use our knowledge, for instance, that Victorine Meurend modelled for Manet's *Olympia*? Presumably what matters is whether or not the artist intended such information to inform our responses. We tend to think that a portrait is *about* the particular identity of the sitter, whereas with nudes that is not the case. The difference is expressed in the distinction between sitters and models. It is not a question of how well the artist knew the person. We place in the portrait category pictures that prompt us to imagine being, or interacting with, the individual depicted. When we look at a nude as a portrait, we tend to ask, not what the figure means, in relation to some system or artistic vision, but rather what the image 'reveals' about the inner person portrayed as well as what they look like. We apply to art skills acquired in life for reading people's characters from their behaviour and body language, recognising in the sitter an equivalent to how we see ourselves.

It may help at this stage to introduce some concrete

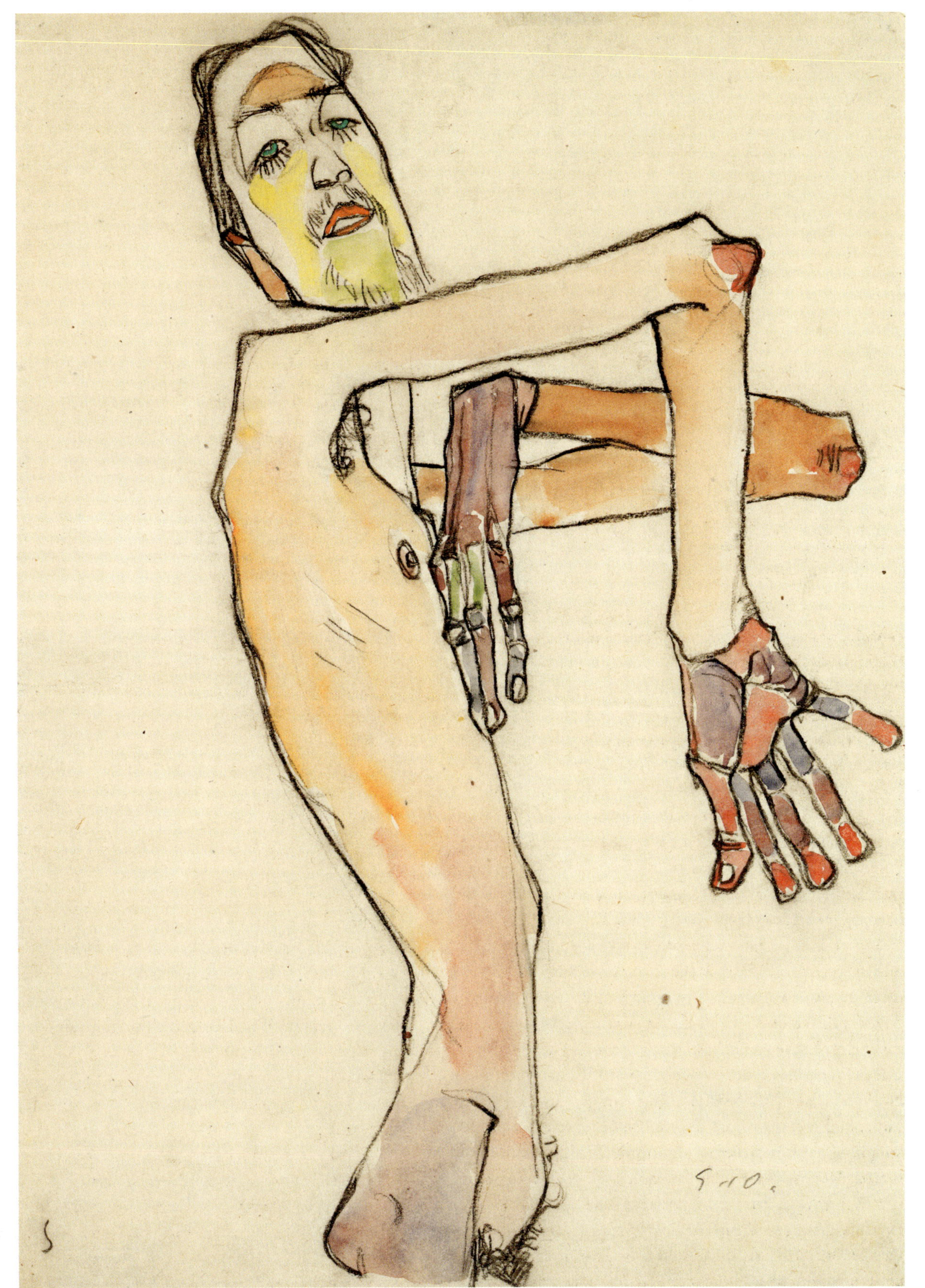

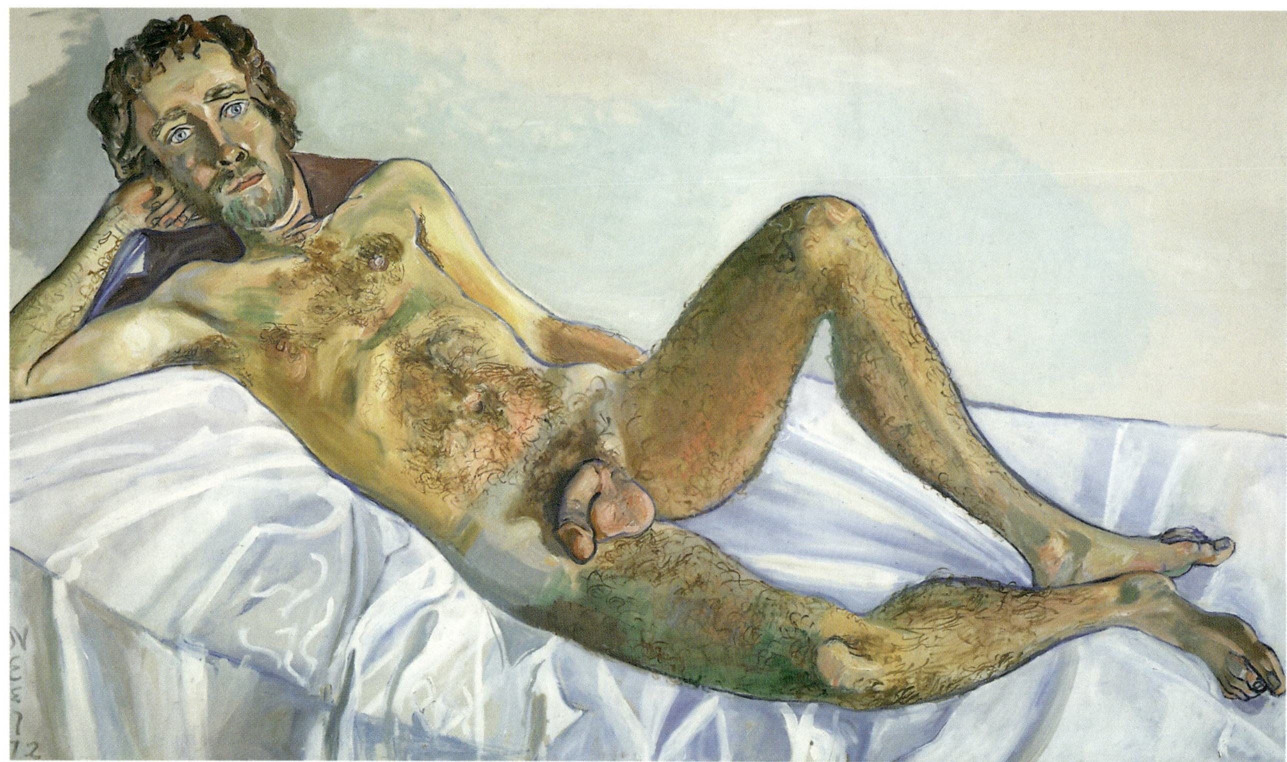

left **8 Alice Neel**
John Perreault, 1972
Whitney Museum of American Art, New York

below left **9 Leon Kossoff**
Fidelma No.1, 1978
James Hyman Fine Art, London

right **10**
Robert Mapplethorpe
Bob Love, 1979
Victoria & Albert Museum, London

far right **11**
Wolfgang Tillmans
Arnd, Nude, Sitting, 1991
Victoria & Albert Museum, London

examples. In Egon Schiele's depictions of his close friend Erwin Van Osen, the stylised gestures produce a powerful sense of individuality, as well as evoking the sitter's own interest in mime performance [plate 7]. A concern with characterisation is evident in Alice Neel's portrait of John Perreault [plate 8], which arose when the young, gay art critic tried to borrow Neel's early portrait of Joe Gould (1933) for a show about the male nude. She wanted to be represented by something more up-to-date, and inveigled Perreault into posing: 'Neel guided me into the living room that was her studio during the day and right there and then placed me on the couch: That's it. Just stay right there. I've always wanted to paint you. You look like a faun or a satyr or like Pan.' The picture is also a witty send-up of the reclining Venus formula. The sitter recalled: 'the relaxed pose is mine – left knee up and legs spread open, left heel resting on back of right shin to form a loopy triangle'.[11] Neel's several nude portraits were one-offs, but in the case of Leon Kossoff's *Fidelma* series [plate 9], it seemed important that the title acknowledge the sitter, just as the body language discloses an autonomous individual: 'the model lapses into moments of unselfconsciousness when something more intimate or unforced is glimpsed. Kossoff's depictions reveal these unguarded moments, vividly recreating an acute, unidealised and physical sense of another's presence.'[12]

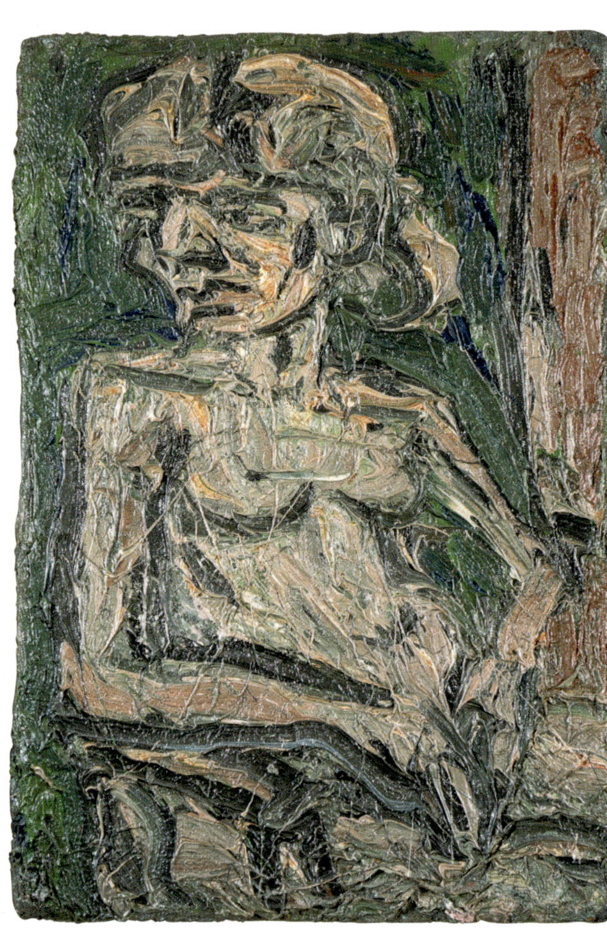

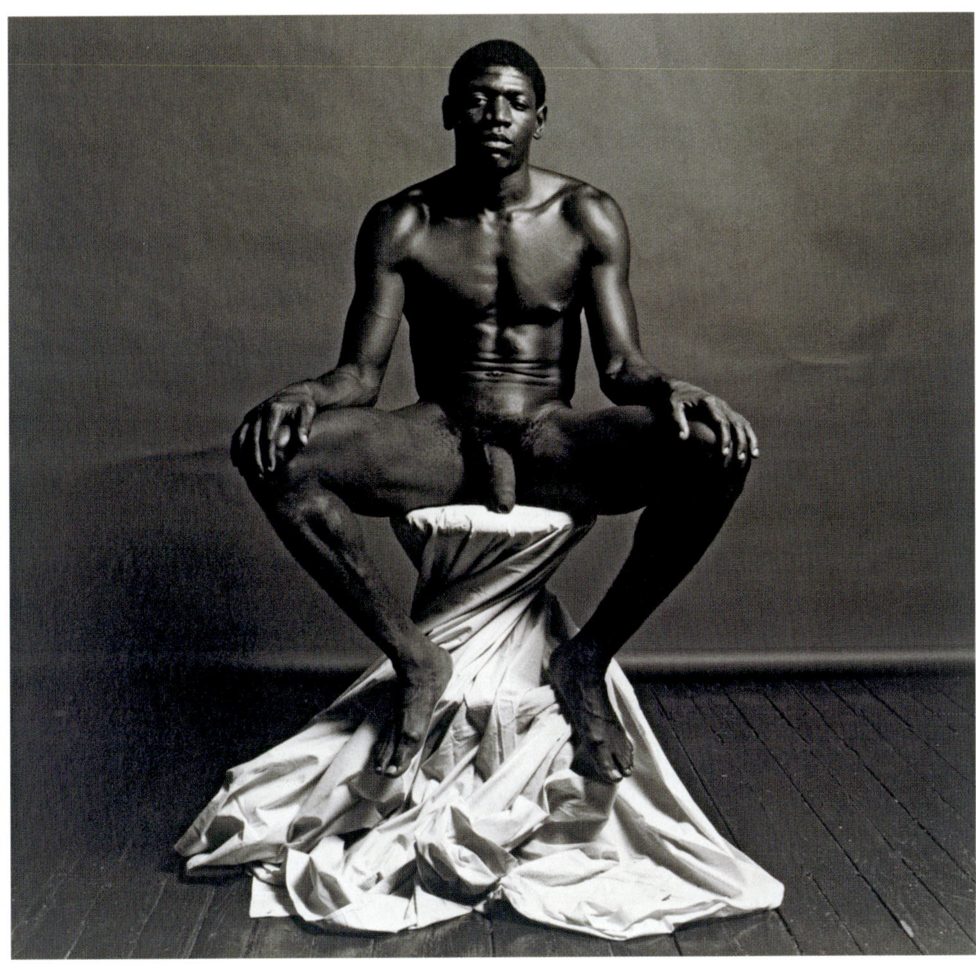

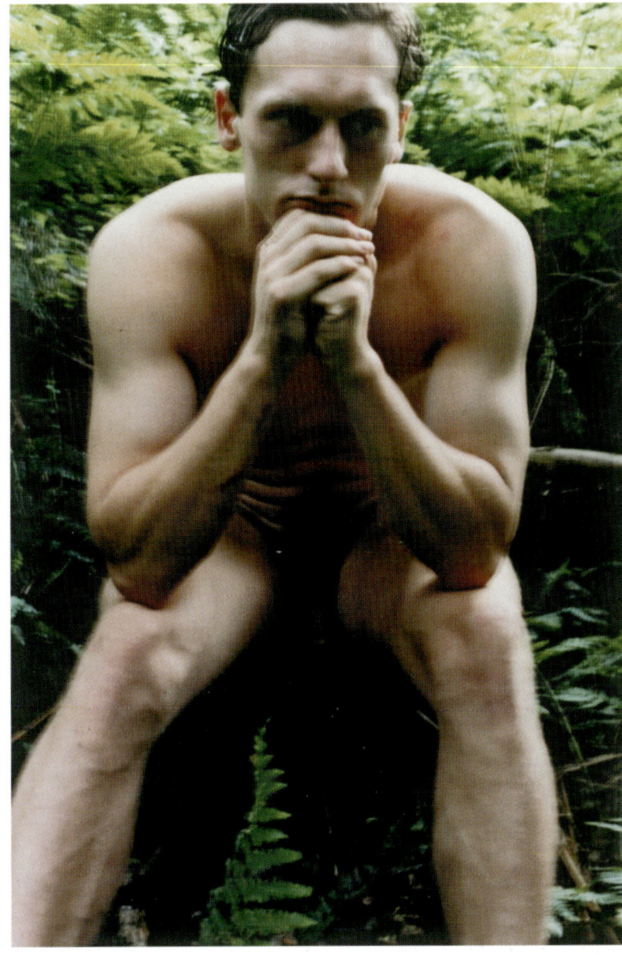

In photography, Robert Mapplethorpe's *Bob Love* and Wolfgang Tillmans's *Arnd, Nude, Sitting* both portray named seated males, legs apart and facing in the general direction of the viewer [plates 10 and 11]. Both could be said to reflect the gay sexuality of their makers. The Tillmans suggests a snap-shot intimacy and informality, conveyed by the colour, outdoor setting, and the sitter's pose, which we register as thoughtful. In contrast, the Mapplethorpe invites us to admire the beauty of the sitter, the play of light on his black skin, and the consummate artistry of the composition.Although the work is presented as a portrait, Mapplethorpe shows little interest in evoking the inner life of his sitter. Early on he remarked: 'I often don't know who these people are. It's not that important to me. I never had heroes.'[13] Mapplethorpe has been taken to task for his detachment, and for stereotyping his black sitters as fetishes for a homosexual subculture.[14]

The work of Peter Hujar, a fellow gay photographer working in New York, has never enjoyed the same success as Mapplethorpe's. Hujar's portraiture, much of it naked, seems far more concerned with introspection and self-projection on the part of his sitters [plate 12]. The almost exaggerated sense of performance recalls early Mapplethorpes, such as the portrait of his close friend Patti Smith [plate 13], or the studies of female body-builder Lisa Lyon. Hujar provides a contrast to what has often been seen as the dearth of human content, and 'hyper-aestheticized' idiom of Mapplethorpe's later photography.[15] Nan Goldin, a friend and fan of Hujar's remarked: 'He was a magician, he hypnotized his subjects. He never forced exposure, he seduced people to want to reveal all to him ... Looking at his photographs of nude men ... is the closest I ever came to experience what it is to inhabit male flesh.'[16] A pictorial equivalent is Francis Bacon's use of body language to characterise an individual. *Study from the Human Body* was virtually his last painting, one of three portraits of Bacon's painter friend Anthony Zych. The Edinburgh *Study for a Portrait* (1991) shows the clothed sitter standing in a doorway.[17] The contrasting naked picture, with its contortion of posture, clearly refers to Zych's interest in body-building [plate 14].

Alternatively, the viewer might register allusions to

portrait conventions. An example is the bust, a type extending back to antiquity which focuses on the sitter's head and upper torso.[18] Nudity is implied in many bust portraits, but modesty preserved by the truncation of the figure. As a sculptural format, in both marble and bronze, this was widely employed by nineteenth-century artists, up to and beyond Auguste Rodin .The formula migrated into two-dimensional work. The depictions by Vanessa Bell and Duncan Grant of their friend David Garnett provide a wonderful example of the relativity of perception: Bell made him boyish and innocent, Grant (his lover) highly masculine and sexy [plates 15 and 16].[19] Self-presentation is dramatised in Robert Mapplethorpe's self-portrait diptych, one example of his many reinventions of the sleek idealisations of the classical bust [plates 17 and 18]. The two images project contradictory aspects of the artist's own sense of homosexual identity, and the naked image is just as manipulated, and psychologically opaque, as its biker counterpart. In Richard Avedon's portrait of a coalminer, connotations of classic perfection are undermined by the off-kilter placement of the sitter and by his unkempt appearance and bleak expression – inserting a tragic note in a format where dignified calm was the norm [plate 19]. A modern equivalent to idealisation is evoked, ironically, in Marc Quinn's *Template for my Future Plastic Surgery*, where the artist's half-length body is adorned with a violinist's ear, a chef's tongue, the hand of his girlfriend on his heart, and a piece of coral as surrogate for his brain, as if to assert an affinity with nature [plate 20].

These varied images demonstrate that portraits are, in the end, what viewers choose to view, in particular ways, as portraits. The problem remains of where to draw sensible parameters. Is it reasonable to see as naked portraits Pierre Bonnard's pictures of women at their toilet, often now seen as conveying the specific identity of his wife Marthe; or Man Ray's nude photographs for which lovers such as Kiki de Montparnasse, Lee Miller, and Meret Oppenheim were the models; or Picasso's distillations of lust in the early 1930s, sustained by his memories of his young girlfriend Marie-Thérèse Walter, whose existence he could not have acknowledged publicly? The issue is brought into focus by particular pictures. We are told that Balthus's *Le Lever*

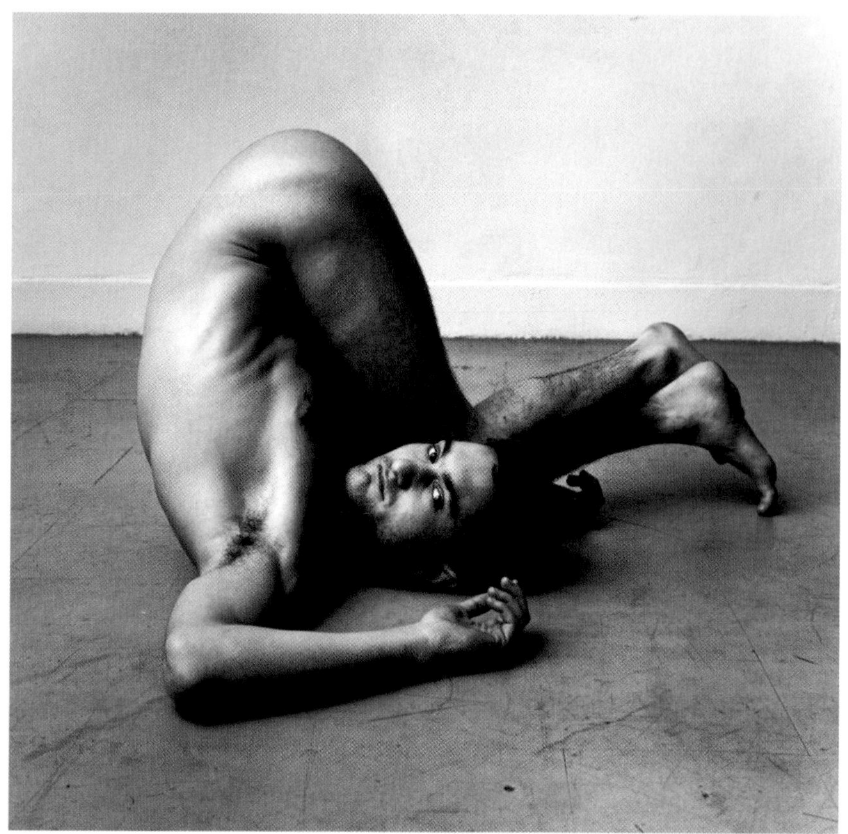

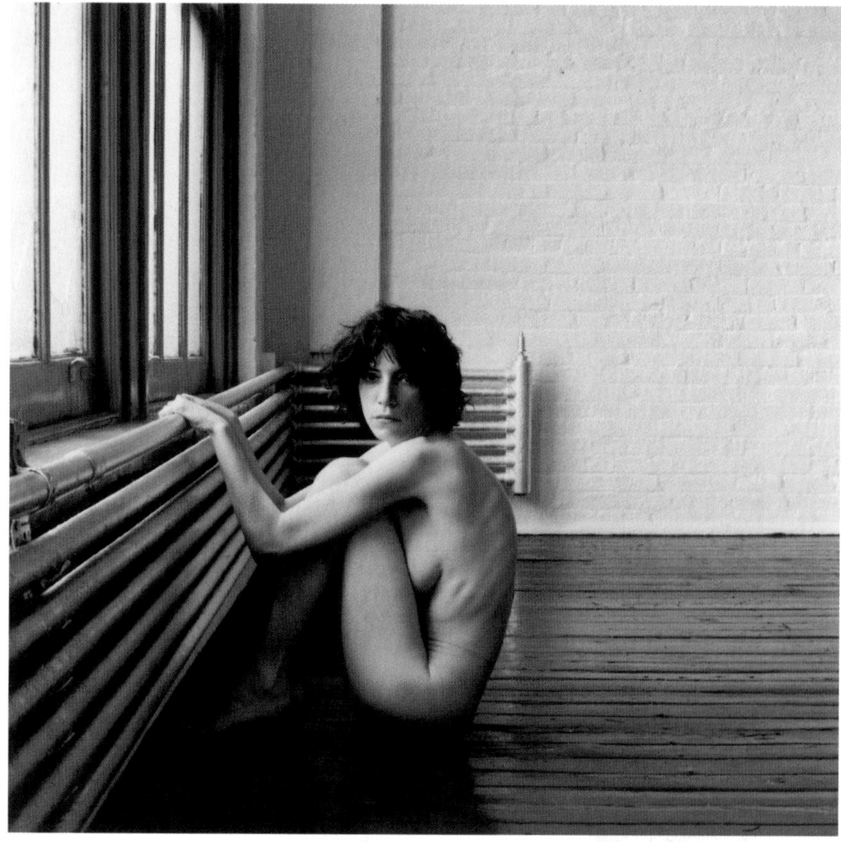

above right **12 Peter Hujar** Gary, 1982

Coutesy Gary Schneider and John Erdman

right **13 Robert Mapplethorpe** Patti Smith, 1976

Private Collection

opposite **14 Francis Bacon** Study from the Human Body, 1991

The Estate of Francis Bacon, courtesy Faggionato Fine Arts, London and Tony Shafrazi Gallery, New York

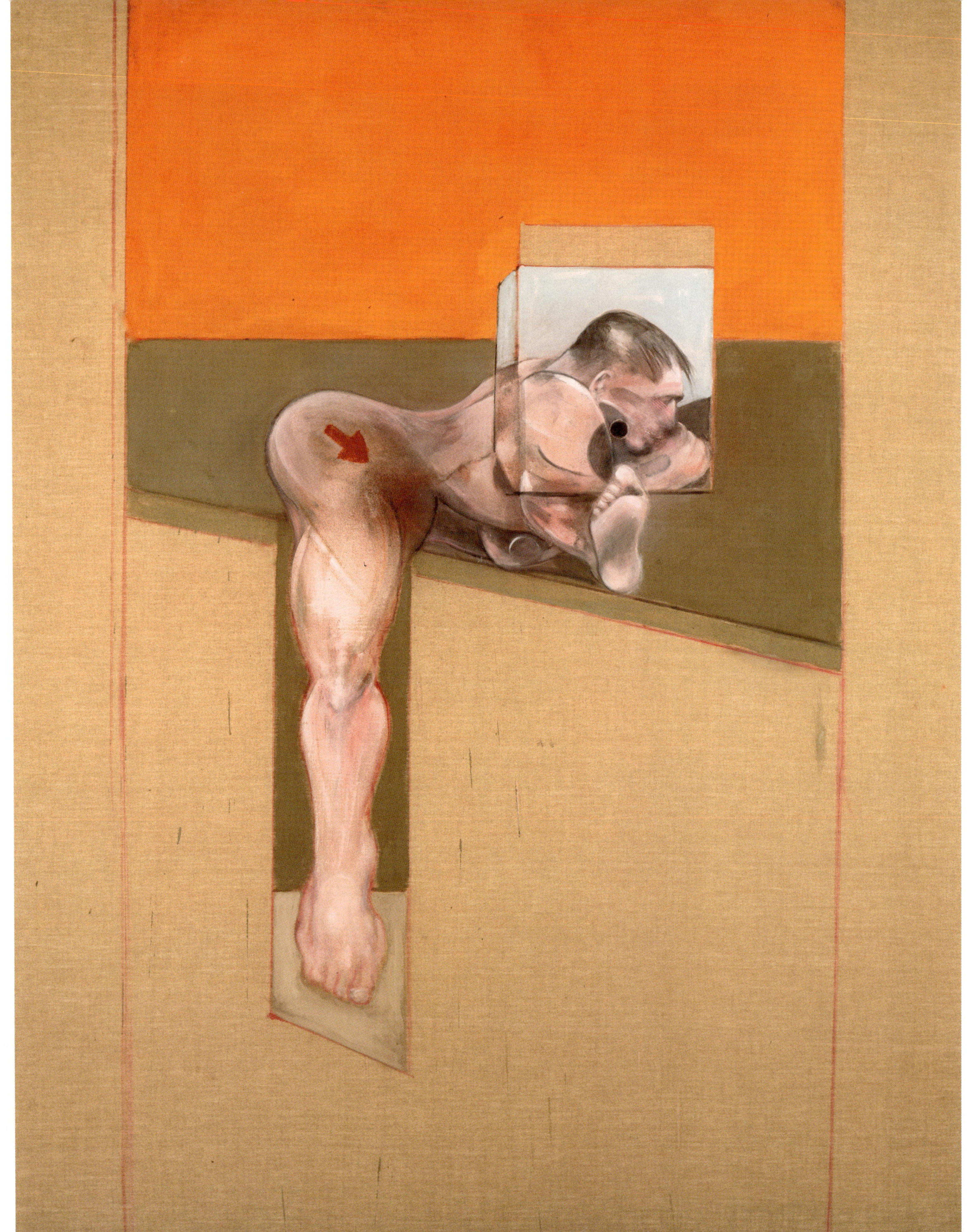

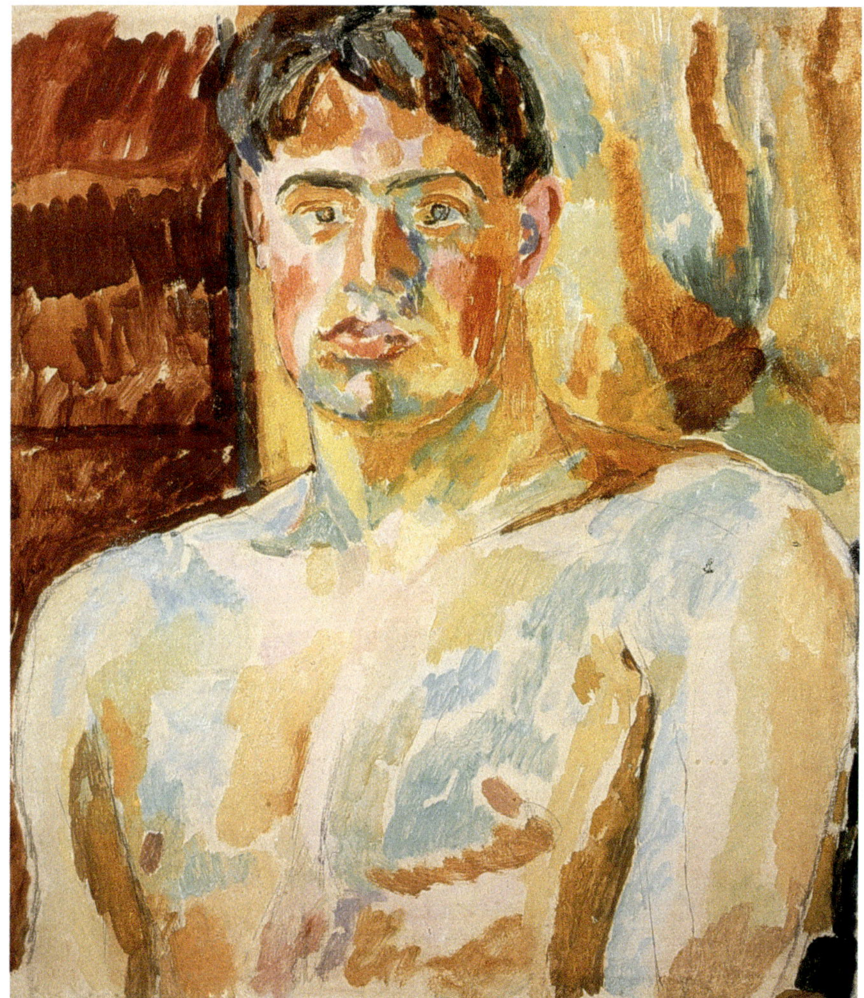

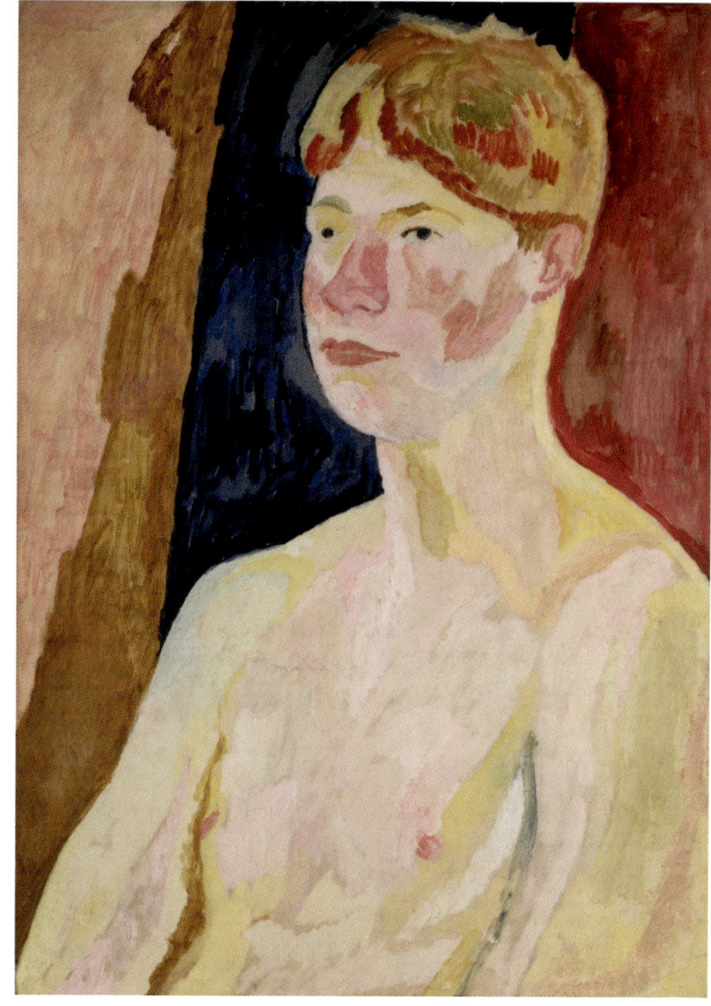

portrayed his niece Frédérique Tison, who, at the age of sixteen, became the artist's 'mistress' and 'favourite model and muse' [plate 21].[20] In the same year he did a conventional, clothed portrait, and she is recognisably the model for several pictures like *Getting Up*, where the angle of the head makes her features barely discernible.[21] *Getting Up* is also part of Balthus's longstanding concern with images of nude or scantily clad pubescent girls, disporting themselves in the repertoire of poses from old master paintings that he admired (an echo here of Caravaggio's *The Victorious Eros*).[22] Do these facts mean that Frédérique was just serving as a model, or can we continue to read the picture, on some level, as Balthus's perception of the individual? And how can we decide, in the absence of clarification from a title or statement of intention? In the case of Roger Hilton's *Dancing Woman* (1963), the title is non-specific, and the image is highly abstracted [plate 22]. Yet documentary evidence indicates that this picture was meant to read as some kind of portrait. Artist and sitter told roughly the

above

left **15 Duncan Grant** David Garnett, 1915
Private Collection, London

16 Vanessa Bell David Garnett, 1915
National Portrait Gallery, London

opposite

top left **17 Robert Mapplethorpe**
Self-portrait in Drag, 1980
Pompidou Centre, Paris

top right **18 Robert Mapplethorpe**
Self-portrait with Cigarette, 1980
Pompidou Centre, Paris

bottom left **19 Richard Avedon**
Hansel Nicholas Burum, Coal Miner, 1985
Collection Fotomuseum, Winterthur,
permanent loan from Andreas Reinhart

bottom right **20 Marc Quinn**
Template for my Future Plastic Surgery, 1992
Scottish National Gallery of Modern Art, Edinburgh

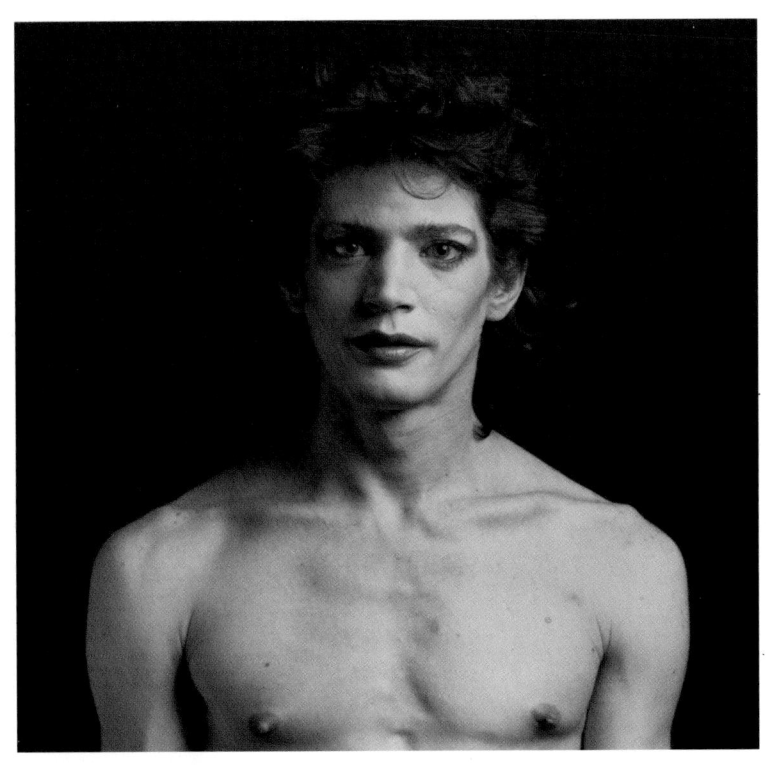

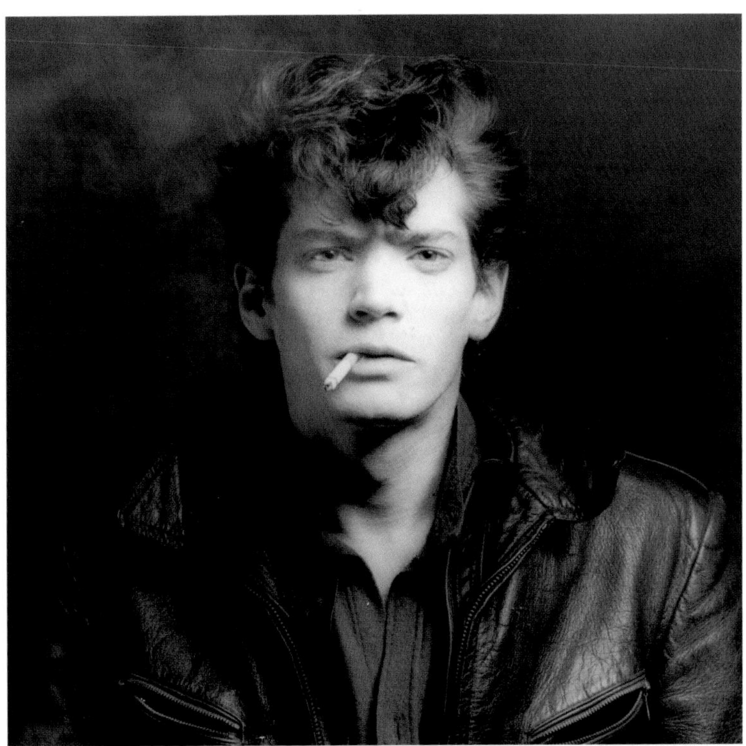

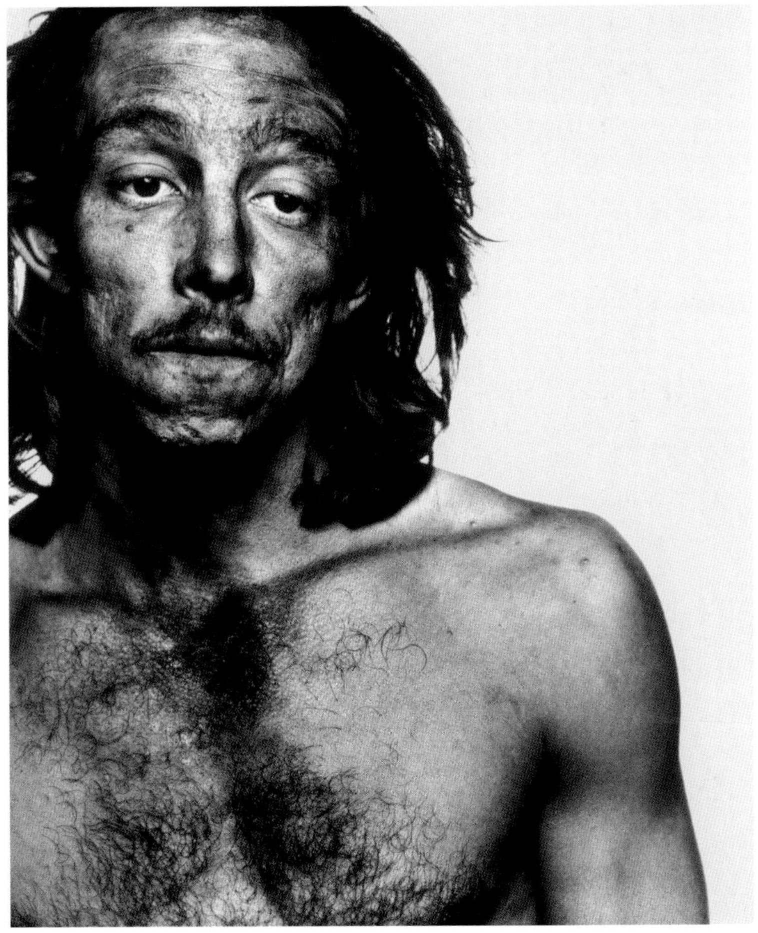

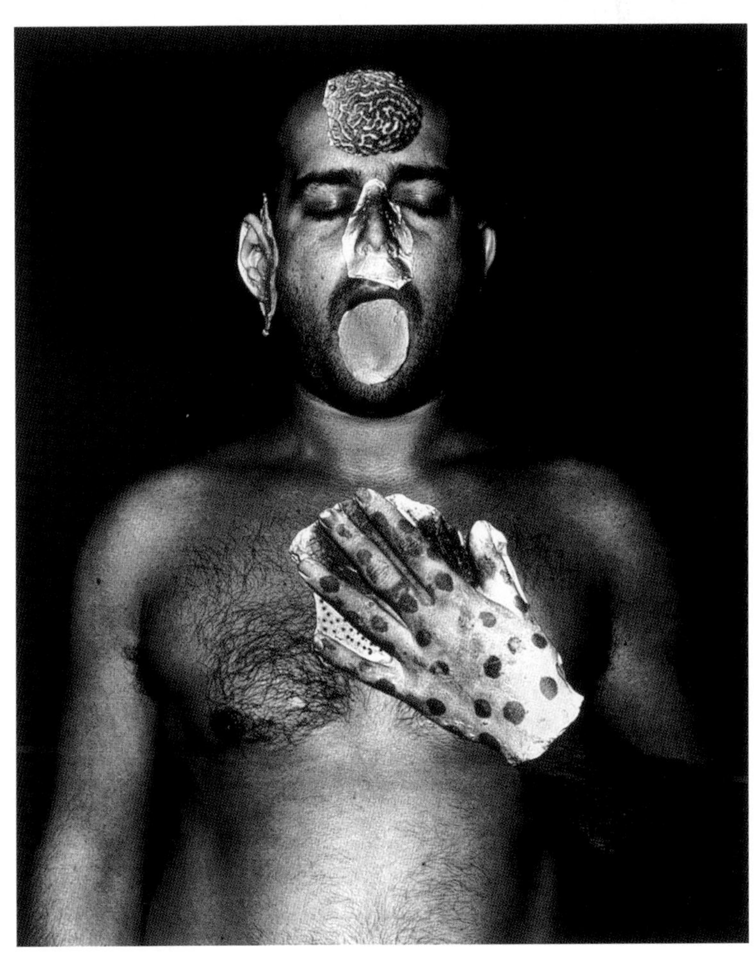

same story about its origin in a family holiday in France: 'It was my wife dancing on the veranda, we were having a quarrel. She was nude and angry at the time and she was dancing up and down shouting "oi, yoi, yoi" [the title of the Tate variant].'[23] Again, was the painting really about his wife, or was the episode merely a pretext after the event for an exercise in the erotically charged, semi-abstract type of painting that preoccupied Hilton in the early 1960s?

In the face of such dilemmas, two extreme positions are possible. The first would maintain that art, especially in the modern period, has been profoundly informed by personal impulses that sometimes become clearer with hindsight. Frank Auerbach reflected this when he commented that even Titian's art is autobiographical: the figures in the subject pictures are 'probably portraits' and his themes 'stand in some sort of way for events in his life'.[24] The contrary argument is that we tend to trivialise artistic expression by projecting biographical concerns onto work that is really about other things. This was one of Barthes's objects of attack in his famous call for a metaphorical 'death of the author'. The authors of a recent book on classical art note how the spurious identifications littering the literature on the portraiture of their period testify to 'the search for authenticity' and 'our ever renewed desire to animate the ancient world with living people'.[25] Are we running the risk of doing something similar here? The difficulty with the first position is that it may leave us without any sense of portraiture as a distinct genre. But being too restrictive about what counts as a portrait is also unsustainable in the modern period, when the entire genre system has lost its hold. A compromise might be to assume that the distinction between, say, the nude and the naked portrait has to allow for a zone of uncertainty. We would have to assess borderline cases on their merits. Does it enrich our understanding of Bonnard or Woodman, say, to consider their work comparatively in a context of naked (self-) portraiture; or does such a classification result in misunderstanding, even gossip parading as art history? Are those pictures by Balthus and Hilton portraits, but only in some marginal sense, rather than definitively one thing or the other? At several points, *The Naked Portrait* invites the viewer not only to consider whether some particular work is a portrait, but also to question assumptions about the nature of portraiture itself.

Art historians draw a distinction between iconographic and iconological analysis. We have been doing the former thus far by trying to construct a category of subject matter. The latter entails understanding patterns of imagery in relation to wider values and belief systems. How, then, might we explain the fact that naked portraiture has become increasingly pervasive during the last century? What is its significance as a cultural phenomenon? Is this study itself symptomatic of what one sociologist has termed our 'striptease culture', in which 'public nakedness, voyeurism, and sexualised looking are permitted, indeed encouraged, as never before'?[26]

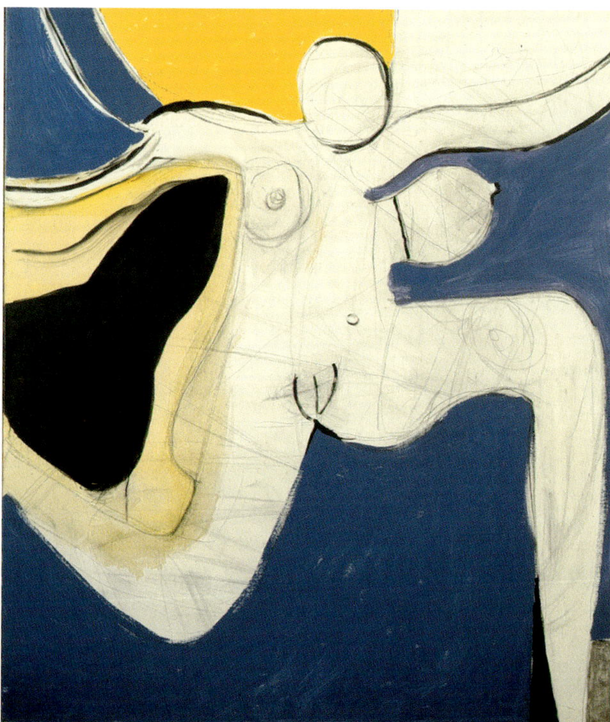

far left **21 Balthus (Balthasar Klossowski de Rola)**

Le Lever (Getting Up), 1955

Scottish National Gallery of Modern Art, Edinburgh

left **22 Roger Hilton**

Dancing Woman, 1963

Scottish National Gallery of Modern Art, Edinburgh

Naked portraiture has certainly coincided with other manifestations of an impulse to expose what is authentic beneath the superficial veneer. Leaving aside science, we might note the psychoanalytical project of stripping away the social to unmask a deep self, with powerful and often repressed instincts; the acknowledgement of sexuality as a key human drive; the post-Darwinian sense of continuity between human and animal, and between so-called civilised and primitive states of human development; the 'primitivist' sensibility in so many areas of modern artistic and cultural activity; and the tendency since Nietzsche to deconstruct the surface of discourse to reveal manifestations of the 'will to power'. Particularly since the 1960s, nakedness has been associated with moral and sexual liberation, especially as experienced by women, gays and younger people. It came as no surprise when Alice Neel asked John Perreault to pose nude: 'Everyone knew she was always trying to get people to take off their clothes. It was a late-'60s, early-'70s thing. Nudity meant you were free.'[27] In 1975, an entire current of sociological thinking was articulated by Howard Kirk, Malcolm Bradbury's fictive 'History Man', when describing his new book *The Defeat of Privacy*:

It's about the fact that there are no more private selves, no more private corners in society, no more private acts … Mankind is making everything open and accessible … You see, sociological and psychological understanding is now giving us a total view of man, and democratic society is giving us total access to everything. There's nothing that's not confrontable. There are no concealments any longer, no mysterious dark places of the soul. We're all right there in front of the entire audience of the universe, in a state of exposure. We're all nude and available.[28]

Even historians have turned their attention to areas of human experience that used to be seen as private, and too subjective for analytical scrutiny. In Theodore Zeldin's *An Intimate History of Humanity* (1994), 'portraits' of living individuals are combined with historical data to evoke the many dimensions of human intimacy.[29] A recent study of photography discerns an impulse to reveal that which is concealed beneath the social façade: 'Much of contemporary photographic portraiture sees a removal of clues and contexts and a highly formal, almost scientific and clinical approach which leaves the sitters with nothing to hide behind. The level of scrutiny involved is obvious, leaving the viewer less room to understand the function and meaning of the work since many frames of reference are removed.'[30] The onus is on the viewer to make sense of the imagery: 'The strength of these works lies in the uncertainty, as it's not only the "who" that fascinates us but also the "why". Why would a person allow such interrogation – not only by the photographer but also by the audience?'

In looking for underlying factors, we might take some bearings from Charles Taylor's book *Sources of the Self: The Making of Modern Identity*.[31] Taylor describes both shifts and continuities between Modernist and Romantic attitudes to the self. The enemy is soulless practicality, 'the world just seen as mechanism, as a field for instrumental reason'. This model seemed 'shallow and debased' to the Romantics, but by the twentieth century its encroachments 'were incomparably greater, and we find the modernist writers and artists in protest against a world dominated by technology, standardization, the decay of community, mass society and vulgarization'.[32] For the Romantics, the antidote was an 'epiphanic art' that would 'bring to light the spiritual reality behind nature and uncorrupted human feeling'.[33] By the modern period, their means had lost credibility; nature had become marginalised and 'there are no more peasants living in symbiosis with it'. According to Taylor, the alternative recourse was 'interiority', that is to say 'the world as experienced, known and transmuted in sensibility and consciousness'; 'this kind of move, which brings philosophers together with artists and critics in an attempt to recover what has been suppressed and forgotten in the conditions of experience, has been repeated many times in the twentieth century'.[34] The concern to retrieve the full vividness of lived experience, as opposed to the ready made categories that we apply for the sake of convenience, is implicit in the thought of Henri Bergson and phenomenologists such as Husserl, Sartre and Merleau-Ponty, as well as a host of artistic and literary projects.

Taylor's perspective has been extended in a recent study of the notion of authenticity. This shows how ideas operating on loftier planes are matched at more popular levels of culture. Our attention is drawn to 'a distinctive set of binary oppositions that governs the way we sort things out in everyday life',[35] and that contain an implicit set of value judgements. Thus the natural is set against the artificial; the masks we assume in the social arena are set against what we see as the real self beneath the façade of ordinary life. This correlates with an opposition between private and public levels of existence, between pure, spontaneous behaviour, on the one hand, and the contrived and calculating, on the other. By extension, we construct interconnecting oppositions between deep and superficial, organic and mechanical, genuine or true and what is fake and illusory. But the 'master dichotomy governing all others' is that between inner and outer, where the former is associated with real value: 'to be authentic, you must be in touch with what lies within, that is, the inner self, the self no one sees except you … one turns inwards because it is within the innermost self that one discovers the ordinarily unseen and untapped resources of meaning and purpose.'[36]

The naked portrait is ostensibly about the bodily exterior rather than interiority. Nevertheless, such imagery takes on a particular resonance. Nakedness signifies the self stripped of outer garments and social posturing. It suggests the concealed, private, inner self. Moreover, the naked body belonging to oneself, a person one knows intimately, or someone encountered more casually, has a specific set of properties. It is absolutely unique, whereas clothing and generic nudity tend towards assimilation to type. It provides a springboard for feelings and instincts that are fundamental to our identity, and are the least encroached upon by the pernicious qualities of modern life which, according to Taylor, have generated cultural despair. In our experience of our own bodies and those of others, we may experience sexual desire, the relishing of powerful sensations through touch, taste, hearing, smell and sight. There may be a heightened sense of our own vulnerability to aging, illness and mortality and of the possibilities and limitations of personal freedom and spontaneity. The image of the naked portrait serves to remind us of our primordial core, what we were when we emerged from our mother's womb and embarked upon the long, slow process of clothing ourselves, not just with garments and other adaptations of our physical appearance, but also with social and linguistic skills, and all the elements that make up personal identity. It offers both a literal depiction of the self beneath the façade, and a metaphorical image of the self stripped back to its 'authentic', pre-modern, pre-social fundamentals. In this way, naked portraiture becomes symptomatic of beliefs about identity in our culture.

Those assumptions are implicit in the widely touted distinction between naked and nude, launched in Kenneth Clark's *The Nude: A Study in Ideal Form* (1956).[37] For Clark, bodies are naked in daily life, while the sanitised version we encounter in art is the nude. The idea that the nude will transcend the particularities of any individual goes back to antiquity, Zeuxis, famously, creating his ideal image of Helen of Troy by merging the best qualities of five naked models, the most beautiful girls in the land. In *Ways of Seeing* (1972), John Berger adapted Clark's terminology:

To be naked is to be oneself.

To be nude is to be seen naked by others and yet not recognised for oneself. A naked body has to be seen as an object in order to become a nude … Nakedness reveals itself. Nudity is placed on display.

To be naked is to be without disguise … The nude is condemned to never being naked. Nudity is a form of dress.[38]

Berger also emphasised the element of male voyeurism in the concept and artistic currency of nudity.

'Naked' has since come to signify not something outside representation, but rather one version of representation. Depicting the naked individual, warts and all, has provided an antidote to the stale, generalised nude. For one critic, 'few nudes are more naked than Schiele's, exposed, their bones protruding, limbs contorted in pain or ecstasy'.[39] Arthur Danto writes of the negative associations that go with nakedness, repressed in the mediated state of nudity: 'Nude goes with beauty as naked goes with shame. The nude has nothing, the naked everything, to hide … nakedness is the natural metaphor for vulnerability … The naked body cries out for cover not so much against cold and rain as against the eyes of the cold.'[40] For Danto, Lucian Freud 'shows us pictures of naked humans, and with enough painterly realism, that we cannot use the conventions of nudity to treat them as beautiful, the way that it was demanded in Lord Clark's book that it do'.[41] Gilbert & George were delighted with David Sylvester's response to the pictures in which they divested themselves of their usual business suits: 'He said that all of the Modern artists … only succeeded in doing nudes … but that we have done naked.'[42] David Bailey sees his portraits in *Bailey's Democracy* as naked rather than nude and remarks: 'Nude is about the photographer, whereas naked is more about the people'.[43] In all such cases, an artistic, even moral, virtue is being made of the 'authentic' connotations of nakedness.

The art of Lucian Freud provides a vehicle for exploring this distinctively modern sensibility in more depth. *Small Naked Portrait* [plate 23] is one of the earliest examples of his use of the term. Appropriately, given the scale of the work, the setting is minimal. Gazing at the figure, in her semi-foetal reclining posture, the eye is drawn, as always, to the face, but also to the details of hand, breast, knee, arm, foot, all subjected to the same scrutiny. Indeed, the body is seen by Freud as a composite of disparate parts, which are varied in structural intricacy as well as in their particular skin colour and texture. Equally, the picture itself is constructed from interconnecting shapes. The facial features, exactly half-way up the canvas, lead into knuckles, an emphatic nipple, and across to the left knee. The same knee is the visual point of departure not just for the left leg, a structural anchor in terms of composition as well as anatomy, but also for the left elbow and lower arm. This forms a right-angle with the right calf, which in turn connects with the face and rhymes with the upper section of the left arm. This combination of structural organisation and vivid representation of anatomy, texture, and the play of light, is characteristic of Freud's naked portraiture.

Freud's engagement with such imagery is obsessive, going beyond artists who may have been catalysts, such as

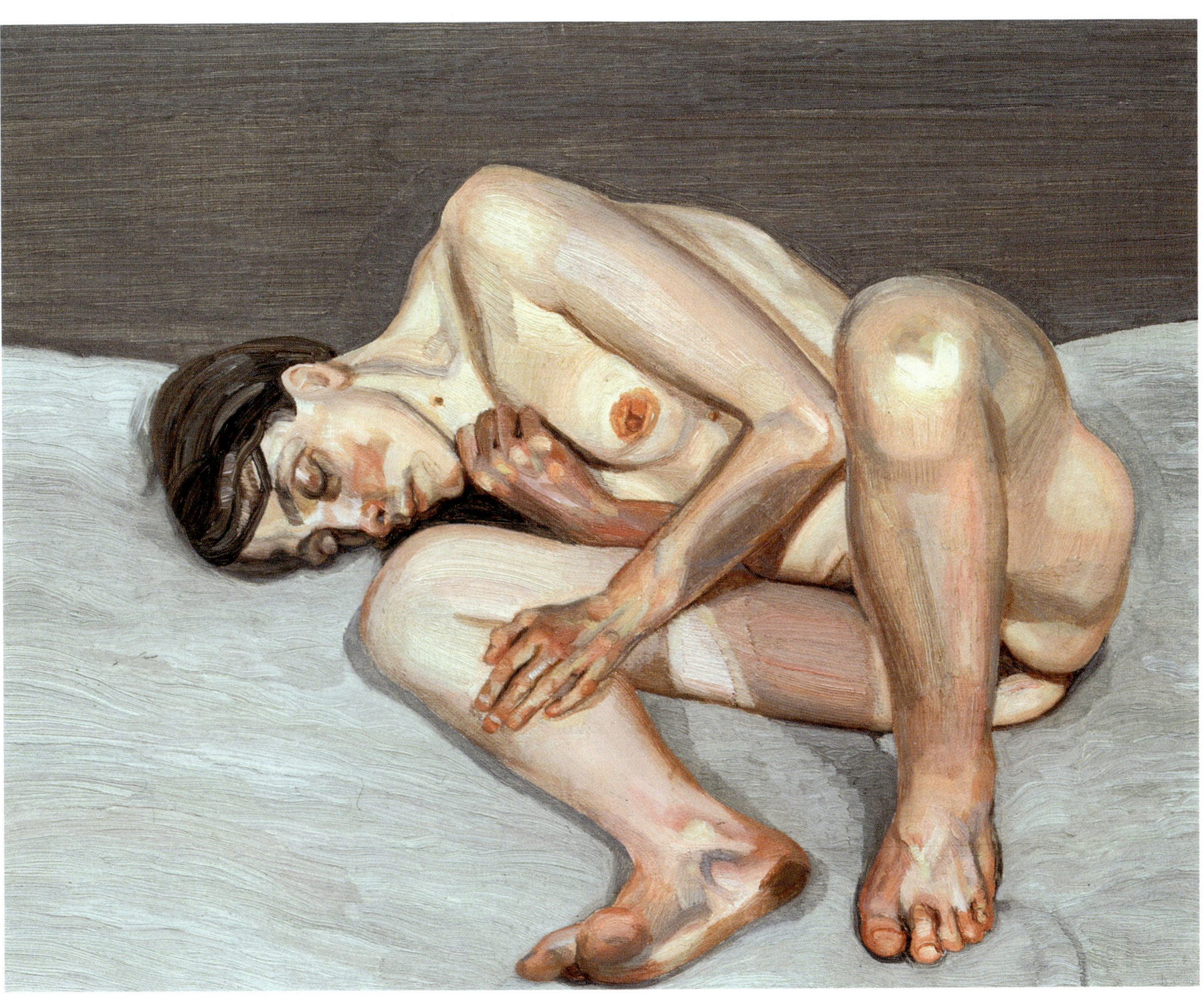

23 Lucian Freud Small Naked Portrait, 1974

The Ashmolean Museum, Oxford

Balthus, Stanley Spencer and Francis Bacon.[44] Surveying the long sequence of pictures from the second half of the 1960s, several continuities become apparent.[45] Their faces are impassive, masking unknowable thought processes. Typically, we seem to be standing, and gazing down onto figures who recline, sit, or sprawl. The details of anatomy and skin are strengthened by frontal illumination, producing slivers of shadow that enhance the sense of relief. Freud's colour range is dominated by shades of ochre, brown, off-white and fleshy pink, enlivened by passages of bright colour or pattern. This austerity complements the unglamorous types and poses of the figures. The emphatic surfaces avoid decorative mark-making; we observe, rather, how paint is applied in very different ways, even within a single picture, to evoke specific substances. The figures sometimes assume twisted configurations, but there is a general absence of gesture or movement. They look as though they are there for the duration, willing victims of an inordinately detailed scrutiny that lasts for months. There is no attempt on either the sitter's or the artist's part to conform to preconceived notions of body language. As Robert Hughes remarked, 'they bypass decorum while fiercely preserving respect'.[46] Genital areas are often prominent, treated with the same uncompromising attention as any other bit of the body. The gaze of the artist, which we are invited to recapitulate, is unselective and omnivorous. Freud comments on his working method: 'I used to leave the face until last. I wanted the expression to be in the body. The head must be just another limb. So I had to play down expression in the nudes.'[47]

It is sometimes said that Freud's pictures subjugate his female sitters, who are treated as so much meat rather than individuals. Yet it is illuminating to compare Freud with Egon Schiele, given the frankness of both artists' work (Sigmund Freud, with his emphasis on sexual instincts, was Schiele's Viennese contemporary and Lucian's grandfather). To a degree, Schiele's *Reclining Woman* of 1917 foreshadows Freud's *Lying by the Rags* from 1989–90.[48] But with Schiele, the splayed legs and recumbent posture evoke the erotic fantasy of a male observer. The body language of Freud's figure allows her independent consciousness, but she also exists as mere physical matter, along with the horizontal zone mediating between the hard geometric floorboards below, and the soft white and grey rags above. If there is erotic resonance, it is only as part of a wider appeal to our tactile imagination. The sense of unremitting substance, on a monumental scale (the figure is virtually life-size), coexists wittily with the floating and sliding suggestions of the composition.

In contrast to Schiele, whose figures tend to be variations on a theme, Freud's physical types are far from the stereotypes of nudity in art and the mass media. The majority are young women of standard shape and size, though there are a significant number of men, and some of the sitters, such as Lee Bowery and Sue Tilley, who posed for Freud in the early 1990s, are dramatically large. Freud's paintings compel us to confront flesh and skin, and its variations of colour, texture, hairiness, and the shapes produced by bone, and tendon, and pockets of fat. The viewer is invited to project their own physicality: '... his images of defenceless and vulnerable bodies, far from rendering us powerful as viewers, induce us instinctively to drop our guard. Rather than yielding passively to our gaze, therefore, Freud's subjects press on it invasively ... By means of the skin of paint and the painted skin, the painting addresses us ... through our own skins and in terms of bodily awareness'.[49]

Apart from the individuality of physique and body language, the pictures are set apart from one another by studio props. Thus different pictures of naked young women include a palette and brush on a table, or a skillet with two fried eggs [plate 24]. The lower parts of a pair of legs are reflected in a mirror behind the sofa on which she poses. A man tenderly holds a rat in his hand, while gazing off into space, and its tail drapes over his thigh. Another woman leans against a great pile of rags. In several paintings, a second figure appears, though there is usually no suggestion of communication, and one senses that each figure posed separately. A semi-naked young woman is joined by Freud's mother sitting in an armchair, facing away from her. A reclining man is flanked by a clothed, standing female painter, for whom he is presumably modelling, though there is no sign of the canvas and easel. Sue Tilley reclines uncomfortably on the bare boards in a painting of 1993, and behind her we see a seated figure, plus a dog sleeping on the bed. What, we may ask, is the expressive purpose of such props? The simple settings again highlight the specificity of the figures.[50] In the naked portraits, the people often lie on a simple bed, covered by white bedding or a patterned quilt, and the tubular metal headboard is occasionally visible. Alternatively, they recline on a stuffed brown leather Chesterfield sofa which has seen better days. The bedding provides textural and tonal contrast with the bodies and a neutral backdrop to the articulation of the human form. In the related etchings, Freud often leaves out the setting. The sofa functions likewise, but Freud also plays on the analogy between upholstery and body, both soft, rounded, and articulated in terms of smaller units, both possessing inner matter and an outer skin, both subject to decay and rupture. The walls, when they appear, comprise nothing more than discoloured, flaking plaster, and the

24 Lucian Freud
Naked Girl with Egg, 1980–1
British Council

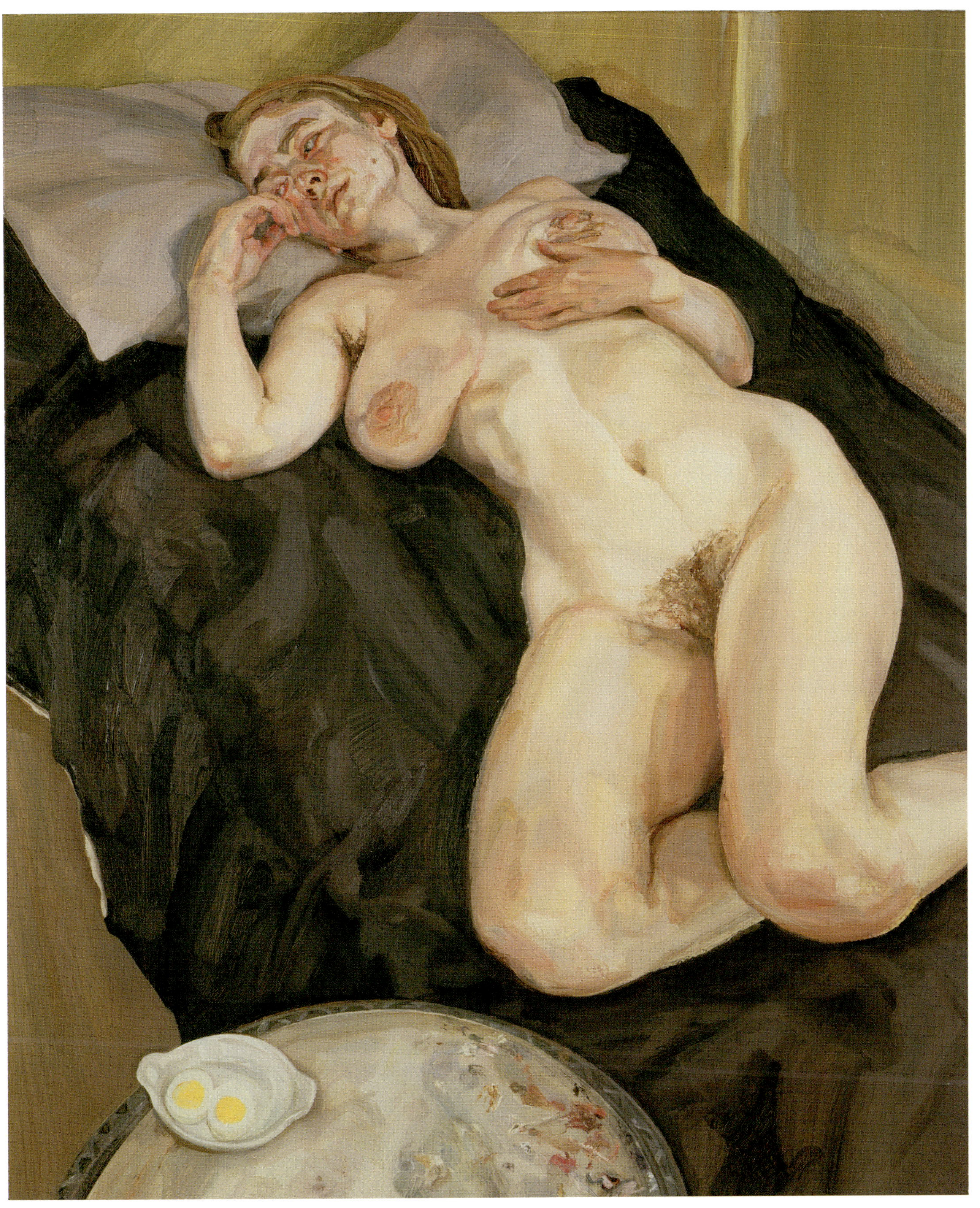

floor mere wooden boards. We infer that the sitters have come to the artist. The ingredients of domesticity, such as sofas, beds and rugs, evoke not just an artist's studio, but also a human habitation stripped of colour, pattern, and signs of social interaction. This slight remove from familiarity reinforces the sense that Freud's sitters have quit their domestic comfort zone, put aside their social façades, and exposed their elemental selves to our scrutiny.

Such self-exposure is not undertaken casually. A further thread in Freud's work, we are told, is that the people in the paintings are mostly the artist's friends or relatives. In 1974 he was quoted as saying:

I get my ideas for pictures from watching the people I want to work from moving around naked. I want to allow the nature of my model to affect the atmosphere, and to some degree the composition. I have watched behaviour change human forms. My horror of the idyllic, and a growing awareness of the limited value of recording visually-observed facts, has led me to work from people I know. Whom else can I hope to portray with any degree of profundity?[51]

The pictures are conceived as representations 'in-depth', a prolonged transaction yielding a distillation of the specific 'aura' given off by an individual. Freud has articulated his sensitivity to this physical manifestation of identity: 'You are very conscious of the air going round people in different ways, to do with their particular vitality.'[52] For Freud, making his pictures is a process of interaction and scrutiny to which the term portraiture is appropriate. From the viewer's position, the facial expressions and bodily poses adopted by sitters are bound to invite psychological interpretation, but predominantly the paintings read as exercises in observing the human body. A recent book about portraiture notes the 'debate about the extent to which Freud's ungainly naked figures should be classed as portraits, as opposed to nude studies'.[53] But his heightening of physical singularity has also been seen to inform 'Freud's great contribution to the "idea" of portraiture':

... it is not so much about 'penetrating character' or illustrating personality traits; it is about the strongest possible presentation of a specific human presence. And bound up with that is an understanding of other people's privacy, their essential solitude ... Even as he scrutinizes his models with the utmost intensity, Freud powerfully registers their unknowability. In doing so, he grants them a great depth of human freedom; this in turn provokes an impulse in the viewer to accord them a genuine, a believable reality.[54]

This is consistent with the fact that Freud's sitters are encouraged to arrange themselves as they wish. However, he often makes changes to the configuration of the body, as well as its setting, as the picture proceeds, and the visual evidence confounds his claims not to be interested in composition. The sitter is granted a measure of liberty, but Freud also exercises his freedom in order to create coherent and compelling paintings.

What illumination is provided by titles concerning Freud's relationship to portraiture? His titling, in fact, is not as consistent as the language of the pictures themselves. Sometimes the genre is acknowledged, as in the *Naked Portrait* and *Night Portrait* series, corresponding to two shifts in his production process. Other titles imply a specific sitter, but do not refer to portraiture, as in *Blond Girl* (1966), *Naked Girl Asleep* (1967 and 1968), *Naked Man with Rat* (1977–8), *Naked Man on a Bed* (1987), *Naked Woman on a Sofa* (1984–5), or even *Seated Nude* (1990–1). Elsewhere the sitter is characterised by what they are doing, and where or when they posed – *Standing by the Rags* (1988–9), *Lying by the Rags* (1988–9), *Evening in the Studio* (1993), or *Sleeping by the Lion Carpet* (1995–6). The latter two paintings feature the same, unmistakeable figure as *Benefits Supervisor Resting* (1994), and *Benefits Supervisor Sleeping* (1995). It is known that the sitter is Sue Tilley, but this is nowhere made explicit. She met Freud through the performance artist Leigh Bowery, who featured in the 1990 *Leigh Bowery (Seated)*, *Naked Man: Back View* (1991–2), *Nude with Leg Up* (1992), and *Leigh under the Skylight* (1994). *Naked Portrait* of 2002 unmistakably depicts Kate Moss. William Feaver confides the identity of certain sitters: Raymond Hall posed for *Naked Man with Rat* and *Naked Man with his Friend* (1978–80), Celia Paul for *Naked Girl with Egg*, Sophie de Stempel for the two rags pictures.[55] Only a few works are identified by first names, such as *Annie and Alice* (1975), *I.B.* (1977–8), *Rose* (1978–9), *Esther* (1980), and *Bella* (1982–3). These are pictures of Freud's daughters, sitters whom one might least expect to be identified by name (see Chapter 5). In the end, it appears to be entirely arbitrary whether a personal name, or terms like portrait, naked, or nude, feature in the titles of any particular picture in this extended sequence.

Freud might regard the matter with indifference, an aspect of marketing rather than the real business of making works of art. Yet he clearly does exercise control over the way his pictures are understood. In books about his work, a few trusted individuals provide the texts, and the images tend to be presented without accompanying captions. In exhibitions, viewers are provided with titles, but Freud forbids anything further, such as descriptive labels.[56] The transaction with his sitter may be crucial to the making of the pictures, but Freud seems to believe that knowing the identity of the sitters would be irrelevant for viewers. Neither words, nor the semiotics of clothing, domestic setting or environment, are on offer to tell the viewer what to think or feel. We are free, empowered even, to respond to the pictures imaginatively. There seems indeed to be a personal ideology in play here. For the subjects, identification might have been seen as an intrusion, given the frankness with which they had exposed themselves – although Freud's fully clothed sitters are usually not named either. The value given to privacy extends to the habitat of the pictures. Some are on public view, but a high proportion of his works are merely described as being in private collections. Freud is famously unwilling to perform the art world rituals; we are often told of his 'jealously guarded privacy, his intimidating reputation as a man so averse to certain social situations that he declines to attend even his own private views'.[57] In a recent film, many of his inner circle spoke about Freud's charisma, but he appears for the merest instant at the very end, walking across the studio.[58] In sum, viewers do not need to be told what to think; sitters do not need to acknowledge their identity; owners should not have to tell anyone what pictures they live with; Freud does not have to do anything he doesn't want to. The imagery of the naked portraits matches Freud's preoccupation with the sphere of existence in which one can simply be what one is.

Freud has remarked of the people in his pictures: 'Human, tired, they are the thing which they themselves feel is essential to them, which is the effect they have by their presence, which is relegated to actually being alive and being there and sitting there.'[59] A primordial mode of being is shared by humans and animals, and there is a raw, animalistic quality to Freud's portrayals of people. Nakedness strips them of names and occupations, allowing purely animal and physical qualities to come through: 'I'm really interested in them as animals. Part of liking to work from them naked is for that reason. Because I can see more: see the forms repeating right through the body and often in the head as well. One of the most exciting things is seeing through the skin, to the blood and veins and markings.'[60] On another occasion he remarked: 'You can't be aware enough. I've always thought that biology was a great help to me and perhaps even having worked with animals was a help. I thought through observation I could make something into my own that might not have been seen or noticed or noted in that way before.'[61] It is interesting that Freud's earliest naked portraiture should have coincided with the publication in 1967 of Desmond Morris's *The Naked Ape*, an exercise in popular zoology that argued that humanity is essentially a species of ape, sharing patterns of feeding, sleeping, fighting, mating and rearing young.[62]

Freud is driven not just to evoke the aura of individual nude people but also to attain a more fundamental idea of the naked truth. It is as though portraiture itself has been stripped naked, as much as the sitter. The pictures assert that painting can convey unique truths that differ radically from the registration of visual facts. The use of the naked sitter, and the equally stripped-back setting, symbolise such basic realities in descriptive terms. Freud's commitment to the notion that profound perceptions stem from engagement and experience over time is implicit in his processes of selection and organisation, in the body language of the people, and in the emphasis on working with sitters to whom he feels a close affinity. The visible build-up of paint and local colour suggest 'hard-won' representation. The paint surface also proclaims Freud's identification with old masters such as Rembrandt, or Frans Hals, and their aim to distil a specific human presence. His painting represents an antidote to the facile glimpses afforded by other modes of painting, or certain kinds of photography. For Freud, the main difference between the two media is 'the degree to which feelings can enter into the transaction from both sides. Photography can do this to a tiny extent, painting to an unlimited degree.'[63] The naked portraits are about the potential of a painting to convey profound truth beneath transient sensations.

But here, as in other respects, Freud looks representative, rather than a lone individual. Although approaches vary, such ambitions have informed the work of many artists and photographers who have engaged with naked portraiture. The lure of such imagery is that it is utterly specific and concrete, but also has rich potential for exploring metaphorical meaning and 'universal' themes.

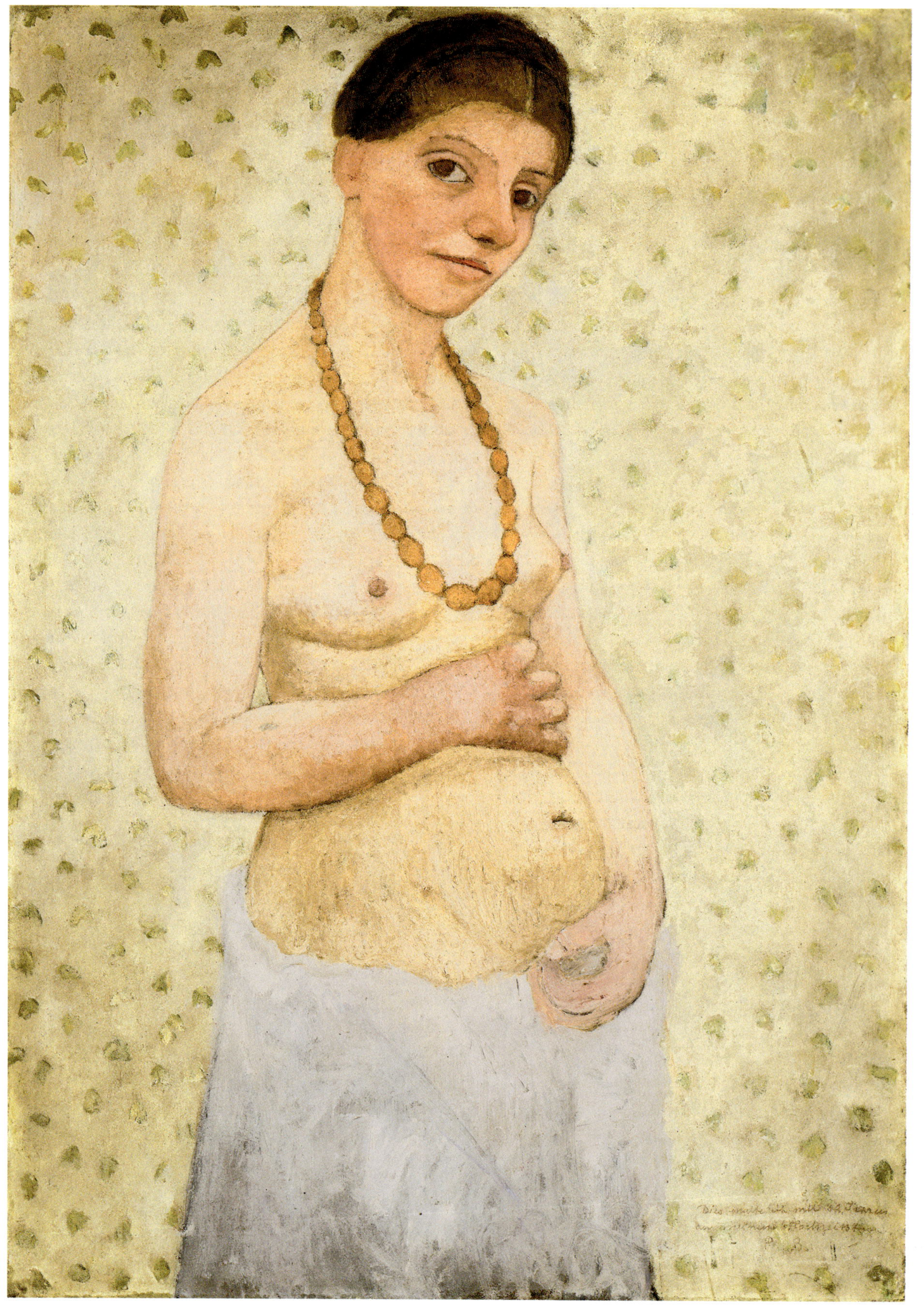
P. B.

Chapter 2 Beginnings

25 Paula Modersohn-Becker
Self-portrait on her Sixth Wedding Anniversary, 1906
Kunstsammlungen Boettcherstrasse / Paula Modersohn-Becker Museum, Bremen

A cluster of pictures from the early twentieth century mark the genesis of the modern naked portrait, although some pointers were provided by the previous generation. In particular, Auguste Rodin's sculpture applied a vivid naturalism to the nude human form, as an antidote to academic classicism. The resulting works were mostly given allegorical or mythic titles (*The Thinker*, *Iris*), but in 1899 Rodin exhibited one reclining nude, without head or lower legs, as *Femme (Adèle)*, acknowledging his point of departure.[1] Public sculptures such as *The Burghers of Calais* or the portrait of Balzac were preceded by full-size nude studies, in some ways more expressive than the final works. In the Victor Hugo memorial, the figure remained naked, as befitted a timeless literary genius. Several of Rodin's bust sculptures were nude by implication, in the antique tradition (see Chapter 1). One sitter at least, the painter Puvis de Chavannes, refused to be portrayed in this manner, because it might detract from his dignity.[2] Although naked portraiture was latent in Rodin, it was the frank vitality of his sculptures and drawings of the female nude that meant so much to subsequent artists, such as Egon Schiele, Alfred Stieglitz or Lucian Freud.

Paul Gauguin's *Aita tamari vahine Judith te parari* [plate 27] is another significant precursor.[3] The Tahitian inscription means 'The child-woman Judith is not yet breached'. It was painted in Paris, between stays in Tahiti, and the model was probably Annah the Javanese (an alternative title for the picture), who was living with Gauguin at the time as mistress and servant. But the title, if not the image, may well refer to Judith Molard, the daughter of friends, on whom Gauguin had a crush. Such enigmatic allusions are just one dimension of the picture's portrait dimension. The painting possesses visual affinities with contemporary society portraiture, such as John Singer Sargent's *Lady Agnew of Lochnaw* [plate 26]. Gauguin's sitter, placidly returning the gaze of the viewer, likewise assumes a relaxed, frontally arranged pose in her ornate chair. The orange monkey adds exoticism, as does the inscription. Otherwise, the main differences are that Gauguin's sitter is black and completely naked, except for a pair of earrings. Her nakedness extends to the audacious inclusion of pubic hair, which artists had always tended to leave out. It is as if Gauguin was debunking the associations of portraiture with finery and social status. Gauguin's sitter seems unembarrassed about exposing her body, yet she has none of Lady Agnew's arch flirtatiousness.

Although this particular Gauguin does not seem to have been widely known, his work inspired the young German artists who in 1905 formed *Die Brücke* (The Bridge), such as Ernst Ludwig Kirchner and Erich Heckel. By painting murals with distorted figures and sexual imagery, making wall hangings and furniture, acquiring tribal artefacts, and by assuming a bohemian garb and mode of behaviour, they transformed the studio into a 'primitive' environment.[4] This provided a suitable setting for their use of models who reinforced a preconception, widely held at the time, that the childlike was directly analogous to the primitive. In addition to generic nudes, Kirchner and Heckel made many images depicting two waifish adolescent girls, Fränzi and Marzella, the daughters of a local artist's widow, who joined their entourage around 1909 (it is now thought possible that they were the same person). These works show young girls possessed of an adolescent sexuality in excess of anything in Gauguin. Thus Kirchner exhibited *Marzella (Nude)* under that title at the group's show in Dresden in September 1910 [plate 28].[5] In comparison with, say, Munch's *Puberty* (1892), one of the key differences in the Kirchner is the specificity, not just of the setting but of the figure's features. The childlike ribbons in her hair, her painted lips and nails, her direct stare and the forward lean of her body all confront the viewer. Yet she crosses her arms and legs modestly, and her uncovered torso reveals that she is too young to have fully developed breasts.[6] While the Munch reads as imaginary, the Kirchner registers as the portrait of an

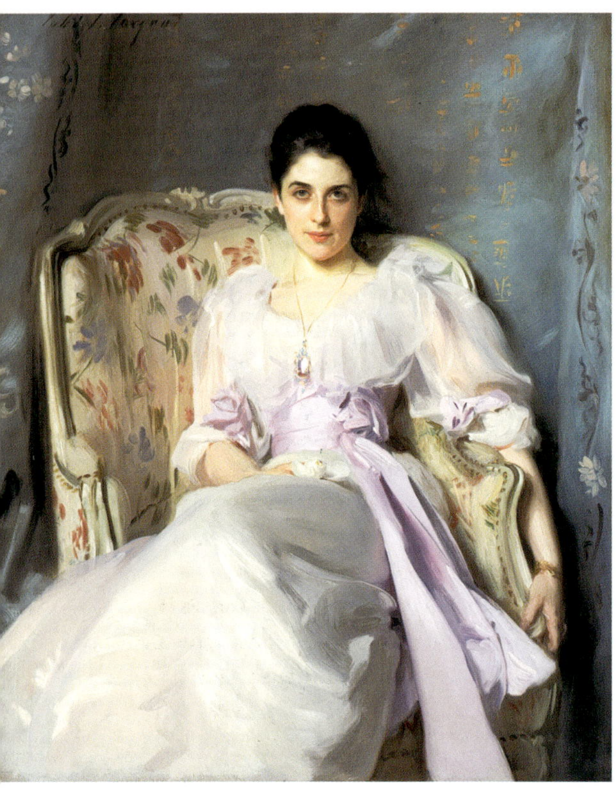

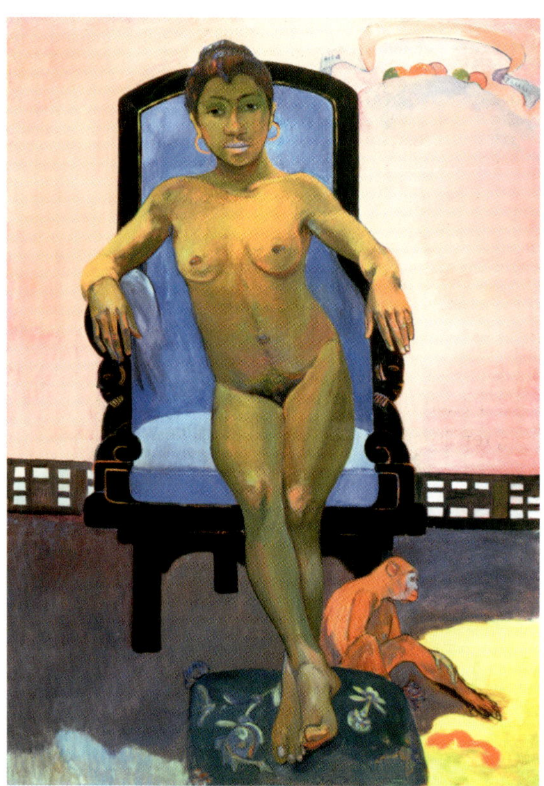

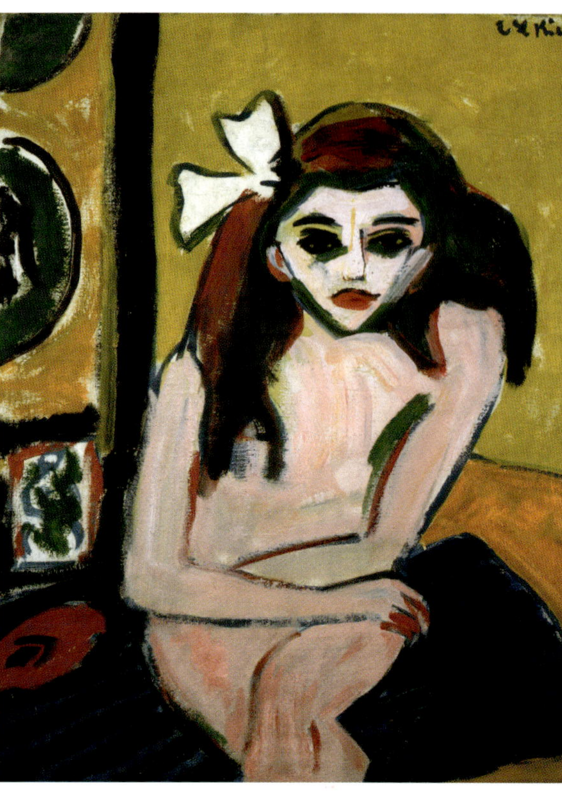

individual, who embodies the subtle transition between childhood and adulthood.

The period witnessed momentous shifts in the understanding of human sexuality, coinciding, above all, with the emergence of Freudian psychoanalysis in Vienna. Just as art assumed a primitivist look, so psychoanalysis trained its focus on the primitive depths of the self. According to Freud, we are far more influenced than we suppose by the subconscious strata of the mind, where memories of early childhood and powerful, often sexual, instincts inform patterns of behaviour and feeling in adult life. Analogies between clothing and the covering up of psychic vulnerabilities came naturally. On his therapeutic methods, Freud commented in 1909 that people 'do not show their sexuality freely, but to conceal it they wear a heavy overcoat woven of a tissue of lies, as though the weather were bad in the world of sexuality ... But when your patients discover they can feel quite easy about it while they are under your treatment, they discard this veil of lies.'[7] One of his most radical departures was to see childhood, not as an age of innocence, as was customary, but as a time of life in which sexuality is already pervasive. Freud's emphasis on candid self-revelation and coming to terms with buried layers of the self offers a suggestive parallel to the emergence of naked self-portraiture, with its connotations of unblinking self-scrutiny.

Indeed, imagery of the self provided the main vehicle for early experimentation with naked portraiture. Artists like Van Gogh and Cézanne had used self-portraiture as a vehicle for pictorial innovation and asserting their avant-garde identity. For artists of the next generation, nakedness came to register one element in an emphasis on fantasy and solitary performance, rather than recording creative activity in the studio. Lovis Corinth painted a self-portrait each year, as a form of physical and spiritual autobiography. His persistent concern with role-playing informs the 1907 *Self-portrait with Glass*, where he exposes his expanse of hairy chest [plate 29]. His head and lower torso are covered by pieces of cloth, suggesting a figure from classical antiquity. The imagery evokes the metaphorical state of intoxication that Friedrich Nietzche had invoked as the essential root of creativity, one in a sequence of works on themes of Bacchanalian ecstasy and excess. In other self-portraits where wine is being imbibed, the artist is clothed and it is his model (also wife) who is naked. The association between creativity and masculinity is also apparent in *Self-portrait with Glass*. Yet the treatment of the features is impassive, permitting us to see a layer of irony, or even despair beneath the immersion in sensual or creative pleasures.

In *Self-portrait in Hell* of 1903 [plate 30], Edvard Munch stripped himself back to the core, offering 'a direct portrayal of inner tensions, for which hell is only a metaphor'.[8]

left **26 John Singer Sargent**
Lady Agnew of Lochnaw, 1892
National Gallery of Scotland, Edinburgh

centre **27 Paul Gauguin**
Aita tamari vahine Judith te parari, 1893–4
Private Collection

28 Ernst Ludwig Kirchner
Marzella (Nude), 1909–10
Moderna Museet, Stockholm

The painting was originally called either *Self-portrait* or *Naked Self-portrait*, and then *Inferno*, before it acquired its present title. It projects a state of psychological crisis whose immediate causes were bound up with the shooting incident that marked the end of his relationship with Tulla Larsen. Munch depicted the aftermath in *On the Operating Table* (1902–3), another depiction of his own Christ-like naked body, surrounded by medical staff who symbolise the oppressive, uncomprehending society by which Munch felt rejected.[9] In *Self-portrait in Hell,* nakedness intensifies the sense of vulnerability created by the flame-like colours, the looming dark shadow, and brush marks that seem to dematerialise his smooth, feminised body. Paradoxically, the passage that contributes least to this expressive reading is the artist's face, which merges with the red background, with few indications of features or expression.

In Corinth and Munch, the neutrality of the features reads as a by-product of their concentration on the picture-making task. Yet the same mask-like quality is apparent in the primitivist self-portraits that Paula Modersohn-Becker and Pablo Picasso created in 1906. Picasso's bust *Self-portrait* registers a more radical archaism, realised during the course of his visit that summer to the remote Pyrenees village of Gósol, which 'temporarily became his ancient Greece, the embodiment of a strong living primitivism rather than an intellectual reconstruction' [plate 31].[10] In the pictures he produced in Gósol, and then from imagination back in Paris, the nude is a recurrent theme, leading to the *Two Nudes* and *Seated Nude.*[11] The impact of Gauguin (there was a big retrospective that autumn in Paris), and as the Iberian heads that he had discovered in the Louvre, informed Picasso's full-length figure paintings, as well as the portraits that formed a parallel stream in his work. His portraiture culminated in images of Gertrude Stein and himself that he completed in the latter part of 1906. The unclothed self-portrait is one of the least discussed works from this group. Picasso kept it, and it was one of the many works to emerge after his death. The picture relates to generalised nudes such as the *Nude on Red Background* and the Chicago *Bust of a Woman.*[12] It corresponds also to the Philadelphia *Self-portrait with Palette*, where the artist is dressed in peasant garb. The heads are especially close,

left **29 Lovis Corinth**
Self-portrait with Glass, 1907
National Gallery, Prague

right **30 Edvard Munch**
Self-portrait in Hell, 1903
Munch Museum, Oslo

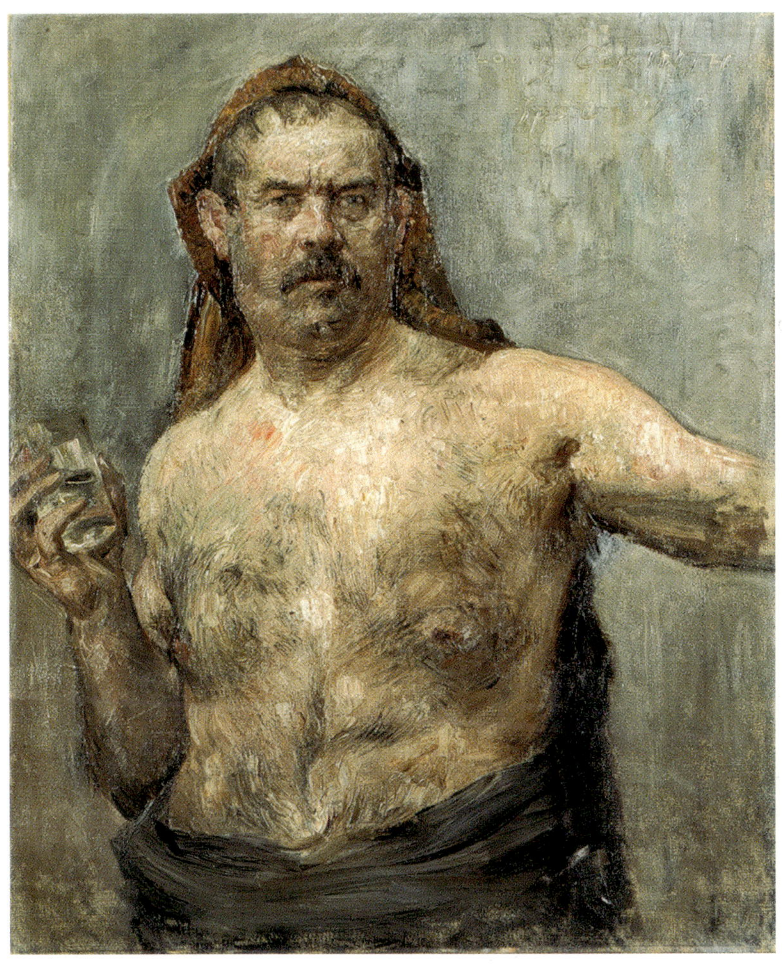

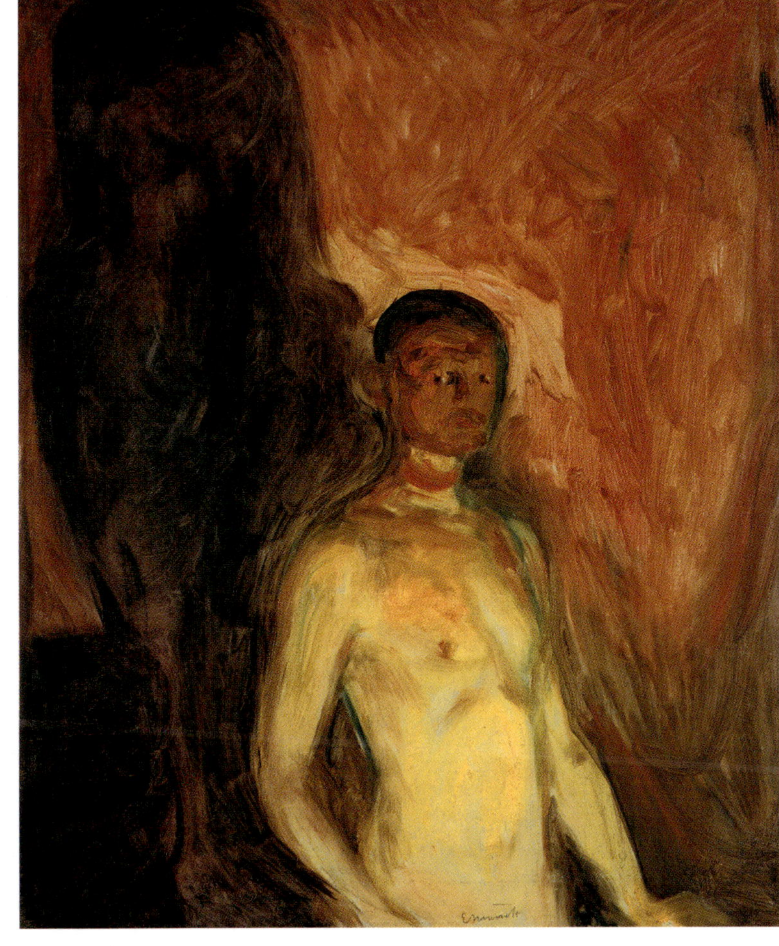

although there is a slight increase in specificity in the clothed picture. The lips, eyes, ears, eyebrows, and, above all the nose, convey more precise observation, as does the description of the neck which becomes a pure cylinder in the Paris painting. Here the greater degree of schematisation reinforces the allusion to archaic classical sculpture. Picasso's features still come across with sufficient vividness to suggest that he conceived the picture as some form of self-portrait. As Tim Hilton remarked: 'It is as though he were not primitivizing art but primitivizing his own self … the age of the artist is now made strangely ungraspable, as though he could be adolescent, or younger, or quite out of time and without age.'[13]

In Modersohn-Becker's *Self-portrait with Amber Necklace* and *Self-portrait on her Sixth Wedding Anniversary* [plate 25], the artist's nudity correlates with the stripping away of detail that characterises her formal language. The simplifications of form and painterly touch indicate an awareness of the art of Gauguin and Cézanne, who were currently being rediscovered by progressive artists in France and Germany. In the *Self-portrait with Amber Necklace*, Modersohn-Becker projects herself as the equivalent to one of Gauguin's Tahitian girls, whose nakedness signifies their closeness to nature. It has been argued from a feminist position that such pictures are a naturalistic and celebratory antidote to the denigrating abstractions of the female body produced by male modernists such as Matisse or Kirchner.[14] Yet, despite her body language, the artist was not actually pregnant when she painted *Self-portrait on her Sixth Wedding Anniversary*. The previous month she had written that she did not want to have a child yet.[15] The suggestion of pregnancy functions metaphorically, to convey the sense of fulfilment that she was experiencing, having left her husband, and Germany, and moved to Paris, to immerse herself in painting. The image is just as much a fictional construct as work by her male contemporaries.

Vienna was the key centre for the production of this type of imagery. In Richard Gerstl's two strikingly large, nude self-portraits, dating from 1904–5 and 1908, the artist seems radically liberated from sexual and social constraints. In the earlier picture, Gerstl appears otherworldly, exploiting to this end both form (symmetry, simplicity, colour) and subject-matter (nudity, absence of setting),[16] so that he looks like a Buddhist monk. Alternatively, he 'depicts himself emerging through a halo of light, wrapped in a white sheet as the baptised, or perhaps newly resurrected, Christ'.[17] In the 1908 *Self-portrait Nude*, the artist's body is permitted to gesture more freely, both as depicted and as the instrument of the picture's spontaneous mark-making [plate 32]. Gerstl has been seen as drawing inspiration from a work that could

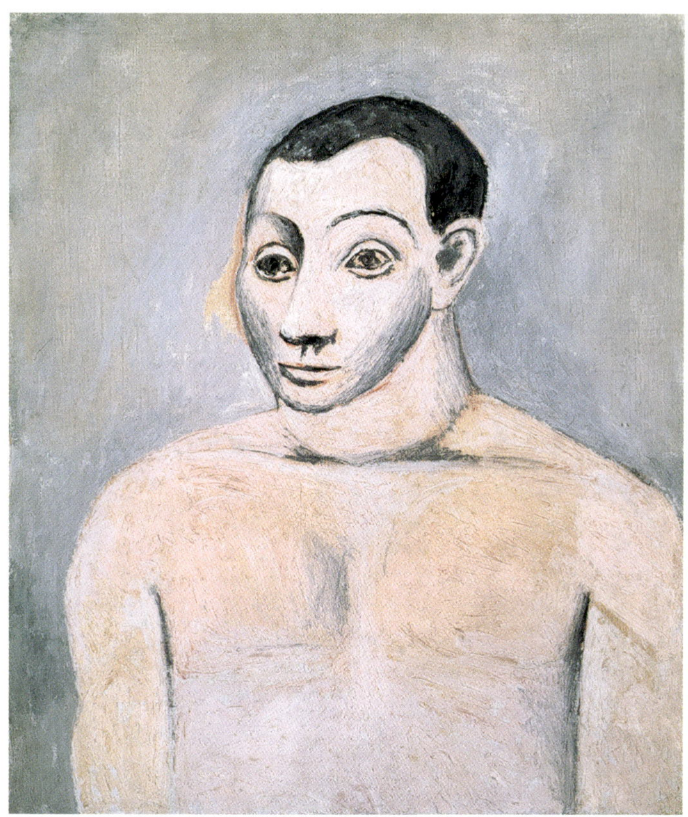

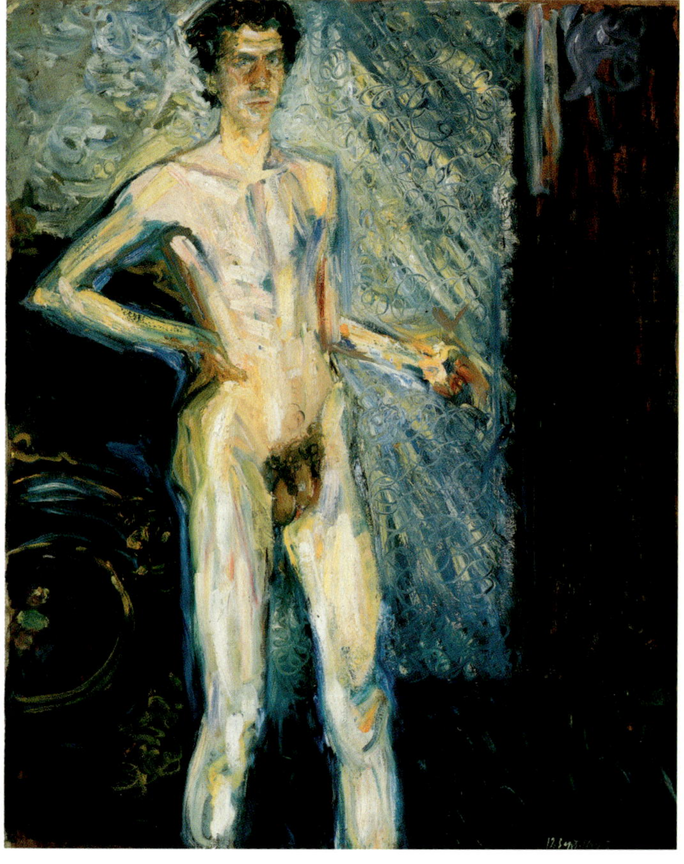

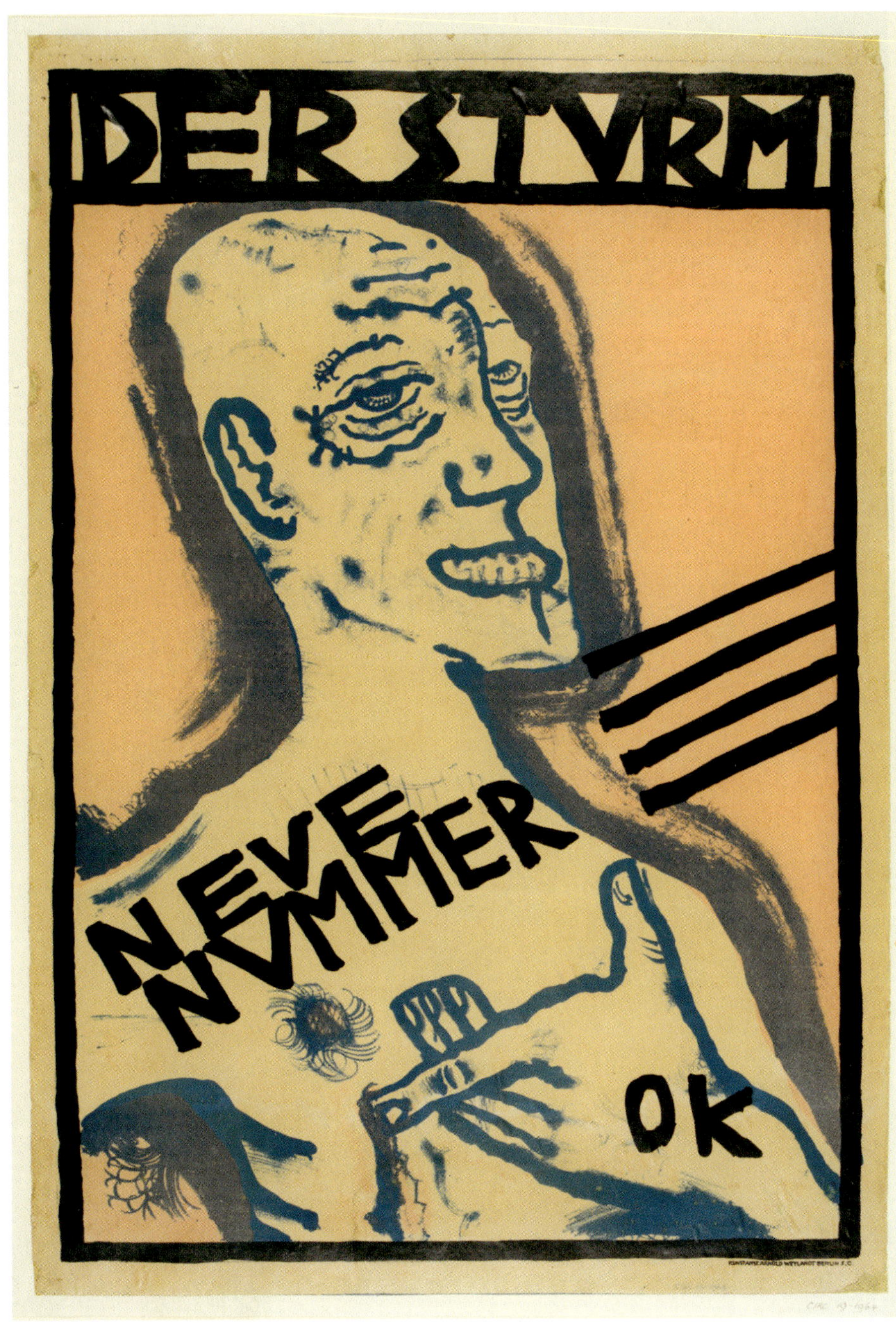

opposite above
31 Pablo Picasso
Self-portrait, 1906
Picasso Museum, Paris

opposite below
32 Richard Gerstl
Self-portrait Nude, 1908
Leopold Museum, Vienna

above **33 Oskar Kokoschka**
Self-portrait, Poster for *Der Sturm*, 1910
Victoria & Albert Museum, London

hardly be more tightly controlled and linear, Albrecht Dürer's nude self-portrait drawing of 1503. Interestingly, the Dürer seems only to have been identified as a self-portrait in 1906, having previously been regarded as a study for a painted *Flagellation of Christ*.[18] The most extreme example of self-portraiture incorporating religious symbolism is the poster Oskar Kokoschka conceived in 1910 for the Berlin journal *Der Sturm* [plate 33]. A recent account states: *Kokoschka deliberately cultivated a theatrical persona as social outcast. He shaved his head like a convict and proclaimed himself, in his appearance as much as in his art, as beyond the pale of bourgeois society. In this brutal and deliberately primitive image the shaven-headed and grimacing artist points to the wound in his side. The wound makes direct reference to Christ, but Kokoschka's probing finger can be read as either making the wound or else as exploring it, suggesting that it is precisely in the exploitation and examination of suffering that the source of his art lies.*[19]

It was Egon Schiele who made a more sustained contribution to naked self-portraiture than anyone of his generation [plates 34 and 35]. Virtually all commentators identify naked portraiture as one strand within a much larger body of work devoted to the nude, starting with the life studies that he made at the Academy of Fine Arts before graduating in 1909. Significantly, the young Schiele was confronted by the example of Gustav Klimt, whose images of the female nude take on an explicitly sexual charge. Schiele also derived from Klimt his commitment to portraiture, and a reliance on the decorative potential of pure line. It was for his elegant portraits, both works on paper and large scale oils, that Schiele first became known. The naked portraiture coincided with a large group of clothed portraits, both painted and drawn, that depicted his circle of friends and admirers, and that constituted his principal means of earning a living and launching his career as a painter. In his nudes, Schiele, like Klimt, worked in many cases from anonymous models, men, women, and children of various ages. However, in both his clothed and nude figure studies, he also made use, especially in 1910 and 1911, of his sister Gertrude, and close friends such as Erwin van Osen, and Osen's girlfriend Moa. The resulting images tend to be named, and therefore read as conveying Schiele's perceptions of individuals to whom he was close [plates 3 and 7]. The same applies to the large body of drawings made by Schiele in front of the mirror recording his distinctive features and hair, which are commonly seen as a remarkable exercise in self-scrutiny. The naked portraits bring together Schiele's interests in the nude and the portrait, which remained firmly demarcated in Klimt's work. The fusion is especially evident in Schiele's 1909 oil painting, *Nude Self-portrait with Ornamental Drapery*.[20] Klimt was an inspiration for the flattened language of the picture. Both in its imagery and in the interplay it establishes between narcissistic self-exposure and aloof detachment, the 1909 picture anticipates the subsequent body of works on paper which commonly appear under a self-portrait heading.

It was from drawings of himself and his sister that Schiele created a group of large painted nudes which he exhibited in 1910. In the paintings, as in the drawings, the figures are defined by means of linear contours, and they

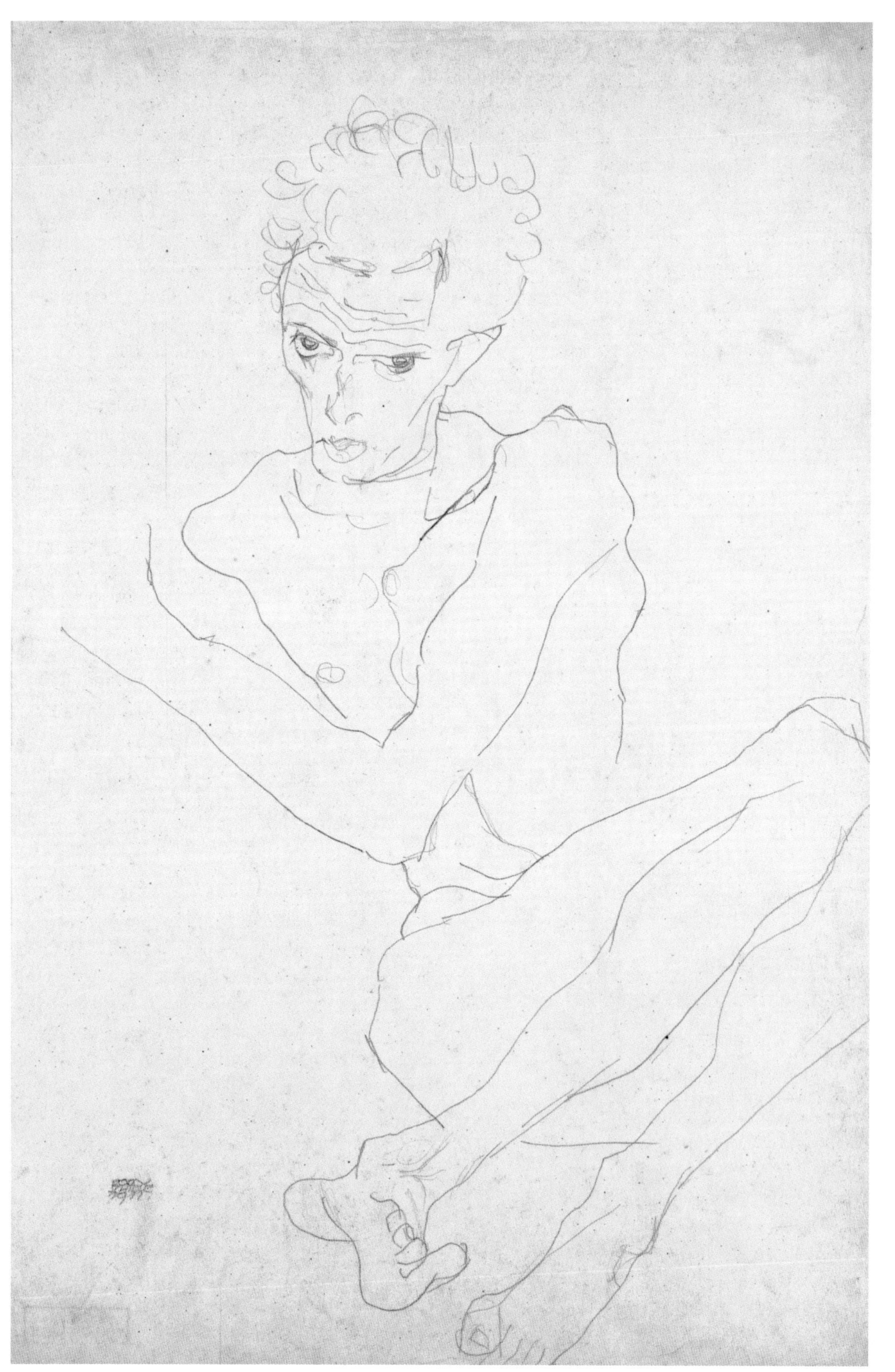

left **34 Egon Schiele**
Nude Self-portrait Crouching, 1912
Leopold Museum, Vienna

right **35 Egon Schiele**
Nude Self-portrait in Grey with Open Mouth, 1910
Leopold Museum, Vienna

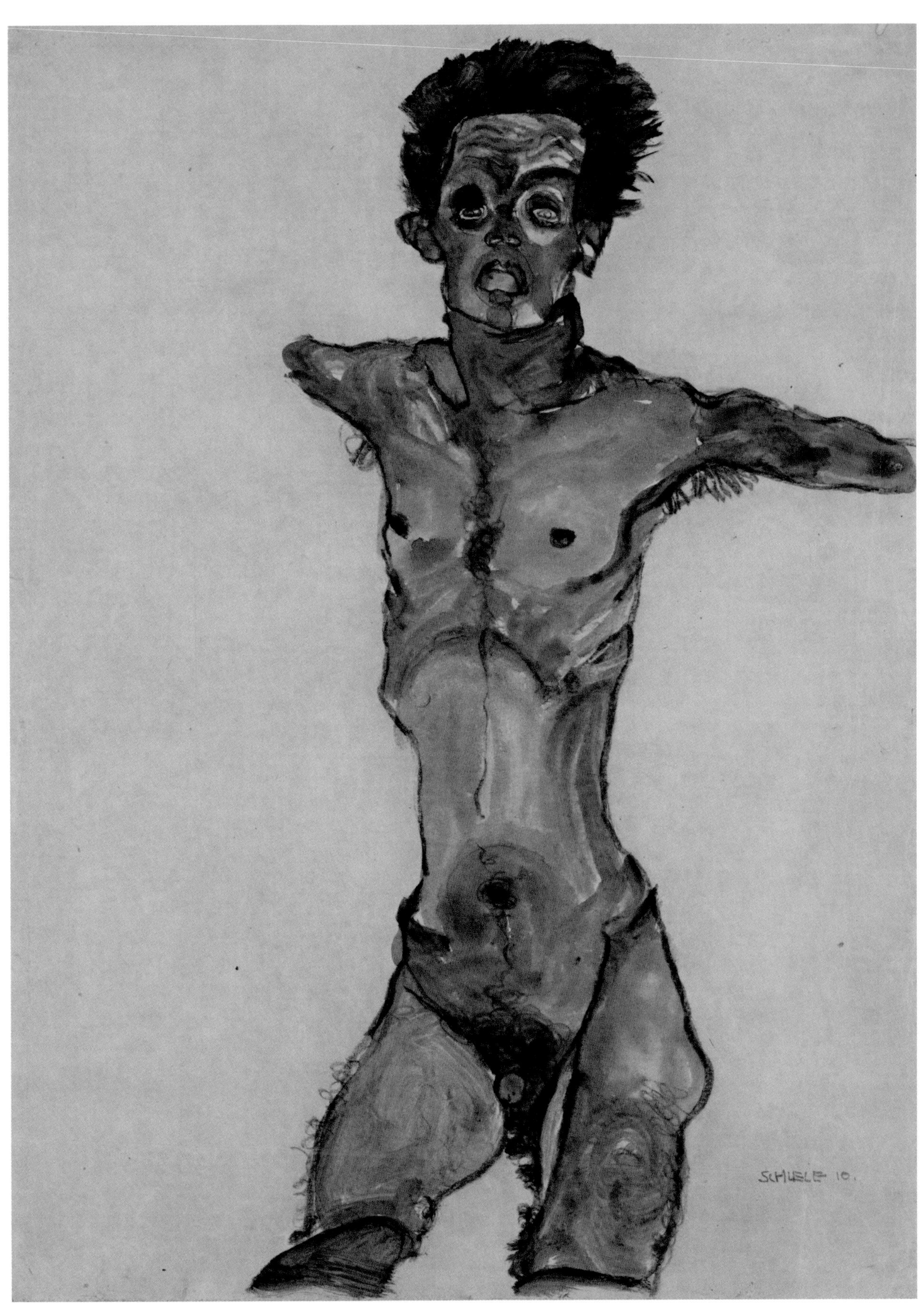
SCHIELE 10.

float against unmodulated white grounds, with no indication of a setting. Only one is recorded in a contemporary exhibition catalogue, under the curious title *Decorative Panel*; and one other survives, in the collection of the Leopold Museum, and, like the related studies, is now known as *Seated Male Nude (Self-portrait)*.[21] In subsequent pictures, Schiele's naked image formed the basis for a sequence of symbolic or allegorical pictures, such as *The Self-Seers* (late 1910), *Melancholia* (1910/11), *Prophets* (1911), *The Poet* (1911), *Man and Woman I* (1914), *The Family*, originally known as *Squatting Couple* (1917/18), and *Two Squatting Men* (1918).[22] Their present titles are frequently bracketed with references to self-portraits. Likewise, a lithograph based on nude studies in front of the mirror was originally titled *Nude* in a portfolio of prints to which Schiele contributed, appearing in early 1912, but it is known now as *Male Nude (Self-portrait)*.[23] This suggests that Schiele either was modest in acknowledging a reference to his naked self, whereas we are able to accept the pictures for what they really were, or that we project onto his work a more literal dimension of self-portraiture than the artist himself intended.

One problem with the works on paper is that many seem to have been acquired at an early date by private collectors. Without the evidence of exhibition catalogues, we do not know whether the artist explicitly conceived them as portraiture or self-portraiture. The drawings are characterised by a wide range of angular, contorted, sometimes spasmodic bodily gestures, which have been compared with the language of mime that preoccupied his close friend van Osen. They feature such innovations as white halo-like borders heightening the contours of the figure, unorthodox cropping of the figure by the edges of the sheet, and editing of the body by eliminating or truncating limbs. The emphasis on body hair and genitalia, the spindly, emaciated anatomy of the figures, the smeary wet-on-wet application of paint, and the exaggerated colours, all serve to distance his work from conventional idealisation. Such subversive features also occur in his drawings of anonymous models. There seems nothing, for instance, to distinguish the drawings of his sister from studies made from other models, and to that extent the mention of her name in titles is irrelevant. One account argues that such images 'do not suggest any intimate interest in these people, who were either relations or close friends. They all adopt the histrionic gestures which Schiele arranged for them.'[24] Is it also the case that in the so-called self-portraits Schiele was only using himself as a model? The one major distinction is the fact that the self-portraits, clothed and naked, like the pictures of van Osen, contain animated facial expressions, such as screams, grimaces and general contortions, and convey a sense of intense, and poignant, self-scrutiny.

We might see such work as essentially introspective, an exercise in psychic autobiography and the revelation of inner depths. The terminology of self-portraiture implies such a preoccupation, whether conscious or otherwise. Parallels are routinely made with Freud, a towering figure in contemporary Viennese intellectual life, especially given the emphasis in psychoanalysis on the profound and pervasive role of sexual instincts in the workings of the human mind, explored, for instance, in the *Three Essays on the Theory of Sexuality* (1905). But one could equally argue that Schiele was an acutely self-aware artist, rather than a solitary figure at the mercy of subconscious urges. In artistic terms, historians have perceived informed responses in Schiele's early work to Van Gogh, Hodler, the drawings of Rodin, the sculpture of Georg Minne, and others. Schiele was also a highly political figure, at any rate in an art world context, and one can presume an equivalent awareness of intellectual currents 'in the air'. One might read the 1909 self-portrait as a visual statement consonant with ideas that he evidently promoted in a manifesto circulated on the occasion of a group exhibition in Vienna in December 1909. According to the revised version printed in 1914, he believed that it was the task of the original artist to 'be, unconditionally, himself; he must be a creator, he must build the foundations entirely alone without recourse to anything that has been handed down from the past. Then he is an artist. Let each of us be one – ourselves.'[25] Stripping away the social façade could well have offered a visual metaphor for Schiele's sense that the artist's fundamental point of departure was the self, the distinctive personal and artistic resources to which he alone had access.

The notion that Schiele knowingly manipulated his self-image underlies Kirk Varnedoe's analysis: 'What seems most tellingly modern about these works is not the directness of their communication, but its obliqueness; not the sense of revelation, but the sense of performance ... The nudity here is not the sign of ideal truth, but of studio artifice.'[26] Others have speculated that Schiele's role-playing reflected an interest in the symptoms, and perhaps their photographic record, of hysteria, insanity, and general mental instability. The treatment of his own features, combined with the emaciated, wraith-like aura of the body, and the frequent implied fragmentations, might also characterise the artist as a tragic visionary, almost Christ-like, an outsider rejected and persecuted by a materialistic, bourgeois society. Parallels have been drawn between Schiele's white haloes and imagery relating to theosophy and spiritualism, then fashionable.[27] The naked self-portraits encapsulated an image of the figure of the artist as an alienated figure, whose sensitivity and inner-directedness nevertheless provided the only effective antidote to the philistinism and materialism of the age. This at any rate was a pervasive assumption in his milieu. Freud and his followers argued that we permit the artist to give free expression to those subconscious and erotic instincts that the smooth running of society requires the rest of us to repress.[28] An assimilation of such thinking about the artist as a type may well have informed Schiele's staged self-portraiture, in the drawings and the allegorical paintings for which they formed a basis.

Self-portraiture came into its own when art was directed inwards, even more so than in the Romantic period. The twentieth century in literature has been described as 'the era of the literary confession, of the literary memoir, of self-exposure and revelation', of 'a pervasive sense that the author somehow expresses something of herself in her writing'.[29] Much the same could be said about the visual arts. Yet, in the wake of debates about authorial control, we tend to distrust too simplistic an idea that art expresses the inner self. We are told that 'such confessionalism is not incompatible with impersonality, that autobiography can be a way of depersonalizing, or disowning, the self, just as the project of impersonality can be bound up with an expression of intense subjectivity'.[30] The naked self-portrait possesses a similar ambiguity. The image suggests an introspective probing of psychic layers beneath the façade that the artist, like anyone else, presents to the world. Yet looking at, or imagining, oneself naked could equally function as a distancing device, a means of separating the imaginary self projected in art from the everyday, contingent self, what Yeats called 'the bundle of accidents and incoherence that sits down to breakfast'. Notwithstanding the 'natural' and revelatory connotations of naked self-portraiture, the theme can as easily become a vehicle for enacting a role or fantasy, for performing a self constructed for the purpose, rather than unveiling some authentic, essential self. Such complexity of purpose will be seen persisting in subsequent explorations of naked self-portraiture (see Chapters 6 and 7).

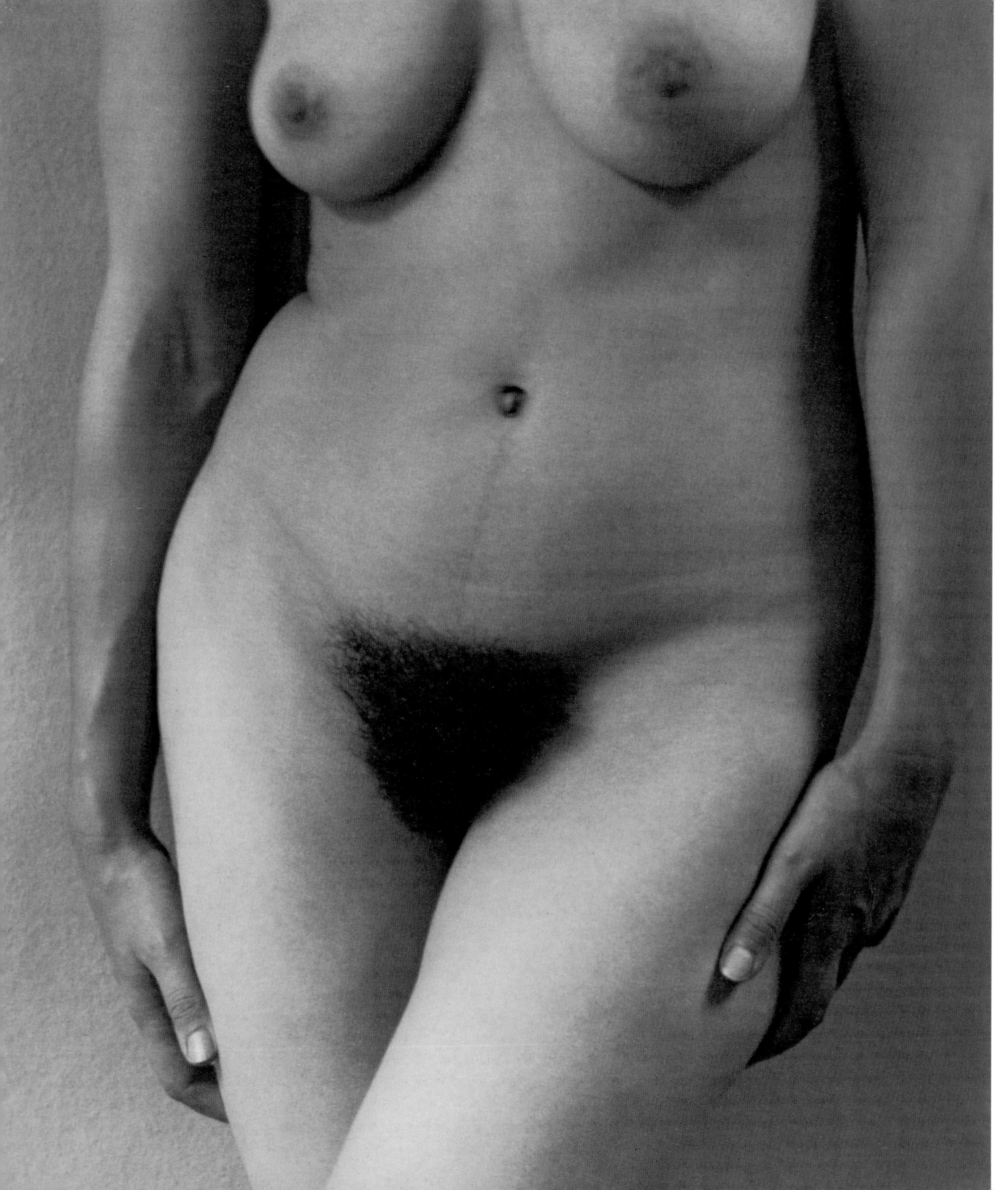

Chapter 3 With Love

36 Alfred Stieglitz

A Portrait Torso (Georgia O'Keefe), 1918

Victoria & Albert Museum, London

It is one thing for an artist to use their partner as a convenient model, quite another to work from the impulse described by Harry Callahan: 'I wanted to photograph the person for whom I had feeling. It wasn't enough to just photograph a nude.'[1] Images of loved ones tend to be decorous, especially if they have public currency, whereas nudity is associated with the private, sexual dimension of a relationship. If an artist makes a naked portrait of a loved one, the intention, we presume, is to encompass feelings of trust, tenderness and desire between artist and sitter. The many manifestations of this approach have even extended to sculpture, with its traditional commitment to the generalised nude, as in Don Brown's recent scaled-down portrayals of his partner Yoko.[2]

Such imagery is not unprecedented. In his critique of the nude, John Berger argued that in a few exceptional 'paintings of loved women, more or less naked', the artist's 'personal vision of the particular woman he is painting is so strong that it makes no allowance for the spectator'. The painter articulated 'her will and intentions in the very structure of the image, in the very expression of her body and face', [3] so that the viewer cannot 'turn her into a nude'. His examples included *Hélène Fourment in a Fur Coat* (1630s), Rubens's painting of his young wife in a pose adapted from the classical Venus, goddess of love.[4] Berger also continued the tradition of reading much of Rembrandt's art as a species of autobiography. His unidealised nudes have been seen as imaginative portrayals, although *A Woman in Bed* has been identified with three women in his life, depending on the date given to the picture [plate 37].[5] This approach has been questioned: public nudity, including posing nude for an artist, was 'considered an immoral and reprehensible act' in seventeenth-century Netherlands, and only prostitutes would have exposed themselves to public scrutiny.[6] It is thus anachronistic to regard the pictures as portraits. Modern reactions to Rembrandt presuppose our own shedding of inhibitions, and affirmation of sexual desire as fundamental to human identity. This drastic cultural shift is associated above all with the thinking of Freud and his followers, whose description of the mechanisms of desire found overt artistic reflection in Surrealism. Yet a more open view of sexuality is a wider phenomenon than can be accounted for by the inspiration of psychoanalysis, and its resonance in art goes beyond the erotically charged images of Surrealism.

Alfred Stieglitz's extended portrayal of Georgia O'Keefe inaugurated a rich photographic tradition of naked portraiture. In the summer of 1918 Stieglitz's relationship with O'Keefe went beyond the friendship and mutual admiration that had grown up between the two artists, he in his early fifties and she more than twenty years younger. After O'Keefe moved from Texas to New York, Stieglitz walked out of an unhappy marriage, and they began living together. He also started photographing her in 'a kind of heat and excitement', as O'Keefe recalled.[7] The photographs now 'became less about O'Keefe as an artist and more about her as a woman and lover, and the sexual passion they shared'.[8] We encounter O'Keefe exposing and kneading her breasts, or standing nude in front of a window against a semi-transparent fabric. A cluster of images scrutinises her body from above the knees to above the breasts, either standing or sitting [plate 36]. Others concentrate on her breasts, hands, feet, or neck. O'Keefe's face, the traditional focus of portraiture, is often omitted altogether. Yet the nude pictures are not overtly sexual when compared to the photographs he made of Georgina Engelhardt or Rebecca Strand.[9] Although Stieglitz choreographed the images, an uninhibited attitude towards nudity was also part of her persona, just as other aspects of the photographs may have originated with the sitter. Her artistic production at this time featured fluid watercolour studies of the nude, including of her own body.[10] Concerning her first summer in New York, and the studio where she and Stieglitz lived, she recalled that 'it was so hot that I usually sat around painting with nothing on'.[11]

O'Keefe's identity as an artist was integral to Stieglitz's attraction, and to his portrayal. In his role as impresario, Stieglitz had exhibited her paintings in 1916 at his 291 Gallery. Following the Rodin drawings show in January 1908, 291 had become the most important venue in America for seeing exhibitions of contemporary art, including Picasso, Brancusi, and, in 1914, the 'primitive' African art that had spurred so many recent innovations. In 1915, for a mixture of ideological and practical reasons, Stieglitz decided to focus exclusively on American artists, showing experimental photography by Paul Strand, and paintings by the likes of Marsden Hartley and O'Keefe. His first, clothed, photographs of O'Keefe dated from her brief visit to the city in June 1917, when she was again featured by the gallery. As with his other portraits of artists, he posed her in front of her own highly abstract pictures [plate 38]. His own photography had become sidelined, but when he had to close down the gallery, straight after O'Keefe's show, he was evolving a new approach to portraits and cityscapes: 'Not a trace of hand work on either negative or prints. No diffused focus. Just the straight goods … everything simplified in spite of endless detail.'[12] Such artistic ideals also disposed Stieglitz to explore naked portraiture, with its visual simplicity and connotations of portraying a true, underlying self. Focussing on limited areas of the body permitted him to fuse sharp and vivid detail with 'abstract' compositional effects, within a modernist shallow space.

An innovatory notion of portraiture was forming in Stieglitz's mind. He articulated his sense of purpose in April 1919:

I am at last photographing again – just to satisfy something within me – & all who have seen the work say that it is a revelation. – It is straight. No tricks of any kind. – No humbug. – No sentimentalism. – Not old or new. – It is so sharp that you can see the [pores] in a face – & yet it is abstract. – All say [they] don't feel they are conscious of any medium. – It is a series of about 100 pictures of one person – heads & ears – toes – hands – torsos. – It is the doing of something I had in mind for very many years …[13]

Stieglitz included a section called 'A Demonstration of Portraiture' in his retrospective exhibition at The Anderson Galleries, New York, in February 1921. This included sixty-one of the 145 photographs in the show. Sixteen consisted of two or three images of different, named sitters, and the phrase 'One Portrait' after the catalogue entries indicated a concern to suggest multiple dimensions of an individual. The remainder of Stieglitz's 'demonstration' comprised:

101–126 A Woman [One Portrait], 1918–1920
127–134 Hands [One Portrait], 1918–1920
135–137 Feet [One Portrait], 1918–1920
138–140 Hands and Breasts [One Portrait], 1918–1920
141–143 Torsos [One Portrait], 1918–1920
144–145 Interpretations, 1918–1920

These diverse images formed the serial portrait of a single individual, who was discreetly anonymous but recognisably O'Keefe to anyone in their milieu. She recalled: 'His idea of a portrait was not just one picture. His dream was to start with a child at birth and photograph that child in all its activities as it grew to be a person and on throughout its adult life. As a portrait it would be a photographic diary.'[14]

In a letter he wrote to Paul Strand in 1918, Stieglitz commented on what the photographs signified to O'Keefe: 'Whenever she looks at the proofs [she] falls in love with herself – or rather her Selves – There are very many.'[15] The notion of composite portraiture may presuppose a view of gender difference that photographer and sitter shared. The diversity of pose, gesture, expression, and dress or the lack of it, could have signalled a multi-faceted condition of selfhood, even an 'unknowability', that both understood as specifically female, in accordance with contemporary trends in psychology. For Anne Wagner, 'it was Stieglitz's great concept to treat the body as if it were a visual guide or index to the plurality of the female self'.[16] Gender differentiation certainly underpinned the unrelenting manner in which he and others read O'Keefe's work as projecting a distinctively female bodily sensibility. In an essay of the period Stieglitz commented:

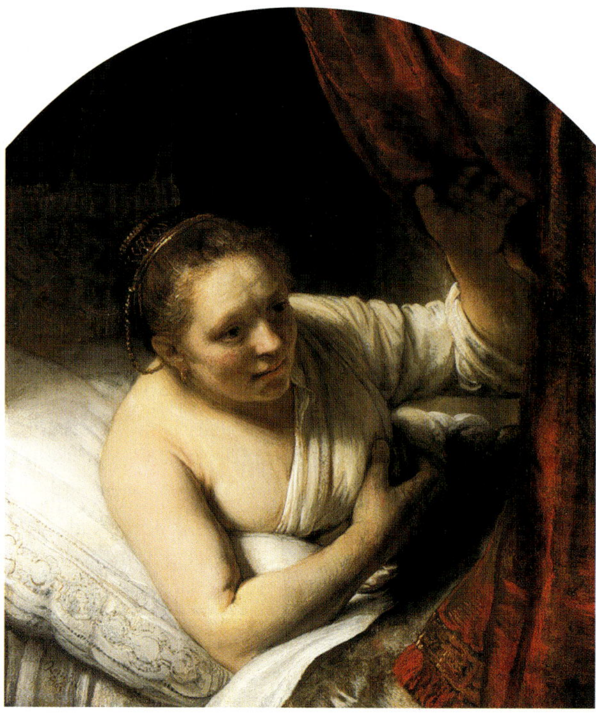

37 Rembrandt
A Woman in Bed, c.1645
National Gallery of Scotland, Edinburgh

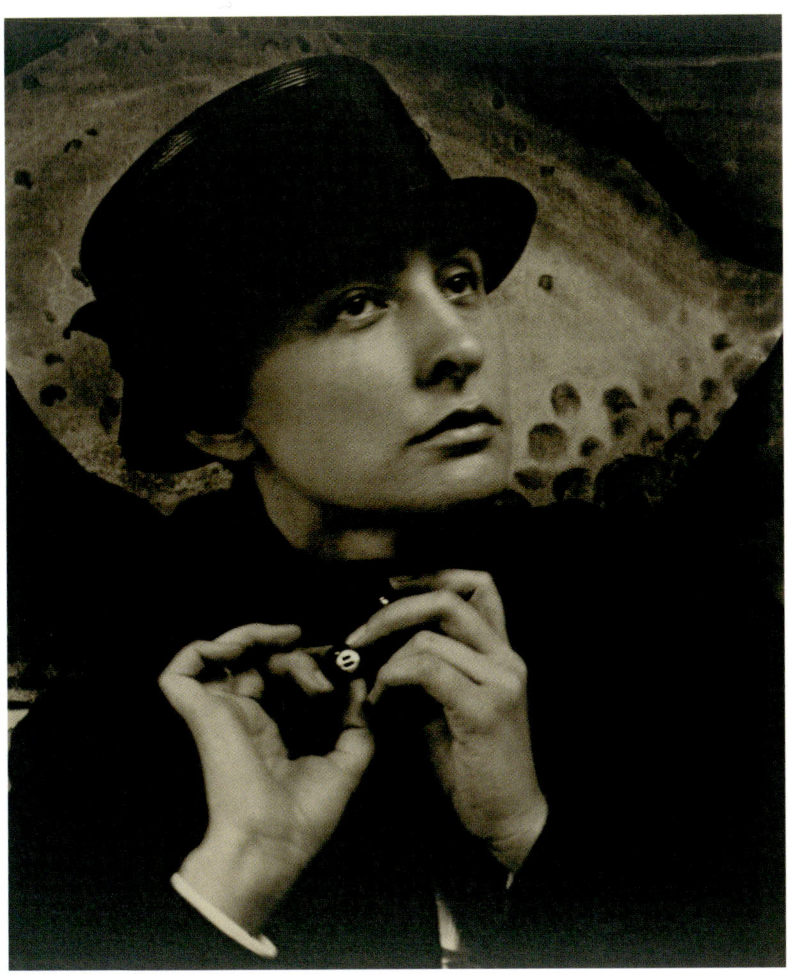

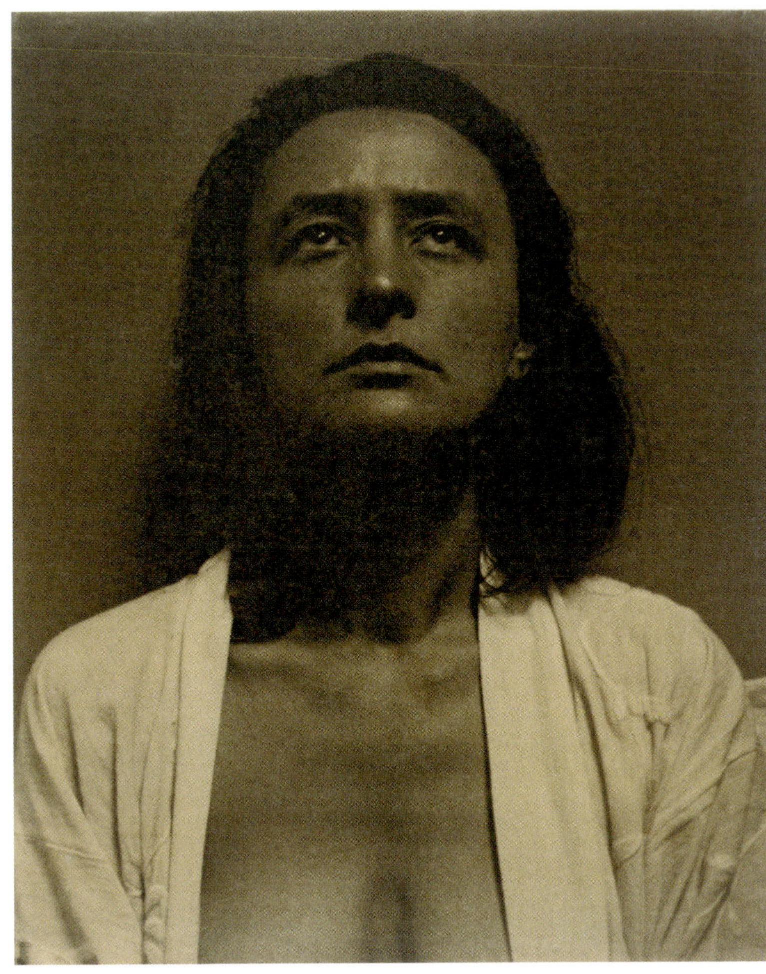

left **38 Alfred Stieglitz**
Georgia O'Keefe, 1918
Victoria & Albert Museum, London

right **39 Alfred Stieglitz**
Georgia O'Keefe, 1918/19
Victoria & Albert Museum, London

Woman feels *the world* differently *than Man feels it. And one of the chief generating forces crystallizing into art is undoubtedly elemental feeling – Woman's and Man's are differentiated through the difference in their sex makeup. The Woman receives the World through the Womb. That is the seat of her deepest feeling. Mind comes second.*[17]

This view of women as creatures of bodily instinct rather than intellect underpinned Stieglitz's focus on O'Keefe's breasts and torso, as well as the emphasis on hands, and thus sensuous, physical touch, as the expression of her female identity. Stieglitz came close to the curvilinear version of modernist style in O'Keefe's painting, promoting it as an expression of the artist's female identity.

Other influences converged in the series. The focus on the body brings to mind not just the ideas of Sigmund Freud, but also the frank treatment of sexual themes in contemporary literature, notably the novels of D.H. Lawrence which were admired in Stieglitz's circle. A photograph of Stieglitz's room in 1891 shows a reproduction of Rubens's *Hélène Fourment in a Fur Coat* on the mantelpiece, an awareness that must have shaped his own exercise in conjugal portraiture.[18] There is also the passion for modern art shared by photographer and sitter. It has often been observed that the silhouetted images of O'Keefe's torso drew inspiration from the Rodin drawings that Stieglitz had exhibited, of which he owned several examples.[19] Modern artists such as Matisse, as well as African sculpture, demonstrated that the nude was ripe for reinterpretation and experimental approaches to portraiture were current in New York Dada circles. Since 1915 O'Keefe herself had been creating abstract 'portraits', reflecting the reinvention of the genre by figures like Francis Picabia and Marius de Zayas, which Stieglitz knew well.[20] Such approaches may well have been a catalyst for Stieglitz's very different experimental 'demonstration'. As a bulwark against excessive European influence, Stieglitz and his friends developed a strong sense of American artistic identity, characterised by a primitive directness. Walt Whitman became a talismanic figure, and Stieglitz's multiple portrait of O'Keefe might have owed something to his poem *I Sing the Body Electric*, whose extended lists of bodily parts were recapitulated in the O'Keefe photographs.

Painters also produced naked portraiture of loved ones at this time. Most are images of women by men, but Christopher Wood's *Nude Boy in a Bedroom* of 1930 shows homosexual passion fuelling artistic expression [plate 40]. Francis Rose, one of Wood's lovers, recalled that he was the boy in the hotel room in Tréboul in Brittany.[21] The picture has been described as 'overtly erotic', with 'an unmistakably post-coital feel'.[22] The conjunction of bed and naked figure seen from the back certainly hints at mutual sexual attraction. The way the figure stands by a wash basin, looking at a picture on the wall, implies a concern to characterise a specific individual.

In contrast to Wood's faux-naïve modernism, the art of Stanley Spencer remained loyal to traditions of direct observation and careful drawing that he had assimilated at the Slade School of Art before the First World War. These methods underpinned the nude studies of his first wife Hilda Carline, whose counterpart was Carline's drawings of him [plates 41 and 42]. These tender images were precursors of the well-known group of paintings from the mid- 1930s, the outcome of Spencer's bizarre relationship with Patricia Preece. The two met in Cookham in 1929, and after Spencer moved back to the village of his birth in 1932 he began to use Preece as a model. In 1935 he completed the first of his naked portraits, a close-up half-length depiction of Preece [plate 43]. More than ten years later, he described the ambition that he thought had been realised here: 'I want to be able to paint a nude from life and do it as a portrait. I mean not so quickly but taking my time.'[23] A concern for warts-and-all realism is conveyed by the treatment of her veined, sagging breasts, the forms and hollows of her neck and collar bone, the variations of skin texture and colour, and by a fixed, uncommunicative facial expression. Hyman remarks on 'the counterpoint between leather upholstery-

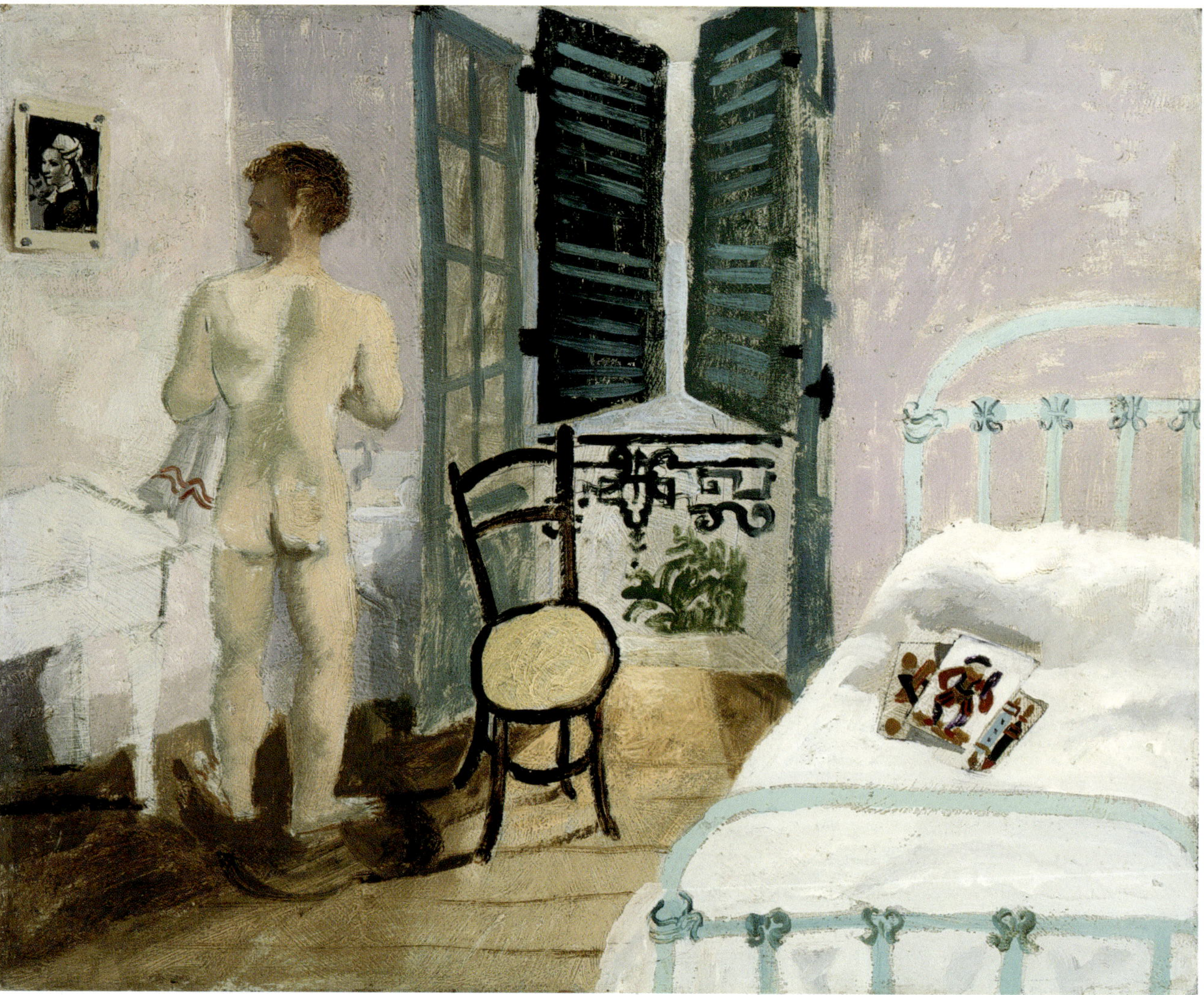

40 Christopher Wood
Nude Boy in a Bedroom, 1930
Scottish National Gallery of Modern Art, Edinburgh

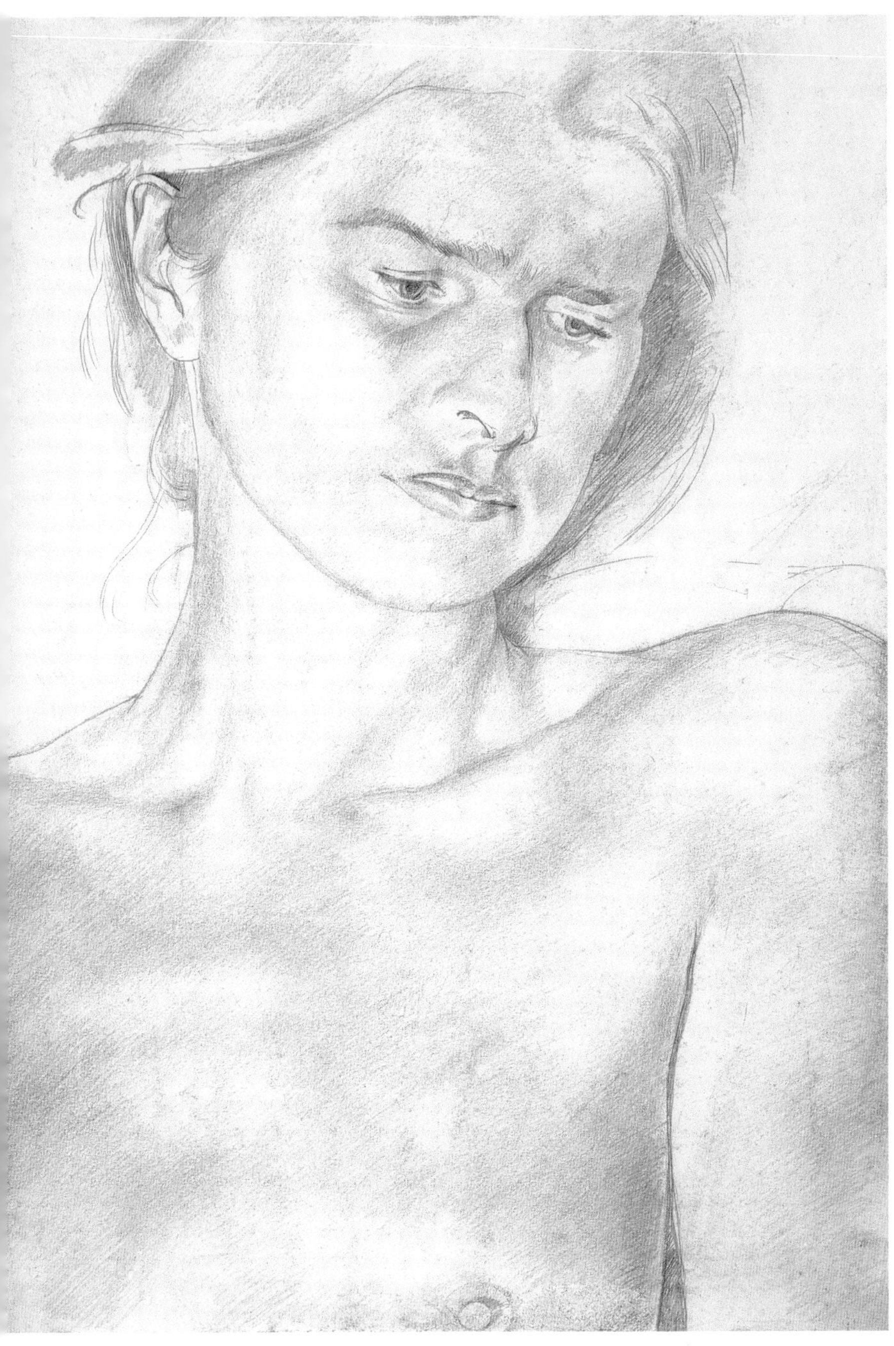

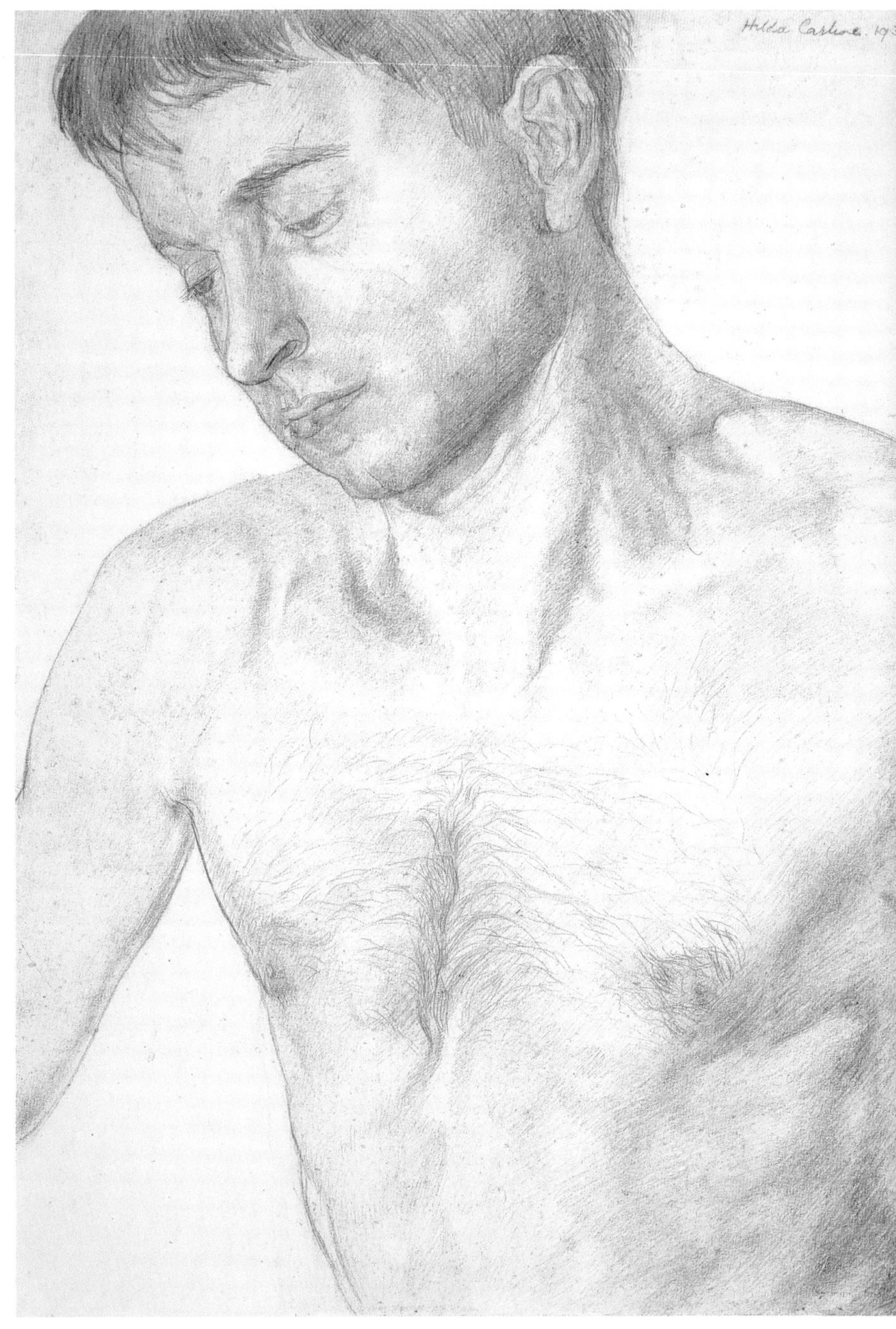

left **41 Stanley Spencer**
Hilda Spencer, 1931
Scottish National Gallery of Modern Art, Edinburgh

right **42 Hilda Carline**
Stanley Spencer, 1931
Scottish National Gallery of Modern Art, Edinburgh

buttons, eyes and nipples; between concave black-leather swirls, and convex white breasts', to which might be added the general leatheriness of Preece's skin.[24] The cropping at the edges, especially in the treatment of the head, reinforce the impression that Spencer started with what really interested him, the upper torso, and then fitted in the other parts of the body. This projection of a middle-aged man's desire was taken up again in his subsequent double portraits (see Chapter 4).

Comparable imagery is treated differently in the work of David Bomberg, a fellow student of Spencer's at the Slade who reacted against this inheritance, first by embracing a geometric abstraction allied to Vorticism, and later by adopting a more descriptive painterly idiom. In his half-length picture of *Lilian*, Bomberg's girlfriend since 1928 and eventually his wife [plate 44], the palette, chiaroscuro, and thick brushwork suggest an immersion in Rembrandt's later manner. The sitter recalled that it was Bomberg's idea to paint her nude. The situation was unfamiliar and to overcome her shyness, Lilian posed with a black dressing gown

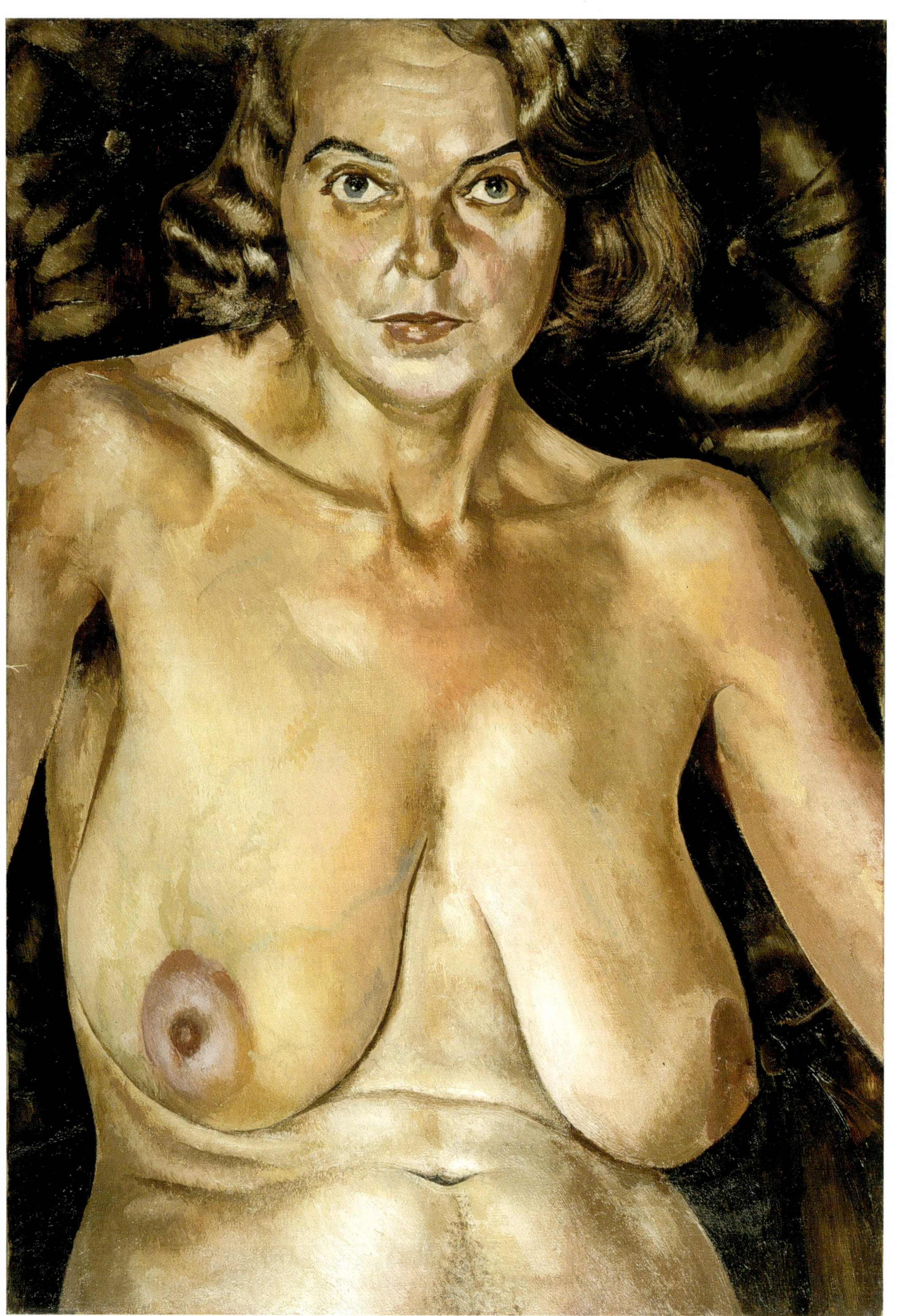

43 Stanley Spencer
Nude (Portrait of Patricia Preece), 1935
Ferens Art Gallery, Hull Museums and Art Gallery

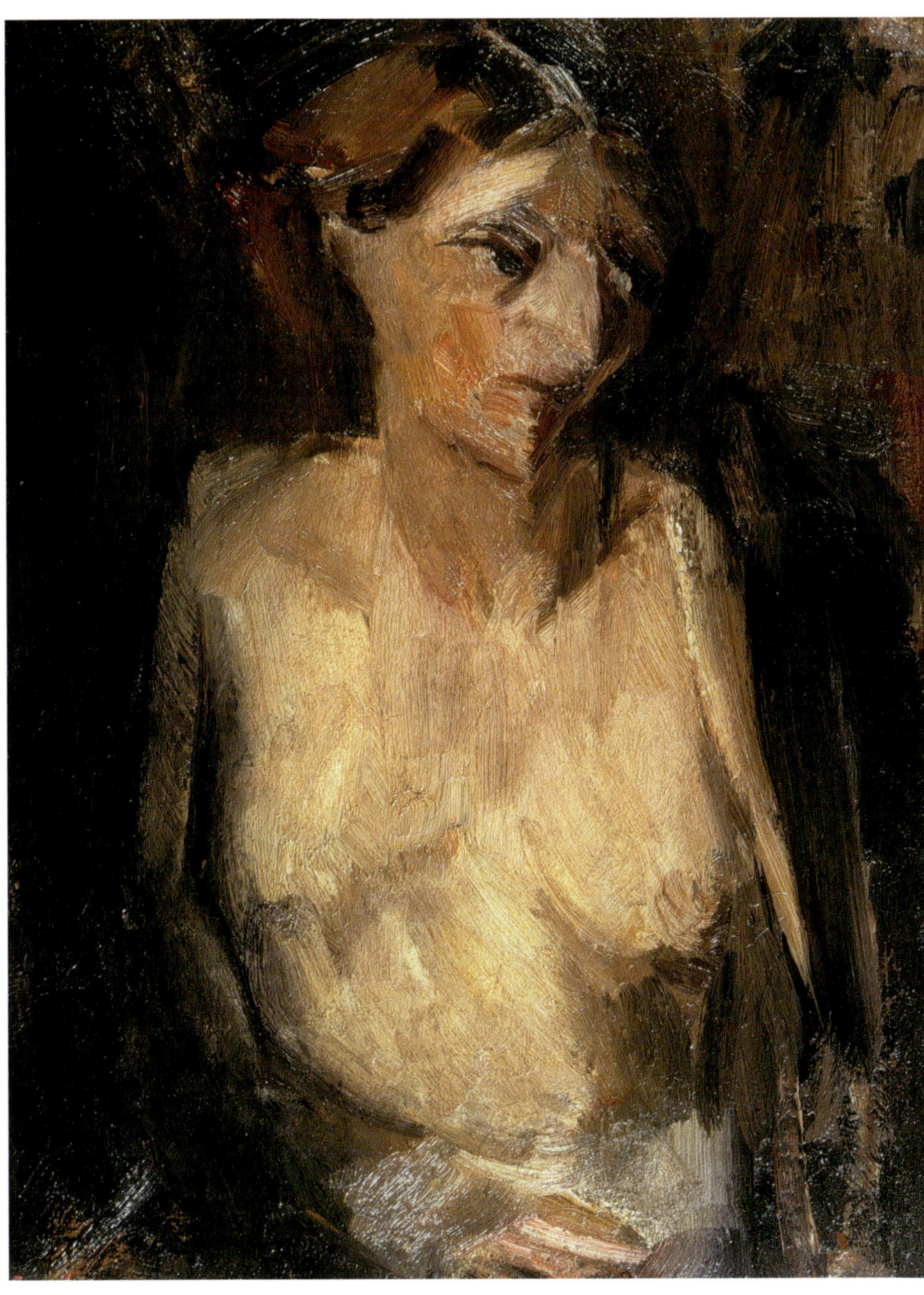

44 David Bomberg
Lilian, 1932
Tate, London

on her shoulders and arms. Nevertheless, she felt an active participant: 'You must give out your whole being, the same as painting. I was giving my whole soul to him. David insisted on my being very still – the stillness was essential to the giving out. And you mustn't talk.'[25] Lilian's availability was doubtless a factor in Bomberg's decision to paint her, as was his own for a current series of self-portraits. But, for Richard Cork, the picture is much more than a study of light effects. The sitter's pale body looks painfully exposed and isolated in the surrounding darkness, and she turns away as though 'unwilling to confront the male eyes scrutinizing her flesh'. The picture reflects her nervousness and 'a despondency in her expression' reflects recent difficulties in the relationship. At the same time, the free brushwork minimises the garment's presence, and has 'a tender and caressing quality which discloses the true depth of his affection'. Cork perceives 'a compassionate image' with complex undertones: 'Even though her gaze is averted, the picture still seems to be animated by the hope that she might soon feel ready to look at him directly again, discard her robe and restore the lost intimacy between them.'[26]

Is there a danger here of reading too much into painting? The same issue arises in another work of 1932, Picasso's *Nude Woman in a Red Armchair* [plate 45]. It belongs to a cluster of works connected to Picasso's relationship with the youthful Marie-Thérèse Walter. The artist's infatuation lies behind the combination of a particular physical type, clearly inspired by the blonde Marie-Thérèse, and a new emphasis on sensual, curvilinear drawing, bold patterning, and bright, decorative colour. The relationship was a closely-guarded secret, and it is no surprise that the pictures were exhibited with titles such as *The Red Armchair*, *The Dream*, *The Mirror*, *Sleeping Nude*, or *Girl before a Mirror*. A trend after the artist's death towards biographical interpretation of his changing patterns of style and imagery culminated in the 1996 exhibition *Picasso and Portraiture*.[27] The Marie-Thérèse pictures, like the clusters of works supposedly inspired by other women in his life, were presented as a species of portraiture, albeit involving formal abstraction, and conveying Picasso's states of mind in his dealings with his sitters. This was helped by the fact that he mostly worked from memory, rather than having the person sitting in front of him. Some of the 1932 pictures can be viewed as images about sexual rapture and abandon, or unreflective serenity, whereas Picasso came closer to portraiture in *Nude Woman in a Red Armchair*. Here the figure is less part of an abstract arrangement, less of a type, than the figure based on the same model in *The Dream*. The figure possesses a more rounded existence and there is a suggestion of an observed condition of light, with a shaft of sunshine playing on her upper body and the remainder cast into half-tones. There is something almost child-like about her gesture of cradling her head, with its reflective expression, between her reversed hands. Its conjunction with the overt sexuality of her body, the round breasts, and exposed vagina, produce an image less easy to assimilate to existing archetypes, though legible as Picasso's vivid recollection of his young lover, perhaps in the wake of a sexual encounter.

The hedonism of such paintings brings Picasso into alignment not just with Matisse but also with Pierre Bonnard.[28] Indeed, Bonnard is the painter of this period whose work has come to be most widely understood as

naked portraiture. A large proportion of his nudes tend now to be read as being in some fundamental sense *about* Marthe Boursin, Bonnard's long-term girlfriend who became his wife in 1925.[29] There was no reference to this at the time, just as Marthe's existence was barely acknowledged, his family only learning that the couple had been married after the artist's death. The strongly erotic early images present her 'as a modern sexually liberated (and for the male, sexually liberating) woman' [plate 46].[30] The numerous subsequent images of women performing their *toilette* are equally specific in their reference to Marthe's appearance and personality. Bonnard himself was a private and solitary man, but this tendency was magnified by living with Marthe. She came from a humble, provincial background, had little education, and subsequently cut off virtually all contacts with her family. She suffered from long-term health problems, possibly asthma but more likely tuberculosis, a debilitating condition that made her weak, breathless, and prone to other illnesses. In accordance with current medical advice, she took to spending many hours each day obsessively cleansing herself, and the couple made frequent trips to spas and secluded villas for a change of air. Marthe became, in one harsh assessment: 'deeply neurotic, an invalid, unable to have children, devoid of understanding of Bonnard's work, unwilling to receive his friends in his house, endlessly nagging, wildly jealous'.[31] Evidence for Bonnard's own outlook is a letter from the winter of 1930–1: 'For some time now I have been living a very secluded life as Marthe has become completely antisocial and I am obliged to avoid all contact with other people. I have hopes though that this state of affairs will change for the better but it is rather painful.'[32] Such hopes were almost certainly dashed, as Marthe retreated into her private world.

Bonnard began making pictures of Marthe in the bathroom around 1908, prompted by Degas's images of women at their *toilette*. As Sarah Whitfield remarked, 'the ceramic tiles, the patterned linoleum and the plain enamel tubs of the modern bathroom offered Bonnard a setting for the twentieth-century nude so dauntingly banal that few others would have dared to appropriate it'.[33] Within this space, transfigured by the play of light and by Bonnard's compositional inventiveness, we encounter the same naked figure, washing, drying, scrubbing, anointing, dressing, or, from the mid-1920s onwards, crouching or lying in her bath [plate 47]. The language of the body has priority over the face, which is often turned away or barely visible. With her short hair and slender figure, the woman is recognisably Marthe, although she remains younger than her actual years. Bonnard's method of constructing his pictures from quick pencil sketches made as the model moved around facilitated this

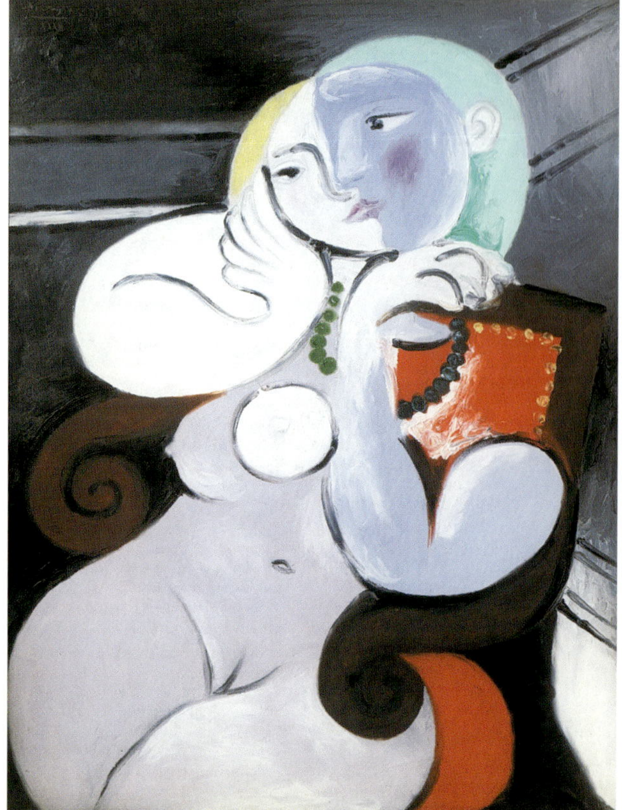

45 Pablo Picasso
Nude Woman in a Red Armchair, 1932
Tate, London

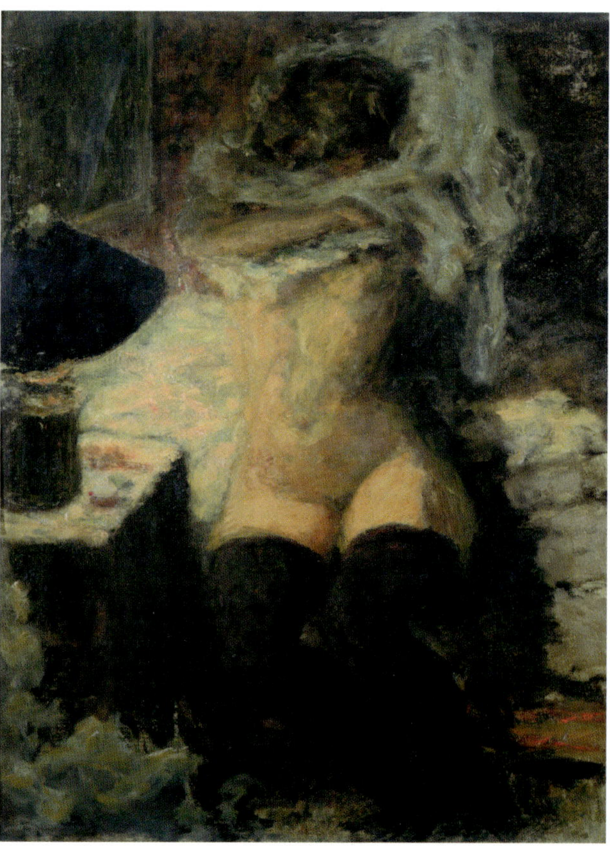

46 Pierre Bonnard
Nude Woman in Black Stockings, *c.*1900
Private collection on loan to Sheffield Galleries and Museum Trust

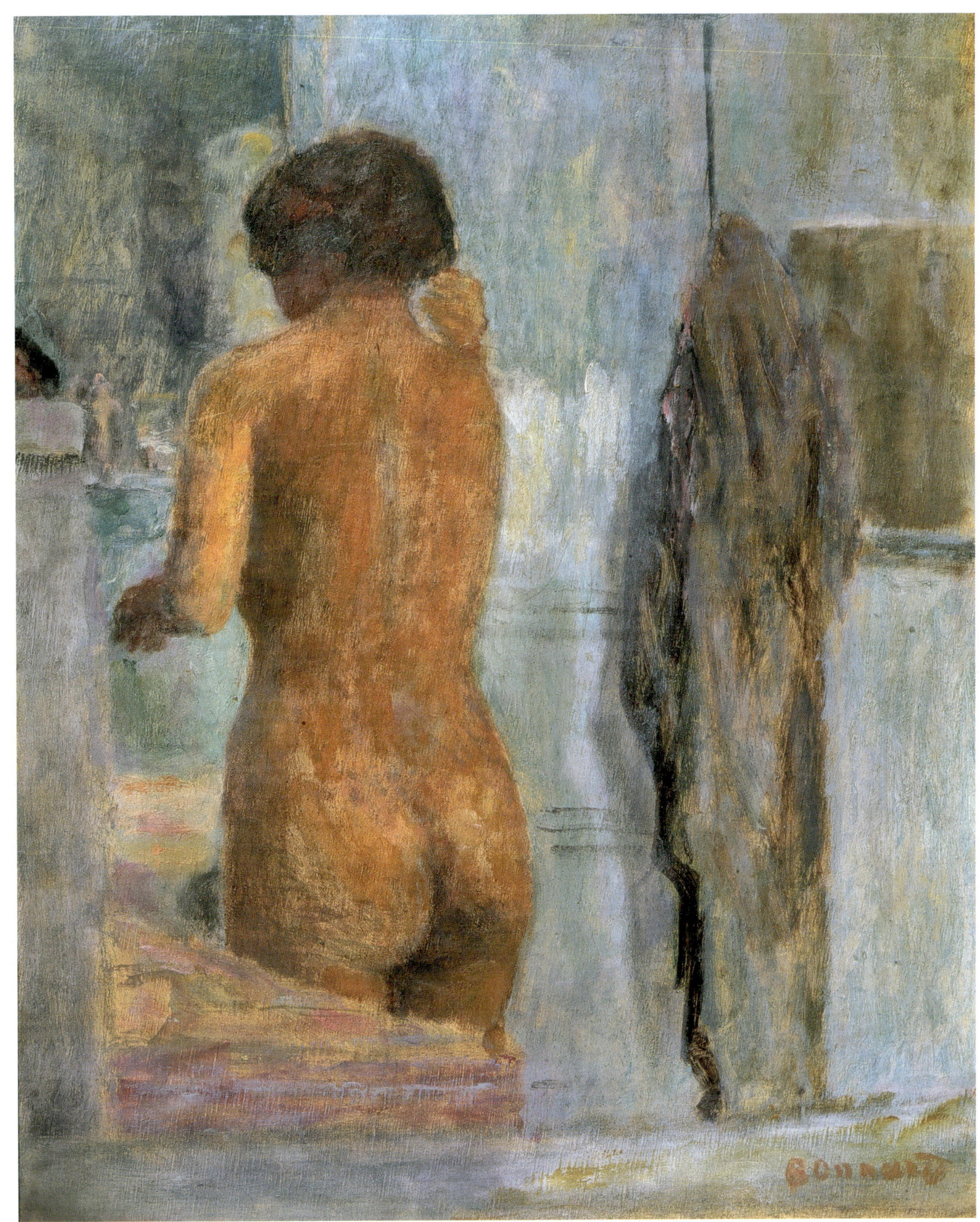

47 Pierre Bonnard

Bathing Woman Seen from the Back, *c*.1919

Tate, bequeathed by the Hon. Mrs A.E. Pleydell-Bouverie through the Friends of the Tate Gallery, 1968

fusion of direct observation with memory and longing. David Sylvester claimed that Bonnard viewed Marthe 'with a complexity of feeling that has hardly been surpassed in art', embracing idealisation, nostalgia, intimations of mortality, 'compassion for her in her vulnerability', sexual longing, and even irony. Faced by the spectacle of the tiny figure naked except for her high heels, Bonnard conveyed 'a rueful wit that is sharply aware of her absurdity'.[34] Vividly present, an invitation to gaze and to touch, she is also set apart, dissolving into colour and light, self-contained within her regime of hygiene, and her sarcophagus-like bath. Sylvester remarked upon the 'extreme ambivalence' in Bonnard's portrayals, which encompassed the celebration of sensual experience and an elegiac sense that the moment passes, beauty fades, and the living succumb to death. If this is what the pictures are about (as well as light and the process of seeing), then the bathroom paintings constitute a sustained exercise in a very particular naked portraiture. They represent not just what Marthe looked like, but also something of what it was like to be her, and what it felt like to be her doting, long-suffering companion.

These paintings by Bonnard are at the opposite pole from the Surrealist preoccupation with the female body as an object of desire and fantasy. This found expression in generic and sometimes abstracted imagery, and portraits of individuals were exceptional. However, Man Ray, court photographer of the movement, although affected by his contacts with Duchamp and Dada circles in both New York and Paris, was also aware of Stieglitz. This underpinned his nude portrayals of girlfriend sitters such as Kiki de Montparnasse and Lee Miller over a ten year period [plate 48]. In the 1934 collection of his photography, Man Ray presumably had such images in mind when he talked of 'autobiographical images' which had been 'seized in moments of visual detachment during periods of emotional contact'. André Breton likewise praised the way the artist had gone beyond 'immediate likeness' to aim for 'profound likeness which physically, morally engages the entire future. The portrait of a loved one should be not only an image at which one smiles but also an oracle one questions.'[35] The portrait aspect seems less important in Man Ray's fully Surrealist imagery, such as the *Veiled Erotic* series in which the artist Meret Oppenheim enacts some mysterious drama, her naked body set against the hard geometric forms of an etching press.[36] Oppenheim was also briefly Man Ray's lover, but she seems to function here as the type of the nubile, androgynous girl. It has been noted that he 'often rises above the level of a specific obsessionalism to a more generalised exploitation of an idealised sexuality'.[37]

In the art of Salvador Dalí, the image of his wife Gala was a familiar theme, and a source of complex mythologising. The naked variants were produced around the end of the Second World War, when the couple were living in America, and Dalí was renouncing his commitment to Surrealism.[38] His engagement with the nude might be seen as a new adherence to traditional values, though this hardly

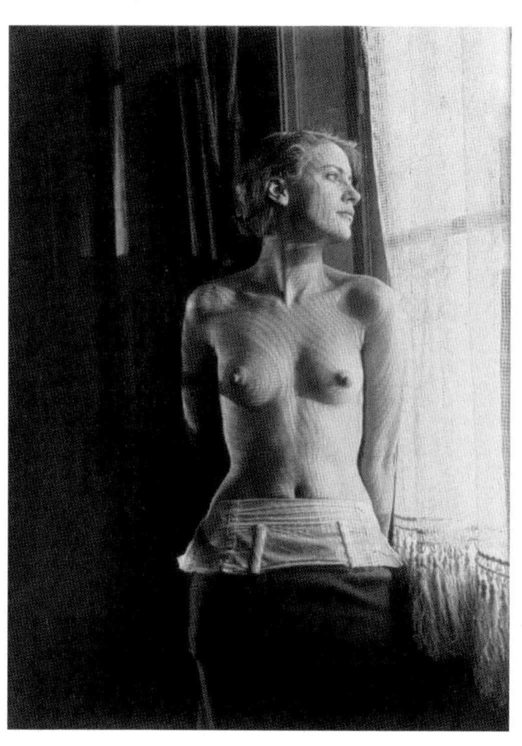

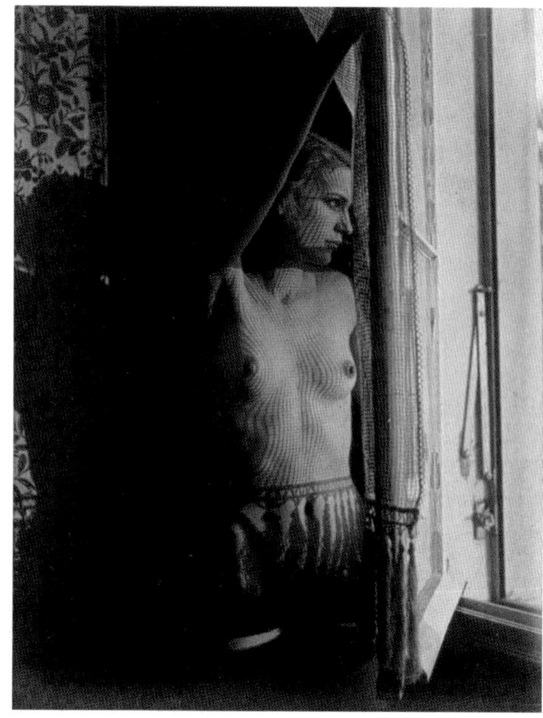

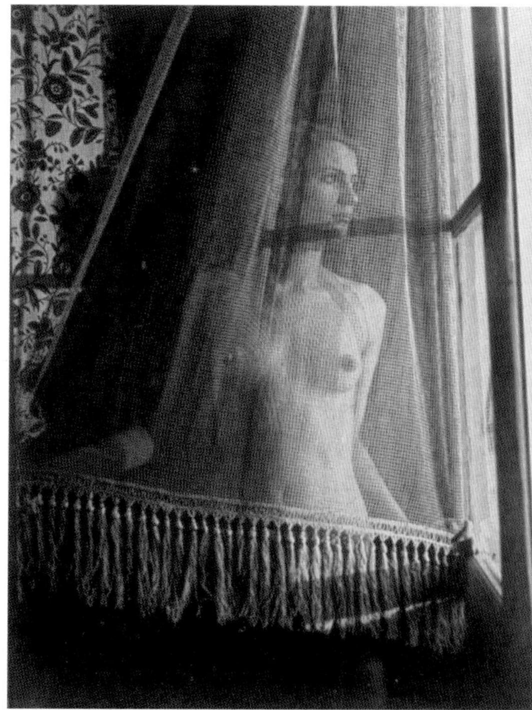

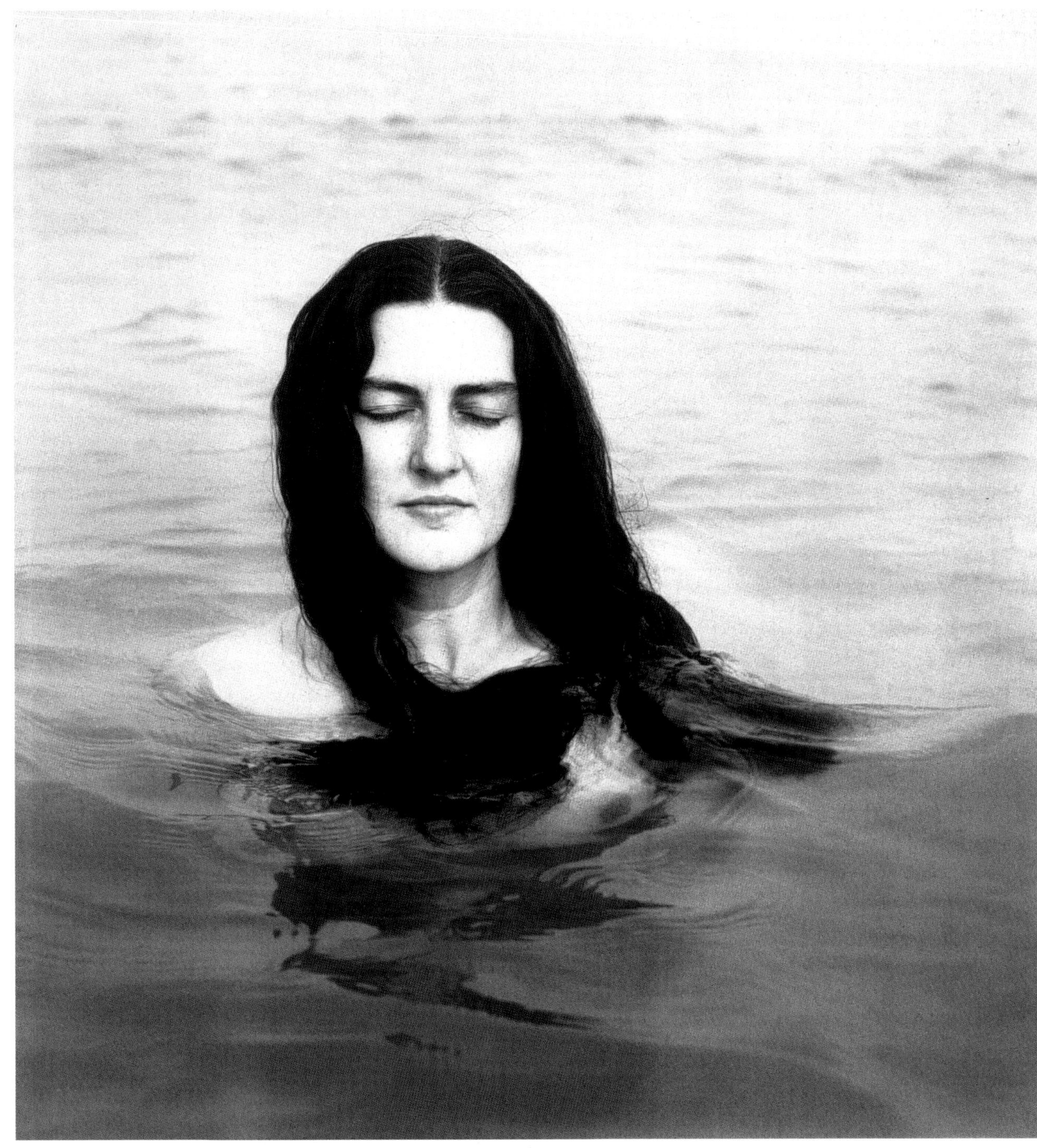

opposite **48 Man Ray**
Lee Miller Triptych, early 1930s
Private Collection, Thomas Koeffer, Zurich

right **49 Harry Callahan**
Eleanor, 1949
Pompidou Centre, Paris

does justice to pictures steeped in fantasy and memory, which have received little notice compared with Dalí's mainstream Surrealist production. The title most indicative of portraiture is *My Wife, Nude, Contemplating her own Flesh becoming Stairs, Three Vertebrae of a Column, Sky and Architecture* (1945), which describes a picture in which Gala, seen from the rear, looks back towards a skeletal architectural structure that echoes her own form. The slightly earlier *Dream Caused by the Flight of a Bee around a Pomegranate, One Second before Awakening* (1944) was also a portrayal of his wife. Her serene, naked figure is incongruously surrounded by the bizarre components of a dream that she had recounted to Dalí. In the foreground, the actual pomegranate that prompted the dream casts a shadow in the form of a heart, indicating that the picture was a form of love letter. Finally, *Leda Atomica* (1947–9) 'exalted Gala as goddess of my metaphysics', embedding the image of his wife in an abstruse allegory that refers to modern science, Christianity and Greek myth.[39] Of the Gala pictures generally, Fiona Bradley remarks: 'When Dalí looks at Gala he sees himself reflected in her. As must we for, as viewers of his work, we see only the Gala constructed by him'.[40] Dalí is an extreme example, but at one level all the works discussed in this chapter could be interpreted as surrogate self-portraiture, representing what the artist finds within himself as well as what he sees in front of him.

The theme resurfaces elsewhere after the Second World War. From 1947, many naked pictures featured in Harry Callahan's serial portrait of his wife Eleanor, on her own or with their young daughter. He was evidently unaware at first of Stieglitz's photographs of Georgia O'Keefe, but their discovery 'clarified' things and 'made me more aware of what I was doing'. Callahan valued Eleanor's freedom from rehearsed body language:

When he first thought of photographing me in the nude, I felt very shy. I thought 'Oh, no, nice girls don't have their pictures taken in the nude.' I protested a couple of times, but I soon got over that. Harry assured me that he would never do anything to embarrass me. I knew that his work was done with an eye to the beauty of the nude.

Before he started making pictures, Harry would have me try out different poses. Not being a professional model, I couldn't invent poses … The arrangement was all Harry's idea.[41]

The image of Eleanor became a vehicle for formal experimentation. Callahan focused on fragments of the body, exploring textural contrasts between skin and fabric, and then manipulating lighting in the studio, and tone within the developing process, to accentuate edges. He remarked of his landscapes of the same period: 'When I began to eliminate tone and show only lines … it was the breaking of tradition for me. At that time it was anti-photography to me'.[42] An extreme instance is the tiny *Eleanor, Chicago* (1947) – Callahan's standard title – where one gradually realises that a linear cruciform floating on an almost blank expanse of luminous white is actually formed by the creases of his wife's bottom, and the divide between two legs pressed tightly together. An interest in symmetry is also apparent in works where Callahan used Eleanor as the central focus, and a curvilinear counterpoint to hard-edged interior spaces. The figure is often seen from the back: she sits on a bed, her dark shape contrasted against the white rectangles of the windows; rises Venus-like from the sea and spreads her bedraggled hair over her arms and shoulders [plate 49]; or leans against a radiator, one leg raised as if in parody of a bird or a balletic pose, her corporeal solidity accentuated by the free linear abstractions painted by a friend on the walls of their apartment [plate 150]. One 1949 picture comprises a tiny image of a distant Eleanor, again standing on one leg, surrounded by total blackness; another focuses on the expanse of her pregnant stomach looming out of darkness.[43] In subsequent works, Callahan used varied viewpoints and settings, out-of-focus effects, and the traditional theme of the naked figure in the landscape, as in *Port Huron* (1954) and a group of double-exposure photographs where Eleanor's body is floated against the landscape around Aix-en-Provence. The very impersonality and discretion of the pictures have been seen as reinforcing their portrait dimension. For Sarah Greenhough, such work avoids trying to 'probe and uncover the innermost workings of Eleanor's psyche'.[44] Rather, Callahan conveys the meaning that their loving relationship held for him: 'through his graceful, elegant presentation – the way he allows her to close her eyes, avert her gaze, or even turn her back to the camera, the way her body and face are always composed and comfortable, never disturbed or surprised – he reveals a relationship of profound trust, ease, intimacy, and, most significantly, respect'.[45]

There are intriguing parallels between Callahan's photography and the exactly contemporary preoccupations of Alberto Giacometti. The portraits of Eleanor, her figure

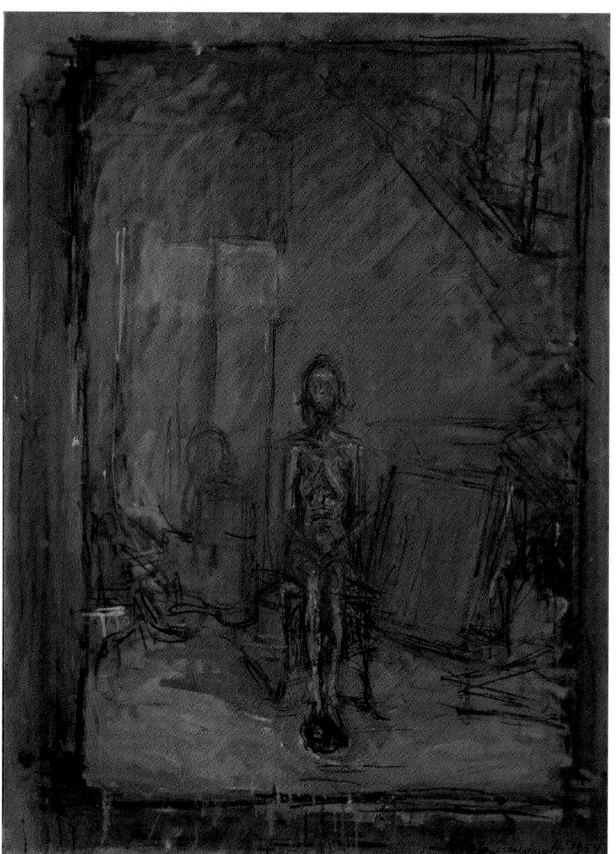

left **50 Alberto Giacometti**
Annette Seated in the Studio, 1954
Hirshhorn Museum and Sculpture Garden

opposite **51 John Bratby**
Jean and Still Life in Front of a Window, 1954
Southampton City Art Gallery

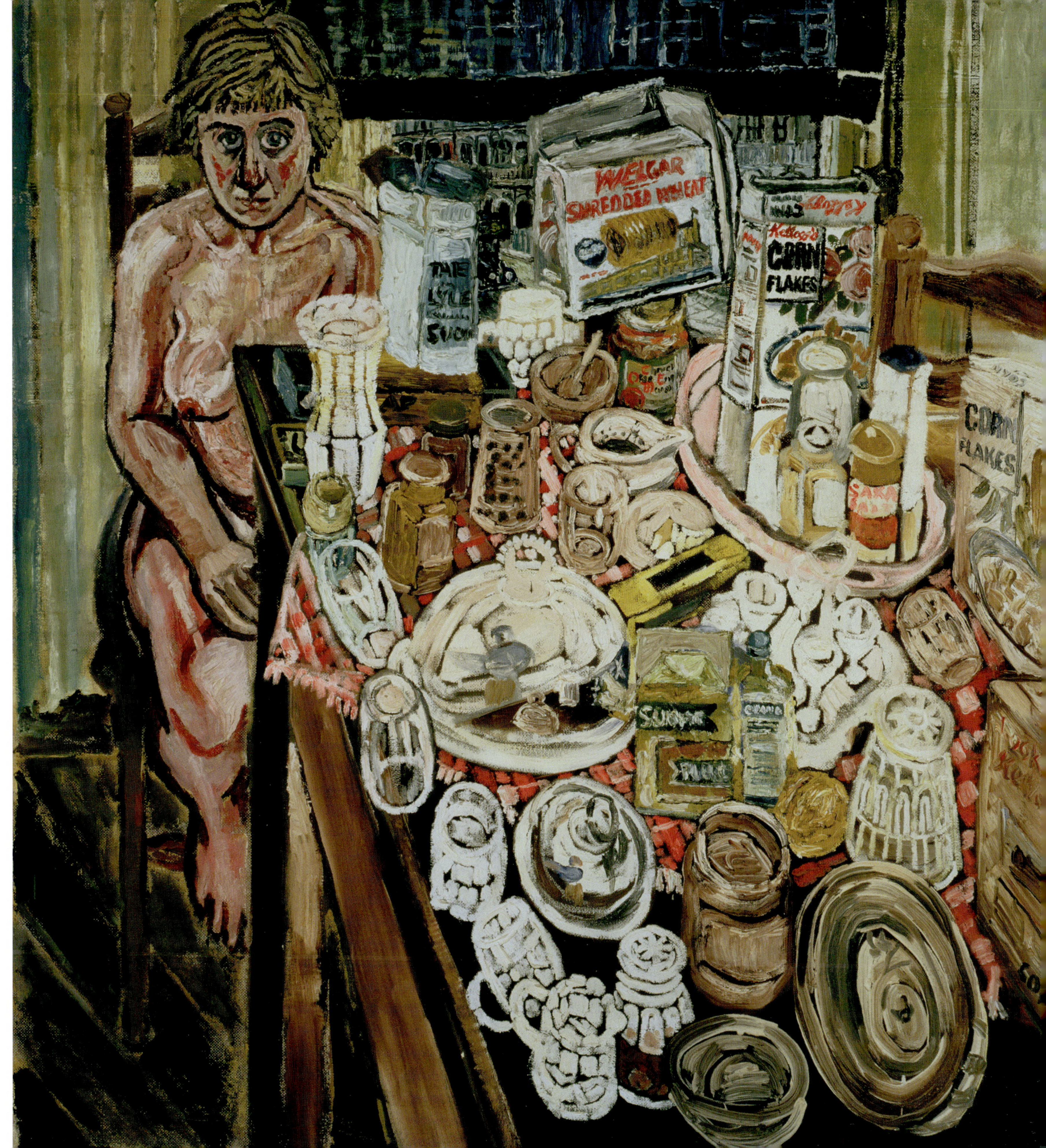
WELGAR
SHREDDED WHEAT
Kellogg's
CORN
FLAKES
CORN
FLAKES

almost dominated by box-like interior spaces, recall Giacometti's paintings of his intimate family, his mother, wife Annette and brother Diego, from the years on either side of 1950. Such works grew out of a wider project to reinvent the image of the human figure, evident in the spindly sculptures that started to become well-known around 1948. The earliest naked depictions of Annette appear in a sculpture from 1953, *Annette from Life*, and in pictures from 1954, marking the point at which a more solid corporeality returns to Giacometti's work in both media [plate 50].[46]

This 'realism' extended in Britain to the work of so-called 'Kitchen sink' painters, such as John Bratby, who experienced critical success when fresh out of art college.[47] Whereas much of this work matched the austerity and emotional bleakness attributed to Giacometti, Bratby specialised in the visual clutter of domestic life. His table-top still-lifes included virtually everything except the kitchen sink – hence the label, coined in 1954. The human presence is added in a picture like *Jean and Still Life*, in which his naked wife looks out sheepishly in our direction from behind a table top of kitchen paraphernalia [plate 51]. The earthiness and sense of *horror vacui* suggest continuities with the art of Stanley Spencer. However, to a 'School of London' painter like Frank Auerbach, the work of an artist like Bratby (and probably Spencer too) looked like 'linear illustrative painting'.[48] Lucian Freud offered an alternative model of sustained scrutiny. Although we are not normally aware which of Freud's naked sitters were also lovers, we do know that the painter Celia Paul sat for his *Girl with Egg*, and that she became intimate with Freud and had a child by him [see plate 24]. In a recent film about Freud, she describes crying a great deal during the making of what she regards as a 'pitiless' but profoundly truthful picture.[49]

From the 1960s onwards, naked portraiture became a widespread preoccupation for painters and photographers. Gerhard Richter and David Hockney both portrayed loved ones in this way. Another affinity between them was working from photographs and acknowledging that reliance stylistically, with a nod to the example of Andy Warhol. In his large oil painting *Ema* (1966) Richter worked from an image of his young wife walking naked down a modern-looking flight of stairs. This was the first time Richter had used a colour photograph and indeed from an image he had taken himself, rather than culled 'ready-made'. The derivation is apparent from the black shadow that forms a halo around the left-hand side of the figure, an effect familiar from the use of flash. At the same time, Richter's painterly technique asserts that this is very much a painting. His

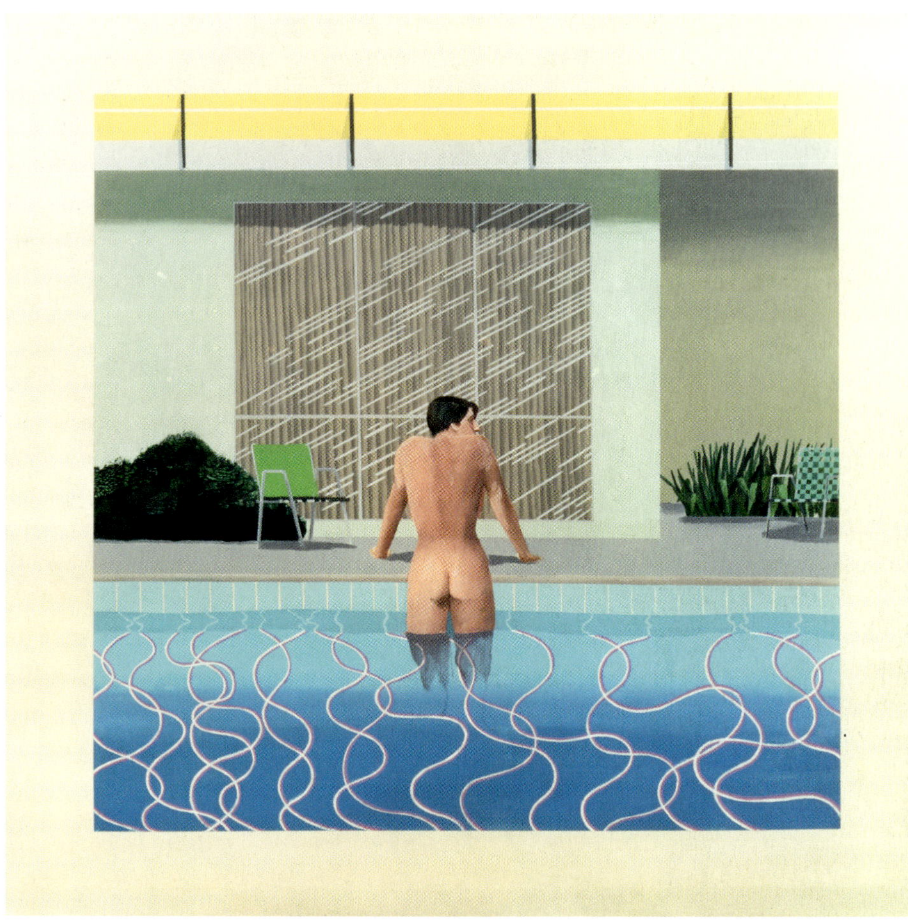

above **52 David Hockney**
Peter Getting out of Nick's Pool, 1966
National Museums Liverpool, Walker Art Gallery

opposite **53 Gerhard Richter**
I.G., 1993
Contemporary Art Collection Fundacion 'la Caixa', Barcelona

method blurs and drains the image of easy legibility and physical substance. Despite, or perhaps because of, the intimate associations of its imagery, *Ema* epitomises Richter's aspiration to a certain fastidious detachment. In the same year, he remarked: 'A portrait must not express anything of the sitter's "soul", essence or character … it is far better to paint a portrait from a photograph, because no one can ever paint a specific person – only a picture that has nothing whatever in common with the sitter. In a portrait by me, the likeness to the model is apparent, unintentional and also entirely useless.'[50] The gulf between image and prototype is heightened by an allusion to Marcel Duchamp, whose art was currently emerging from decades of obscurity and inspiring many neo-Dada and Pop artists. Richter accepted that 'there was certainly an influence', but noted that 'it may partly have been an unconscious antagonism – because his painting *Nude Descending a Staircase* rather irritated me. I thought very highly of it, but I could never accept that it had put paid, once and for all, to a certain kind of painting. So I did the opposite and painted a "conventional nude".'[51] *Ema* typifies the ambivalence and obliqueness to which his work aspired, in reaction against the bold

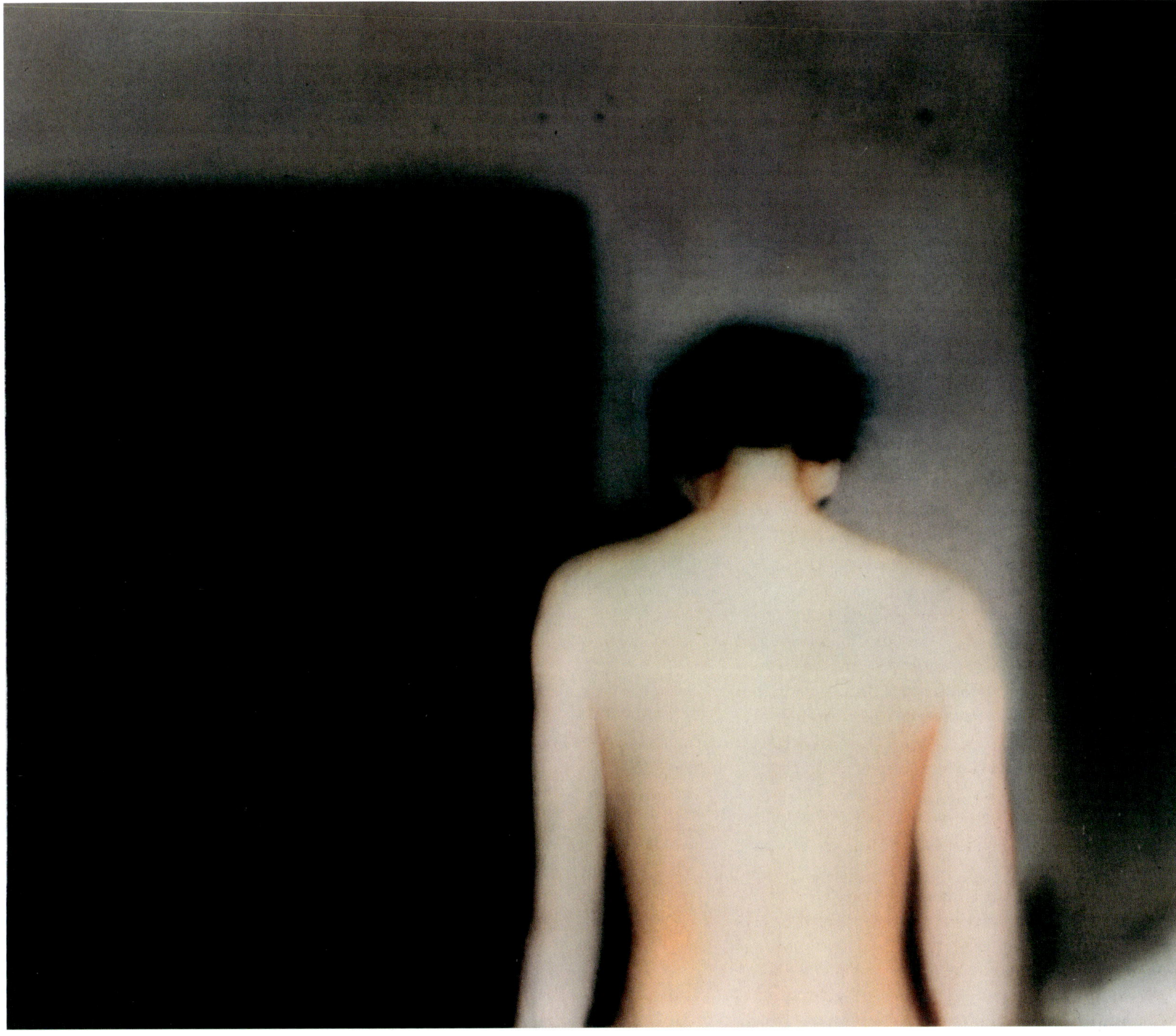

visual and semantic simplicities of the American Pop art that currently seemed so irresistible to German artists and collectors. Subsequent naked portraits of *I.G.*, Richter's third wife, equally disdain portraiture's concern with psychological revelation [plate 53].

Hockney likewise evolved an unfashionably naturalistic style around 1966, after moving from London to Los Angeles. His new boyfriend, art student Peter Schlesinger, became the subject of paintings, drawings and prints. Hockney's painting *Peter Getting Out of Nick's Pool* [plate 52] distils the liberated homosexual subculture that he found so captivating in L.A., and whose novelty to someone British was matched by the environment of white-painted modernist buildings, exotic foliage and swimming pools, all defined by bright sunshine. The effects of light reflected from the surfaces of glass and water are evoked through graphic conventions that acknowledge the impossibility of reproducing such transient things more literally in paint on canvas. Indeed, the image as a whole proclaims its status as an Arcadian fantasy. The detail of the figure was actually imported from a black and white snapshot of Schlesinger leaning against a car.[52] In the painting, the remove from direct observation is heightened by overt allusions to photography. The image proclaims the trademark square Polaroid, with its white borders, while the heightened colour and clarity evoke the commercial photography encountered in travel brochures. As in Richter's *Ema*, we encounter in *Peter Getting Out of Nick's Pool* an interplay between intimacy and detachment. A striking precedent for Hockney's presentation of the naked Schlesinger from behind is Christopher Wood's *Nude Boy in a Bedroom* [plate 40] from thirty five years earlier. It is not known if Hockney knew Wood's painting, though it was owned by the actor John Gielgud and may have been known in the gay community.

In photography, Americans have been the most interesting practitioners of naked portraiture. Emmet Gowin and Nan Goldin epitomise two different generations and aesthetic outlooks. Gowin wrote his student thesis about the affinity he felt with the Stieglitz tradition, and in 1965 went to study under Callahan, whose work conveyed 'a poetry of feeling and intimacy – and the revelation of a secret, unrecognised dimension in the commonplace'.[53] The experience clearly predisposed Gowin to find his subject matter in his new wife Edith Morris, her close family and their rural surroundings in Virginia:

I admired their simplicity and generosity, and thought of the pictures I made as agreements. I wanted to pay attention to the body and personality that had agreed out of love to reveal itself … My pictures are made as a part of everyday life … In this situation, both the sitter and photographer become part of the picture. Sometimes my photographs resemble home snapshots, which are among the richest resources of images I know. But I always want to make a picture that is more than a family record.[54]

In 1967 Gowin embarked upon an extended series of portraits of Edith, often nudes [plates 54, 55 and 56]. The pictures comprise a monument to his devotion to his wife, and a frank study of the inexorable process of aging. In the most recent picture, we see Edith, seated and akin to an Egyptian goddess, through a transparent fabric densely covered in moths, an arresting image but also a reinvention of ancient metaphors concerning the inherent ephemerality of life. By comparison with the self-effacement of Callahan's Eleanor, Edith comes across as a strong, independent person. In contrast to Stieglitz, we are presented with all or most of Edith's body, frankly and frontally displayed. Her face is often turned away, avoiding eye contact with the viewer. Her body language and facial expressions read as emanations of the sitter, rather than contrivances imposed by the artist. The least snapshot-like aspects of the works are the rich tonality and strong compositional sense of Gowin's black and white prints, exploiting textural contrast and integrating the sculptural form of the figure with often natural surroundings. The pictures are also informed by technical experiments, such as fusing her body and organic imagery in the development process to create montages, in the tradition of admired figures such as Callahan and Frederick Sommer. Another series exploits the distorting effects of a circular lens.

Gowin and Nan Goldin highlight qualities that are distinctive to the other's work. Gowin espouses a traditional 'artistic' idiom, a complement to such old-fashioned virtues as family and community, and what he describes as the 'spiritual' harmony between man and the natural world. In Goldin's work, we encounter the conditions of modern urban life, specifically the Lower East Side in New York, in their heightened, bohemian form. The use of colour and snapshot-like informality are attuned to a life-style of heady, transient, youthful pleasures of sex and stimulants, in a setting of sensory profusion, even squalor. The images started as quick-fire slide shows, accompanied by music, which Goldin would show at clubs and parties, before they migrated to fat, illustrated books and densely hung exhibitions. We are invited not to linger too long over each image, but to scan pictures in quantity, picking up on themes, narratives and atmosphere. The subjects are mostly Goldin's close friends and lovers, both male and female, who make up what she too refers to as her 'family'. The photographs comprised an autobiographical 'visual diary', an exercise in seizing the moment: 'The camera is as much a part of my everyday life as talking or eating or sex. The instant of photographing, instead of creating distance, is a moment of clarity and emotional connection.'[55]

There is a distant echo of Stieglitz in Goldin's commitment to serial portraiture: 'Maybe more than other photographers I don't believe in the single portrait. I believe only in the accumulation of portraits as a representation of a person.'[56] The two lovers who appear most often in Goldin's earlier work are Brian [Burchill] and Siobhan [Liddell]. We see Brian sleeping, watching TV, masturbating and generally hanging around. He comes across as 'blokeish', stereotypically masculine in his demeanor and body language. This squares with the passage about him in

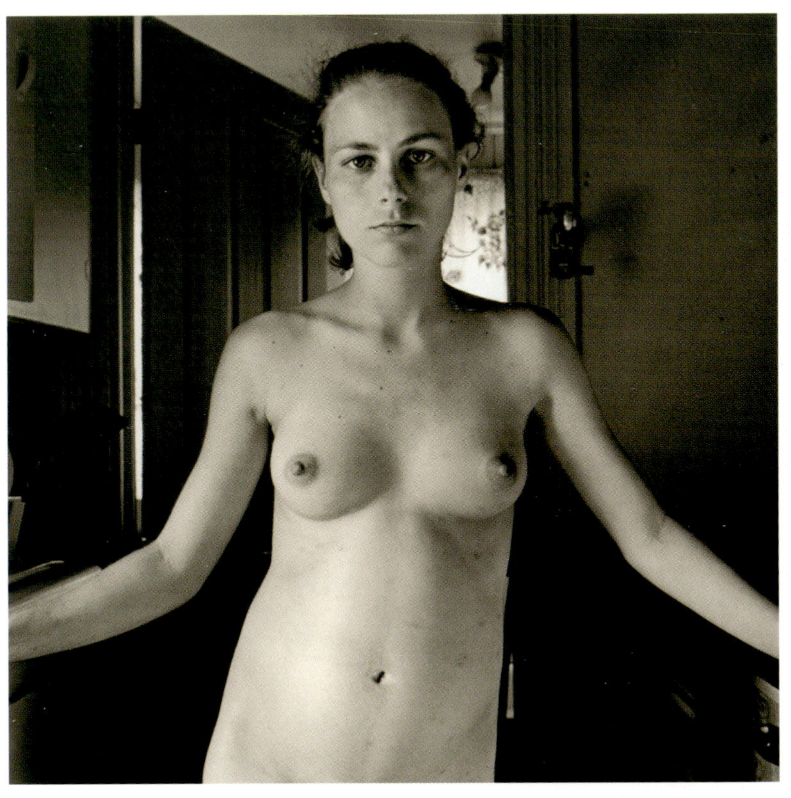

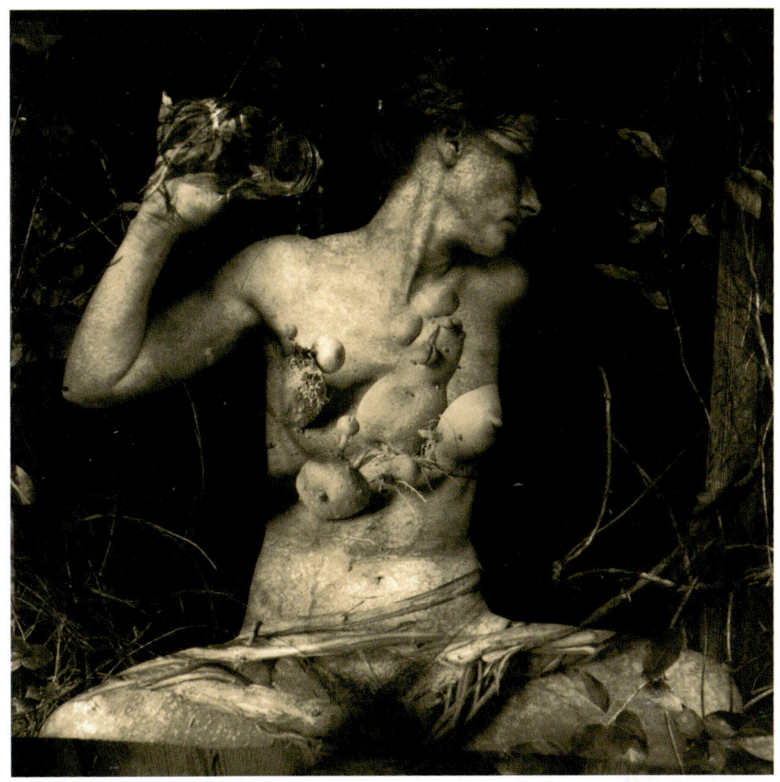

above left **54 Emmet Gowin**
Edith, Danville, Virginia, 1967
Courtesy Pace/MacGill Gallery, New York

above right **55 Emmet Gowin**
Edith, 1986
Courtesy Pace/MacGill Gallery, New York

right **56 Emmet Gowin**
Edith, Newtown, Pennsylvania, 1974
Courtesy Pace/MacGill Gallery, New York

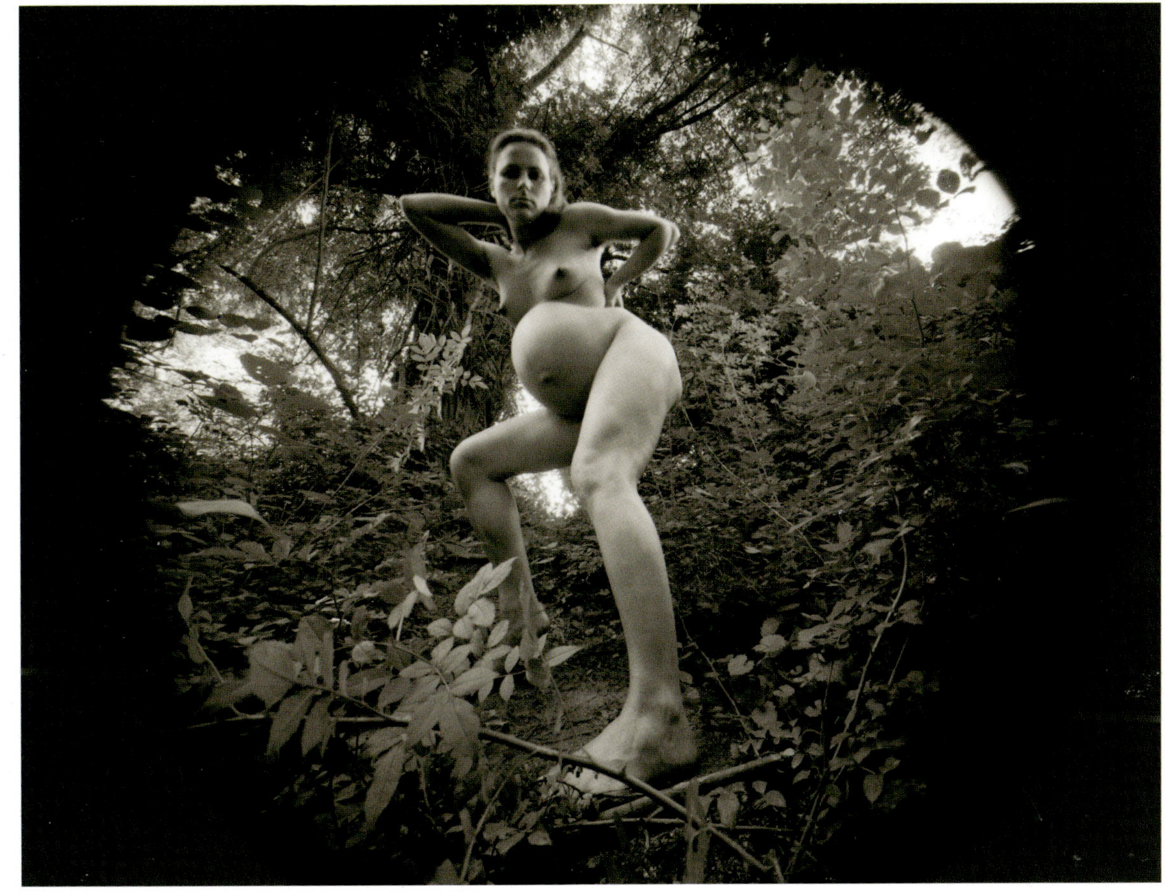

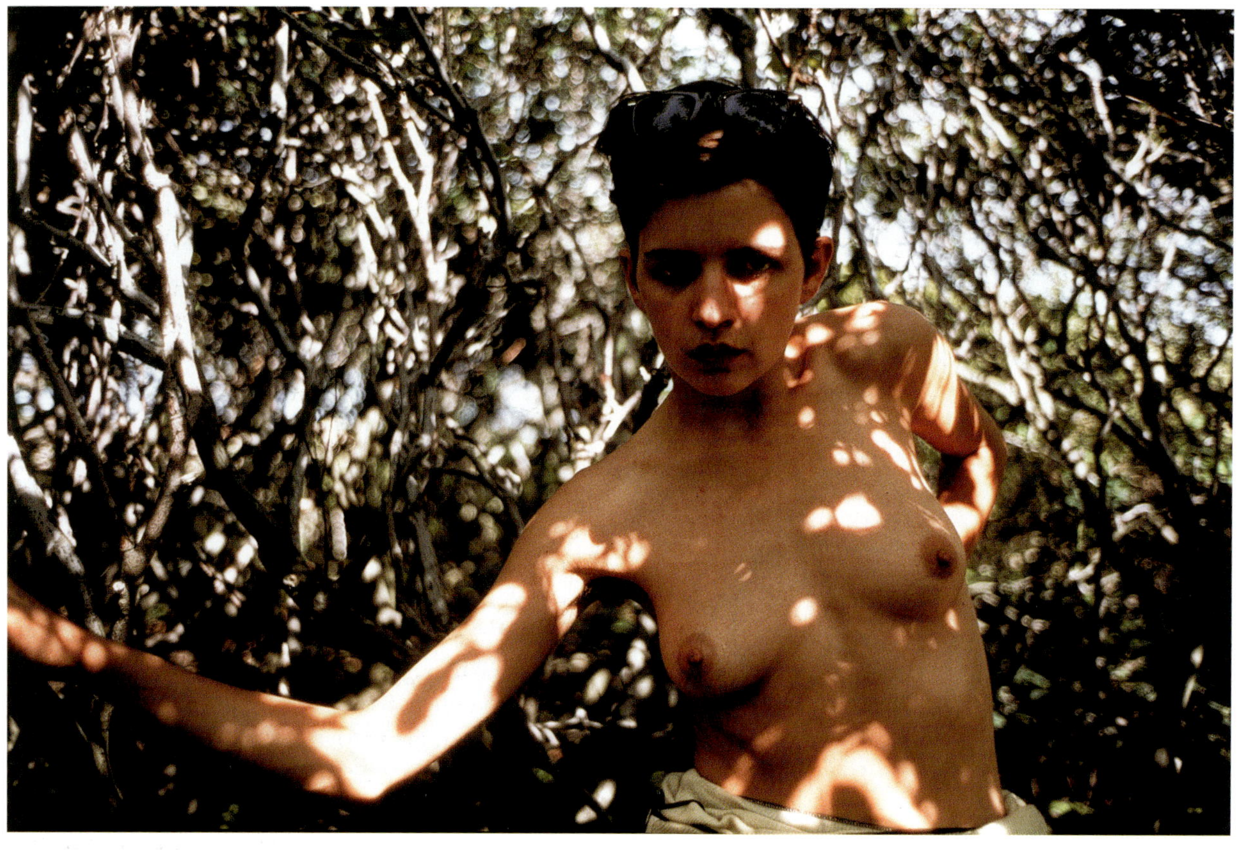

57 Nan Goldin
Siobhan in the Woods,
Provincetown, 1991
Collection Fotomuseum, Winterthur

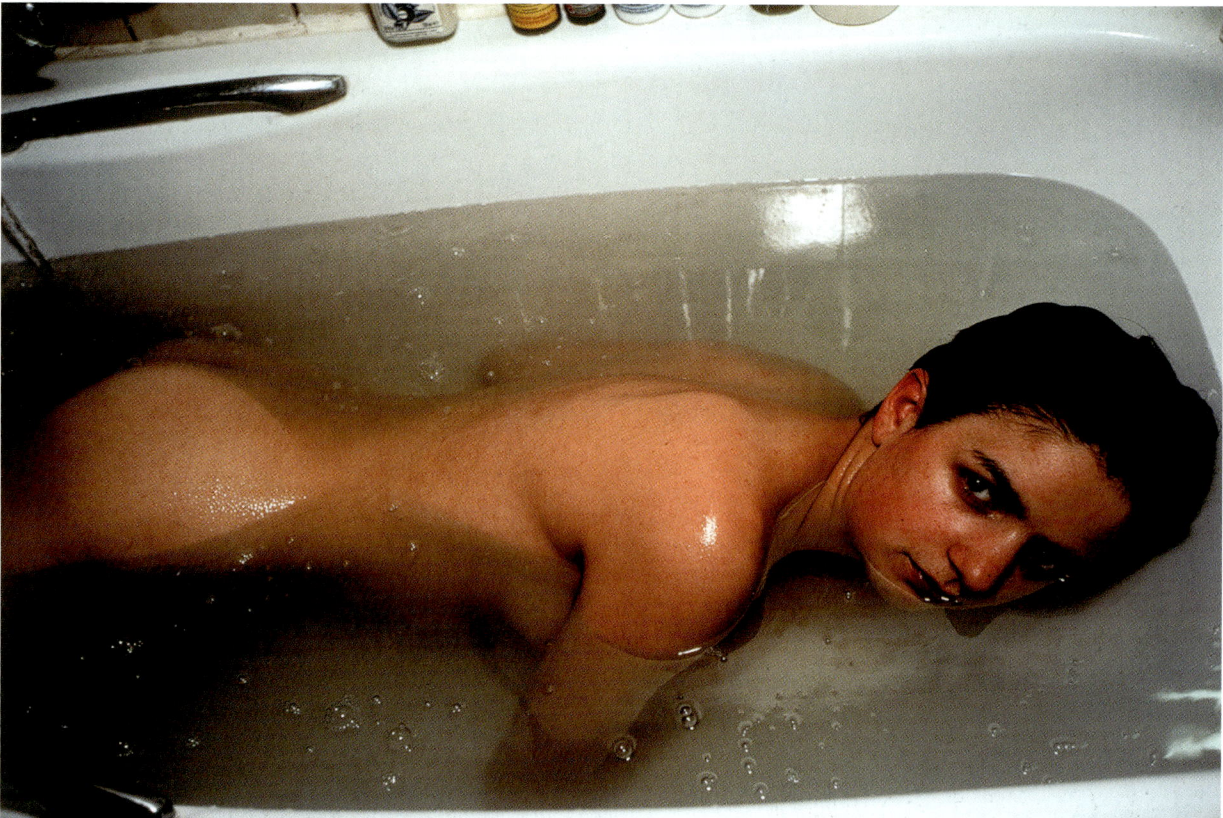

58 Nan Goldin
Siobhan in my Bathtub, Berlin, 1992
Collection Fotomuseum, Winterthur

the book where many of his pictures appeared, the celebrated *Ballad of Sexual Dependency*: 'We were well suited emotionally and the relationship became very interdependent. Jealousy was used to inspire passion. His concept of relationship was rooted in the romantic idealism of James Dean and Roy Orbison. I craved the dependency, the adoration, the satisfaction, the security, but sometimes I felt claustrophobic ...' Sexual obsession kept them together when the relationship began to collapse, but eventually he severely battered her, reducing her to a condition in which Goldin memorably photographed herself. In 1988 she was successfully treated for drug dependency. Her subsequent work was characterised by the discovery of natural light, and an expanded repertoire of subject matter, which included a focus on her new lover Siobhan [plates 57 and 58]. As with other female subjects in her work, Siobhan's domain is often the bathroom. Such images read as a soft, gentle antidote to Brian's self-absorbed harshness, but also as a metaphor for some wider process of cleansing or purification. The compositions are simpler than many of the works collected in *Ballad*, and the sitter projects a more subdued presence and sensuous eroticism. There is a certain convergence with Gowin, epitomised by the juxtaposition of *Siobhan* (1991) and the 1973 picture of Edith, and by Goldin's remark: 'it's really about giving back to the people, who gave so much of themselves to me'.[57]

With Goldin we should not confuse the immediacy with an unmediated realism. A recent study notes: 'As works of art, her photographs are as much products of cultural myths and her aesthetic training as they are documents of lived experience.'[58] Critics have noted a pictorial aspect to her work. For instance, the bathroom imagery of the Siobhan photographs, their luminosity, heightened colour and emphatic patterning, suggest an awareness of the paintings of Bonnard. It has also been suggested that 'the powerful sobriety' of these works reflected the example of Lucian Freud.[59] Such comparisons raise the question of what distinguishes Goldin's work from the casual vernacular photography they aspire to look like. What is their artistic dimension? She tends to approach this issue by maintaining that her imagery transcends the anecdotal: 'The people and locales in my pictures are particular, specific, but I feel that the concerns I'm dealing with are universal.'[60] This is an important part of their appeal, although the people and storylines seem unexceptional. But the photographs possess a compelling intensity, perhaps because they are highly factual, in the tradition of social documentary, but at the same time they are highly inventive in their approach to colour and organisation.

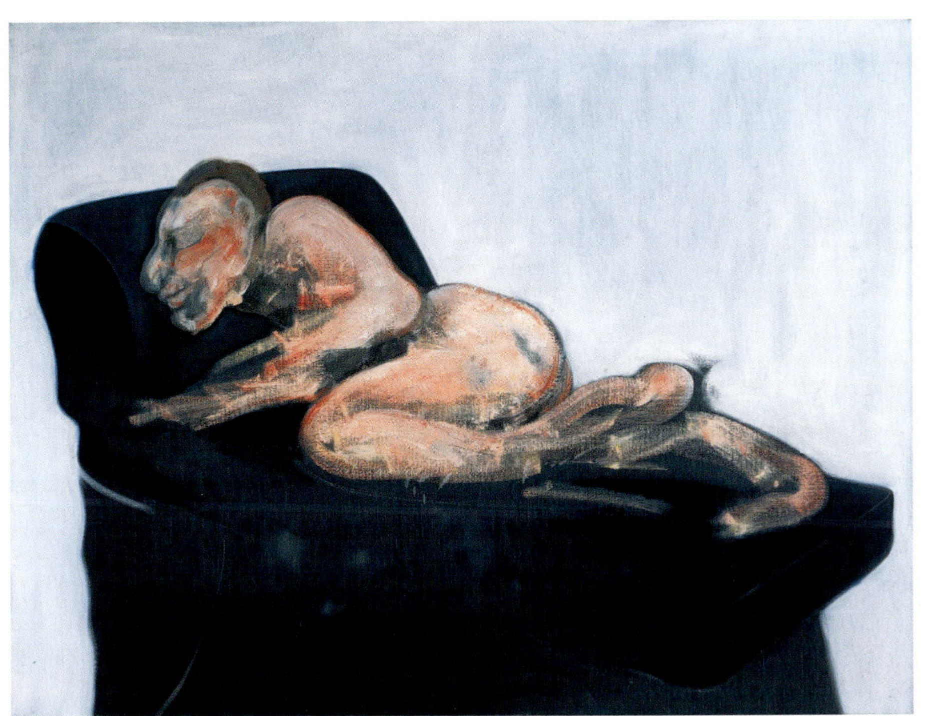

59 Francis Bacon
Sleeping Figure, 1959
Private Collection

The impulse to affirm tender feelings towards a loved one derives some of its urgency from an awareness of transience. Desire fades and we ourselves and the people we love will die. In two clusters of images, an elemental nakedness establishes a link between the body that is known intimately, and the fact of mortality. The naked human form had been a preoccupation in Francis Bacon's work since the late 1940s, but this assumed a portrait dimension with pictures such as the *Sleeping Figure* (1959), a tender image of his lover Peter Lacy reclining, perhaps sleeping, on a couch [plate 59].[61] The picture foreshadows Nan Goldin's images of Brian on a bed. Naked portraits subsequently become one component in a wider blossoming of portraiture in Bacon's art. He mostly worked not from direct observation but rather from photographs of his sitters commissioned from John Deakin.[62] This was the case with Bacon's lover George Dyer, who featured in many pictures after 1963. In *Portrait of George Dyer Staring at a Blind-cord* (1966), Bacon extracted the seated figure from one of Deakin's studio portraits (showing Dyer in the underpants that he was too modest to remove), and made it into an embodiment of existential crisis. The setting is at once ordinary (the empty chair, carpet, blind cords) and baffling (the curved wall, linear space frame, dark shadow-like forms on the floor). Likewise the figure of Dyer, with his legs casually crossed, is rendered disconcerting by the removal of his chair, so that he seems poised to spring sideways, and by the reinvention of his anatomy in highly painterly, smeared brushmarks, with the head appearing to

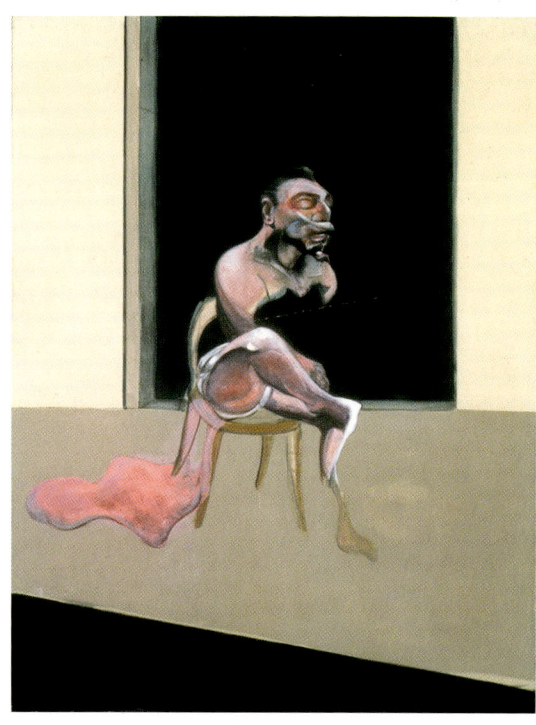
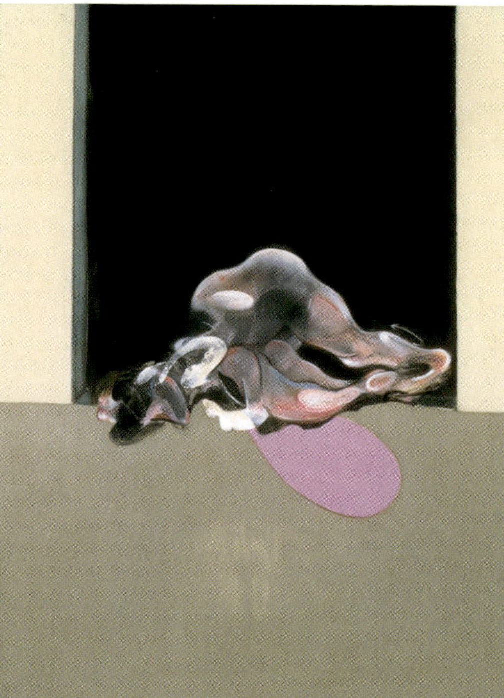
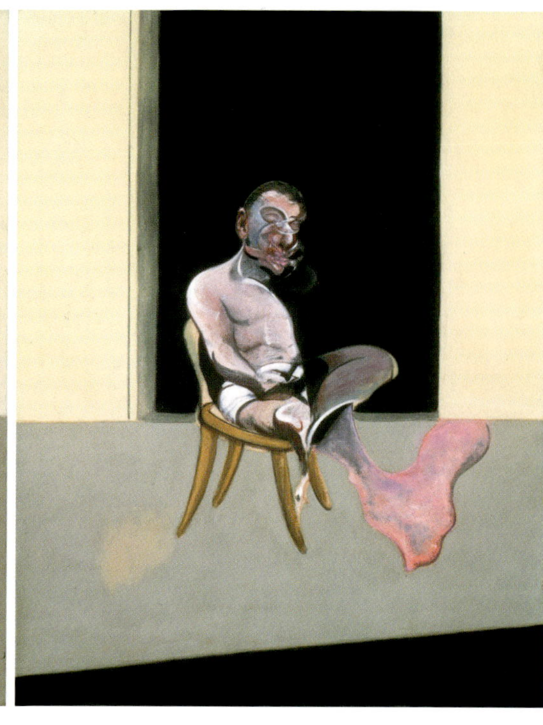

60 Francis Bacon
Triptych: August, 1972
Tate, London

twist on its axis. A sense of life's transience is intimated both viscerally – the animation of the body, the ejaculation-like flick of white paint emanating from Dyer's leg – as well as symbolically – the watch, the fragile blind-cords which might at any moment shut out the light.

The theme becomes more explicit in the pair of great triptychs that Bacon painted in the wake of Dyer's death in October 1971. As Bacon was preparing for the opening of his big show at the Grand Palais in Paris, Dyer succumbed to a cocktail of alcohol and sleeping pills and died sitting on the lavatory in their hotel room. In the outer panels of *Triptych; August 1972* Bacon worked once again from Deakin's photos of the seated Dyer, but now with less distortion. There is a sense of the body being eaten into by the surrounding space, and of the life force seeping out of the figure in the form of pink ectoplasm-like forms [plate 60]. The central image celebrates their intimacy through the reworking of an image of two intertwined males that Bacon had derived from a Muybridge photograph of wrestlers. If this painting is elegiac in mood, *Triptych May-June 1973* is Bacon's stark visualisation of Dyer's final moments, throwing up on the right, slumped on the toilet, naked and dead, on the left. In the centre, Dyer's profile confronts a Fury-like shadow of death and a bare light bulb. Both triptychs are notably simple, and use large expanses of flat black as a component of their morbid theme. In each case, Dyer's nakedness intimates the basic conditions of life and death.

Bacon's channelling of his grief finds a remote photographic parallel. Seiichi Furuya, having moved to Austria from Japan, embarked on obsessively photographing his wife Christine Gössler in 1978, the year of their marriage. When he exhibited the portraits the following year, he remarked: 'I saw in her a woman who passes me by, sometimes a model, sometimes the woman I love, sometimes the woman who belongs to me. I feel obliged continuously to take pictures of the woman who has different meanings for me.'[63] In many of the photographs, the sitter's nakedness testifies to the intimate bond between artist and sitter, but also suggests a fundamental state of being. Her facial expressions and body language soon begin to hint at the depressive illness that eventually caused Gössler to commit suicide in 1985 [plate 61]. During the twenty years since her death, Furuya has compiled many exhibitions and publications which assemble in different ways his imagery of his wife and of their life together, under titles such as *Mémoires*. The pictures have been described as 'a requiem, a lament for the dead', terms which could equally be applied to Bacon's triptychs.[64]

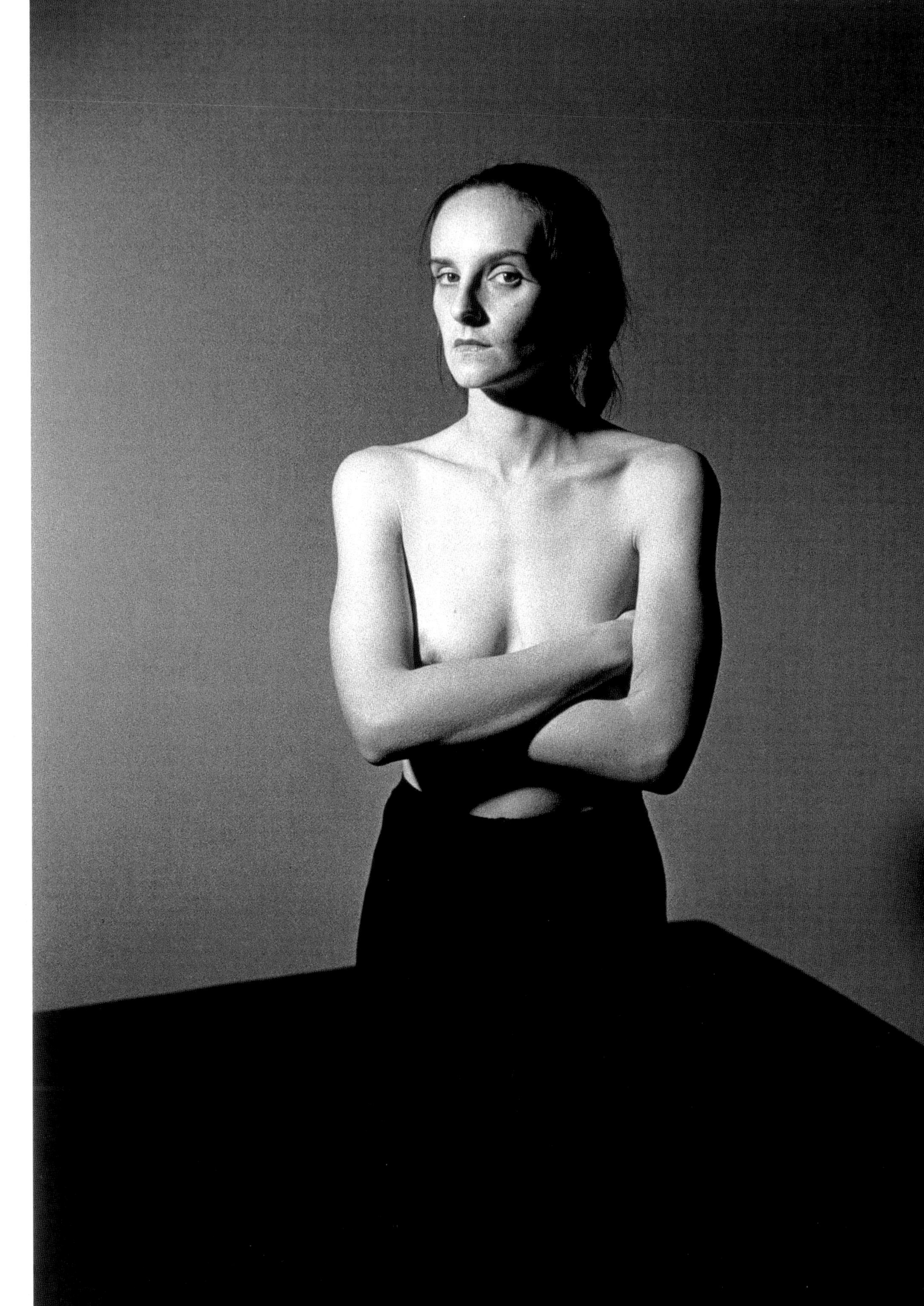

61 Seiichi Furuya

Portrait of Christine Furuya, Vienna, 1982

Collection Fotomuseum, Winterthur, Gift of Seiichi Furuya

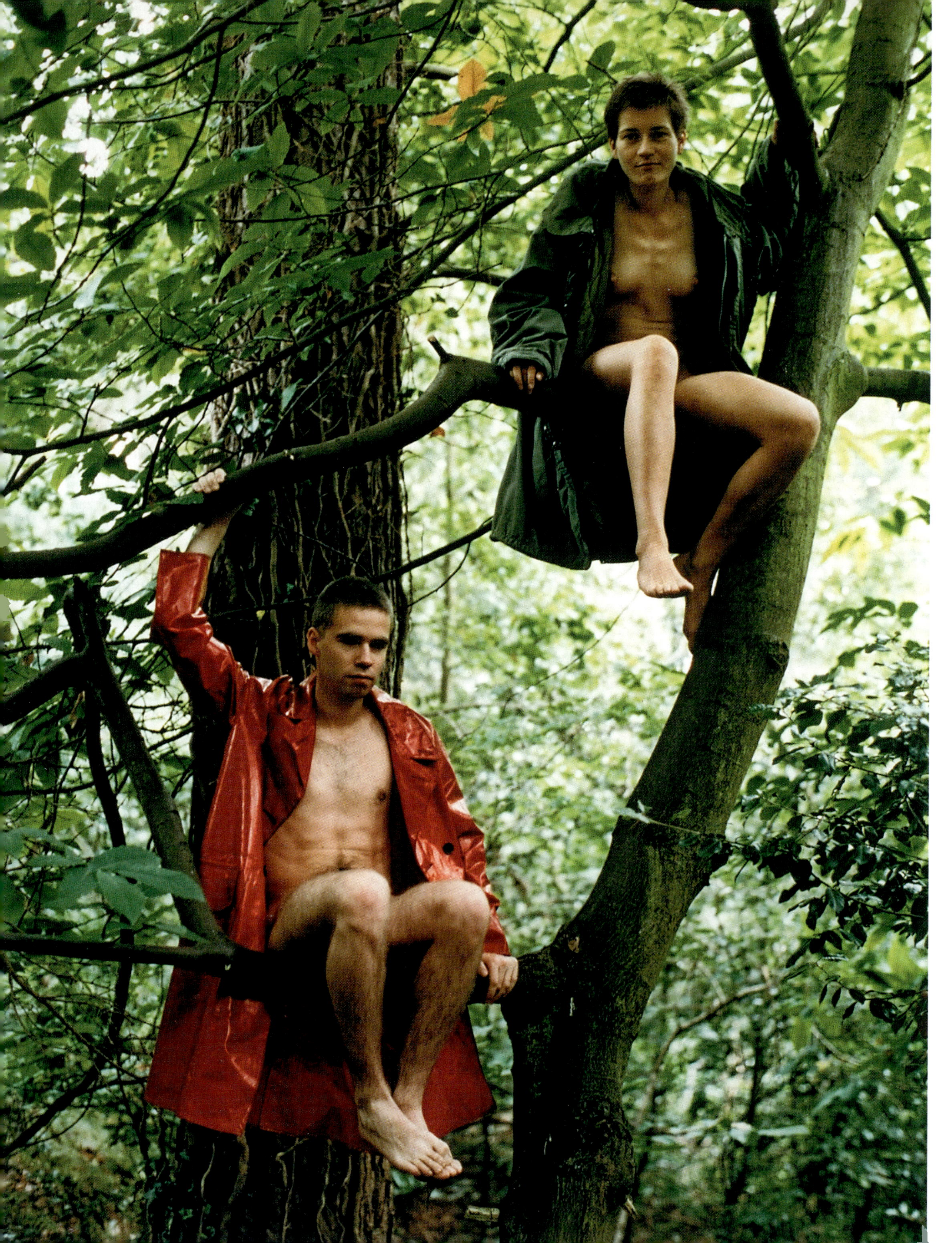

Chapter 4 Two More Naked Than One

62 Wolfgang Tillmans
Lutz and Alexandra Sitting in the Tree, 1992
Victoria & Albert Museum, London

The double portrait, often of a married couple, has a long tradition in Western art. This chapter looks at modern variations in which both (or occasionally just one) of the figures happen to be naked. Sometimes they just stand next to each other [plate 63]. Or they might interact with one other, physically or psychologically, in a wide variety of ways. The artist is a frequent protagonist. Mostly, it is evident that the two people are a couple, but at times we have no way of knowing. The viewer is likely to apply a common yardstick. When two naked people are gathered together in an image, we seek the distillation of a personal relationship, even though we may accept that a single, silent, static picture can hardly be expected to cut through the complexities of actual experience, and that temporal media such as the novel or film are better equipped to divulge it. This expectation has doubtless been reinforced by the increased willingness to talk openly about the joys and sorrows of relationships, and in particular about sex, that has been such a striking feature of Western social history over the past hundred years.

With liberation has come anxiety and frustration. We are now told that men are from Mars and women from Venus, but exploring the desires and incompatibilities of intimacy has been a longstanding preoccupation. One critic notes that Freud and D.H. Lawrence were in their different ways 'talking about the same thing, an epochal sickness with deep roots in the past ... a malfunction of sexual relationships within the culture'.[1] Visual archetypes were also available for artists who sought to represent the intimacy experienced by two individuals. Rodin's *The Kiss* (1901–4) expresses overwhelming desire, the absolute physical and psychological union between a man and a woman; Munch's *Man and Woman* (1898) embodies tension, alienation, and the mutual destruction that can enter a relationship between two lovers.[2]

Bonnard's *Man and Woman* provides a starting point [plate 64]. It is customary to read this picture as referring not only to the relations between the sexes, but also to an early stage in the artist's own liaison with his future wife Marthe (see Chapter 3). *Man and Woman* is set unambiguously in the bedroom. The figures are contrasted in gendered terms. The man is visually and psychologically dominant. The angular forms describing his bony frame confer masculine hardness, and the shadows that engulf him, heightened by contrast with the pile of white bedding behind, define his mood as brooding or melancholy. We might conclude that he is dressing after sex, but also beginning to disengage psychologically. The Marthe figure is smaller, set further back in space, and the strong light falling on her reinforces the cheerier state of mind implicit in her gesture of playing with a kitten, a symbol perhaps of femininity and domesticity. Alternatively, *Man and Woman* could be a pre-coital image. The man could be taking off his robe, and about to move towards the bed and woman. It is uncertain whether the yellow light is morning sunlight coming in through an imagined window, or artificial light. Critics have frequently noted the important role played by the dark, vertical accent of the screen, aligned with the lighting fixture above. On one level, it provides a phallic commentary on the implicit sexual undertones. But it also creates an emphatic division between the two figures, as though the contrasts already noted were symptomatic of some deeper existential divide between the two individuals, or between men and women generally. Metaphorically, the screen sets them apart rather 'as the Tree of Knowledge separates Adam and Eve'.[3] Or Bonnard may simply have thought that the picture required a central axis, to avoid what would otherwise be an inconsequential pocket of space at the heart of the painting. No one reading can be definitive. Little is actually spelt out, just as faces and genitals are veiled by shadow and loose brushwork, but the artist has provided us with sufficient clues to trigger a process of interpretation, mobilised by a 'play between intimacy and distance' in the interactions between the two figures.[4]

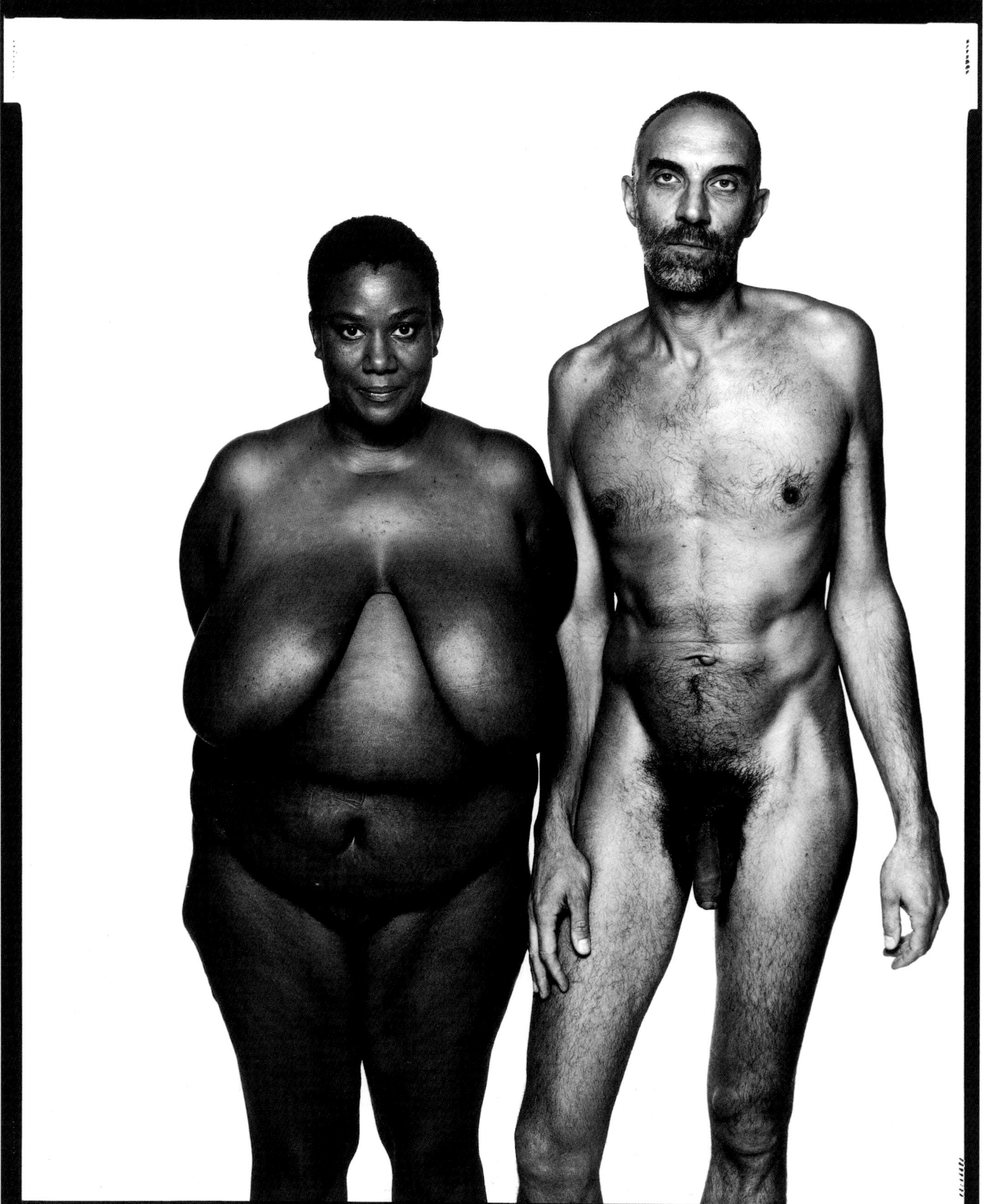

opposite **63 David Bailey**
Denise and Andrew Ward, Actress and Writer, 2002
David Bailey (Camera Eye Ltd)

below left **64 Pierre Bonnard**
Man and Woman, *c.*1899
Musée d'Orsay, Paris

below right **65 Oskar Kokoschka**
Two Nudes (Lovers), 1913
Bequest of Sarah Reed Platt, 1973.196
Museum of Fine Arts, Boston

This phrase was coined to evoke a 'chief characteristic' of Bonnard's art, but it can be applied to other artists who transposed private imagery into a public key. Expressing purely personal experiences becomes intertwined with exploring the contradictory emotions inherent in men and women's dealings with one another. Munch, for instance, introduced a directly personal note in pictures coinciding with an acute personal crisis, which culminated in a breakdown in 1908. He projected the cause of his anguish onto a traumatic episode from 1902, when a confrontation with Tulla Larsen, who could not let Munch go, resulted in a minor, self-inflicted gunshot wound to his finger. These events became an obsessive theme of his art and of his mental life. One friend reported: 'Then come endless lamentations about the woman who ruined his health. It was like a murder ... there are endless variations on it, and whatever type of conversation you try to start, it always goes back to the same old thing.'[5] In his art, descriptive depictions of the incident as he remembered it led to a more mythic treatment in the two large-scale paintings, which he called *The Death of Marat* (1907). Both protagonists are naked, the man lying on the bed, his hand bleeding profusely, the woman standing frontally and gazing at the viewer, indifferent to the man's plight.[6] The pictures had a profoundly personal significance, and it is notable that even though Munch used models, the figures look unmistakably like Larsen and himself. At the same time, Munch introduced visual and verbal references to Charlotte Corday's murder of the French Revolutionary leader in his bath, memorialised in the famous picture by David. He intended the imagery to suggest a literal crime of passion, but also to carry a wider resonance of woman's capacity to exert destructive power over man, and especially through sex.

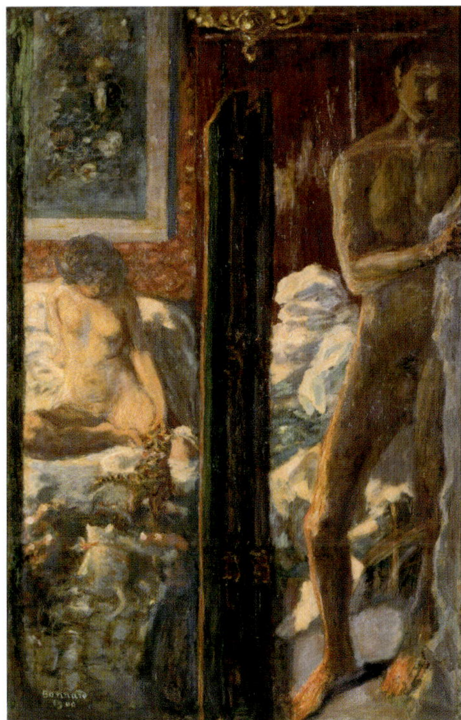

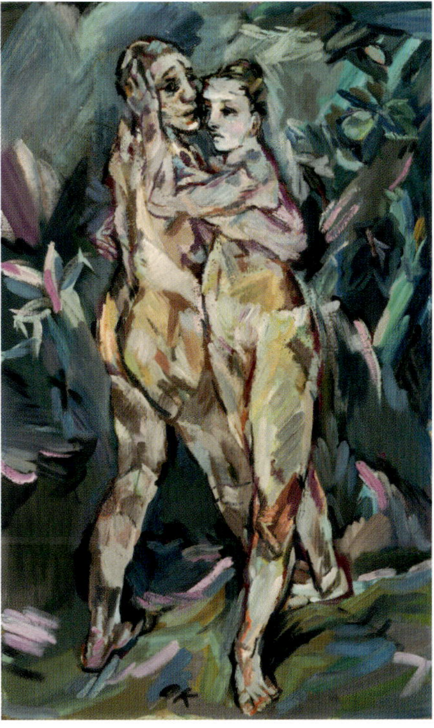

Oskar Kokoschka's distillations of his love affair with Alma Mahler in *Two Nudes (Lovers)* and *The Tempest (Bride of the Wind)* of 1913 seem more celebratory [plate 65]. They are staged in a landscape, recalling their trips together to the Dolomites, and project the couple's psychic and sexual union as a force of nature. The imagery is lifted beyond the mundane by the artist's use of flickering, dematerialising brush marks. Alma recalled the relationship as 'a single violent lover's quarrel'.[7] Both pictures have also been seen to possess poignant undertones: *Two Nudes* becomes 'a tragic dance', in which the figures 'are depicted, naked and embracing, in a rhythmic step; but while the two bodies are entangled, the long strides being taken by both suggest a desire to disentangle'.[8] *The Tempest* was his most ambitious work to date, a paean to his and Alma's intimacy, but filtered through Kokoschka's preoccupation with Tristan and Isolde, the archetypal tragic lovers. For Carl Schorske, 'Alma's smoothly textured body sleeps in eloquent contentment on her lover's passion-coruscated breast. Oskar lies tensely awake, his jaw clenched, his head as rigid upon his neck as if he stood erect. The tired eyes, wide open, stare fixedly into the void; the seared and swollen hands, entwined uncertainly over his groin, bring to a focus his tumescence of the spirit, so hopelessly out of phase with Alma's serenity'. Even the tempest that bears them above the moonlit sea is ambiguous: 'Is it a cloud of hope, a sturdy vehicle of baroque fantasy to draw them upward? Or is it the trough of a wave of despair that will engulf their fated love?'[9]

The Tempest foreshadows Schiele's *Man and Woman I* (1914), which has likewise been associated with 'the end of the relationship between Schiele and his model and mistress Valerie Neuzil ("Wally")'.[10] The Schiele seems an explicitly post-coital image, although any sensuality or intimacy is undercut by the striking contrasts between the two figures: the unmistakeable tension, even anguish, conveyed by the contorted body language, emaciated anatomies, and the intense, confrontational gaze that the man directs towards the viewer; and the almost grisaille palette, crumpled texture and wiry drawing that are used for all components of the scene. Whatever the personal meanings, the image goes beyond the specifics of portraiture.

The theme is revisited in a group of pictures by Christian Schad and Stanley Spencer produced in the period between the two World Wars. In his 1927 *Self-portrait with Model*,

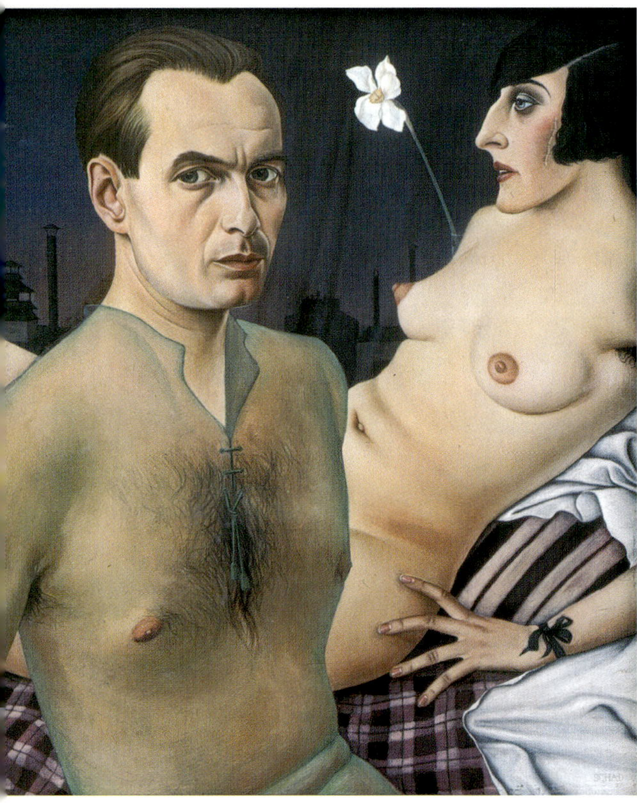

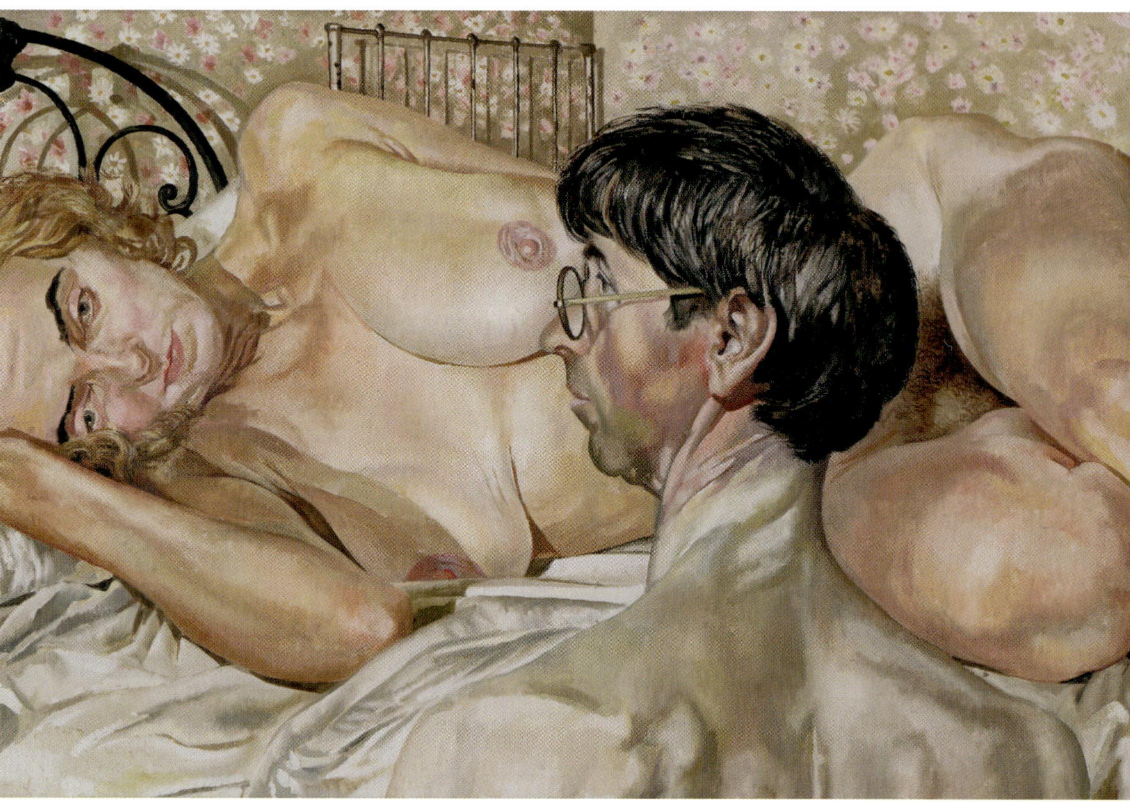

left **66 Christian Schad**
Self-portrait with Model, 1927
Tate, London

right **67 Stanley Spencer**
Self-portrait with Patricia Preece, 1936
Fitzwilliam Museum, University of Cambridge

Schad employs a diaphanous shift that does little to veil his nakedness, a Berlin cityscape also seen through a veil, a stylised image of his naked wife, and a narcissus flower, in order to project himself as a type of modern urban consciousness [plate 66]. Schad's painting provides an uncanny precedent for Stanley Spencer's pair of pictures created in England a decade later and in the wake of the artist's meeting with Patricia Preece (see Chapter 3). In *Self-portrait with Patricia Preece* (1936) and *Double Nude Portrait: the Artist and his Second Wife (The Leg of Mutton Nude)* (1937), the artist and Preece are both nude [plate 67]. Spencer fell in love with her on the rebound from his relationship with Hilda Carline – he and Hilda separated in 1934 and were divorced in 1937. Spencer responded to Patricia's social status, stylishness, veneer of sophistication and worldly self-confidence. Clearly under Preece's spell, Spencer had limited success in achieving the physical intimacy he craved, for she was essentially a lesbian, living with her long-term partner Dorothy Hepworth. She was adept at exploiting Spencer's emotional naiveté, primarily for her own financial purposes, though she may also have sought the 'respectability' of a public relationship with a man. By 1935, he had transferred the ownership of his house to her, and continued to lavish on her extravagant gifts of jewellery and clothes, so that he ended up badly in debt and under pressure to churn out the landscapes that he saw as a distraction from his figurative work. It is difficult to determine whether she was completely cynical, or whether she bore Spencer genuine affection.

From Spencer's perspective, the relationship was clearly not easy, given that Preece's behaviour was often confrontational. He would say things like: 'Hate describing or talking to her about my thoughts, & since she does not agree with anything I think & says so, it is not my fault that I complain' (April, 1934). Or, in a letter to Preece: 'Why should you think I should put up with what you would not tolerate for five minutes, namely someone other than yourself putting some restriction on your behaviour & conduct telling you what you would or would not be allowed to do'.[11] Spencer and Preece married in May 1937, but she immediately returned to her lover, and the marriage was apparently never consummated. Having got her hands on Spencer's worldly assets and a regular allowance, Preece's idea was now that he and Hilda should get back together.[12] Finally, in the wake of being ordered to get out of Cookham, Spencer told Preece that he wanted to return to Hilda: 'the strain of being with someone whose practice was to be always incensed against me was too much even for my *giant* strength'.[13]

Spencer subsequently acknowledged that his art never

became so 'sex-ridden as it did in the long sexless period from 1933 to 1938. I say sexless, then, because while at that time there were incidents with Hilda and Patricia, it was a starvation period.'[14] It is not difficult to see the two naked double portraits as compensatory. In *Self-portrait with Patricia Preece* Spencer's frank anatomical scrutiny extended to the hips, upper legs and pubic hair. The two figures are tied together in certain ways: her nipple is rhymed with his rounded lens, his head takes the place of her stomach (does this suggest a subconscious urge to return to the womb or a maternal embrace?), and a single line describes the contours of his shoulder and neck and her right thigh and leg. The two heads are horizontally aligned, but that is their only connection. Her face implies inwardness rather than communication with her companion, whose profile view fails to engage with her. Whereas Schad's companion is schematised into a sexual fetish, Preece is highly individualised in physical and psychological terms, and it is the artist who is made to appear marginal. In its presentation of Preece's indifference, in her receipt of his abject adoration, the picture suggests Spencer's masochism. In a letter of 1936 he remarks: 'the more severe and austere [she is] the bigger the thrill. Every inch I gain with Patricia is a real achievement – it is so extraordinary to get near *at all*.'[15]

In *Double Nude Portrait*, realistic scrutiny is infused with fantasy and longing. The picture is a frank compendium of bodily details, which barely cohere anatomically, but the one bit missing from both parties is hands, which would imply contact and real intimacy. The artist gives himself more space, though it is still a squeeze, but he remains emotionally subordinate, the priest behind the altar at which we are invited to worship. A poem from around 1935 had used exactly this terminology:

> *I worship her*
> *In the chancel of my garden*
> *I adore her on the altar*
> *Of my dining room fire*
> *I praise her from morning until morning* …[16]

Both images are a sustained exercise in worship from afar. The term has sexual and religious connotations, which Spencer refused to separate in his commitment to an art rooted in love: 'Purely carnal desires may be sometimes ends in themselves & sometimes stepping stones to something further & others. There are two things in this life I love to "suck up" to. One is woman & the other is religion …'.[17] For Spencer, the Preece pictures were 'A great urge for self-expression; a wish to arrive at myself; to be & to behave as I would if in Heaven.'[18]

Schad and German New Objectivity provide a revealing context for looking at Spencer. Yet the double portraits also coincided with the highpoint of British interest in Surrealism, marked by the vast *International Surrealist Exhibition* at the New Burlington Galleries in summer 1936. It is not known if he visited this infamous event, and if he did he would probably have been horrified by most of it. Nonetheless, there is a dream-like quality, a savouring of fantasy, to much of Spencer's work around this time and there are suggestive parallels between some of his imaginative pictures and works by Surrealists.[19] Equally, it is tempting to juxtapose the *Double Nude Portrait*, with its bizarre inclusion of chops and leg of lamb, and Dalí's 1933 picture *Gala with Two Lamb Chops on her Shoulder*.[20] This particular work was in fact exhibited, along with two more portraits of Gala, in a major Dalí show at the Lefevre Gallery coinciding with the *International Surrealist Exhibition*, just months before Spencer embarked upon his *Double Nude Portrait*.[21] Certainly, it is plausible that Dalí's hallucinatory realism would have interested him. The affinity raises the question of whether Spencer's willingness to channel his pent-up sexual desires into his art, initially in the Patricia Preece pictures and then more explicitly in other images, might have been galvanised by an awareness of Surrealism.[22] Of course, the movement reinforced more open attitudes towards sex that were already in the air, thanks for instance to the writings of D.H. Lawrence and Freud, with the latter now accessible, and widely discussed, after the appearance of English translations. We might also note the appearance in 1936 of Lawrence's posthumous *Pornography and So On*. One can well imagine Spencer enjoying the title essay defending 'natural fresh openness about sex' as the antidote to pornography, which comes from puritanical inhibition and 'sex-hatred'; and equally, in 'Introduction to Painting', Lawrence's vehement denunciation of the hatred of the body endemic historically in English artistic culture, and now reinforced by modernist formalism: 'We don't live in the flesh. Our instincts and intuitions are dead, we live wound round with the winding-sheet of abstraction.'[23] The problem with Spencer is that his profuse diaries and letters make it all too easy to interpret the pictures as autobiography rather than considering where they belong in wider contexts.

Several painters since the Second World War have explored such imagery. In the work of Alice Neel, a nude double portrait such as *Cindy Nemser and Chuck* (1975) was part of the artist's obsession with persuading her sitters to remove their clothing.[24] Around the same time, Joan Semmel depicted male and female figures lying next to each other on a bed, from an ideological perspective crystallised in titles such as *Antonio and I* and *Autonomy-Intimacy* (both

1974).[25] A parallel strand of gay imagery runs through David Hockney's *Illustrations for thirteen poems from C.P. Cavafy* (1966). Despite the literary catalyst, these images have been used to support the argument that Hockney's 'drawings of naked people were portraits rather than nudes'.[26] In the case of *The Beginning*, there is no direct reference to the poem or to Cavafy's own life; 'rather it is two naked men in bed watching someone draw them' [plate 69].

In the work of Lucian Freud, the conjunction of two figures is a persistent theme. Both figures are sometimes nude, sometimes only one.[27] In the Edinburgh picture, we gaze down on two sleeping men, one face-up and clothed, the other naked and lying on his front [plate 70]. The picture represents a gay couple, Cerith Wynn-Evans and Angus Cook, which is evidently typical of Freud's choice of male sitters, and emerged from working with the same two models on *Two Men in the Studio* (1987–9).[28] The conjunction of naked and clothed, along with the suggestion that both figures are asleep, downplays any suggestion of sexual interplay, though we might read an involuntary tenderness into the gesture of hand laid onto bare leg. The painting is notable for the relative shallowness of the pictorial space, created by the high viewpoint and by the barely modulated white sheet as backdrop for the figures, interrupted only by the triangle of floorboards top left. The contrast between the two figures is counter-pointed by the visual rhymes and axes that bind them together, as in the continuous diagonal line connecting the edges of black trousers, blue shirt and naked right side. There are contrary progressions of shapes from naked left knee through to clothed right elbow, and from naked left foot to the clothed man's right hand, buckle and belt. Such structural rigour might be highlighted by comparing *Two Men* with the naked double-portraits of Leon Kossoff, where the emphasis is much more on the human presence of the sitters and their intimate contact [plate 68].

In photography, the most sustained exploration of the naked couple is found in the work of Nan Goldin [plates 71, 72 and 73]. Her explorations of the theme, in the *Ballad of Sexual Dependency* (1986) and since, have included tender embraces between lovers, scenes of explicit love-making, in which she herself features with male and female partners, and images of what seems to be tension and alienation, in post-coital scenarios. In her essay for *Ballad*, Goldin emphasised that the images are rooted in personal circumstances, but that their implications transcend the merely anecdotal: 'The people and locales in my pictures are particular, specific, but I feel that the concerns I'm dealing with are universal.' The photographs are, she asserts, about 'the nature of relationships'.[29] In her experience, men and

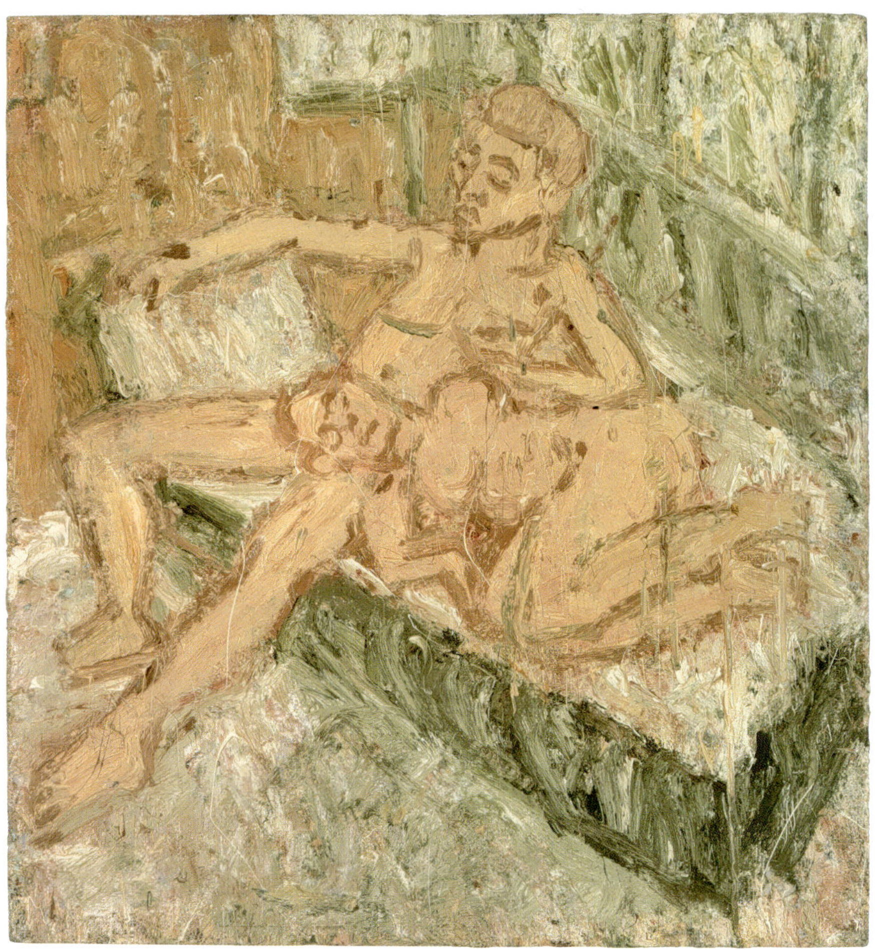

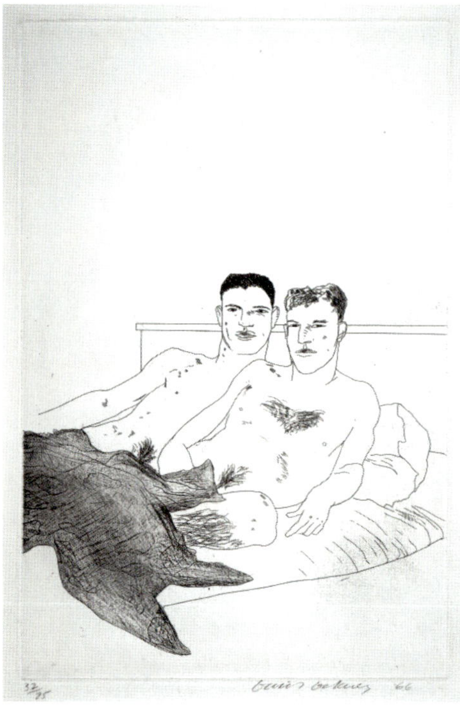

above **68 Leon Kossoff**
Summer in the Studio, Pilar and Jacinto II, 1997
Annely Juda Fine Art, London

left **69 David Hockney**
The Beginning, 1966
Scottish National Gallery of Modern Art, Edinburgh

opposite **70 Lucian Freud**
Two Men, 1987–8
Scottish National Gallery of Modern Art, Edinburgh

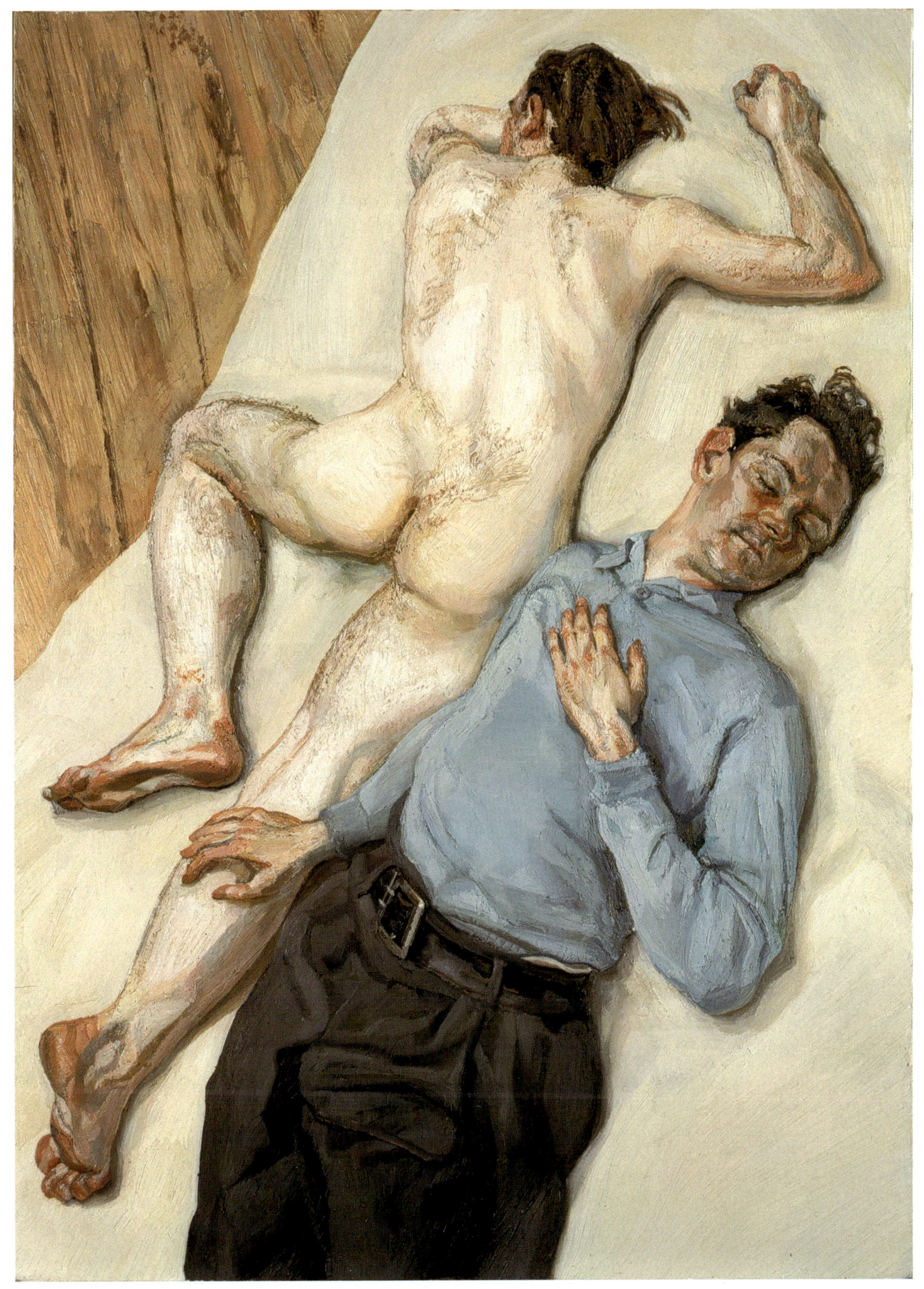

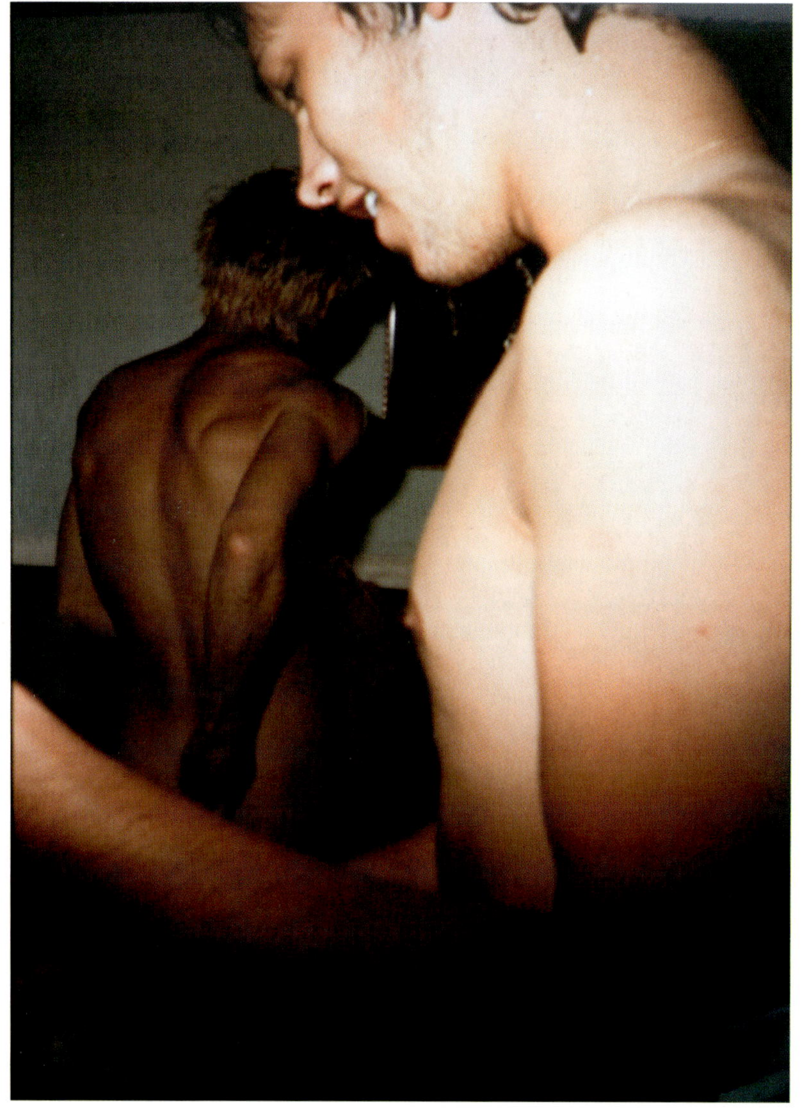

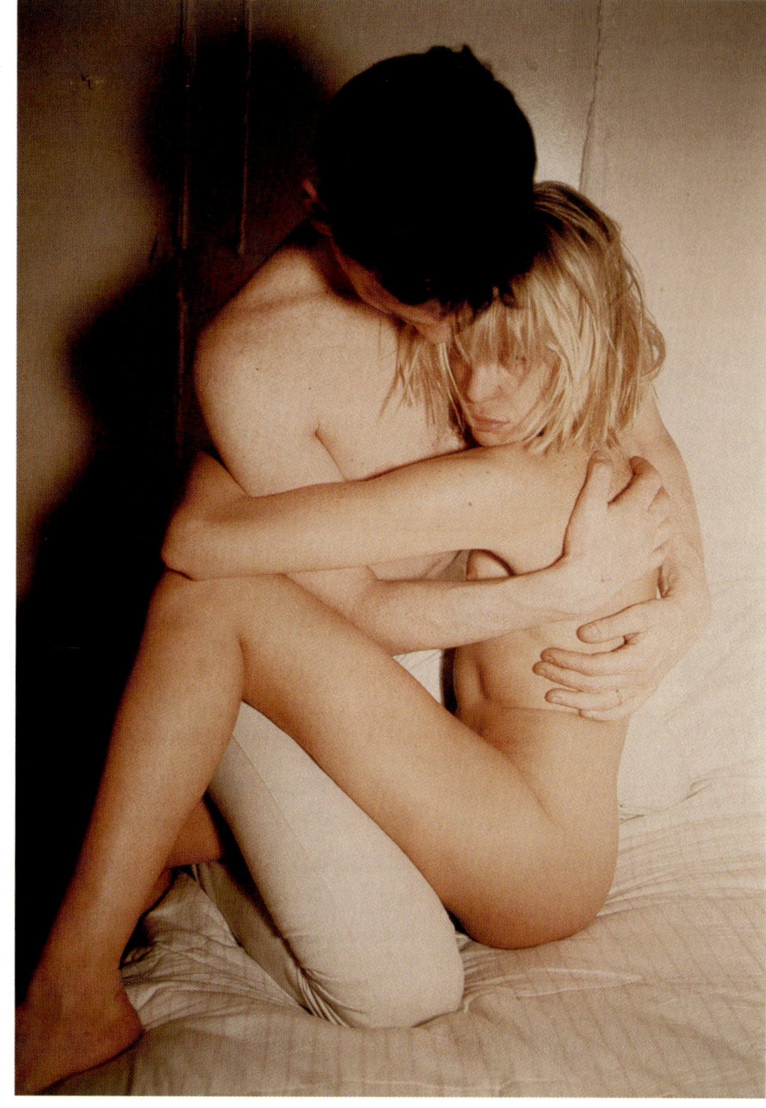

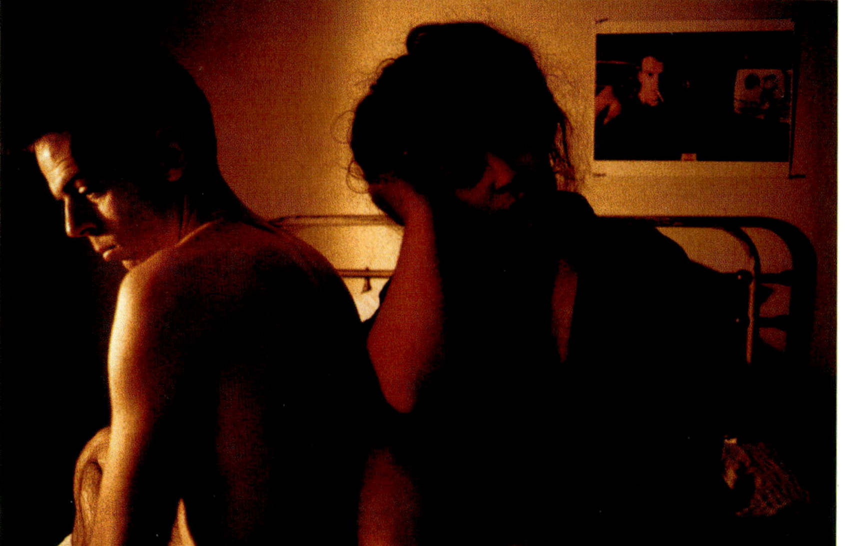

above left **71 Nan Goldin**

David and Bruce after Sex, Provincetown, 1975

Private Collection, London

above **72 Nan Goldin**

Patrick and Teri on their Wedding Night, New York City, 1987

Collection Fotomuseum, Winterthur

left **73 Nan Goldin**

Self-portrait in Kimono with Brian, 1983

Collection Fotomuseum, Winterthur, Gift of Andreas Reinhart

opposite **74 Elinor Carucci**

PMS, 1997

Courtesy Edwynn Houk Gallery, New York

women are 'irrevocably strangers to one another, irreconcilably unsuited'; they 'have different emotional realities and speak a different emotional language'. The 'construction of gender roles' is instilled in childhood, and becomes 'one of the major problems that individuals bring into a relationship'. Nevertheless, 'there is an intense need for coupling in spite of it all. Even if relationships are destructive, people cling together'. The 'universal problem' becomes 'the struggle between independence and autonomy'. On the basis, clearly, of her own private traumas, Goldin describes how 'the friction between the fantasies and the realities of relationships can lead to alienation and violence'. A part of her 'is challenged by the opacity of men's emotional makeup and is stimulated by the conflict inherent in relationships between men and women'. She also feels 'better suited to be with a woman', which in her own case evolved from friendships characterised by 'deep tenderness' to sexual relationships. Such sentiments provide an illuminating commentary on the photographs focusing on the sense of alienation within sexual intimacy, as vividly conveyed in pictures of herself and Brian [plate 73]. The compulsion to couple is evoked in the many images Goldin has made of two naked people embracing or having sex with one another, seemingly oblivious to the presence of herself or the camera.

Other photographers have been required to establish where they stand in relation to a growing and ever more explicit tide of pornographic imagery, aimed at a mostly male audience.[30] A cluster of works by Nicholas Nixon shows the intertwined, fragmentary bodies of pairs of lovers, who are denoted by initials though their faces are not included. The pictures, at the opposite pole from the depersonalisations of pornography, seek to explore 'how we share our lives, feelings, thoughts and bodies'.[31] We come back full circle to Rodin's *Kiss*. Nixon acknowledges that 'intimacy is probably impossible to get at in a picture, but showing how it can look is my way of loving to fail'. Several pictures in Elinor Carucci's *Closer* evoke her relationship with her husband Erin. *PMS* deals with the theme of menstruation, a taboo in visual imagery generally, let alone in art photography [plate 74]. The sombre mood leads us to speculate that a period has come as bad news, generating psychological as well as sexual apartness between the two individuals. Some less definable drama emanates from Odalebe Bamgboye's *The Lighthouse* [plate 149]. While the white girl lies fast asleep in bed, with only her head and face poking out of the duvet, the naked black male, who we may learn to identify as the artist himself, faces and leans against the back wall, his head completely out of view. The gesture is one that we might read as despairing, as sexually available, or even as reminiscent of a police strip-search, a familiar enough experience for black youths. The scenario is enigmatic: 'Is it only the viewer of the lightbox – a tool of the advertising business – or is she, too, dreaming of this black body, this "wild black animal"?'[32]

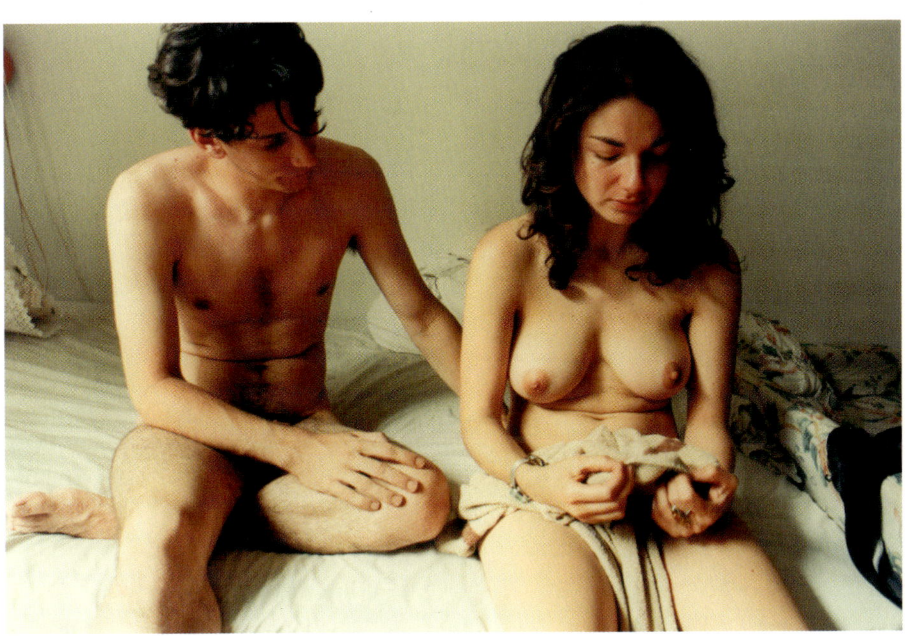

If each of these images might almost be interpreted as a still from some cinematic narrative, the several naked portraits by Wolfgang Tillmans of his friends Alexander and Lutz proclaim their own artifice. In *Lutz and Alexandra Sitting in the Tree* (1992), the couple sit on the branches of a tree, dressed only in smart coats, suggesting a fashion shoot while parodying a Germanic ideology of back to nature [plate 62]. Tillmans flirts with the spectator's disposition to unearth a story, though the contrast with painting is hardly true:

I always try to resist the viewer's appetite for explanation. That's what happens with photography – the viewer wants to know how, when, what, where. I look at pictures as pictures. When you look at paintings you don't ask these questions, you just accept that this is the vignette or situation you're given. That's very much how I see my pictures. I want to keep those questions out so that it doesn't matter if it's staged or not.[33]

In many large-scale photo-pieces from the mid-1990s, such as *In the Piss*, Gilbert & George confront us with an apparently unselfconscious exposure of their middle-aged bodies [plate 75]. The effect is charming, on the face of it, and this is reinforced by the two men's body language, which projects an affectionate, non-sexual intimacy, as though we were contemplating an image of gay marriage. Straightforward readings are encouraged by the artists: 'For us, being naked in front of the public, we are trying to make ourselves vulnerable in front of the viewer … this kind of

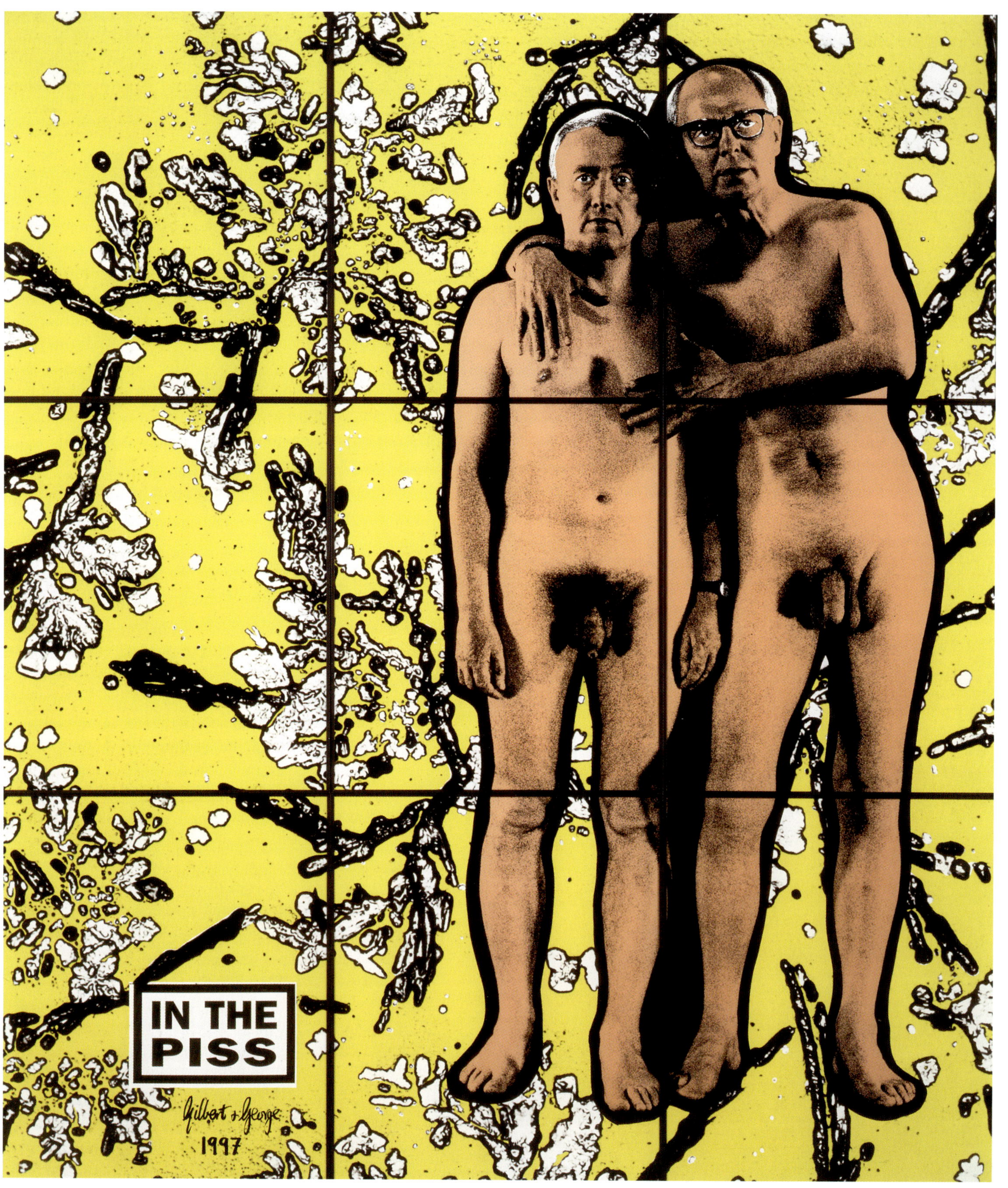
IN THE
PISS
Gilbert & George
1997

picture in some way is showing the world what we actually are inside. It's all the difficulties, all our problems, all our complexities.'[34] Direct lines of communication with the ordinary spectator, who is excluded from most modern art, and engaging with the universals of the human condition, are constant ambitions. This particular cluster of images is said to address 'the human reality that there is no nakedness without a viewer: we are not naked when we are alone'. Whereas pornography objectifies the performing models, preserving the viewer's detachment, 'people looking at our pictures where we are naked are looking at their own nakedness as well. It's not just us. They realise their own nakedness under their clothes at that moment. In that way the pictures are as much about the viewer as about us really'.[35] Nevertheless, confronting the viewer with two nude males is particularly challenging:

GILBERT: *It's strange: a naked lady is wonderful; two naked ladies, very interesting; but two men naked …*

GEORGE: *One man naked is a male study; more than one … well, that's quite serious – two men naked are more naked than one.*[36]

The artists' technique permits the inclusion of large-scale photographic imagery, but it also evokes the slick impersonality, bold outlines and exaggerated colours of advertising imagery. The backdrop of *In the Piss* is highly decorative, suggesting the treatment of blossom trees in Japanese prints. However, it actually originates, as we infer from the title, in microscopic photography of urine. Such an allusion to base bodily processes coexists with intimations of religious imagery, especially Adam and Eve in the Garden of Paradise before the Fall. As ever with Gilbert & George, the vulnerability that the images claim to convey turns out to be performative. The poses and expressions look staged, and the viewer has no real prospect of unearthing their problems and complexities, let alone discerning the nature of the two artists' relationship or gleaning any sense of intimate contact. For all their humanist rhetoric, the pair also recall Morecambe and Wise, and we might even suspect that we too are 'in the piss', in the sense that the artists are perhaps taking the piss, flirting with our impulse to read profound messages about the human state into a picture of two old queens in the buff. Or was the combination of nakedness and urine simply a desire to shock the beholder, perpetuating the artists' reputation as provocateurs at a time when a generation of Young British Artists, such as Damien Hirst and the Chapman brothers, were taking their cue from them but at the same time threatening to outdo them in sheer sensationalism? Although the common man is their ostensible target audience, Gilbert & George operate very strategically in relation to the mechanisms of success in the contemporary art world.

In a series of four triptychs by Melanie Manchot, *The Fontainebleau Series*, it is two naked women who feature, identified by their first names [plate 76]. The body language is staged and formal, just as the images are frontal and symmetrically composed, exploiting the bold colours, forms and textures that Manchot extracted from the locations she chose, a different old-fashioned bathroom for each pair. One of the images in each triptych refers unmistakably to the famous sixteenth-century school of Fontainebleau painting showing one nude half-length female touching the nipple of another (evidently Gabrielle D'Estrées and her sister).[37] In Manchot's variants, the gesture registers as a symbolic distillation of physical and emotional intimacy, rather than as an actual manifestation of tenderness. By such means, and through large-scale formats, a certain formality and distance are inserted, paradoxically, into a context associated with spontaneous behaviour (a bathroom, two naked figures). Manchot subverts our expectations, not just those we bring from life but also from painters and photographers like Bonnard and Goldin. In their work, informality signifies a narrative of the private realm and intimate feelings. In *The Fontainebleau Series*, visual detachment allows us to imagine whatever we like, since we know nothing about the people and their relationship. The bathroom paraphernalia serve to protect the sitters, in their naked vulnerability, and to keep the viewer at bay. Revelation is promised, and withheld.

opposite **75 Gilbert & George**
In the Piss, 1997
National Portrait Gallery, London

below **76 Melanie Manchot**
The Fontainebleau Series: Emma and Charlie I, 2001
Fred (London) Ltd and the Artist

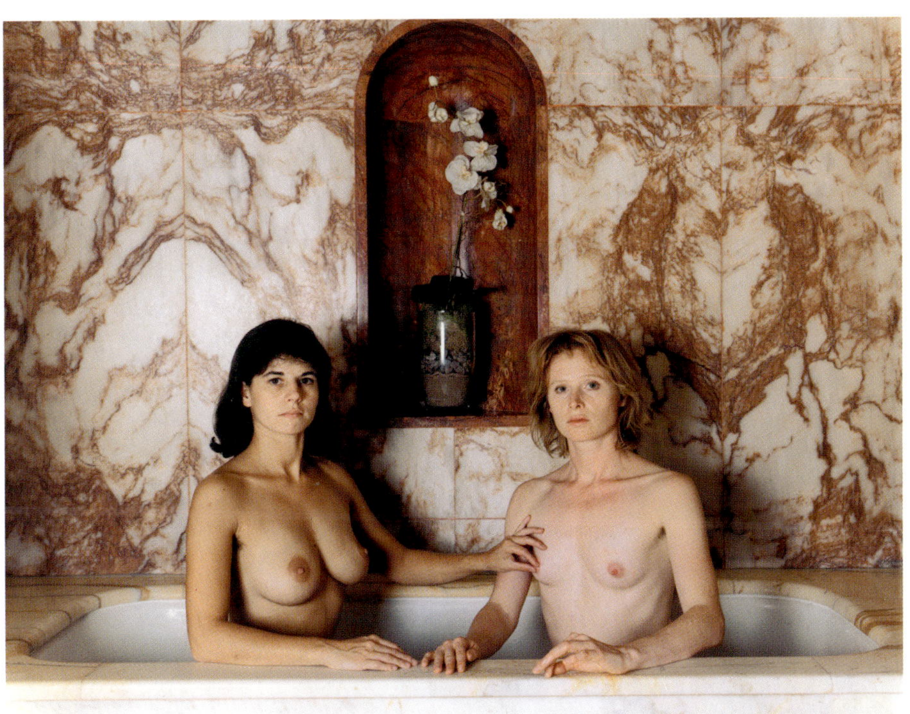

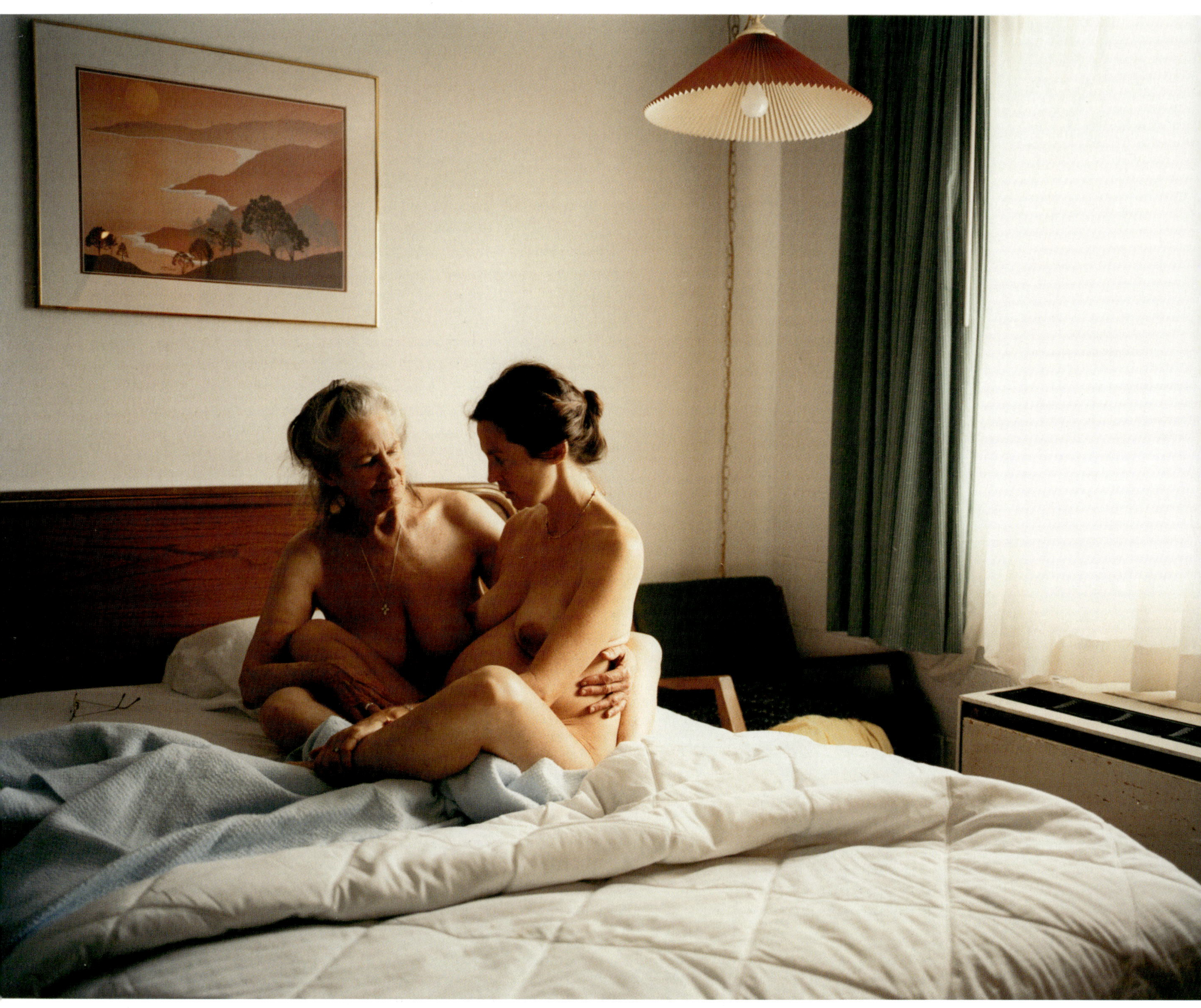

Chapter 5 In the Family

77 Tierney Gearon
Untitled (from The Mother Project), 2003
Courtesy Yossi Milo, New York

In everyday life, our utterly formulaic images of family members and events are enshrined in the idealised narrative of the family album (albeit now in cyberspace rather than on the bookshelf), that universal repository for pictures of special occasions and rites of passage. We all want such pictures to affirm that we value the same things as everyone else. But artists, mostly female, when they have engaged with family imagery, have sought to subvert such clichés. That ambition has extended to presenting their children or parents naked, an appropriate expression of the tenderness and lack of inhibition inherent, ideally, in such family relationships. But viewers' expectations in this area tend to be especially conservative. The work we are going to look at has raised questions of propriety and caused offence, in turn generating distress and frustration for its makers. Some audiences have resisted having to look at older, less obviously alluring bodies than the stereotypes of the mass media. Many more have protested at artists' depiction of their own children naked, in a social climate so aware of child sexual abuse.

Following a chronology of human life rather than the history of art, let us begin with very young babies. These are the one type of sitter everyone depicts naked. Babies seem beyond even the most warped forms of sexual desire. When Alice Neel, as a very old lady, painted her grandson Andrew at five months old, in the midst it appears of having his nappy changed, she captured both how remote babies are at that age from the proportions and upright posture of humans in general, but also how the child is already father of the man, in his attentive facial expression and in his prominent penis [plate 78]. The difference a short period of time can make at that stage is apparent when we turn to David Williams's depiction of his son Sam, luminous with paternal feeling [plate 79]. The state of parental bliss, akin to falling in love, is evoked in his *Triptych: Williams Family Portrait*, in which Williams and his wife converge, blurred and insubstantial, on the diminutive, crystal clear figure of Sam, who walks hesitantly towards us, and into whatever future lies ahead [plate 80].

To such artists, making pictures of young children when they are undressed seems perfectly natural. The images register the tenderness, protectiveness, and fascination that most parents feel towards their offspring. Images of naked children speak to our sense that childhood is a time of innocence, before the corruptions of self-consciousness and the onset of puberty. However, they might also suggest what parents and carers must always have known, that children start behaving in recognisably sexual ways when they are still quite small. Sigmund Freud believed that being open about this was one of the key contributions of psychoanalysis. In 1909 he remarked:

It is certainly not the case that sexual instinct enters into children at the age of puberty in the way in which, in the Gospel, the devil entered into the swine. A child has its sexual instincts and activities from the first, it comes into the world with them … There is even no difficulty in observing the manifestations of these sexual activities in children; on the contrary, it calls for some skill to overlook them or explain them away.[1]

The sexuality of childhood is broached in the work of several photographers. Edward Weston's pictures of his son from the early 1920s are modest in what they show, but seem to transform Neil into a classical Greek statue, with his curls and artfully twisted pose [plate 81]. Weston's most direct successor was Robert Mapplethorpe, who produced several none too subtle pictures of young children unselfconsciously exposing their genitals.[2] Weston may also have provided a catalyst for the more inventive images of their young children, sometimes naked, created by Sally Mann and Nicholas Nixon. Nixon's pictures of Sam and Clementine were created in the 1980s, and Mann's of Emmet, Jessie and Virginia made over several years were collected in her book *Immediate Family* in 1992. Both photographers experienced the revelation described by Nixon:

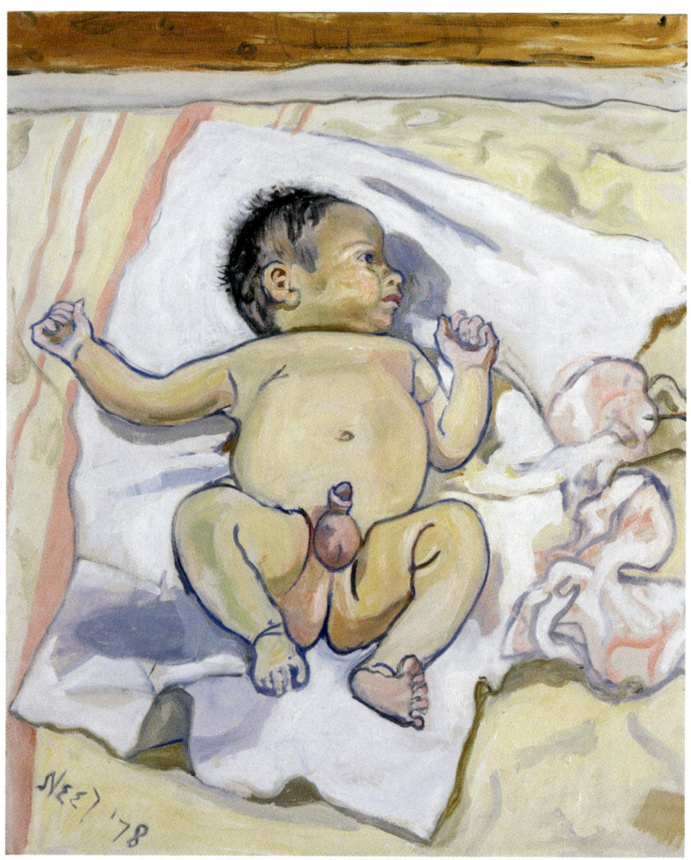

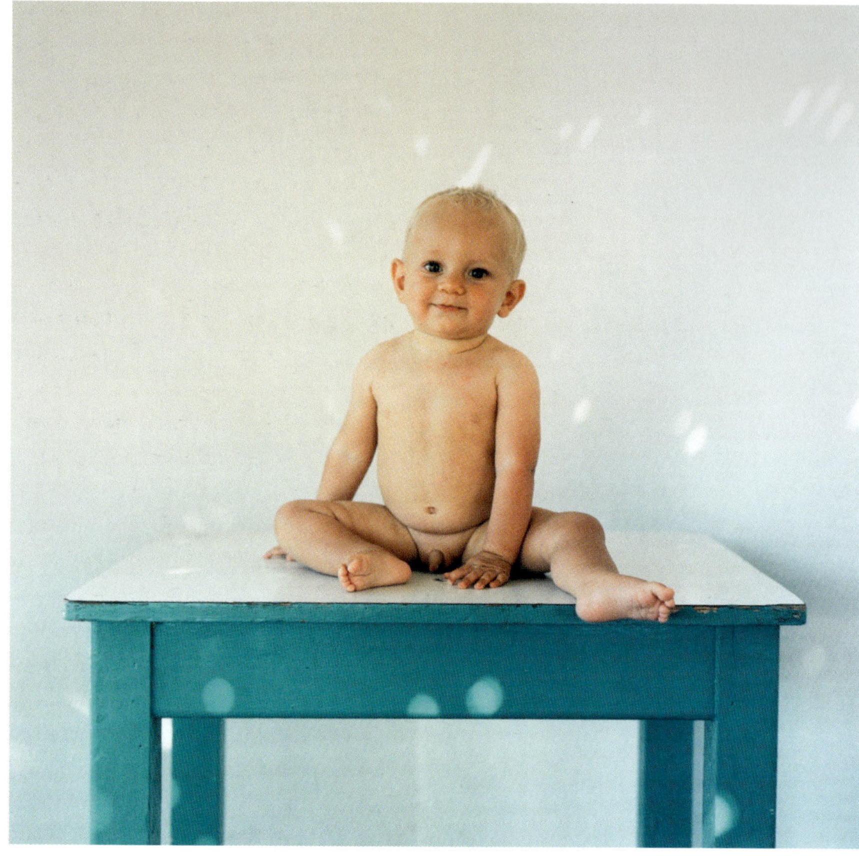

left **78 Alice Neel**
Andrew, 1978
Tate, London

right **79 David Williams**
My Son Samuel, Kos, Greece, 1998
The Artist

opposite **80 David Williams**
Triptych: Williams Family Portrait, 1999
The Artist

'It never occurred to me that having a family and making art could be exactly the same. All of a sudden, what I cared about most in life and in art was two feet away.'[3] Mann and Nixon are Americans of similar age, and both use large format cameras to produce black and white pictures notable for their clarity of detail and tonal subtlety. In the naked portraits of their respective children, the subjects are always identified by name by Mann, and often by Nixon, establishing a relationship to the terrain of the family album. Nixon could again be speaking for both photographers when he commented: 'Maybe part of my artistic ambition is to keep the lively part of snapshots and get rid of the dull, studied part of portraits, but maintain the best juice of both.'[4]

Nixon's images of his children are towards the snapshot end of the spectrum, compared to the formality of his *Brown Sisters* series. He has described his fascination with the qualities of the children's young bodies: 'I just loved their skin. It was so fresh and wonderful ... They seemed like beautiful, pliable, wonderful creatures with this covering that was changing daily.'[5] They are frequently photographed close up, and cropped by the framing edges. The pictures imply, as does the children's body language, that things are happening beyond the picture's edges. The gestures that relate to the intense feelings impelling movements of body and face are difficult to interpret, emphasising that children occupy their own world and are, to a degree, alien to adult comprehension.

In Mann's images, the figures are commonly orientated towards the viewer, in conventional portrait manner, and they seem to be performing for the camera. The children's involvement in their mother's project is suggested by their sense of assurance. In Mann's own words,

Many of these pictures are intimate, some are fictions and some are fantastic, but most are of ordinary things every mother has seen – a wet bed, a bloody nose, candy cigarettes. They dress up, they pout and posture, they paint their bodies; they dive like otters in the dark river.

They have been involved in the creative process since infancy. At times, it is difficult to say exactly who makes the picture. Some are gifts to me from my children: gifts that come in a moment as fleeting as the touch of an angel's wing.[6]

Sometimes the facial expressions and body language seem to mimic adult norms, which, when read in conjunction with their nakedness, evokes that sense of precocious sexuality that has upset Mann's critics, who accuse her of producing what amounts to pornography. *Immediate Family* had the misfortune to appear at a moment of hysteria, when an official panel of childcare experts had concluded that 'child abuse and neglect in the United States now represents a national emergency'.[7] Other viewers, however, admired the frankness of her work which acknowledged the emotional actualities of childhood: 'To look at Sally Mann's photographs of her children as unfeeling or immoral is simply not to be looking at them, to be pushing away something complex and difficult ... and demanding a cliché in its place'.[8]

For Mann, her children epitomise a state whose very impermanence produces a mingling of joy and pathos: 'Their strength and confidence, there to be seen in their eyes, are compelling – for nothing is so seductive as a gift casually possessed. They are substantial; their green present is irreducibly complex. The withering perspective of the past, the predictable treacheries of the future; for the moment, those familiar complications of time all play harmlessly around them as dancing shadows beneath the great oak.'[9] Yet this sense of living in the present is counterpointed by a sense of duration. The children dress up as teenagers or adults, and so look ahead to future excitements. There is also a retrospective dimension. Mann has emphasised the links with what she remembers of her own childhood, growing up in rural Virginia. The children's activities are staged in settings that evoke a world before modernity, and their knowingness coexists with a feral quality, evident not just from physicality, but from their being dirty, damaged, or associated with animals, both dead and alive. In *Jessie Bites* (1985), a dolled-up little girl has regressed into a painted savage, and we can read in her pensive features an emerging consciousness of her own, and life's, complexity. Mann's affinities are with Emmet Gowin (see Chapter 3).[10] The photographic language of Mann also suggests continuities between the present and a past stretching back to the nineteenth century and the dawn of the photographic medium, with echoes of the poetic intensity achieved by Julia Margaret Cameron.

Mann had encountered a great deal of criticism, and the issue was widely debated again on the occasion of a 2001 exhibition in London that included pictures by Tierney Gearon, in some of which her children were playing naked. The police were called in and the popular press had a field day. Gearon was unknown, and the pictures could be viewed unfairly as only blown-up snapshots, which meant that defences of the work tended to be sociological rather than artistic. Commentators argued that such ubiquitous imagery served psychological purposes: 'The idea of childhood innocence – often signified in pictures by children's unselfconscious nakedness – is a convenient myth that we parents need in order to maintain that image of ourselves as members of a contented, loving family, without the usual undercurrents of conflict, competition, jealousy and anger.'[11] Family photos kept the realities of family life at bay:

Nudity often figures in these snaps. It is generic, almost, thematic: because we delight in their lack of self-consciousness, like cherubs or Christ-children in Renaissance paintings, our unclothed children are required to signify an ideal of innocence,

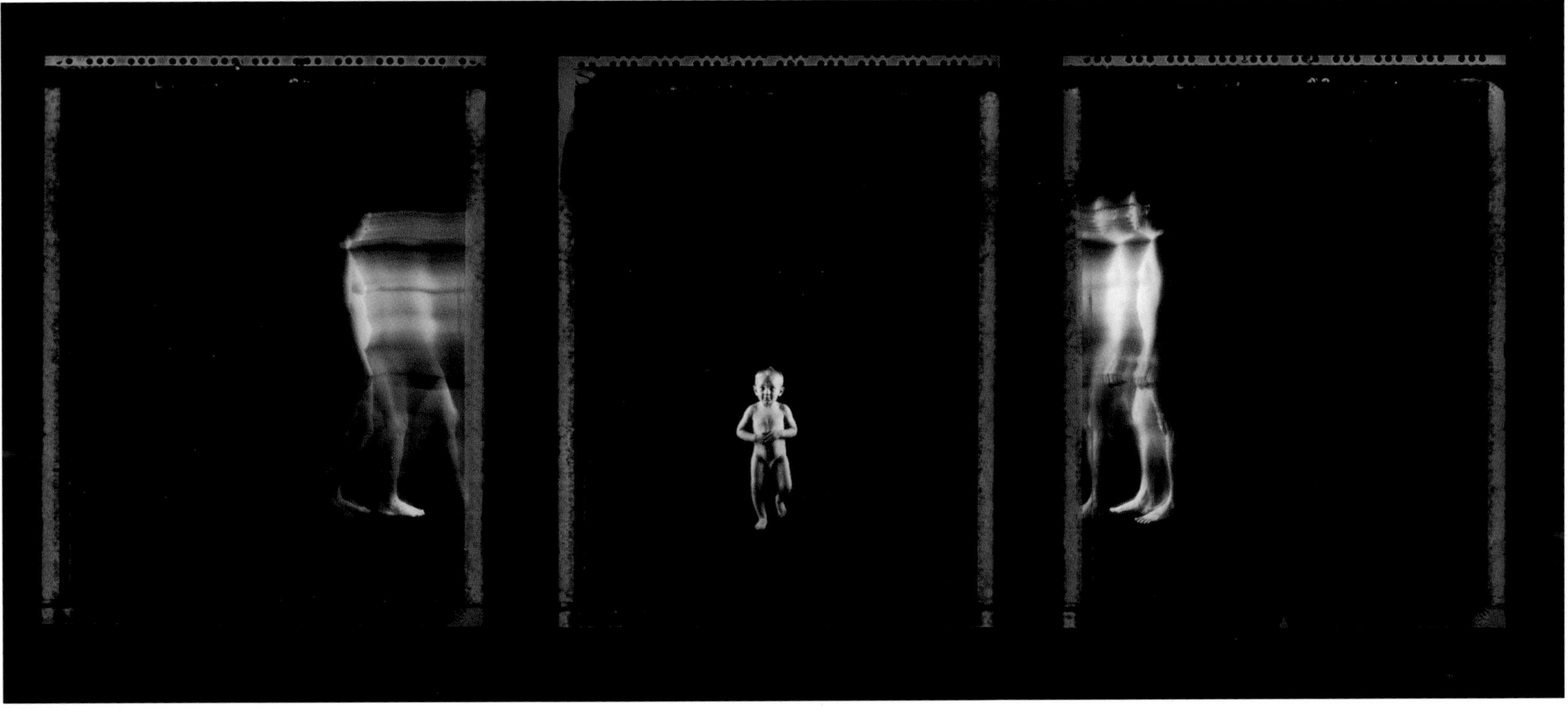

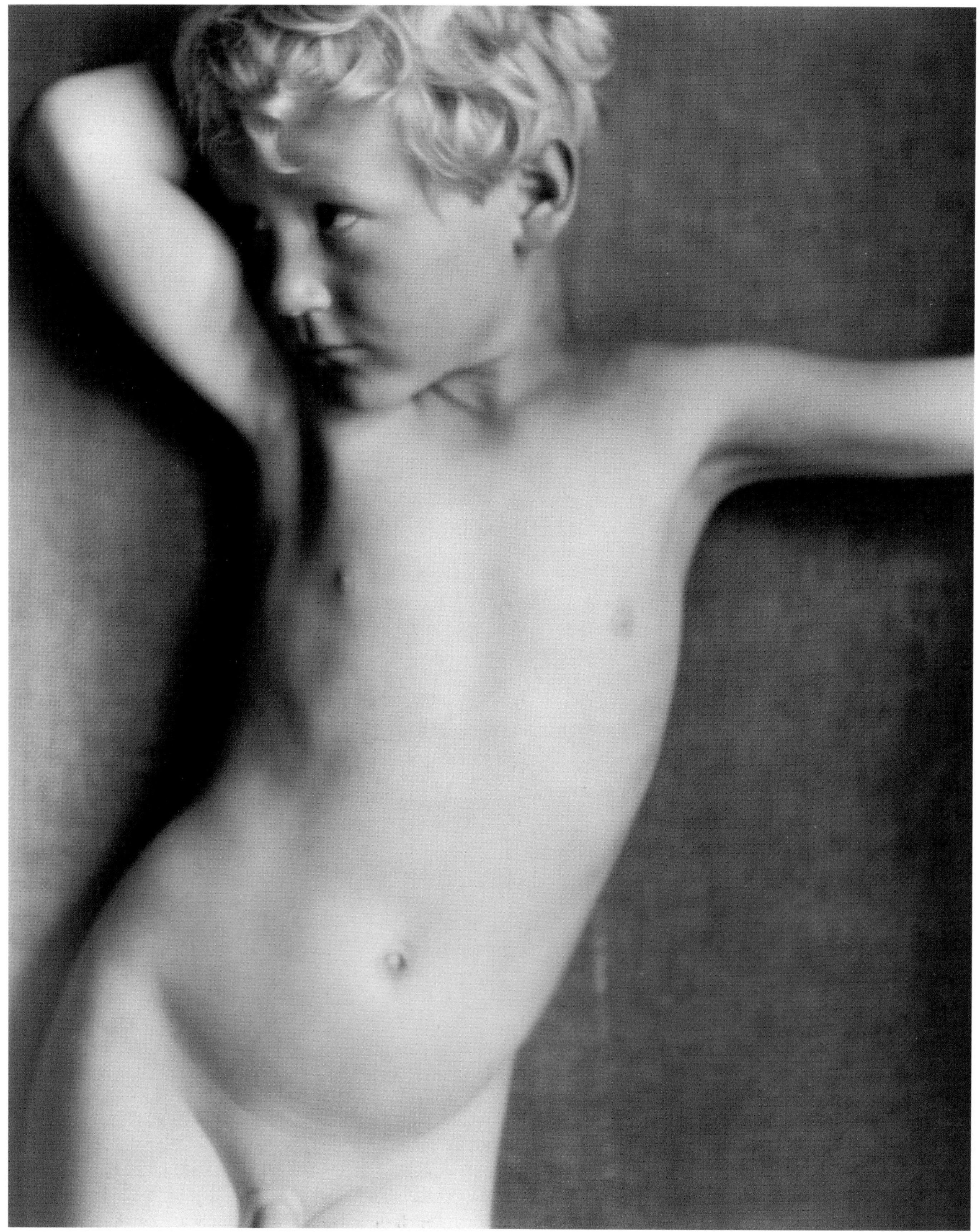

opposite **81 Edward Weston**
Neil, taken 1922, printed 1960s/70s
Victoria & Albert Museum, London

below **82 Melanie Manchot**
Mrs Manchot: Hands on Hips, 1996
Fred (London) Ltd and the Artist

a perfect pre-lapsarian purity. Sexuality within the family is felt to be dangerous and threatening, but you don't need to be a shrink to see the Oedipal complex at work – you only need to have been the parent of a three- or four-year-old boy. Any boy. Or any girl, come to that. Their innocence is our construction.[12]

Gearon herself protested that she felt she had done nothing wrong, either as a mother or an artist, and the journalist Polly Toynbee insisted that that the whole controversy was 'the legacy of paedophile hysteria.' She noted that: 'Children do take their clothes off, do run about gardens and beaches and are photographed by parents to capture just such never-again innocence. But the current obsession with child sex forces everyone to view the world through paedophile eyes. The abhorrent aberrant has won, making us all dirty voyeurs by proxy.'[13]

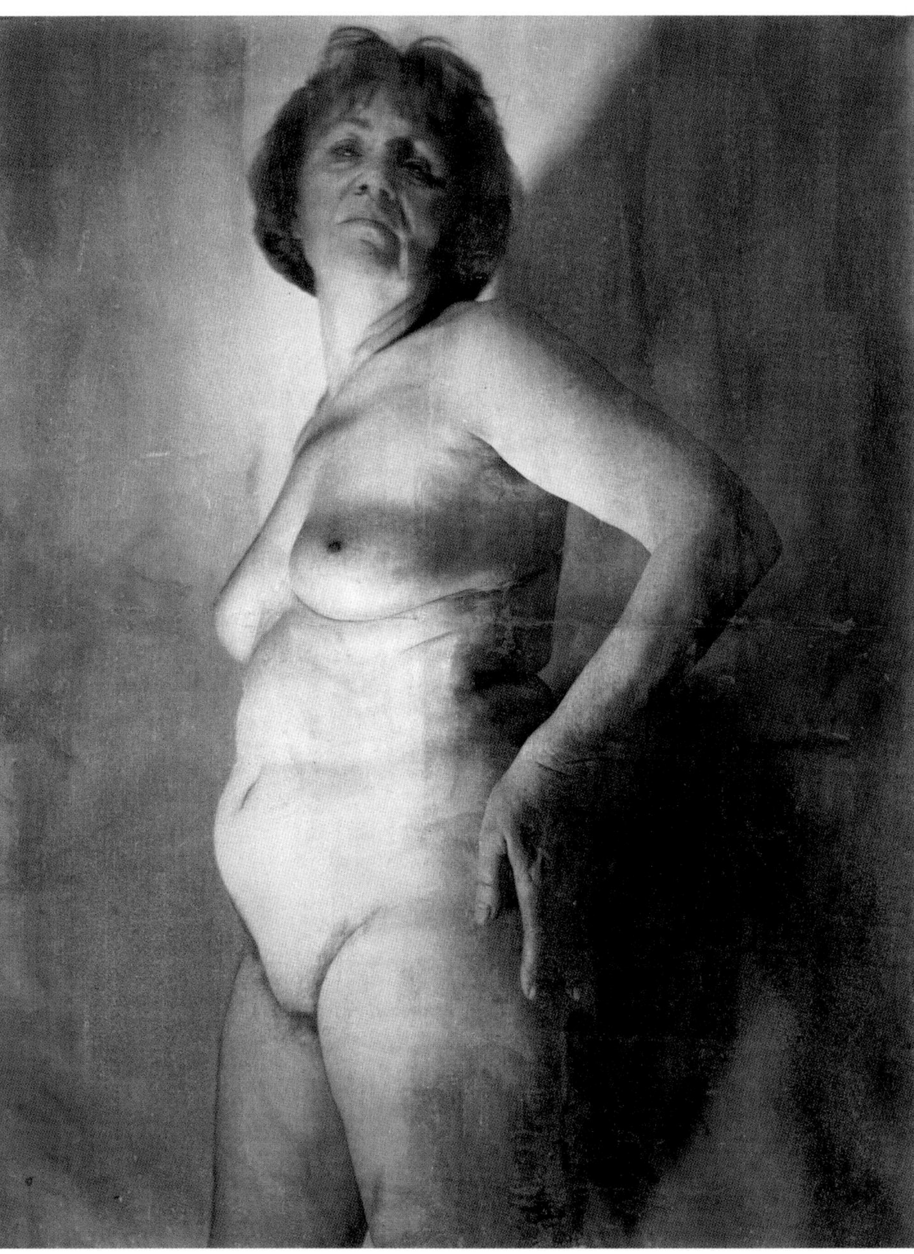

This episode recalled the ethical qualms that had arisen in connection with pictures of certain rather older children. A sequence of pictures by Lucian Freud from around 1980 came with titles such as *Rose*, *Esther* and *Bella*, instead of the usual generic naked portrait tag. It soon became widely known that these young females were in fact the artist's own daughters, from a variety of relationships. Apart from their titles, there is nothing to distinguish such paintings, with their frank exposure of intimate bodily details, from all the other male and female sitters whom Freud has scrutinised, but permitted to retain their privacy. What, then, is at stake for both artist and sitter in this public acknowledgement of a familial connection? The artist asserts that 'my children have nothing to be ashamed of' and that having a naked person in front of him tended to invoke 'consideration': 'You could even call it chivalry on my part: in the case of my children, a father's consideration as well as a painter's. They make it all right to paint them. I don't feel I'm under pressure from them.'[14] According to William Feaver, 'to name them was to acknowledge them'.[15] Freud's children had little to do with him when they were children, and evidently found modelling an important means of establishing an emotional bond. The paintings arose from unusual personal circumstances that may cast doubt on Freud's aptitude for parenthood, but surely do not suggest any morally suspect motivations.

Nakedness has also featured in work based on artists' parents. For several years, Melanie Manchot used her mother, a woman in her sixties, as the model for large-scale works that belied the intimacy and vulnerability that might have been expected. Although their personal relationship made the project possible, this was less important than projecting a wider statement about attitudes in our society towards the bodies of older people:

I wanted to study a body that was in the process of aging. The natural conclusion was to ask my mother because there was a direct link between the two of us. The reason I wanted to work with an older woman was that I'd started to think more and more about female representation and the ways in which the media depicts women in particular but also the body in general. There is this constant reaffirmation of the body as eternally beautiful, youthful, slender, in the media and fashion industry. Unless the body is perfect it's almost as though you're not meant to have it, you are disembodied. But as we get older, no matter how we struggle against it, our bodies can't be perfect. I wanted to find beauty in an older body and celebrate it, accept its condition rather than conceal it.[16]

In the first sequence of portraits, we see Mrs Manchot

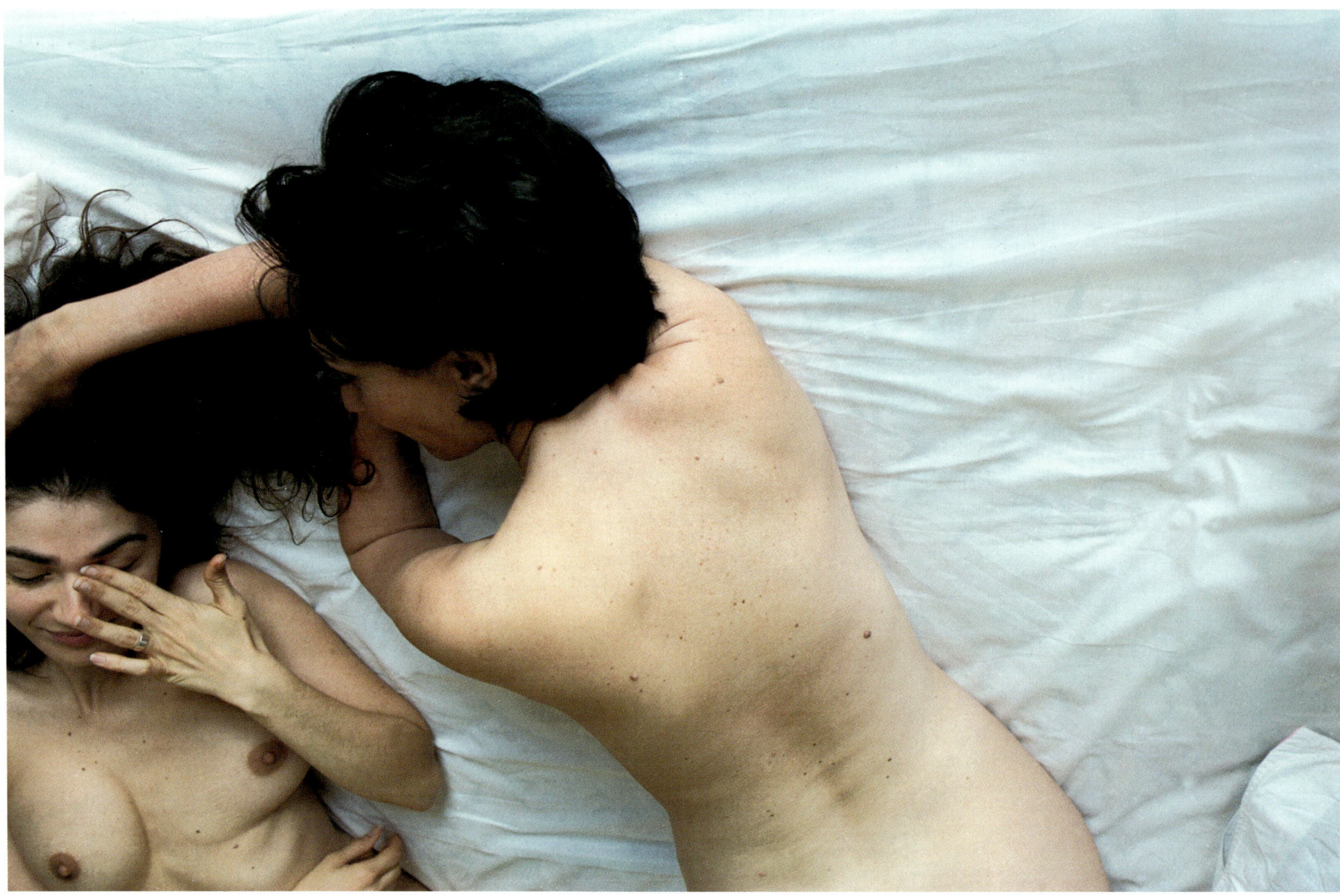

above **83 Elinor Carucci**
My Mother and I, 2000
Courtesy Edwynn Houk Gallery, New York

opposite **84 Melanie Manchot**
Liminal Portrait – with Mountains 1, 1999–2000
Fred (London) Ltd and the Artist

shedding her inhibitions and making the transition from model to participant, manifesting pride rather than shame [plate 82].[17] Initially, her head and face are not included; by the end, she is fully revealed and involving herself in the staging of gestures and expressions, which sometimes recall the repertoires of artistic tradition or current glamour imagery. One constant feature is the elimination of any setting, except in some cases for emphatic cast shadows that have a filmic quality, and only the hair style indicates that the sitter is of our time. Another is the use of technical processes that elide the distinction between pictorial and painterly effect: 'A canvas is prepared with primer, pigment, even sand, then covered in the darkroom with light sensitive emulsion. The negative is projected through an enlarger onto the canvas and out through the developer and fixed like any ordinary photograph. Its surface is then further disrupted by graphite, charcoal or paint.'[18] The 'aging' of the surface of the photograph seems appropriate to her subject-matter. Indeed, the strong chiaroscuro and textured surface of the works establish references to a painter like Rembrandt, whose depictions of Biblical figures such as Susannah and Bathsheba convey to a remarkable degree the sensuality and expressive resonance of bodies remote from a youthful ideal.

In the subsequent *Liminal Portraits*, the artist's mother is naked and highly sculptural, but she is now supplied with a variety of outdoor settings [plate 84]. There is a sense of disjunction between the figure and its surroundings, in part because the nudity seems to conflict with the exposed setting. Whatever their associations for the sitter or artist, the settings and lighting ironically evoke the clichéd backdrops of glamour advertising imagery. Yet the figure is not wearing anything that we are being seduced into buying, and the studio lights linger over bodily details and skin textures that we are not used to admiring. It is as though conventions associated with our longing for material goods and travel experiences have been appropriated as a surrogate expression of Manchot's feelings for her mother, accumulated over decades of family life.

Where the artist herself is included, this kind of naked portraiture encroaches on autobiography. In Helen Chadwick's allegorical installation *Lofos Nymphon* (1987), one component was a series of double naked portraits of Chadwick and her mother, set against backdrops of the Athenian cityscape where her mother had grown up.[19] More recently, Elinor Carucci's photographs, collected in her 2002 book *Closer*, have focussed on the family environment in which she has lived as a young adult. Over several years, her work recorded the domestic existence of her parents, brother, new husband, and more extended family [plates 74 and 83]. She frequently turned the camera on herself, either on her own or in such company. Many pictures focus on two figures, such as her parents, and evoke the closeness of their relationship (see Chapter 4). Her work alludes to the family album, but reveals feelings that are more private and intimate than the imagery usually encountered there. The work of photographers like Nan Goldin gave Carucci a precedent to work in this vein, but the result is gentler in tone and simpler in visual terms. Some images hint at narrative, both pleasurable and strained, but overt animation is rare. Many of the pictures are more obviously portrait-like than much of Goldin's work, visually seductive with strong, inorganic colours and tending towards clarity rather than profusion of detail. Colour aside, *Closer* has more of an affinity with the work of Nicholas Nixon.

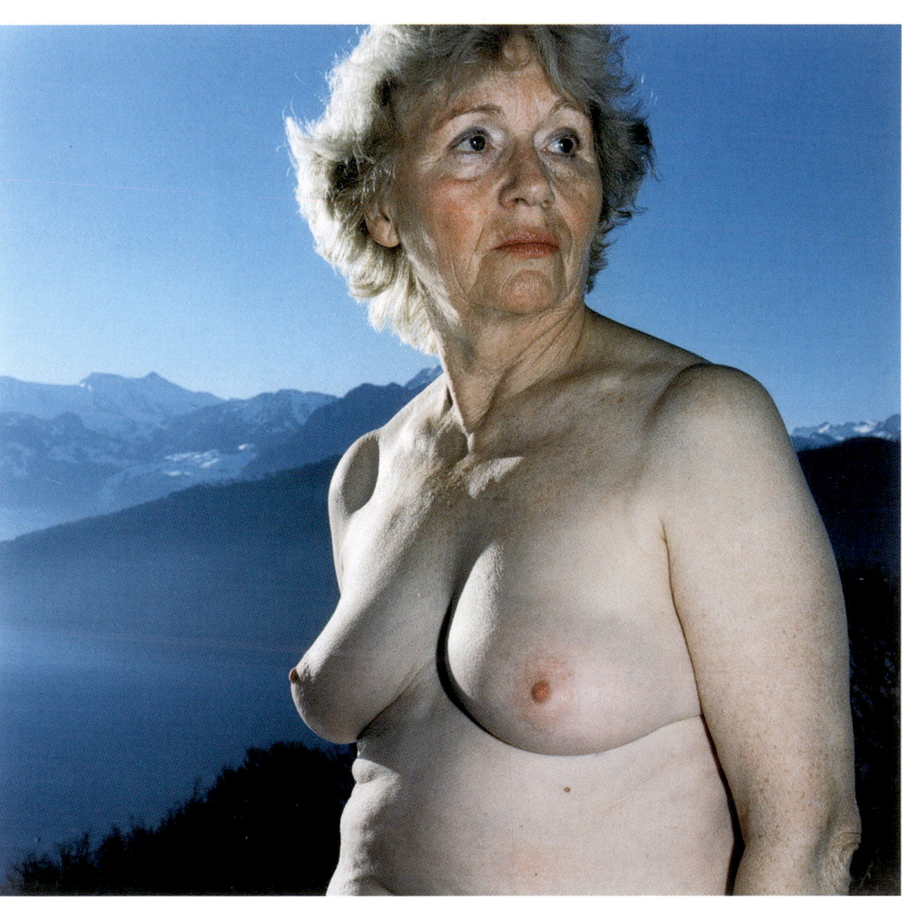

Carucci sought to avoid intrusiveness in photographing her loved ones: '[my pictures] thrive on intimacy and they can't afford to undermine it. I can't show intimacy in any general way, if there is such a thing as general intimacy. I can only say something universal about intimacy through actual intimacy. Mine. The actual real relationships I have with specific people. With these people that I love. The deepest I can reach is within what is most familiar and close.'[20] Yet a consistent aesthetic establishes a certain distance. Carucci describes the camera as 'both a way to get close, and to break free. It was a testimony to independence as well as a new way to relate to the world. A boundary, a distance, as well as the documentation of closeness. I could see my mother, my husband, my father, at once in a detached and a related way'.[21] As the project evolved, she began to use colour, and to focus on details, another sense of 'closer': 'Moving in turned out to be moving out. Work on minute details – a mark on the skin, a stitch, a hair, an eye, a kiss – carried the work beyond the boundaries of my family.'[22]

The imagery in Tierney Gearon's recent *The Mother Project* strikes a different note, recalling rather the idiom and shocking impact of Mikhailov's *Case History* (see Chapter 8). Gearon's subject is a woman who has suffered mental illness for much of her adult life, and lives alone in rural surroundings.[23] Her implied remoteness, of several kinds, is counterpointed by an intimacy that is registered by the nakedness of both artist and mother, as they interact in the mother's home. In one picture, a pregnant Gearon is cradled in the lap of her mother, who is also naked, as if to transmit some primordial wisdom about maternity [plate 77]. In another, her own mother suckles a child, who we assume is the artist's. Naked portraiture becomes a vehicle for exploring the elemental cycles of human life.

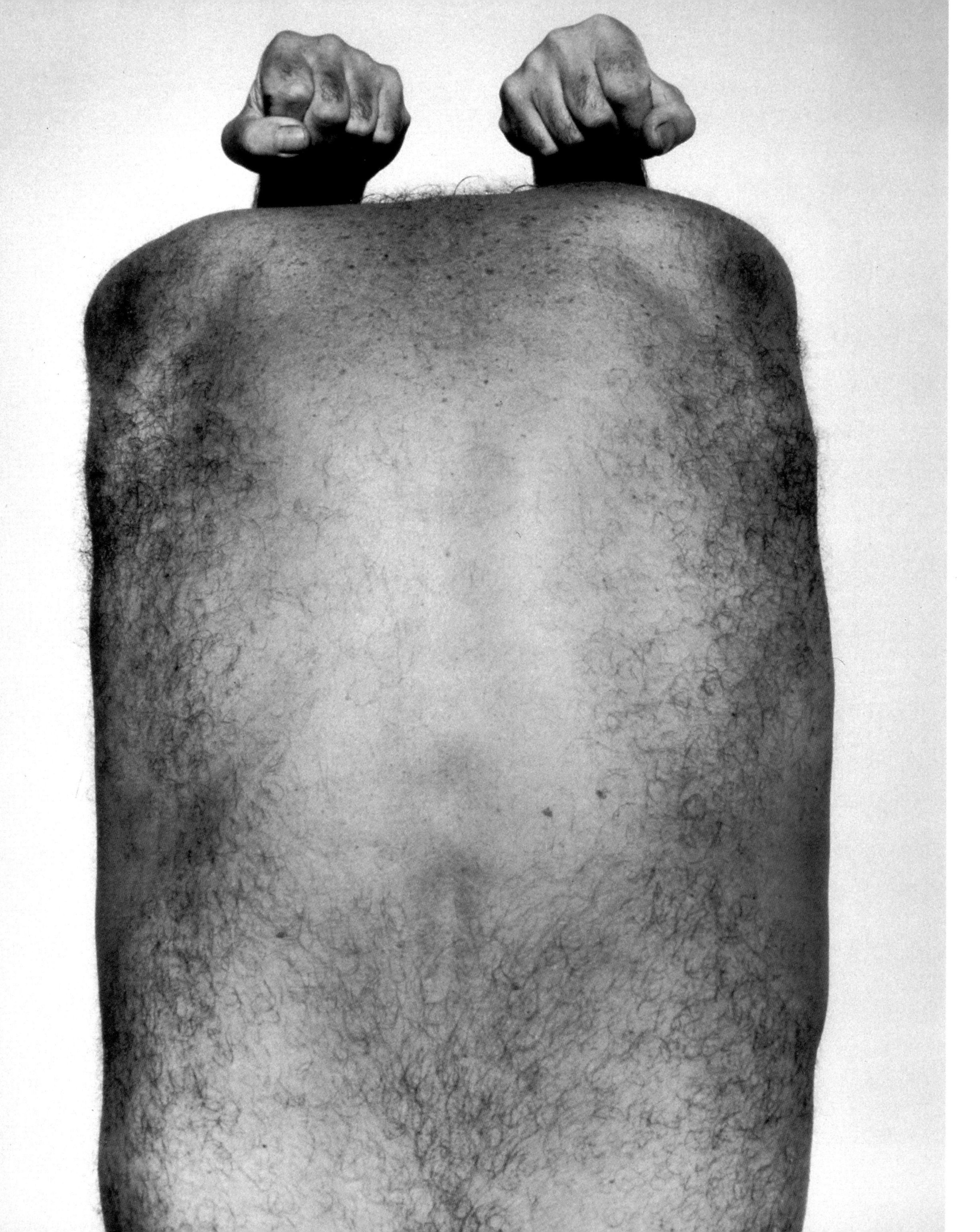

Chapter 6 A Crisis of Masculinity?

85 John Coplans

Self-portrait (Back with Arms Above), 1984

Tate, presented by the American Fund for the Tate Gallery, courtesy of Marsha Plotnitsky, 2000

We turn now to self-portraiture, and the variety of ways in which male and female artists have approached it. The decision by several artists, mostly men, to engage with this form around 1910 marked a decisive moment in the emergence of naked portraiture (see Chapter 2). Such artists tended to characterise themselves as outsiders, their alienation represented by an anguished inwardness. Between the wars, naked self-portraiture is rarely encountered. The most interesting examples emanate from artists conscious of being marginal to the progress of avant-garde art. Two large full-length drawings by Stanley Spencer from the late 1930s, in the wake of the Preece *débâcle*, have been read as psychologically motivated: 'His own nakedness is his "tabula rasa", a place from which to begin again his life and his art. It is as though, standing before us, he is a kind of "Ecce Homo" figure.'[1] The Spencer has a pathos and vulnerability comparable to Schiele, but with none of the latter's theatricality. The late bust self-portraits by Bonnard, such as *The Boxer* (1931) and *Self-portrait in the Bathroom Mirror*, are likewise notable for their naturalism and air of melancholy [plate 86]. Nearing the end of his life, Bonnard seems to confront not just his aging frame but also his fate, firstly with ironic defiance and then with monastic resignation.

There are a number of naked self-portraits by more recent artists, who have likewise tended to see themselves as outside the mainstream. These pictures also evoke a consciousness of personal mortality. In Avigdor Arikha's *Nude Self-portrait from Back* (1986) there is a self-dramatising dimension [plate 87]. The practical gesture of raising his arm to apply brush to canvas acquires an enigmatic force through the way the arm is cropped. The bespectacled face is turning away rather than looking over the shoulder towards the mirror and viewer. According to his friend, Duncan Thomson, 'the artist leans into the void of dense grey, seeking, his back a towering rampart of flesh, with the scars of the bullets that nearly killed him in Palestine clearly visible on his side and on his spine.'[2]

Not surprisingly, the form has been explored by artists conscious of their passage to middle- or old-age. Around 1990 Robert Medley cast himself in the role of Watteau's *Gilles*, restating something of the melancholy of the historic image, with evident reference to what it feels like to experience the slow, steady deterioration of the body and spirit [plate 89]. It is said that seeing a version of the Medley composition in a London collection was a catalyst for another aging male painter, Lucian Freud, to embark upon his own naked self-portrait, the celebrated *Painter Working, Reflection*. This is a very literal image of the artist at work, wielding a palette knife in one hand and holding his palette in the other, wearing a pair of big soft boots to keep splinters at bay, but otherwise standing completely naked, his body gnarled, concentrating on the task at hand [plate 88]. The artist sees himself, factually and candidly, without historical allusion or symbolic reference. While working on the picture he reached the age of seventy, and agreed to give an interview in which he expressed distaste for the modern cult of the artist. He refused to be photographed, and acknowledged that he disliked looking at himself in the mirror. He recalled getting some timid students to paint naked self-portraits, so 'now the very least I can do is paint myself'. But a more existential issue was at stake: 'you see the thing about this self-portrait is that I couldn't scrap it because I'd be doing away with myself'.[3]

The Freud invites similar readings to Arikha's *Painting on a Hot Day* (1991), painted a couple of years earlier.[4] In each case, the courting of a certain indignity encapsulates the two aging artists' images of themselves as uncompromising observers of raw fact, equipped by force of personality to penetrate beneath the veneer of sentimental perceptions. However, when Freud's picture was first exhibited, one reviewer was struck by how different the artist himself looked in this picture from 'the dejected passivity of his other sitters'.[5] This suggested that *Painter Working* was 'a subtle exercise in self-promotion and although it might

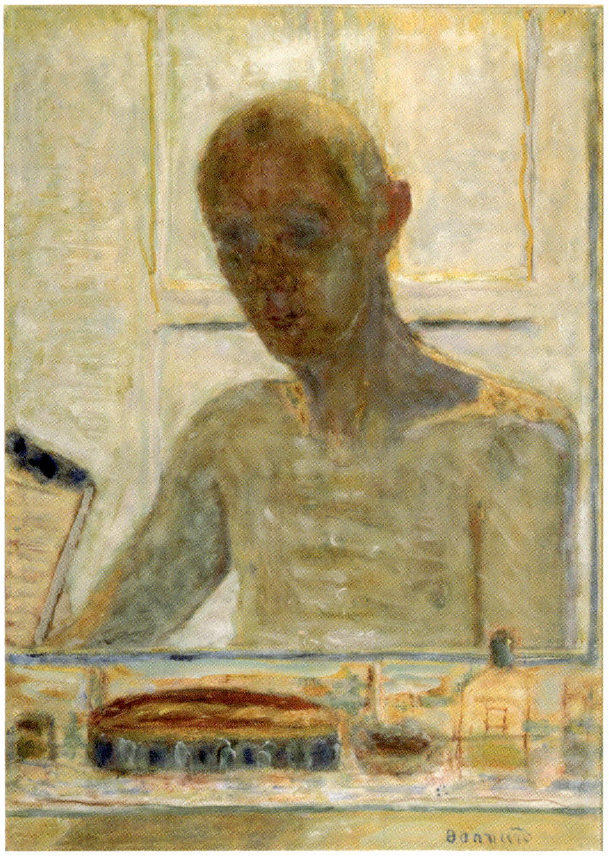

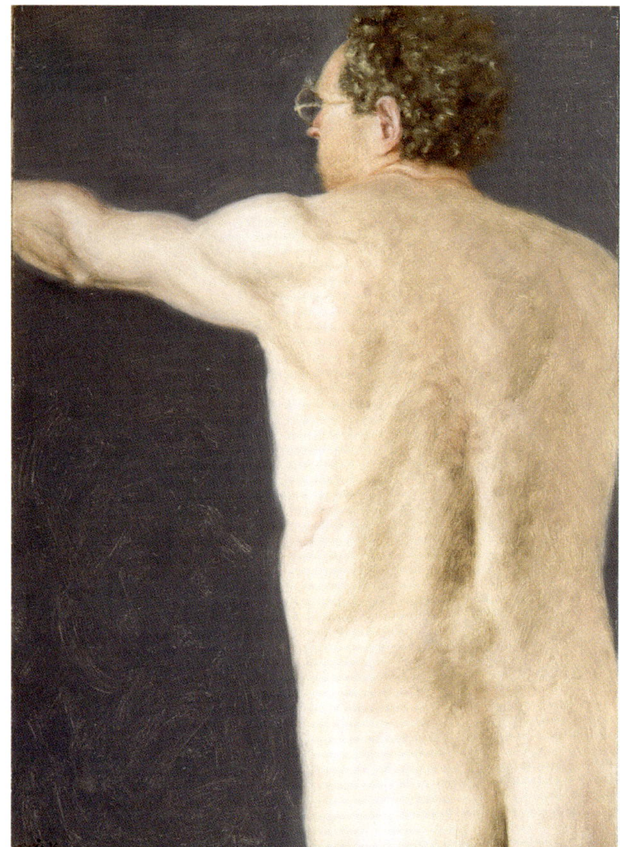

far left **86 Pierre Bonnard**
Self-portrait in the Bathroom Mirror, 1939–45
Pompidou Centre, Paris

left **87 Avigdor Arikha**
Nude Self-portrait from Back, 1986
The Artist

ostensibly be a *vanitas* there is nonetheless a kind of vanity behind it'. Freud had depicted himself 'as a mischievous deity, the artist as shaman, waving his palette knife like a wand. There is truculence and a kind of satanic good humour in his gesture and his expression.' Danto's reading was more lurid: 'Laces are removed from the boots of prisoners who it is feared may do themselves injury if they are allowed to keep them, though it is anyone's guess as to what the symbolism here is. Freud poses himself like some mad maestro, the knife his baton, and there he stands, in a kind of Lear-like wildness, ruler of the night studio, sovereign of naked souls. It is a very scary picture.'[6] Another viewer, already offended by Freud's objectification of his female sitters, took the artist to task for rampant male egocentricity: 'Freud seems in this self-portrait literally to "reflect" the mythology constructed around him; heavy with Rembrandtian overtones, this is a portrait of the aging artist as the traditional old master … In his nude – no naked – self-portrait, the aging painter reveals "himself" to his audience: flabby but powerful, armed with palette knife and penis, the pathos of his fading physical strength allegorically deployed to contrast with his undiminished creative powers.'[7]

left **88 Lucian Freud**
Painter Working, Reflection, 1993
Private Collection

opposite **89 Robert Medley**
Self-portrait after Watteau's *Gilles*, c.1985
Private Collection, courtesy James Hyman Fine Art, London

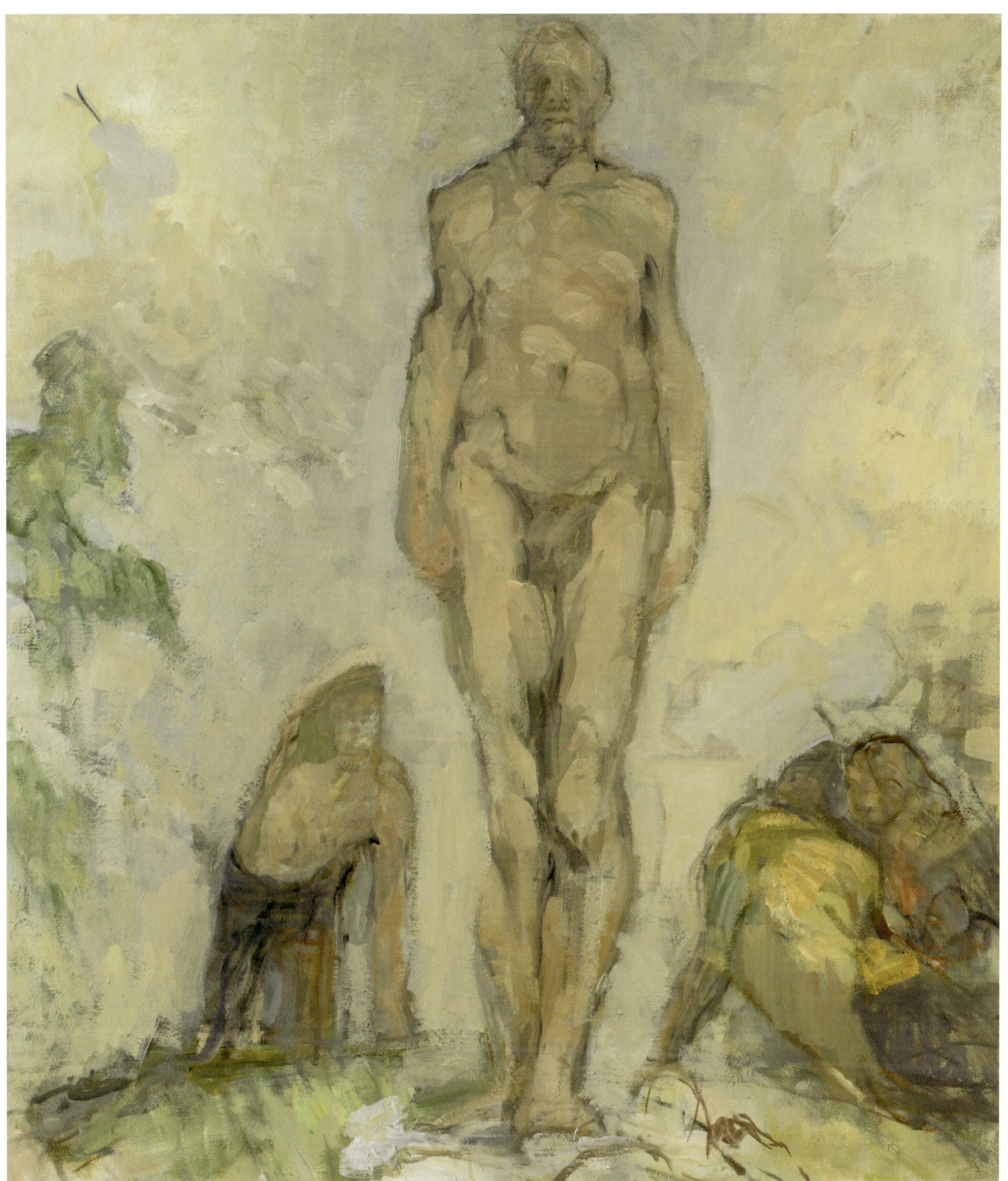

Consciousness of mortality is overt in Francesco Clemente's *Self-portrait with Skull*, and in Ken Currie's *Unfamiliar Reflection* of 2006 [plates 90 and 91]. The former was created around the time of Clemente's fiftieth birthday. There is something of a fallen gladiator about it, and the expression is one of wide-eyed anxiety. The skull propped against his hip accentuates the metaphysical dimension, while the stylised drawing emphasises the boniness of the artist's body and takes us back to the charged self-portraiture of Schiele. Currie's painting, a direct response to the concept of *The Naked Portrait* exhibition, became a meditation on his sense of personal and artistic identity. The artist stands in front of a canvas, whose solid, illusory presence, like his palette with its globules of paint, heightens the soft immateriality of his body, and of his ghostly reflection in the schematic mirror. The paint in these passages is thinly applied, inflected by blotches of flicked turpentine that evoke the disfigured surfaces of old mirrors and aged skin. The reflected figure, whose expression is profoundly sad, is associated in Currie's mind with his father, to whom he bore a remarkably strong resemblance, and who had died of lung cancer the previous year. The artist looks back into the past, but also forward to his own aging and death. His stooped, twisting posture enacts the movement involved in the painting process, but also expresses the pathos, and even horror, of these eruptions of feeling within his act of self-scrutiny. The canvas and mirror make reference to the greatest of all self-portraits, Velázquez's *Las Meninas*, dramatising the gulf between Velázquez's confident occupancy of his social role and the isolation of contemporary man, for which nakedness is a telling metaphor. In another echo of the Baroque, the random drips of red paint on the edge of the stretcher match those on the side of the actual canvas before us, implying that the artist is creating the picture we see, and even suggesting that the canvas itself is bleeding.

The pathos emanating from such paintings contrasts with the more playful naked self-portraiture produced since the 1960s by several artists who have used photography as their medium. Here we become aware of the artist's bodily display as a performance. The works look staged, so that the transient body language invites us to project some interpretative response, rather than seeking distillations of more fundamental states of mind. Nakedness becomes a role or even a costume that the artist has chosen to adopt for particular purposes. Such work epitomises the pervasive presence of the mask and invented persona, as noted by Max Kozloff:

In a critical way, masks underline the difference between artistic portrayal of the self, and the self that is portrayed. The gallery

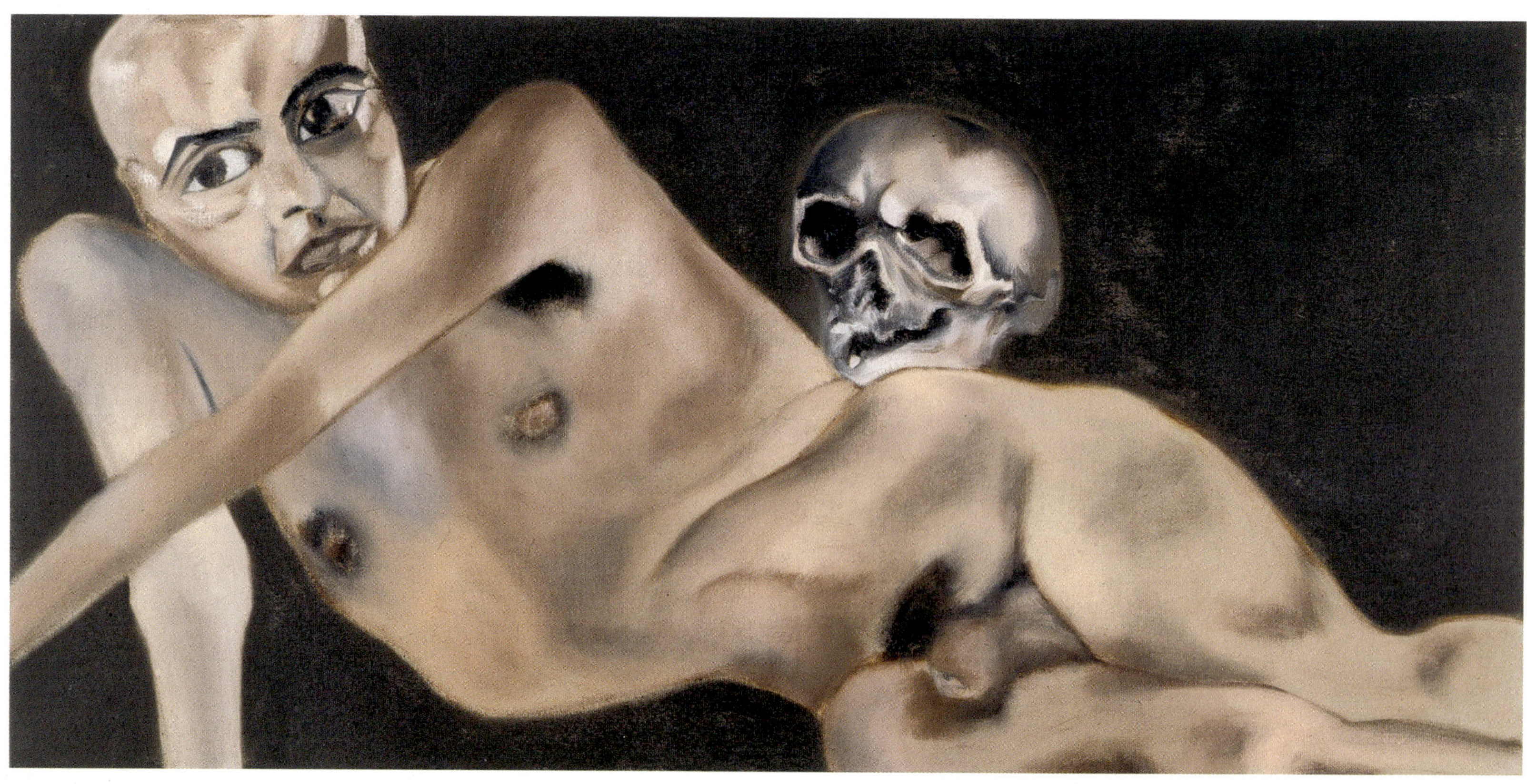

opposite **90 Francesco Clemente**
Self-portrait with Skull, 2002
Private Collection, Thomas Koeffer, Zurich

right **91 Ken Currie**
Unfamiliar Reflection, 2006
The Artist

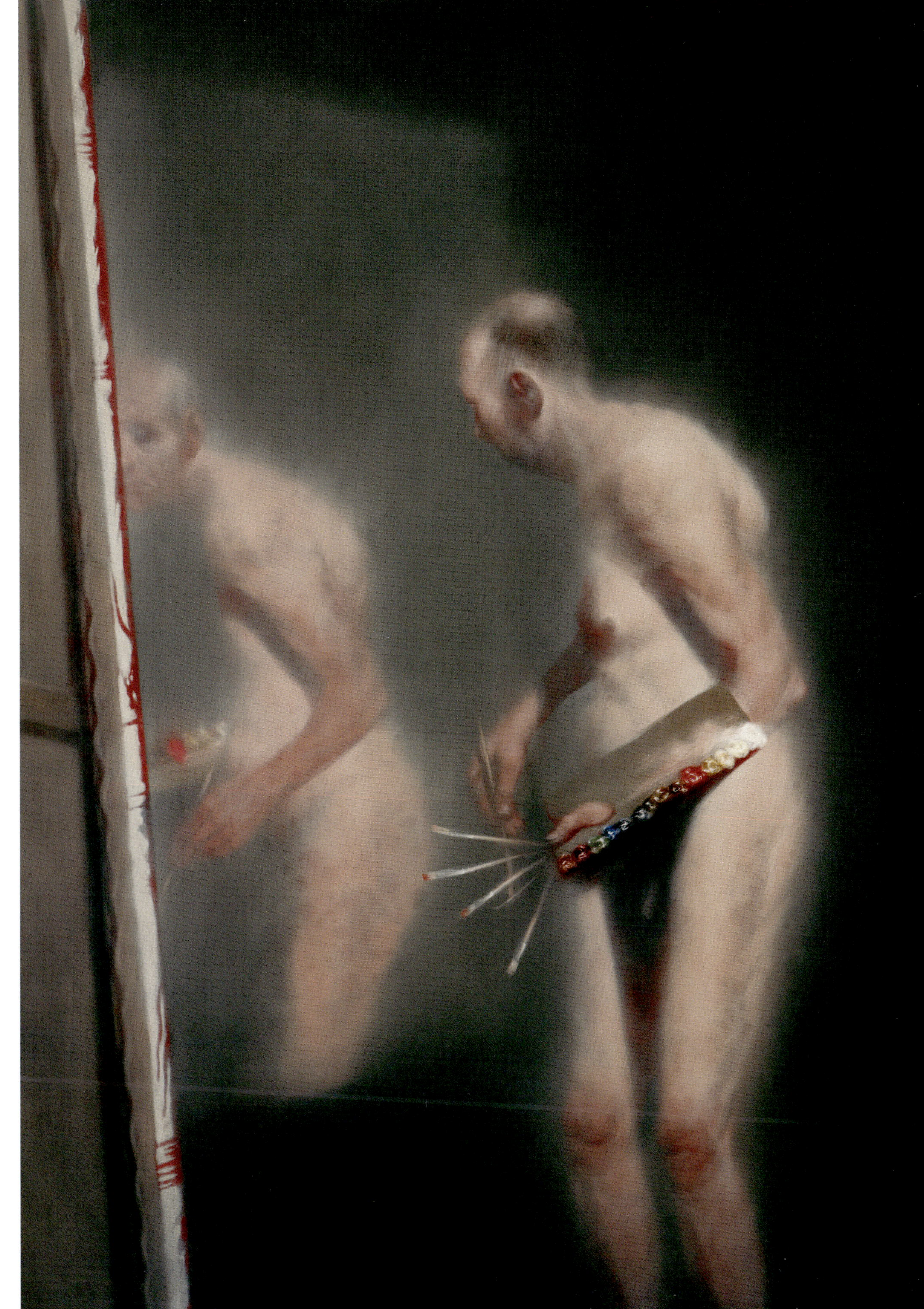

of self-representations in recent photography and art is marked by a high incidence of masks, distorting mirrors, impostures, allegorical staging, disinformation, clowning and melodrama. Many of these performances exert a disfiguring pressure upon self-portraiture, the genre to which they nominally belong. For what we intuit in artistic self-portraits are fantasies constructed for the sake of the image rather more than they are in accord with the ego.[8]

This strand of photographic imagery parallels work in performance art, which became a significant current in the same period. Many live artists have also used their naked bodies as their basic means of expression, including Marina Abramovic, Paul McCarthy, and Bob Flanagan.[9] Certain other artists we shall be considering, male and female, have also operated in this medium. This raises the issue of whether performance pieces might usefully be considered in the context of naked portraiture. Some live art practitioners have stronger autobiographical concerns than others. However, one of the earliest American commentaries on body art emphasised that self-exposure was not the point: 'The artists feel no need to vent their personal emotions in their work. The artist's own body is not as important as the body in general. The work is not a solitary celebration of self. As someone said, "It's more about using a body than autobiographical." The personality refines itself out of the work, impersonalises itself.'[10] Our response to performances, and their record in videos or still photographs, is probably conditioned by the theatrical expectation that the performer is acting a part. The constructed images of fine art and photography predispose us to look for revelation, even when none is intended, because we have internalised a notion of portraiture as capturing the self through the representation of bodily externals. Such an expectation can be manipulated by the artist but also subverted.

Robert Morris was a key figure in the early history of performance art, and an innovatory contributor to naked self-portraiture with *I-Box*, one of a group of works that he exhibited the following year in New York and that proposed a radical redefinition of the genre [plate 92]. *I-Box* comprises a small plywood box, with a suitably I-shaped, hinged door, painted a pinkish shade of grey, that opens up to reveal a black and white photograph of the nude artist. Letter and image provide two alternative means by which the artist represents himself. The work is replete with puns: the 'I' reveals the I belonging to the artist, but also allows the *eye* of the viewer to regard Morris, as if in a peepshow. The 'I' also suggests not just the letter but also the I-beam in engineering construction. And Morris's facial expression is nothing if not beaming – unless it is 'cocky', which also chimes with the imagery.[11] This jokey air, along with Morris's stance and expression, mock our expectations of personal revelation. As a structure, the work suggests a dichotomy between public exterior and private interior, but this refuses to correlate with notions of the outer, social, material self and the more authentic inner spiritual self. Inside turns out to be just another outside. *I-Box* parodies the inflated rhetoric that accompanied Abstract Expressionism, then the dominant aesthetic. Morris expresses his allegiance to the alternative Duchamp/Jasper Johns tradition, both in his imagery and his incorporation into the work of the banalities of photography and commercial lettering. In particular, the work responds to Johns's *Targets* (1955), which replaced high-flown abstraction with the pattern of a target, surmounted by little boxes that the viewer could open up to reveal painted casts of body parts. Like *Targets*, *I-Box* abstains from grand statements, and offers an opportunity for the viewer to have imaginative fun while questioning, in a quasi-philosophical manner, received wisdom about inner/outer, and public/private distinctions, or reflecting on the status of language and image as representations of 'reality'.

Morris's *I-Box* set the tone for much of the naked self-portraiture subsequently produced by male photographers. Its camp aspect is taken up in the work of gay artists, who articulated their sense of sexual identity in opposition to

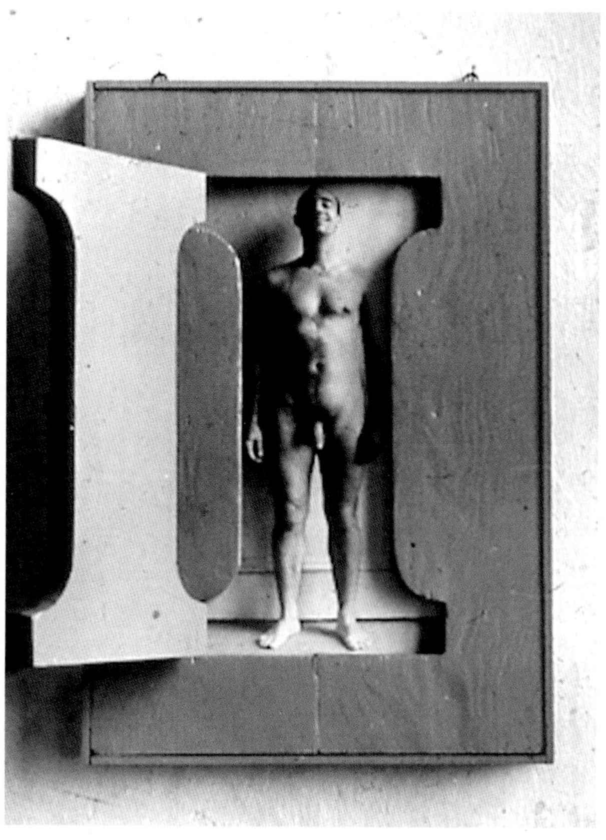

92 Robert Morris
I – Box (open), 1962
Castelli Gallery, New York

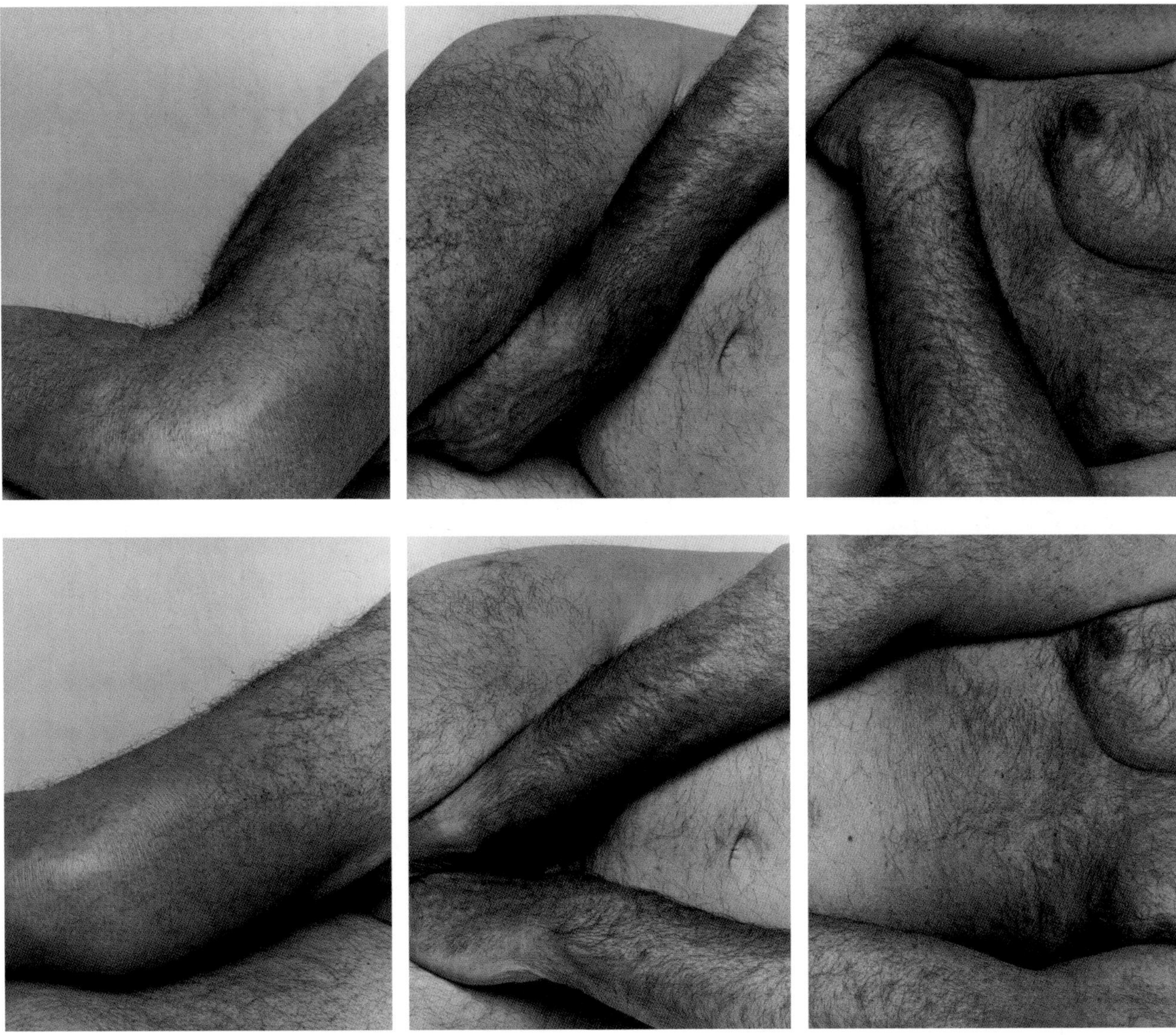

93 John Coplans
Self-portrait: Reclining Figure, Two Panels, 1996
Scottish National Gallery of Modern Art, Edinburgh

macho values. In his 1970s self-portraits, Robert Mapplethorpe capered before the camera as if to subvert the genre's associations with serious self-scrutiny. In *Artist and Model* (1973/4), David Hockney characterised himself as a naked and vulnerable figure, sporting only spectacles and bobby socks, and gazing deferentially across the table towards the great modernist Picasso. Hockney plays on his sense of artistic subordination as well as his detachment from Picasso's legendary heterosexual potency. The naked self-portraits created by Gilbert & George from the mid-1990s onwards seem directly descended from Morris's wry detachment (see Chapter 4). The work of Lyle Ashton Harris is a more recent manifestation of this tradition, by a gay black artist concerned to overturn stereotypes of masculinity.[12] Not that camp is an exclusively homosexual mode. The occasional heterosexual artist has reasserted his laddish sexuality, albeit with tongue-in-cheek irony.[13] The obvious case is Jeff Koons, who in 1991 appropriated the marble classical bust format for a self-portrait sculpture, projecting himself as the hero that we deserve in the late capitalist marketplace.[14] Lucas Samaras has been working sporadically with Polaroid naked self-portraits since late 1969. These emerged out of self-referential work in performance, film and autobiographical writing.[15] Subsequently, Samaras has employed his own body, changing as the artist has aged, in a bewildering variety of roles and settings, and employing a wide array of Polaroid techniques for manipulating the prints in order to overlay or distort the image of the figure. In the *Sittings* series (1980) Samaras himself appears, clothed and compositionally marginal, while others are nude and the focus of his highly theatrical portraiture.[16]

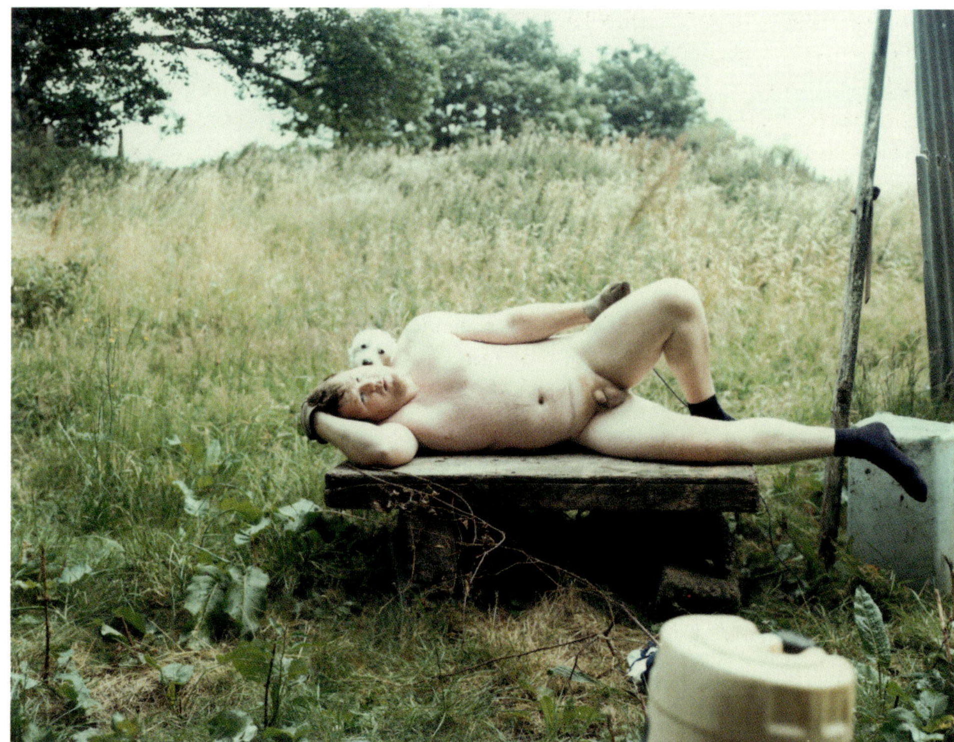

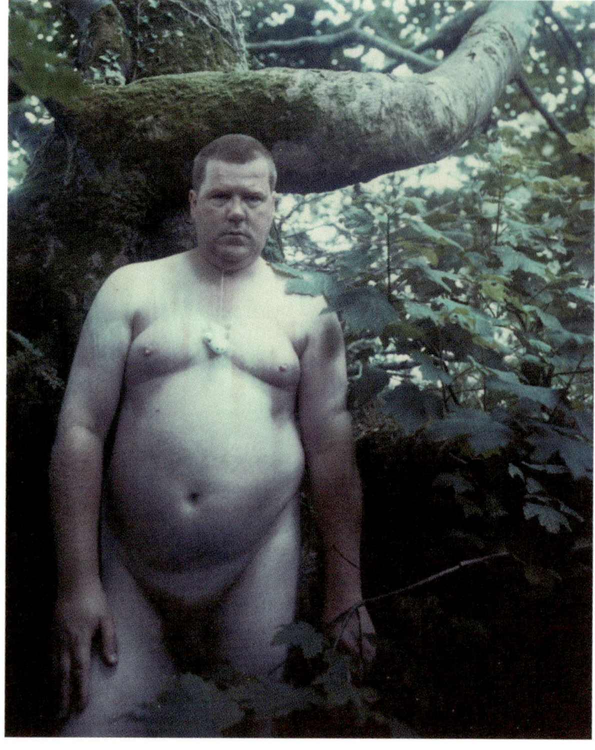

left **94 Steven Tynan**
Untitled (Self-portrait), 1997
The Artist

right **95 Steven Tynan**
Untitled (Self-portrait), 2000
The Artist

John Coplans was around sixty when he embarked upon photography in earnest, after a successful career as an art critic, editor and curator. His own naked body became his subject matter in 1984, and for the next twenty years he created nothing but extremely simple, often large-scale, naked self-portraits [plate 85]. He lambasted the 'slickness of Robert Mapplethorpe's imagery. His prints are diffused to look like sexy advertising photos put out by women's hairdressers. In contrast, my prints are straightforward; only their size and sharpness are subject to adjustment.'[17] Mapplethorpe's complacent celebration of the body beautiful epitomised what he wished to counter. In Coplans's work, we are confronted by magnified, monolithic fragments of an aging male. Although the titles inform us that the artist himself is the model, the head, the prime indicator of inner states and personal identity, is the one element that is always left out. The images convey intimations of mortality, but they also oppose the cult of youthful perfection in contemporary culture. They require us to share his discovery of the unexpected beauty of flab, wrinkles, veins, body hair and the infinitely varied textures of skin with a history. Removed from context as blown-up details, such elements sometimes take on a metamorphic dimension. We find ourselves imagining animal imagery, especially elephantine, or recalling craggy rock formations (Coplans was a great fan of the nineteenth-century sublime landscape photography of Carleton Watkins). In *Torso, Front* (1984), a great slab of hairy chest and stomach starts to read as a face, with a little down-turned mouth. A comment Coplans made in 1980 about the late figurative paintings of Philip Guston could be applied to his own work: 'He parodies himself and his subject matter, menacingly playing the clown at the same time that he ironically solicits our sense of pity'.[18]

Coplans's procedure entailed an assistant taking the pictures, using a 4 × 5 inch Polaroid camera which could speedily produce both an image and a negative. After a period of relying on roughly drawn sketches and trial and error, Coplans gained a greater degree of control by setting up a video camera and monitor in the studio, so that he could look, from the perspective of the model, at the exact configuration in the camera's field of vision, and adjust his position according to his conception. Decisions concerning scale and tonality were then taken. The absence of colour ties in with Coplans's preference for clarity and boldness in the disposition of forms against the plain white ground. As a counterpoint to their vivid realism of detail, the shapes and textures of the body yield purely abstract rhythms and correspondences. A recurrent device in the earlier work was symmetry, as in the frontal pictures of torsos, feet, backs with hands coming over the shoulders, and legs with hands resting on the knees.

Such formal qualities reinforced the grandeur and emotional intensity of the subject matter. In choosing to employ the image of his own body, Coplans pursued a photographic equivalent to the Abstract Expressionist ideal of a direct and primordial art, rooted in the deepest layers of the self and affirming 'the outstanding fact of humanness'.[19] This aspiration is implicit in his account of the fantasies that inform his art: 'In my dream I travel down my genes and visit remote ancestors, both male and female.' When posing for the photographs, he found himself becoming 'immersed in the past … before I know what has happened, I am lost in a reverie; I am somewhere else, another person in another life …'[20] Coplans's work conveys a vision of our humanity, what we have in common with one another in the present, and with all our ancestors of whatever age or gender, stretching back to prehistory. In several works he incorporated allusions to female attributes, as in the image from 1985 where the hands rest just above the knees and the alignment of the two thumbs suggest female genitalia placed immediately beneath his own sex. In the two-panel *Self-portrait: On Back* of 1991, the cropping and slight arching of the back serve to evoke the body and pubic hair of a reclining female, modifying the masculine aura of profuse body hair. The body language avoids the predictable postures or gestures that we are used to from social interaction, or mass media imagery. Equally, the neutral white backdrop eliminates associations with the contemporary world: 'Nakedness removes the body from the specificity of time: unclothed, it belongs to the past, present and future. It is classless, without country, unencumbered by language, and free to wander across cultures at will.'[21]

Coplans's art belongs to a shift towards self-denigration, verging on the grotesque. We have been invited to contemplate bodies that are sagging, hairy, or in some way ludicrous. It is tempting to correlate such imagery with a debunking of old-fashioned ideas of virility. The period coincides with the rise of feminism, and Coplans acknowledged the impact: 'A compelling influence on me has been the feminist movement and the re-examination of men's roles in relation to women. In response it is not only necessary for me to deal with the historical surface of consciousness, but also to examine the deeper, unconscious drives and images of manhood.'[22] Artists have had to situate themselves in relation to a deeply rooted historical association between creativity and masculinity. Feminists have argued that artistic activity is rooted in a wilful egocentricity permissible only to the gender with real social power. By removing the façade of outer garments, an artist can both reinforce and subvert such associations, given that, his gender and sexual identity are that much more explicit, and that, the vulnerabilities and absurdities of his body are more open to scrutiny. In his large-scale photographs *I am not I* (1992), the naked Boris Mikhailov assumed the role of jester, exploiting his flabby middle-aged body and his richly expressive features. He enacted a wide variety of poses, with a dildo as his most frequent prop. The images are hilarious and wonderfully tasteless, but for the artist they offered a distillation of post-Soviet life:

When I started playing with my own image – imagining I could be this or that – I realized that putting my real self forth could be more interesting than creating some subjective expressionist things. For me, this 'I' represented a hierarchy of the era, when I was joining the ranks of the heroes, or becoming an anti-hero. If in the Soviet era we knew who the heroes were … now the very idea of a hero was undermined. At the same time, the transition to capitalism was supposed to bring forth a new hero. And this hero was born: an anti-hero as hero … The anti-hero provided an important reflection of the post-Soviet era.[23]

Over the past ten years, Steven Tynan has produced a body of imagery that vividly evokes a post-feminist sensibility [plates 94 and 95]. Tynan's recurrent subject matter is his own naked body, somewhat overweight and middle-aged.[24] His Polaroid images are modest in scale. They are funny and often touching, combining aesthetic refinement and variety with a persistent playfulness and obliqueness. They include a wide range of indoor and outdoor settings, as well as 'props' such as children, animals, toys, items of clothing, and furniture. All were extracted from Tynan's house and the surrounding countryside in which he and his family live in rural Cornwall. There is a sense of ordinariness, implying that the artist is just like the rest of us, rather than a being of higher sensibilities. Yet Tynan's images possess an intriguing ambiguity, which his nakedness reinforces. One cannot be sure whether he is consciously revealing through his work some introspective and 'authentic' sense of what it feels like to him to be, say, a middle aged father of young children, and a refugee from urban existence; or whether he is performing, acting out memories or imaginary scenarios in front of the camera, in the manner of Lucas Samaras. The one constant is the impassivity of his features, suggesting a bemused detachment from the ludicrous situations in which he places himself and the activities in which he is engaged, yet projecting an unlikely dignity as he returns the spectator's gaze. In Tynan's pictures the old male ego has been definitively cast aside, and the process seems surprisingly painless.

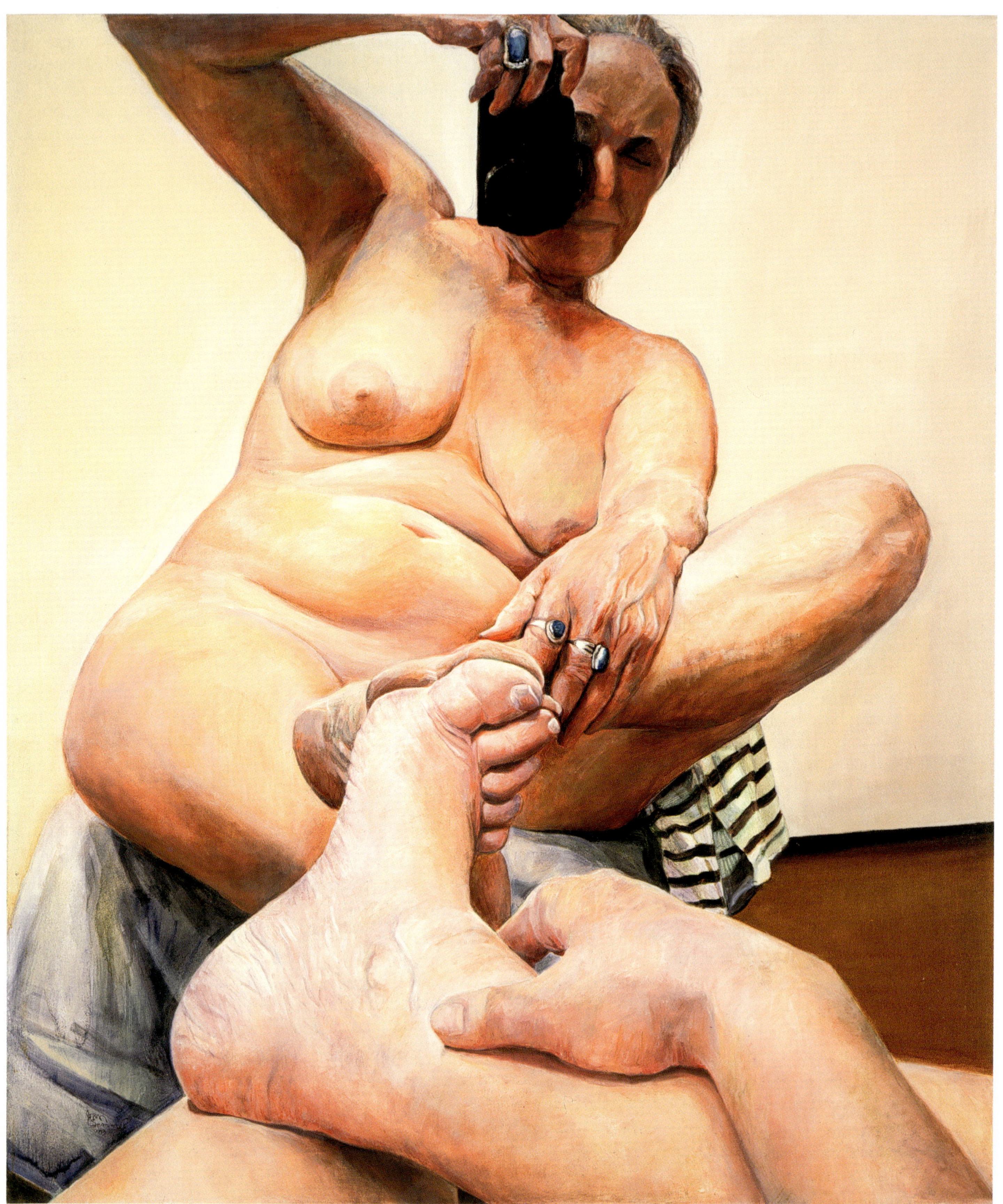

Chapter 7 Our Bodies, Our Selves

96 Joan Semmel
With Stripes, 2003
The Artist (New York)

In recent decades, many women artists have used their own naked bodies as their means of expression. They have sought to redeem the female nude, seen as being entrenched in both artistic tradition and mass advertising as a vehicle for feeding the insatiable male gaze. The continuity between these twin manifestations of female subjugation ('the old master/*Playboy* tradition') was asserted by John Berger in his widely read *Ways of Seeing* (1972).[1] Such imagery operates as 'a tyranny of *in*visibility, as a tradition for *ex*clusions' of bodies remote from the idealised stereotype.[2] In reaction, women artists have celebrated their own sense of bodily and sexual identity, representing what it feels like to occupy their own bodies. Such ambitions have been stimulated by the dramatic impact of feminism in Western societies from the late 1960s onwards. The title of this chapter adapts that of an influential book, first published in 1973, proclaiming the need for women to take control of their own health and sexuality.[3] For their part, artists have claimed 'the right to self-representation', and have aimed 'to make visible new female subjectivities'.[4]

Linda Nochlin's celebrated question in 1971 as to why there were no great women artists has prompted the invention of a proto-feminist tradition. This includes the once marginal work of Paula Modersohn-Becker, especially her naked self-portraits (see Chapter 2). Frida Kahlo, whose obscurity before 1980 is even harder to imagine given her current fame, included her own naked form in such dramatisations of her personal torments as *Henry Ford Hospital* (1932), recalling her experience of miscarriage, and *Broken Column* (1944), which employs a Surrealist idiom to display her spinal injuries. If the work of Modersohn-Becker has sanctioned celebratory, naturalistic explorations of the artist's body, the example of Kahlo has emphasised fantasy and performance, and a darker mode through which women artists have conveyed their sense of being victims in a male-dominated society. The priority of message over modernist formal values has also encouraged belated appreciation of Cecile Walton's *Romance*. This shows the artist holding her newly born son, with her first son looking on and a nurse washing her feet [plate 97]. When exhibited at the second Edinburgh Group Exhibition in 1920, a critic noted its 'frank treatment of an intimate subject' and its 'quaintly primitive manner, suggestive of some earlier painter's "Nativity"'.[5] Such stylistic allusions are typical of the period, but they serve here to confer solemnity on a scene of intimate family life. In choosing such private, quintessentially female imagery, which was taboo, Walton is likely to have been asserting her sense of personal identity, a theme explored in her 1926 essay about gender equality:

The question as to whether women will achieve equal supremacy with men … has given rise to an equally wrong attitude in relation to our own sex. It is obvious that our powers have certain qualities and values of their own, which play a subtle and peculiar part in our social life. To surrender those at our present stage of development in order to acquire those characteristics which are more peculiarly masculine is merely to be unaware of that intrinsic appeal of personality that has made women the equal of man [throughout history].[6]

Since the 1970s, some female artists have continued to operate within tradition, notwithstanding painting's historical association with the nude. A case in point is Alice Neel. Her naked *Self-portrait* was her first self-portrait, though naked portraiture became a major current in her later work, under the influence of a growing climate of support for feminism [plate 98]. The picture makes a fascinating comparison with images about their sense of mortality by male contemporaries such as Medley, Freud and Arikha (see Chapter 6). The Neel is equally elemental, but the humour, down-to-earth quality, absence of vanity, and faux-naïve economy contrast with the self-dramatising tendency encountered in such male counterparts. The inclusion of the brush and rag indicate her profession, but otherwise Neel presents herself with the same wry detachment that she had applied to other occupants of the stripy chair.

The identity of artist and sitter is asserted polemically in the work of her fellow American, Joan Semmel. Semmel belonged to a younger generation of politically-motivated artists, and has employed naked self-portraiture in much of her work. *Out of Darkness* [plate 2] is a nocturnal variant on her better known *Me without Mirrors* (1974). Both paintings unambiguously present Semmel's perspective on her own body, in both optical and psychological terms. The powerful physicality of such pictures was based on photographs she had taken. Semmel's later works, including *With Stripes*, frequently make explicit the procedure by which they were made [plate 96]. We are compelled to occupy the viewpoint, and therefore also the gender and outlook, of the artist, whom we see photographing her own reflection in the mirror, as well as in the form of those bits of her body that come into the picture space. The inclusion of the camera makes all the difference to the implied relationship between artist and spectator. In literal terms, a male viewer is excluded from the circuit of representation. At the same time he is forced to assume the passive role, traditionally the female prerogative, and to become the object of an implied gaze, even while he looks at a naked female form. This conceit effectively celebrates Semmel's own aging body.

Semmel chose to tackle the nude on its own territory of monumental painting. From the start, however, the medium of choice for much feminist production has been photography, precisely because painting seemed so closely associated with exploitative imagery. Photography seemed more 'democratic' in its reproducibility. Like performance, it seemed to present the artist's body directly for the viewer's contemplation, without pictorial mediation. It also opened up possibilities for using serial imagery, through which artists might suggest narrative. In America, nude self-portrait photography was used inventively by first generation feminist artists such as Eleanor Antin, Adrian Piper, and Lynda Benglis.[7] The close alliance between photography and performance was epitomised by the art of Hannah Wilke, whose activity in both media frequently focused on her own naked body, at first young and undeniably glamorous, later shockingly diminished as she succumbed to the cancer that killed her.

Super-T-Art exemplifies the kind of photographic work that grew out of Wilke's provocative live events [plate 99]. In a sequence of twenty images, standing on a small pedestal against a plain white backdrop, she 'performs' her femininity, wearing high heels and a voluminous white sheet that she partially removes, and gracefully wraps

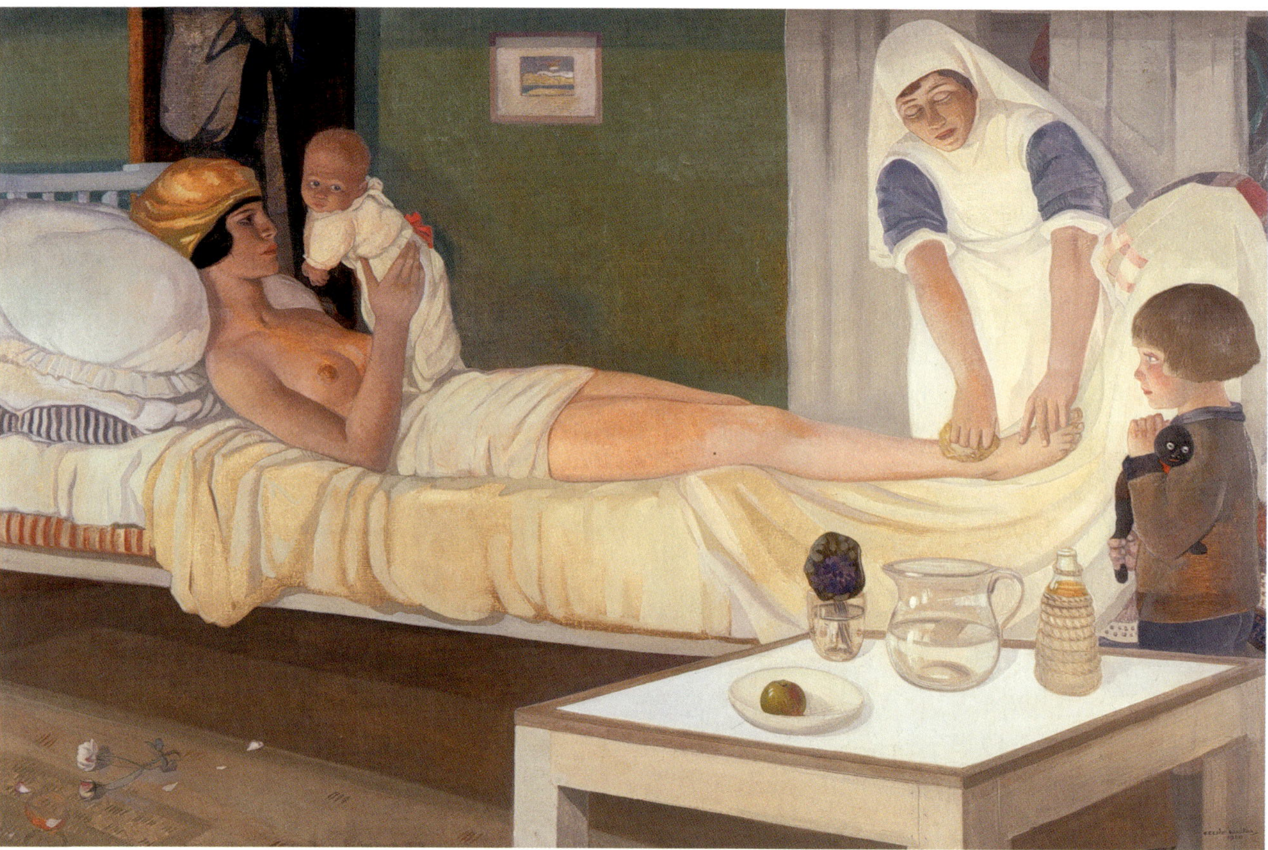

left **97 Cecile Walton**
Romance, 1920
Scottish National Portrait Gallery, Edinburgh

opposite **98 Alice Neel**
Self-portrait, 1980
National Portrait Gallery, Smithsonian Institution

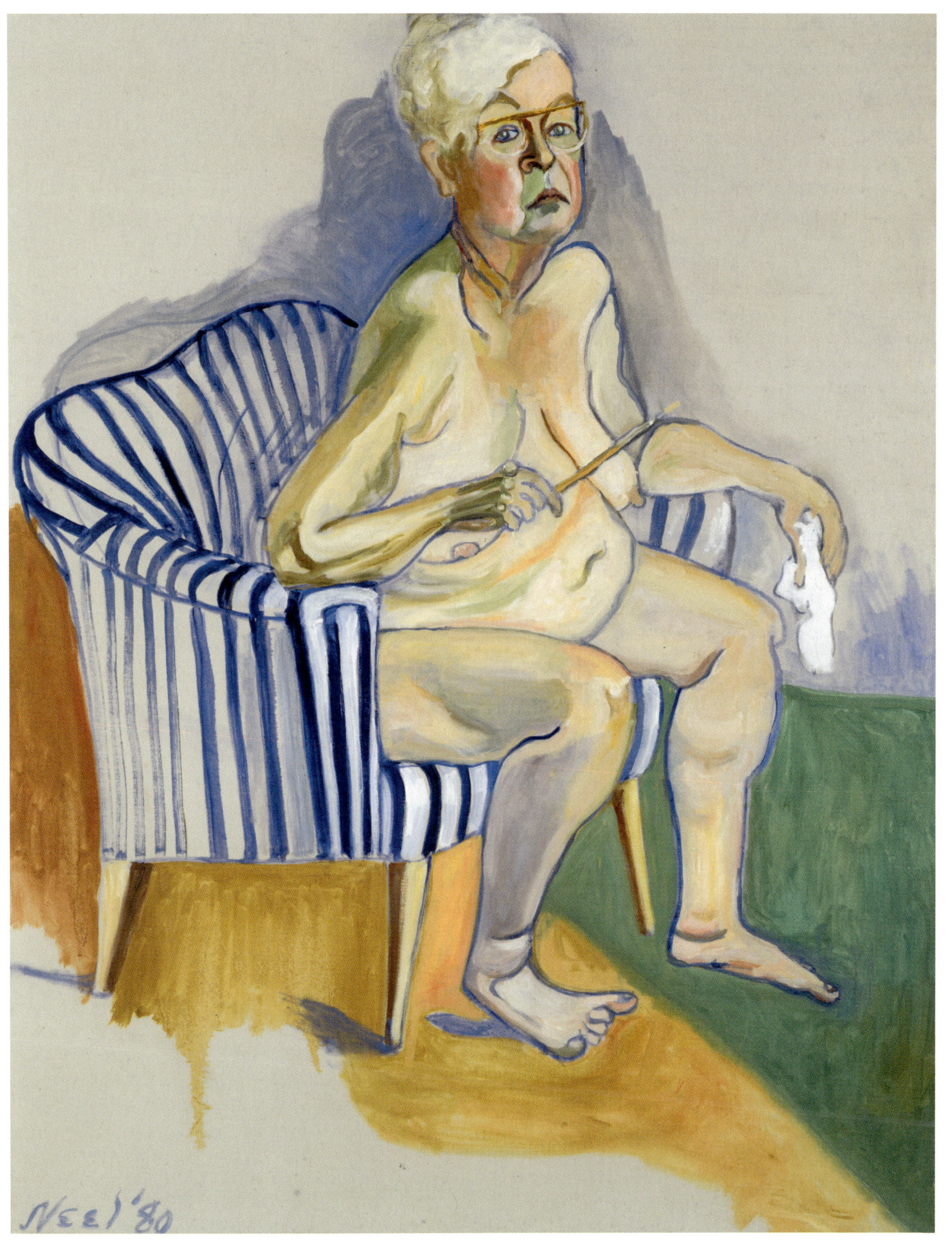
Neel '80

around her lower torso. In terms of body language, the pictures give off multiple suggestions of stereotypical female imagery, ranging from fashion photography to pornography, and even extending to striptease, that quintessential accommodation to male desire. But even as we are seduced by admiration for Wilke's feminine charms, the sting in the tail is our growing recognition of poses that refer to a stylised heroic masculinity, including, by the end, Christ's crucifixion, an allusion echoed by the loin cloth and Wilke's long dark hair. Such imagery is patently subversive, but nevertheless ran into the prohibition amongst puritanical feminists against any use of the female body. In an early survey of female performance art, Lucy Lippard remarked: 'A woman using her own face and body has a right to do what she will with them, but it is a subtle abyss that separates men's use of women for sexual titillation from women's use of women to expose that insult.'[8] From Wilke's point of view, the hostility her work aroused amounted to 'Fascist Feminism'.

The photography of the slightly younger Francesca Woodman was spared such strictures. Because she was so young when she made her pictures, and dead when they came to the art world's attention, any such moralising would have been tasteless. Woodman's work made unremitting use of her own naked body, and conveyed a strong sense of adolescent sexuality. Wilke flaunted her body, and challenged the viewer to look beneath the surface for evidence of an ironic and politicised intelligence. By contrast, Woodman revealed her body, only to submerge it in various ways in the surroundings where she staged her images, in Rhode Island, Rome or New York. She often concealed her facial features, and employed a range of gestures and props that all seemed to deny the viewer any illusion of access to her interior self. The tiny pictures in the *Self-deceit* series are typical of Woodman's oblique approach [plates 100 and 101]. Their dream-like narrative recalls Surrealism.[9] In a forbiddingly bare interior, with pock-marked walls, Woodman's naked form interacts with a roughly shaped piece of mirror. She crawls on the floor, turning away from us, metamorphosing into a near-transparent blur, and reveals her face only once, via a reflection in the mirror. She animates the scene, but at the expense of her own tangibility. The pictures distil some urge to self-effacement, to retreat from an oppressive world of social interactions into a private, melancholy sphere, in which the self is stripped bare. Such readings are facilitated by our knowledge of Woodman's youth (shades of teenage angst) and the fact that she killed herself at the age of twenty-one, suggesting (we presume) some complex history of depression and self-doubt. Feminist perspectives have also constructed 'a vulnerable, paranoiac female subject camouflaging itself against the predatory structures of gendered vision'.[10] But a friend of the artist's has recently queried whether Woodman's work really was so narcissistic:

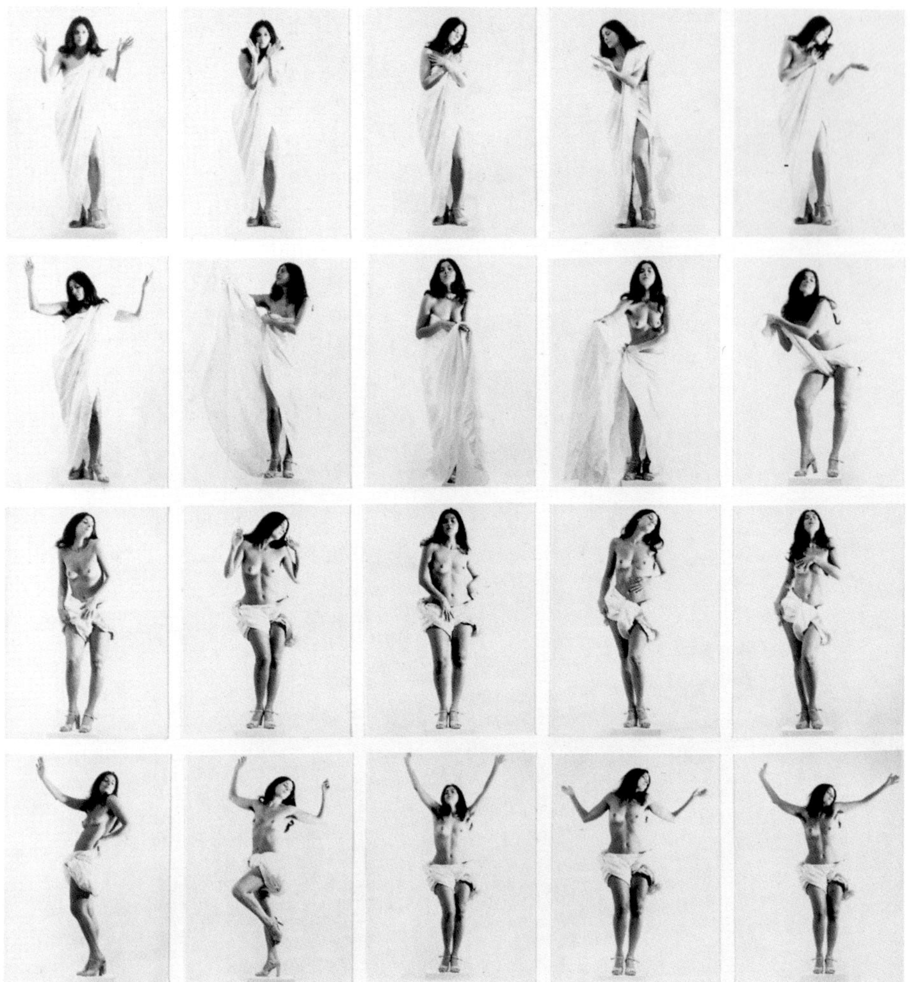

Yes, Francesca had a streak of narcissism ... But once again it was a source of conflict. Francesca was ashamed that she took so many pictures of herself and was irritated by the simplistic self-portrait label attached to her work. She tried using models ... but the reality was she was her own best model because she alone knew what she was after. And as she was the first to say, she was the one who was always available.[11]

This raises the issue of what exactly Woodman was after in her work. In recent criticism, her concerns tend to be aligned with other artists and photographers of the period, normalising her as an emerging figure. Yet this does not exclude the possibility that an exploration and performance of self was at least one element of her creative processes.[12]

We have looked at serial portraiture, employed to give a richer sense of the individual, in the work of photographers like Alfred Stieglitz and Nan Goldin. Other possibilities were opened up by the widespread engagement with serial formats in advanced art of the 1960s and 1970s, as echoed in the work of Wilke and Woodman. In Britain especially, women artists chose to adapt the series idea to exploring autobiographical content. They were inspired, in part, by the feminist conviction that the personal is political. Bringing women's lives and experiences into the public arena was an ideological gesture, since the dismissal of such experiences as merely private was one means to keep women in their place. This was the strategy of much of Jo Spence's work before her death in 1992.

A case in point is *Narratives of Dis-ease* (1990), the culmination of Spence's extensive use of photography as a therapeutic tool and as an attempt to empower other women, and compel viewers to question prejudices about illness and representations of the female body. The five images were chosen from a larger number made during a session with her psychotherapist, in which she re-enacted her experiences since her diagnosis in 1982 with breast cancer and subsequent mastectomy. The photographs they made together were 'very painful since they showed the ways in which my body is not only badly scarred and damaged, but also aging, overweight and deteriorating'.[13] When *Narratives* was exhibited, Spence described her motivation as 'giving expression' to the last eight years of her life; the images marked 'the beginning of a "subject" language' which allowed her 'to start the painful process of expressing my own feelings and perceptions, of challenging the "ugliness" of being seen as Other', and in the process ceasing to be 'a victim' and becoming 'an active participant in life'.[14]

The images depart further from documentary realism than Spence's previous work about cancer treatment and the passivity expected of the patient/victim [plates 102, 103 and 104]. They seek 'to represent the multiplicity of split-off fragments which go to make up an apparently coherent identity'.[15] The figure is spot-lit theatrically against a dark backdrop, and enacts a condensed symbolic narrative of coming to terms with the pain and fear associated with acute illness. In *Excise*, Spence looks down and away from the viewer, suggesting distress as well as an attitude of humility in the face of a medical system that is, we infer, viewed as insensitive and even male in its rationalist ethos. A hospital gown covers her deformed body, and a teddy bear indicates the infantilisation to which, she feels, cancer patients are routinely subjected. In *Exiled*, she exposes her own body, stigmatised as monstrous, and conceals her face behind a mask that implies dehumanisation, but also, perhaps, an impulse to assume a position of power. In *Expected*, Spence is fully naked, except for the high-heeled red shoes that she reaches down to remove, as if to shed her pretensions to conventional femininity. *Expunged* is a pun on 'booby prize', a reward for a fine pair of breasts, and as the consolation awarded to the loser. Finally, Spence shows

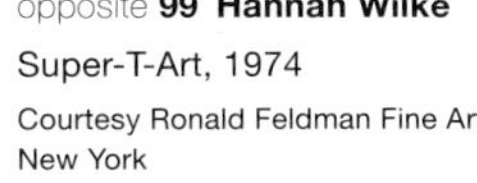

opposite **99 Hannah Wilke**
Super-T-Art, 1974
Courtesy Ronald Feldman Fine Art, New York

left **100 Francesca Woodman**
Self-deceit #4, 1977–8
Scottish National Gallery of Modern Art, Edinburgh
Purchased with the assistance of The Art Fund, 2005

right **101 Francesca Woodman**
Self-deceit, 1977–8
Scottish National Gallery of Modern Art, Edinburgh
Purchased with the assistance of The Art Fund, 2005

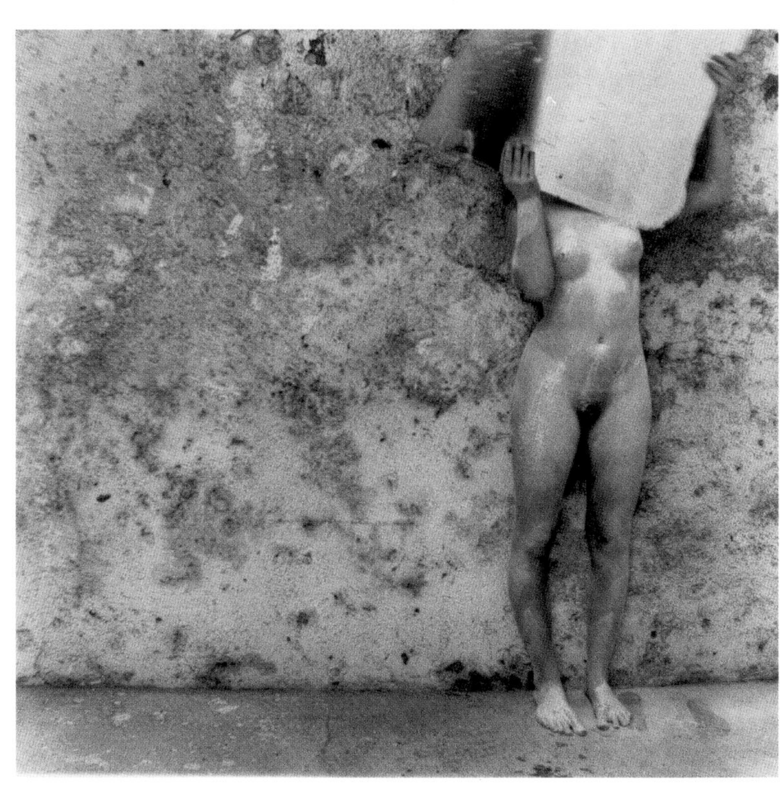

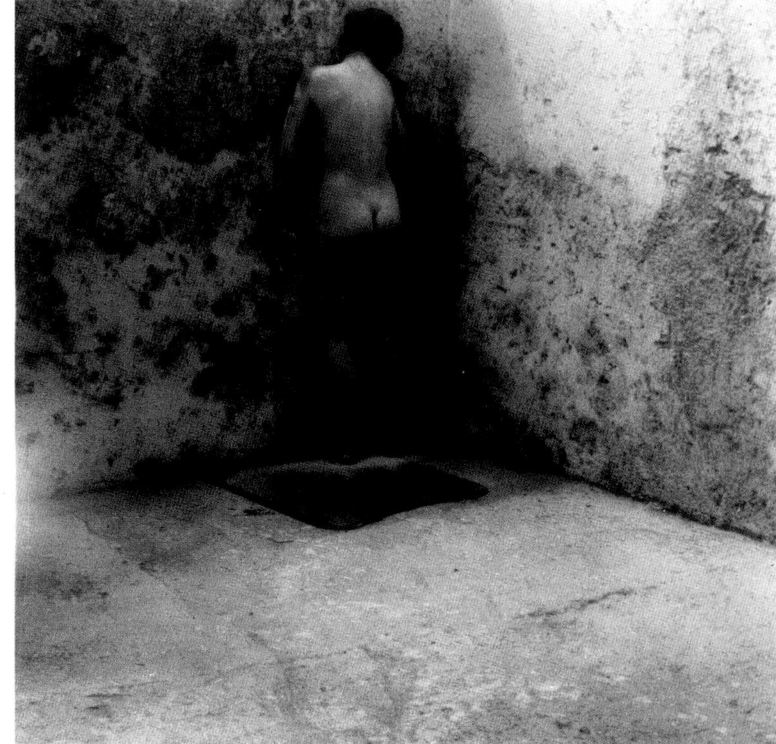

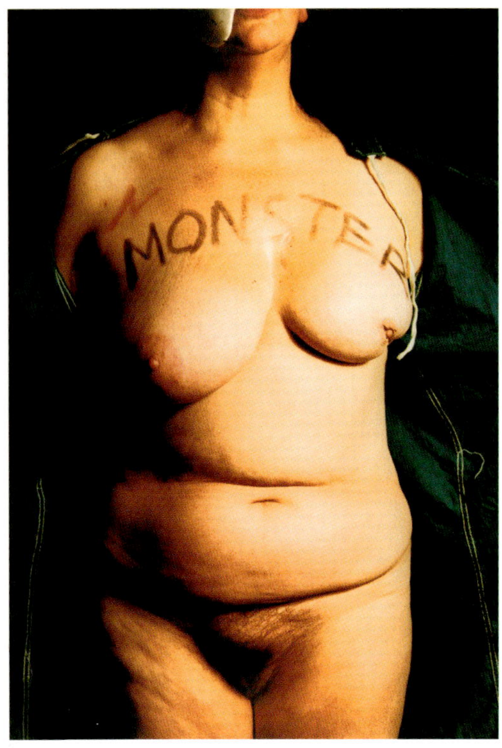

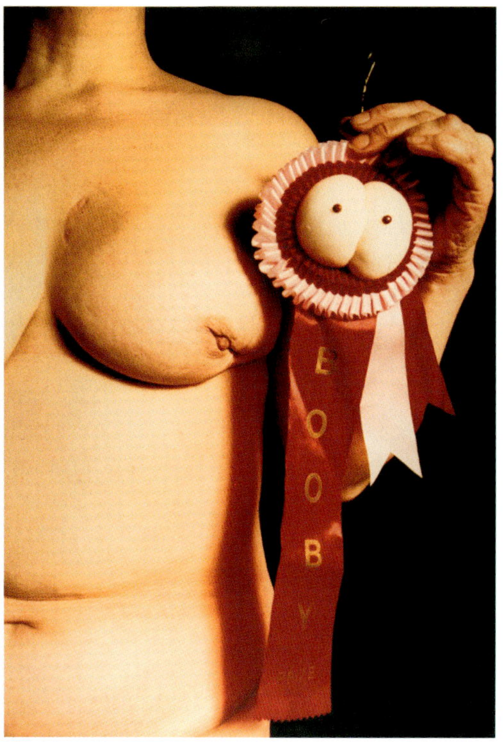

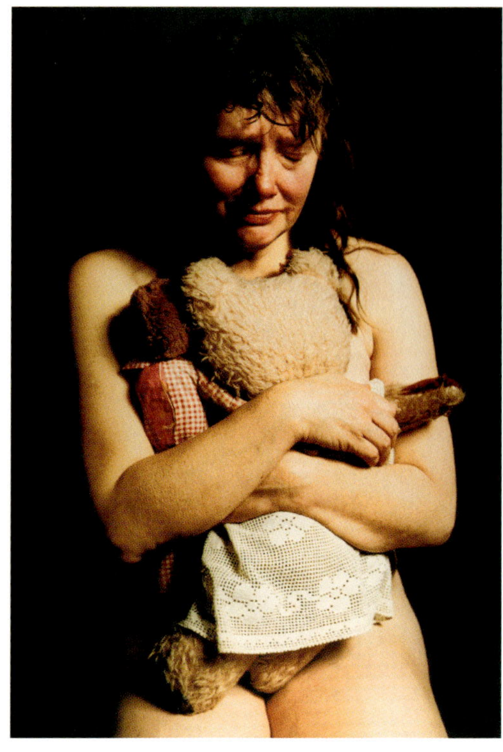

us her own grieving features in *Included*, clutching clothed teddy bears to her naked body as if to console herself, to accept her vulnerability, and to assert her 'inner child'. The title expressed her sympathy with alternative medicine; the term 'dis-ease' suggests the absence of ease, or harmony of body and spirit, that often accompanies physical degeneration. It implies that dealing with illness is as much a psychological as a physical process. The sequence as a whole combines pathos and self-deprecating humour with a strong polemical undertone.[16]

Although her work looked very different, Helen Chadwick acknowledged that it reflected her admiration for Spence, 'perhaps because of the way she is investigating the body and psychic well-being'.[17] Chadwick's early installation *Ego Geometria Sum* [plate 106] is even more explicit and elaborate than Spence's photography in putting naked self-portraiture at the service of a personal narrative. Indeed, *Autobiographies* and *Growing Pains* were alternative titles for this work in which the entire, complex process of growing up is distilled into ten minimalist geometric forms. These schematically describe objects from her childhood: an incubator, font, pram, wigwam, bed, piano, gym horse, cube and vertical column. Thanks to Chadwick's technical inventiveness, all are made to bear photographic and, by implication, memory traces of her present bodily self. That self is naked, reduced in size to the appropriate age, and interacting with these objects. When installed, the forms

above left **102 Jo Spence**
Narratives of Dis-ease: Exiled, 1989
Glasgow City Council (Museums)

above centre **103 Jo Spence**
Narratives of Dis-ease: Expunged, 1989
Glasgow City Council (Museums)

above right **104 Jo Spence**
Narratives of Dis-ease: Included, 1989
Glasgow City Council (Museums)

opposite **105 Helen Chadwick**
Ego Geometria Sum: The Labours I–X, 1983
Eric Franck

below **106 Helen Chadwick**
Ego Geometria Sum, Aspex Gallery, Portsmouth, 1984
Courtesy of Henry Moore Institute (Archive) and the Helen Chadwick Estate

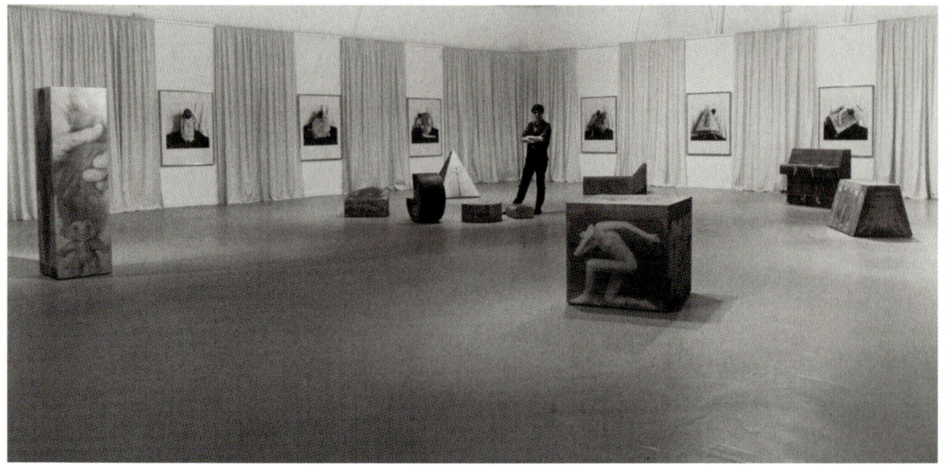

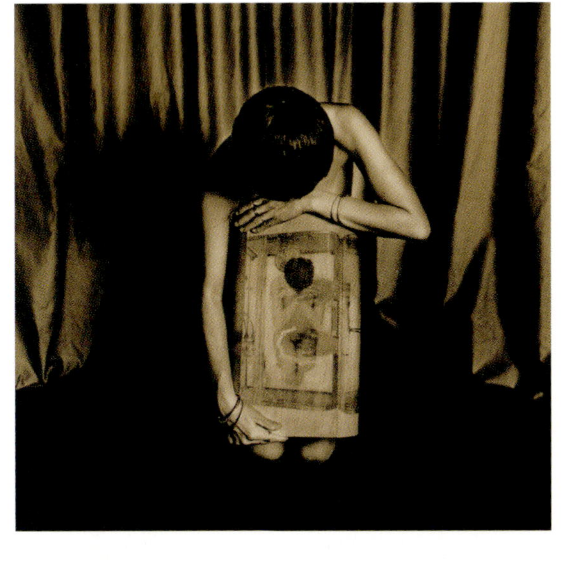
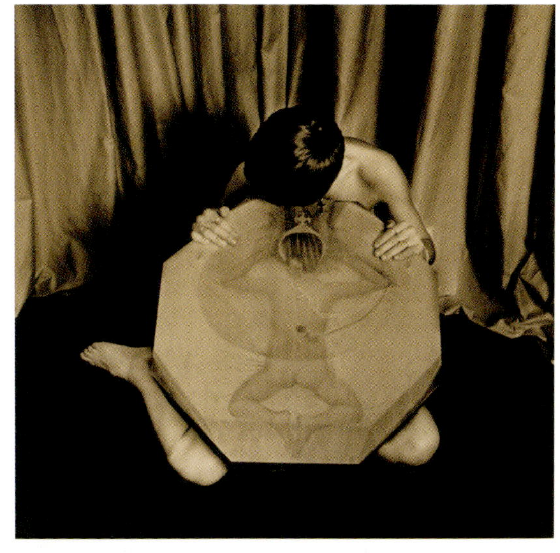
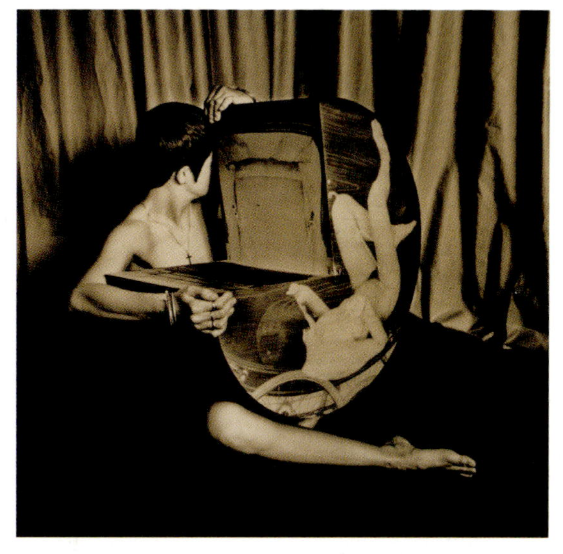
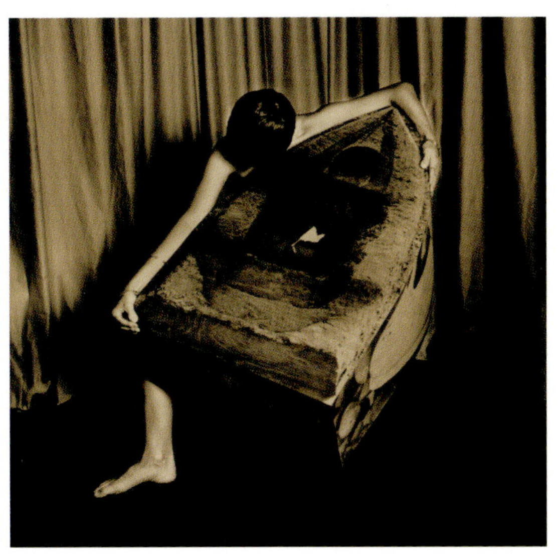
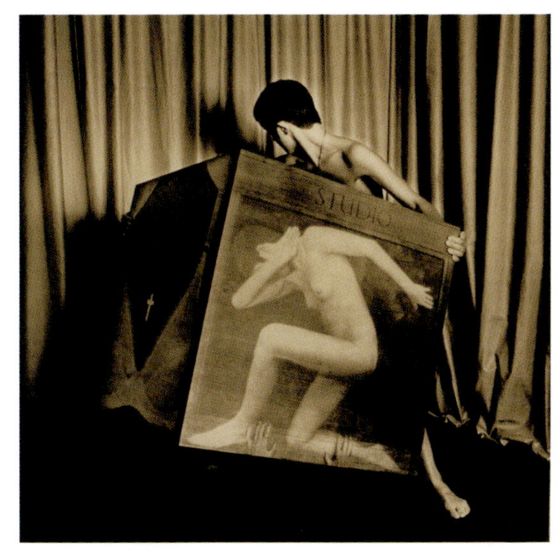
STUDIO
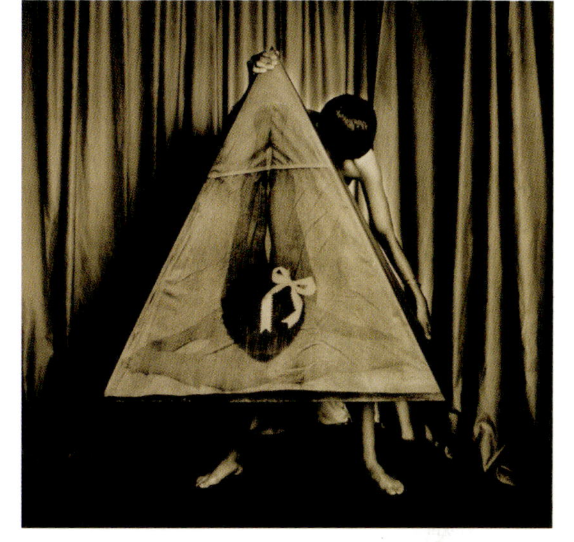
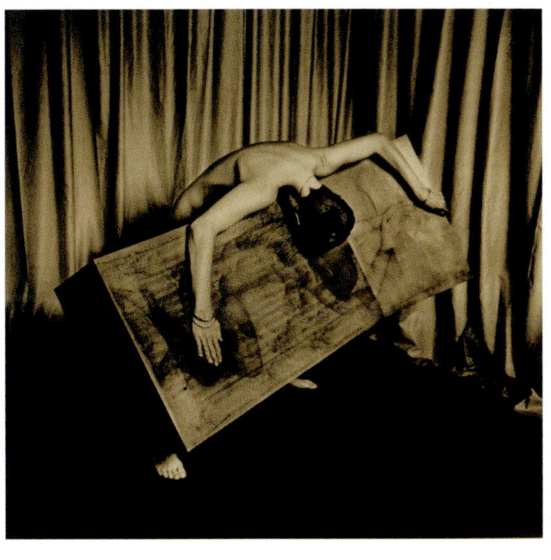
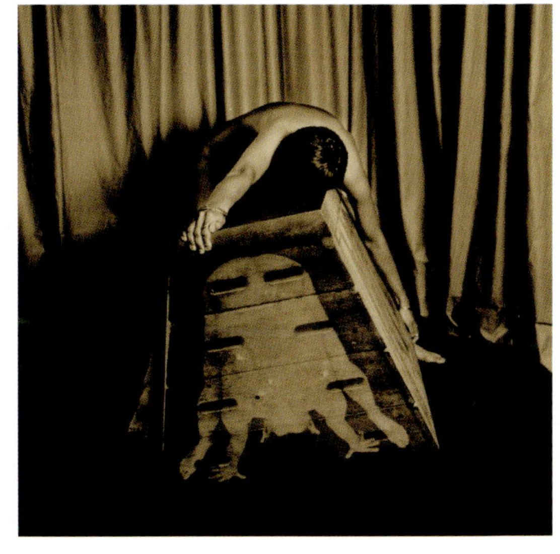
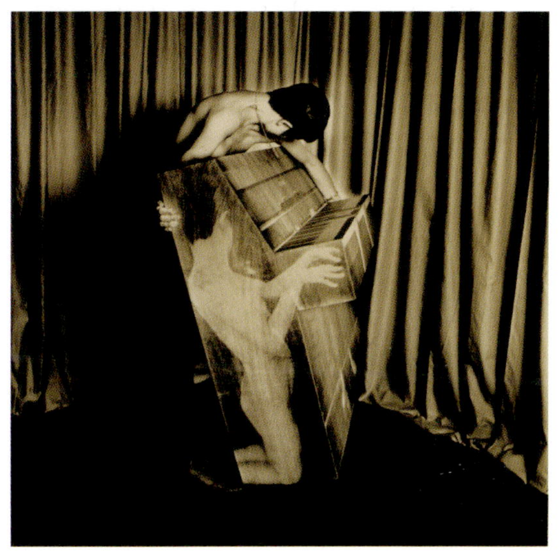

are arranged into a spiral formation which symbolises the universal process of natural growth. But the presiding geometry also conveys the disquieting limitations on personal growth inherent in the upbringing to which children are subjected. In the surrounding series of photographs, *The Labours*, the artist again appears naked, but she is now empowered by personal and artistic maturity to bear, even wrestle with, her own past history, symbolised by the ten sculptures [plate 105], a process of looking 'back to gain equilibrium by throwing the past off'.[18]

Chadwick's *Vanitas II* quotes a strain of titillating imagery that straddles soft-porn magazines and illustrations of Rococo art. The nude female body is surrounded by soft textures and cosmetic accoutrements [plate 107]. She undermines the male gaze by intruding herself in place of the usual unattainable model. Allegorically, Chadwick asserts that the self is an absolute fusion of body and mind, and that her art integrates both visual and intellectual impulses. Like Hannah Wilke, Chadwick was heavily criticised from within feminism for her 'regressive female narcissism', and her complicity with male enjoyment of the naked female form ('I've been accused', she remarked, 'of driving men out to rape young girls').[19]

Twenty years on, it seems unproblematic for 'post-feminist' women to use the image of their own bodies. Liberation from traditional roles and codes of behaviour seems to be taken for granted. Another feature of contemporary naked self-portraiture is the degree of artistic and historical awareness in the work. A significant element in the viewer's response is recognising allusions to previous traditions, including that developed by women artists in the recent past. The artists of the 1970s proceeded from an urge to develop artistic languages that broke free from precedent, something that expressed other kinds of independence. Artists of the present day seem more concerned to position themselves in relation to the mainstream, assuming in effect that being a woman need no longer be such an impediment to critical and commercial success.

Recent manifestations include work by two artists of a slightly older generation, Joyce Gunn-Cairns and Lucy Jones, both now in their fifties. Each has her roots in the earlier twentieth century. In particular, they both seem to take their bearings from German Expressionism, adapting a strand of alienated self-portraiture that male artists had pioneered nearly a hundred years previously. If Gunn-Cairns draws on the tradition associated with a figure like Schiele, Jones owes something to the strong colour and bold brushwork of artists such as Kirchner. Gunn-Cairns has created many naked, sometimes quite harrowing self-portraits that explore, through degrees of abstraction and

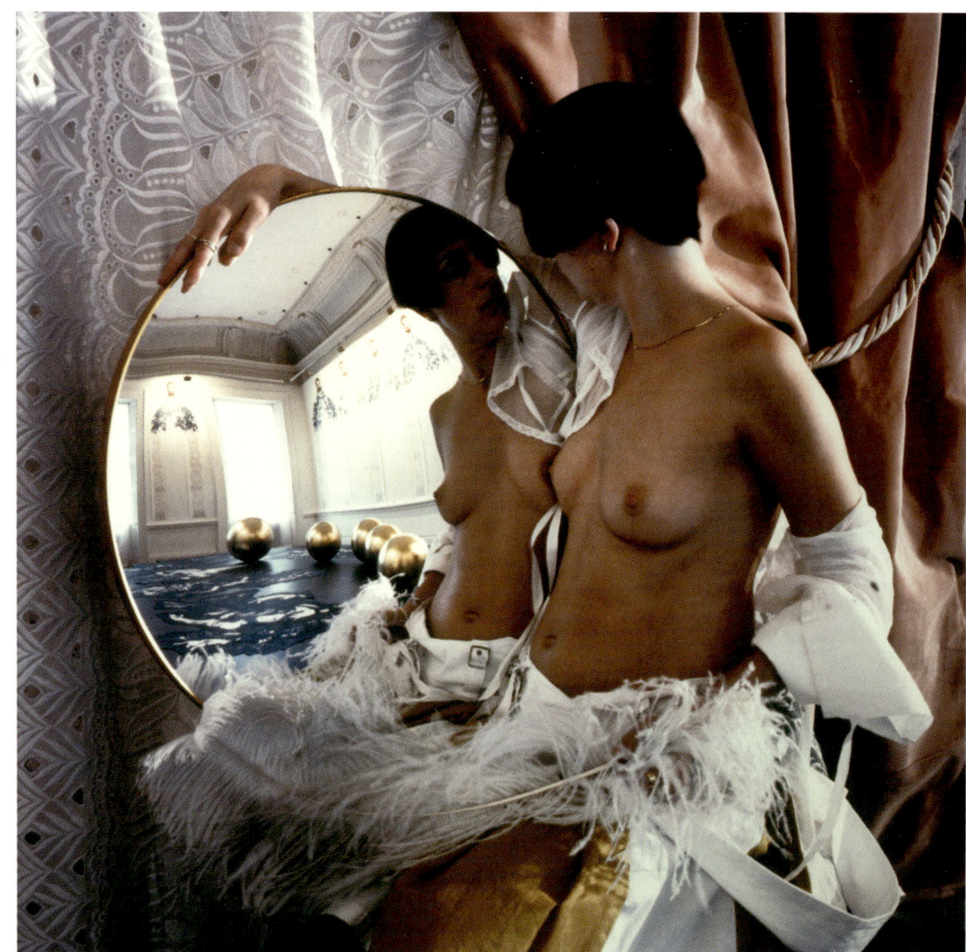

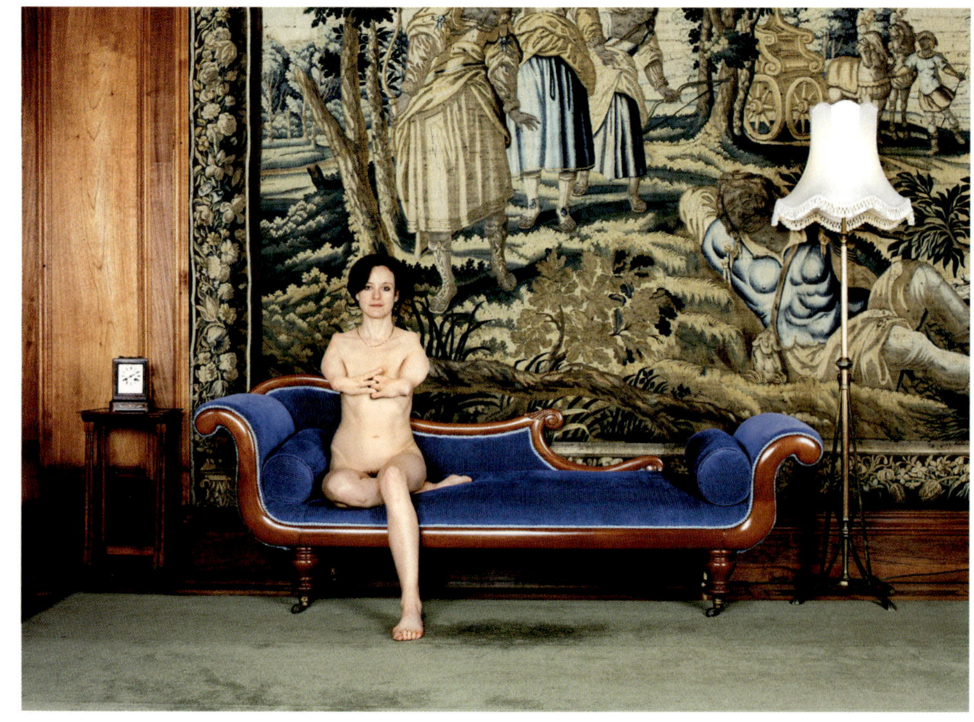

opposite above
107 Helen Chadwick
Vanitas II, 1986
National Portrait Gallery, London

opposite below
108 Alexa Wright
'I' no.3, 1999
The Artist

distortion, not what her body looks like but rather what it feels like, from the perspective of growing older and the experience of long-term depression centred on her physical appearance [plate 109]. She has described what she is aiming at: 'A full-bodied/blooded acceptance of and celebration of my unique humanity in all its many and vibrant manifestations; a refusal to be less than the unique person I am, in all my strengths and in all my flawedness; in my unique creativity, and in my physical imperfection. I want to celebrate and not deny all my physical and emotional idiosyncracies.'[20] She could just as well be speaking for Lucy Jones, who has produced an extensive series of self-portraits, many naked in recent years, that register her own coming to terms with cerebral palsy [plate 110]. Her experience of the condition is conveyed through what we might regard as awkward body language and the presence of her stick, which seems to float or walk of its own accord, its geometric perfection highlighting her difficulties. She has remarked that her motivation is neither cathartic, nor a plea for sympathy: 'The work is sometimes like a mask. I'm not concerned with a physical likeness. I'm after the inner likeness that's constantly changing … By looking at myself, I'm trying to reflect something about being human.'[21]

The narcissism that may be inherent in self-portraiture is challenged in the photography of Alexa Wright. Her *I* series (1998–9) comprises eight photographs that recall the clichéd format, inherited from traditional portrait painting, of the individual in the idealising surroundings of an aristocratic interior, complete with antique rugs, furniture, paintings, and marble statuary. The pictures themselves are symmetrical or otherwise highly ordered. The other constant is the face, which we know to be Wright's. The

left **109 Joyce Gunn-Cairns**
Self-portrait, Deposition, 1998
The Artist

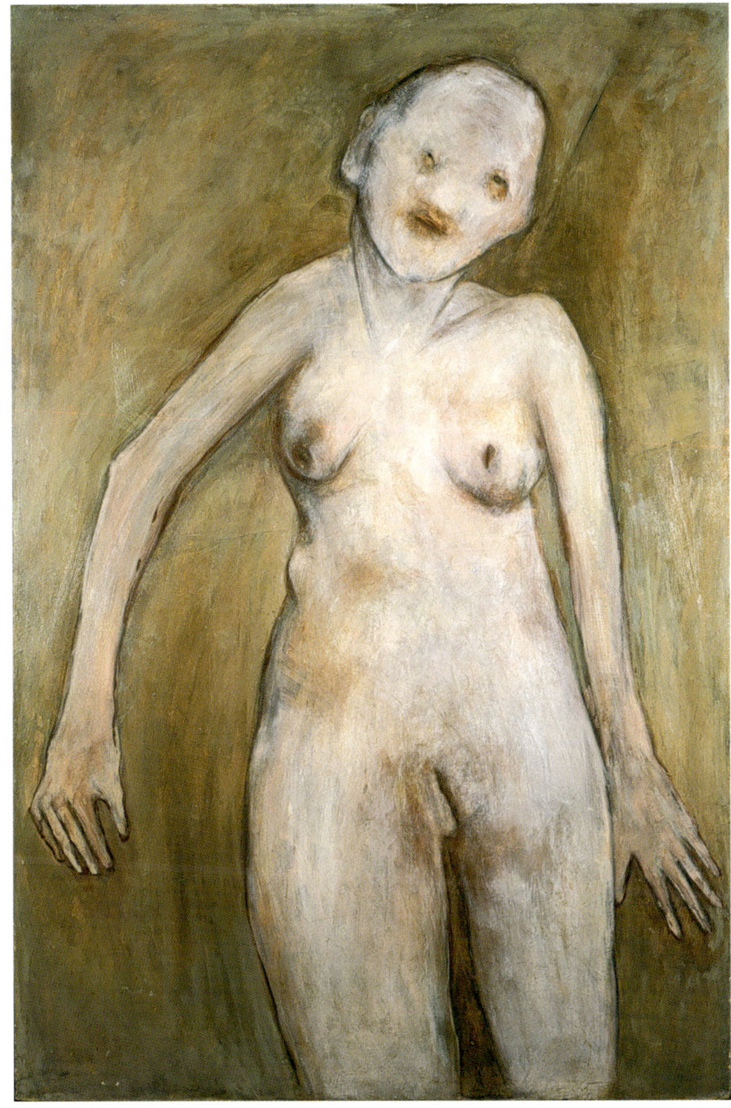

right **110 Lucy Jones**
Asleep, Seeing or Dead, 2000
The Artist, courtesy Flowers

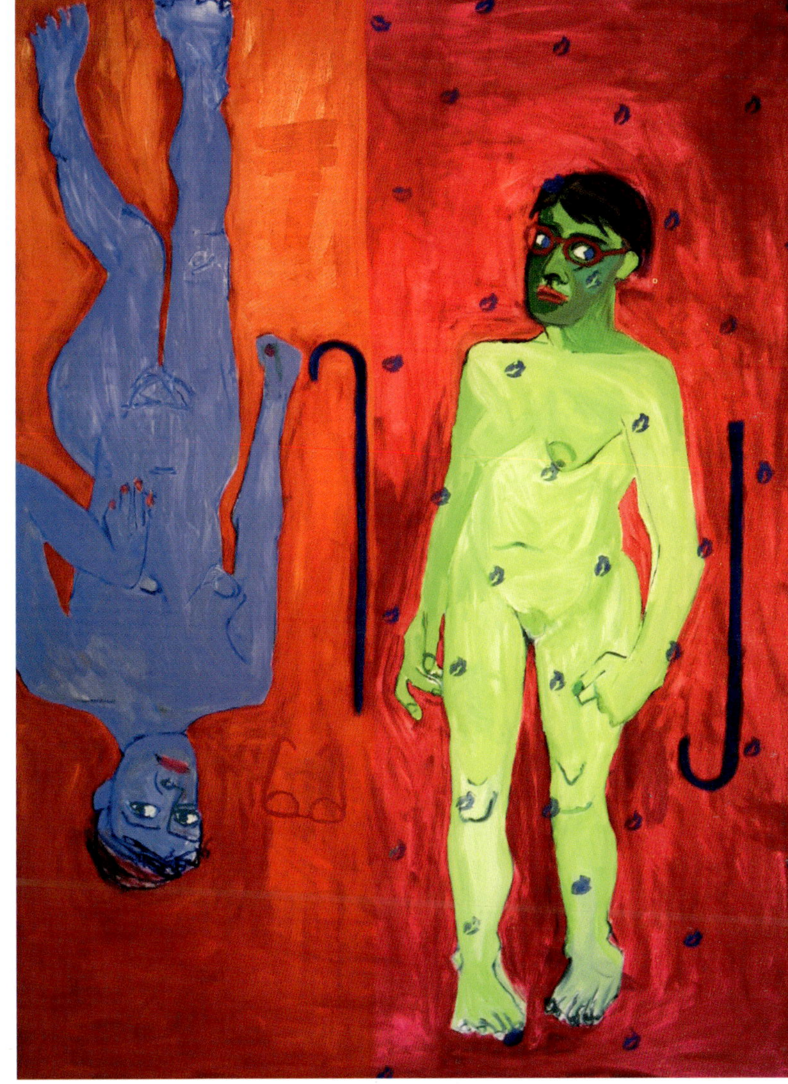

attached bodies are very different from one another, but all have missing or deformed limbs. To make this plain, some of the figures are naked, or partially undressed [plate 108]. One is seen from the back, seated at the piano, the only case where Wright's own features are not included. It becomes clear that she has identified with certain severely disabled women, to the point of exploiting computer software to fuse her own features with their bodies. The same, repeated face serves to focus our attention on the bodies, and their extreme differences not only from one another but also from the normal healthy frame that most of us imagine we possess. The 'perfectly proportioned' objects in the vicinity heighten our awareness of bodily deviations from a stereotype extending from classical statues to the glamorous models who often perform for fashion shoots in such settings.

By inserting her face, the usual sign of identity, Wright is encouraging us to question our attitudes towards disabled people. Do we acknowledge and engage with their individuality, or do we pigeonhole them as 'other', or even freakish? Do we avoid them, although admiring from a distance how brave they are, and how clever at compensating for physical defects? Do they puncture our illusions about our own physical and emotional normality? How do we deal with our own sense of guilt that it is they and not us who so flagrantly fail to fit in? Wright's photographic conceit ends by being an invitation to imagine being a person with that particular body, but with a personality as complex and contradictory as the rest of us. We are also asked to reflect on the disparity between the surroundings in which these images are made, and the institutional and impoverished circumstances in which we know the disabled often exist in our society. But, in addition, the conventions deployed, rather like the marble of Marc Quinn's nude sculpture, confer heroism and worth on people who often have had to cope with enormous difficulties. The feminist project of reclaiming one's own subjectivity and body has become a springboard for a wider acceptance of departures from the mythic bodily norm.

Famously, Jenny Saville made a dramatic impact with a group of monumental paintings of the female body in the early 1990s, when virtually straight out of Glasgow School of Art. Their virtuosity aside, her confrontational images challenged the pressures on women to conform, by means of diet and even cosmetic surgery, to the nubile 'perfection' of media stereotypes. They demonstrated, to borrow the title of a widely-read book by Susie Orbach, that fat was indeed a feminist issue.[22] The pictures sought to convey what it felt like to occupy a young female body, eliciting feelings that might run the gamut from disgust to pride. The generalising effect is reinforced by titles such as *Branded* or *Prop*, but from the start her own body was a key point of reference, although the pictures had a more ambivalent relationship to self-portraiture than Semmel's or Spence's. Saville remarked on how she moved in and out of personal identification with the body in the picture, making specific reference to *Branded*:

The head is mine. In fact this painting is really based on me. I use me all the time because it's really reliable, you're there all the time. I like the idea of using yourself because I want to be in *the work. I don't like the idea of just being the person* looking. *I want to* be *the person. Because women have been so involved in being the subject-object, it's quite important to take that on board ... You're the artist but you're also the model. I want it to be a constant exchange all the time.*[23]

The work of Joan Semmel provides one point of reference for Saville's pictures though the latter involve a greater degree of manipulation and abstraction. But in their preoccupation with body image and occasional inclusion of writing on the body, Saville's early paintings may have been more directly informed by the photography of Jo Spence, whose *Narratives of Dis-Ease* were shown in Glasgow in 1990.[24] Saville has always used photographic sources, her own and those of others, but her increasingly painterly idiom proclaims her admiration for artists such as Rubens or Willem de Kooning, who both put the substance of paint to the service of describing flesh. Like Freud, she maintains her distance from the clinical objectivity of photography. Yet, for a period, Saville produced photographic works alongside her painting. The *Closed Contact* series were made in collaboration with a fashion photographer [plate 111]. Under her direction, Glen Luchford took photographs from below of Saville lying on top of a sheet of glass, parts of her body flattened by her own pressure. These works, whose distorted imagery is barely contained within the frame, are replete with the sheer visceral presence of flesh. If the early paintings made reference to Freud, Saville's photographs recall the sense of the body as raw stuff rather than structure that is found in Francis Bacon's painting.

The sexual realism of work like Nan Goldin's made possible the approaches to self-representation of Sarah Lucas and Tracey Emin, friends and sometime collaborators. The monoprints of Tracey Emin aspire, on the face of it, to eliminate artistic detachment, as well as to push at the aesthetic and technical frontiers of the fine art tradition. They look utterly spontaneous and direct, an effect reinforced by her chosen technique of drawing and writing into ink spread on glass, so that the one-off impressions come out in reverse. The writing is crude and littered with spelling mistakes, like the imagery we might expect to encounter

111 Jenny Saville and Glen Luchford
Closed Contact No.4, 1995–6
Aberdeen Art Gallery and Museums Collections

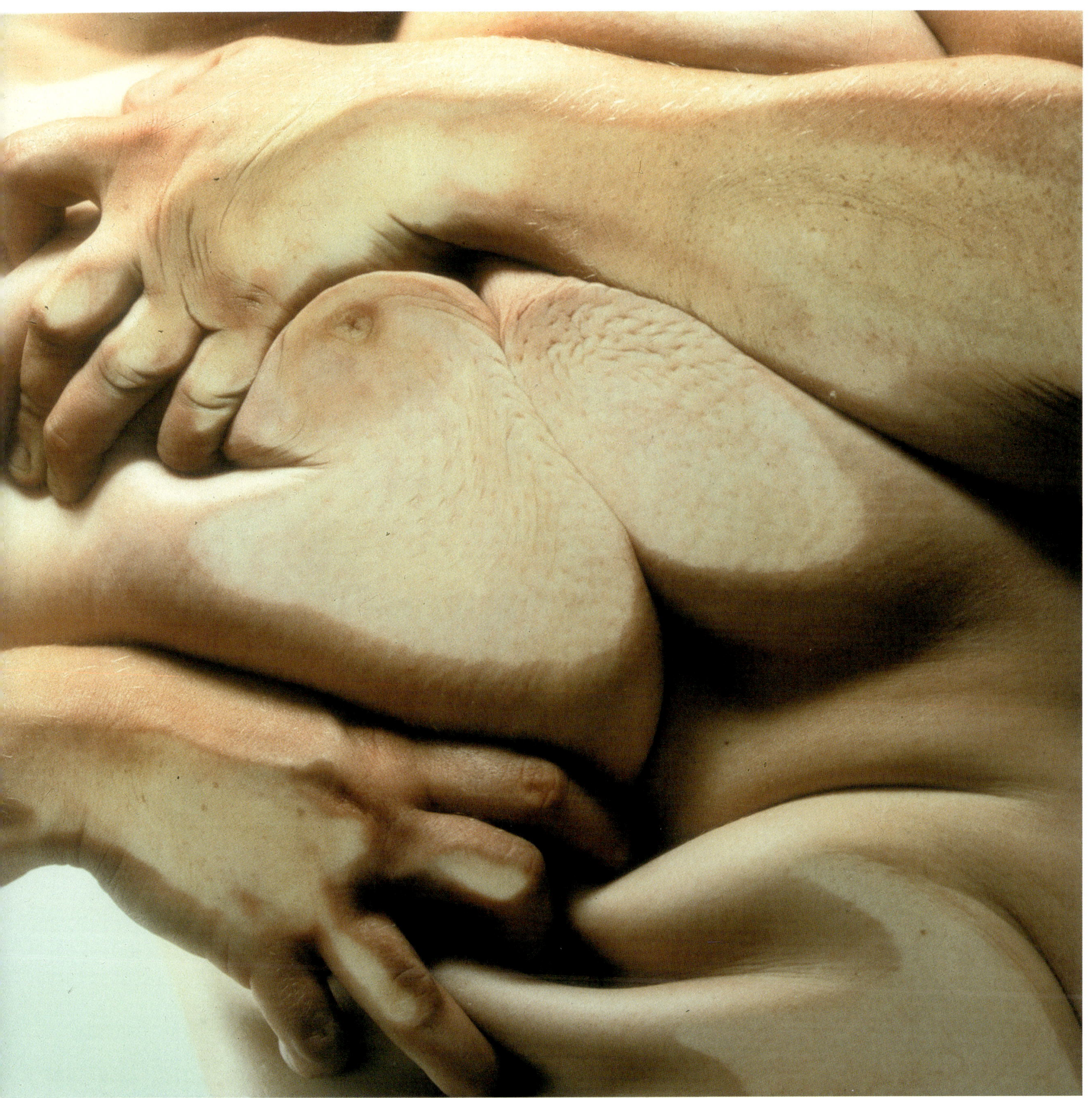

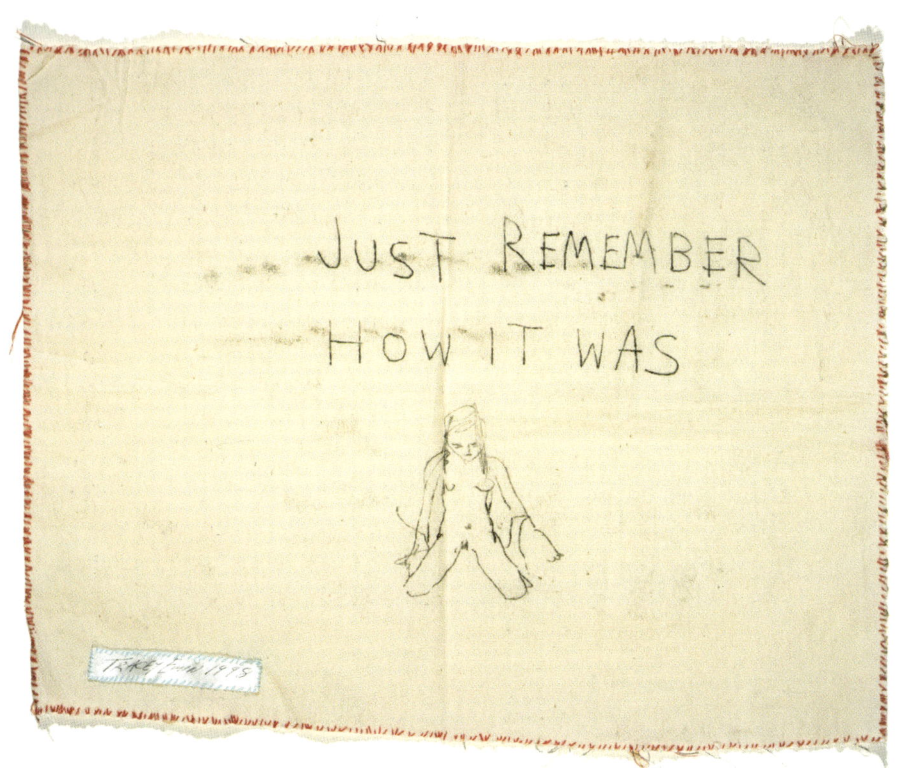

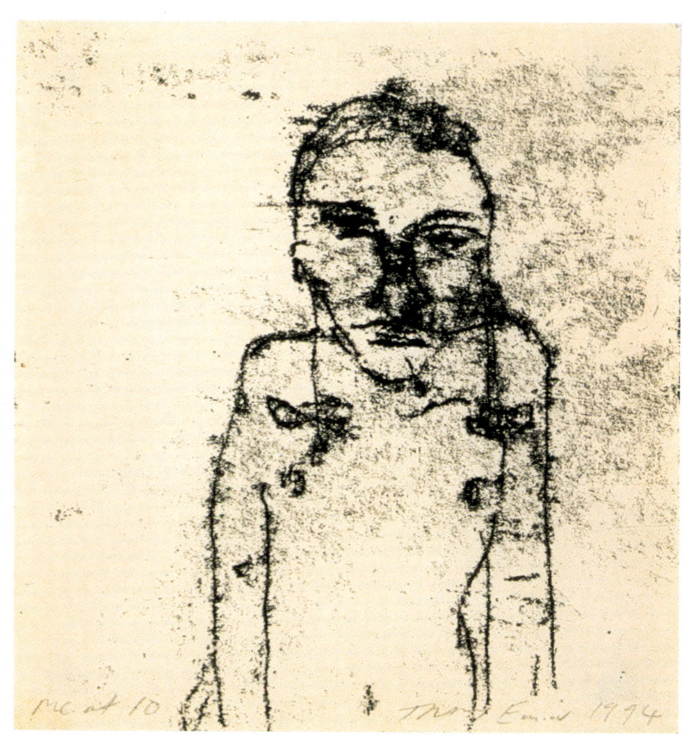

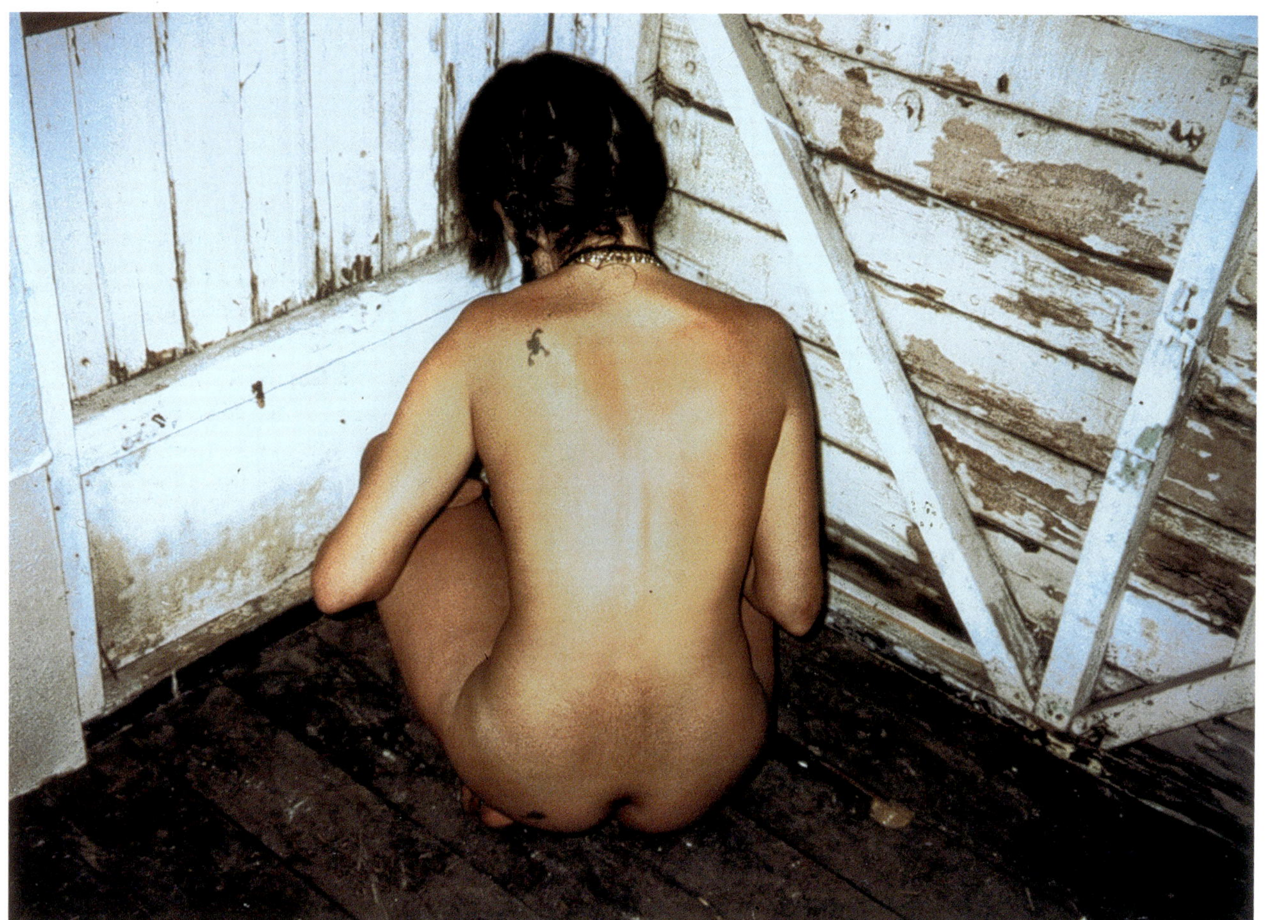

above left **112 Tracey Emin**

Just Remember How It Was, 1998

Scottish National Gallery of Modern Art, Edinburgh

above right **113 Tracey Emin**

Me at 10 (from Family Suite), 1994

Scottish National Gallery of Modern Art, Edinburgh

Purchased with assistance from The Art Fund, the Patrons of the National Galleries of Scotland and the Gibson Bequest, 2005

left **114 Tracey Emin**

The Last Thing I Said to You was Don't Leave Me Here II, 2000

Tate, presented by Anne-Katrin Meier zu Sieker, 2002

opposite **115 Sarah Lucas**

Self-portraits 1990–1998
(Human Toilet II, 1997)

Scottish National Gallery of Modern Art, Edinburgh

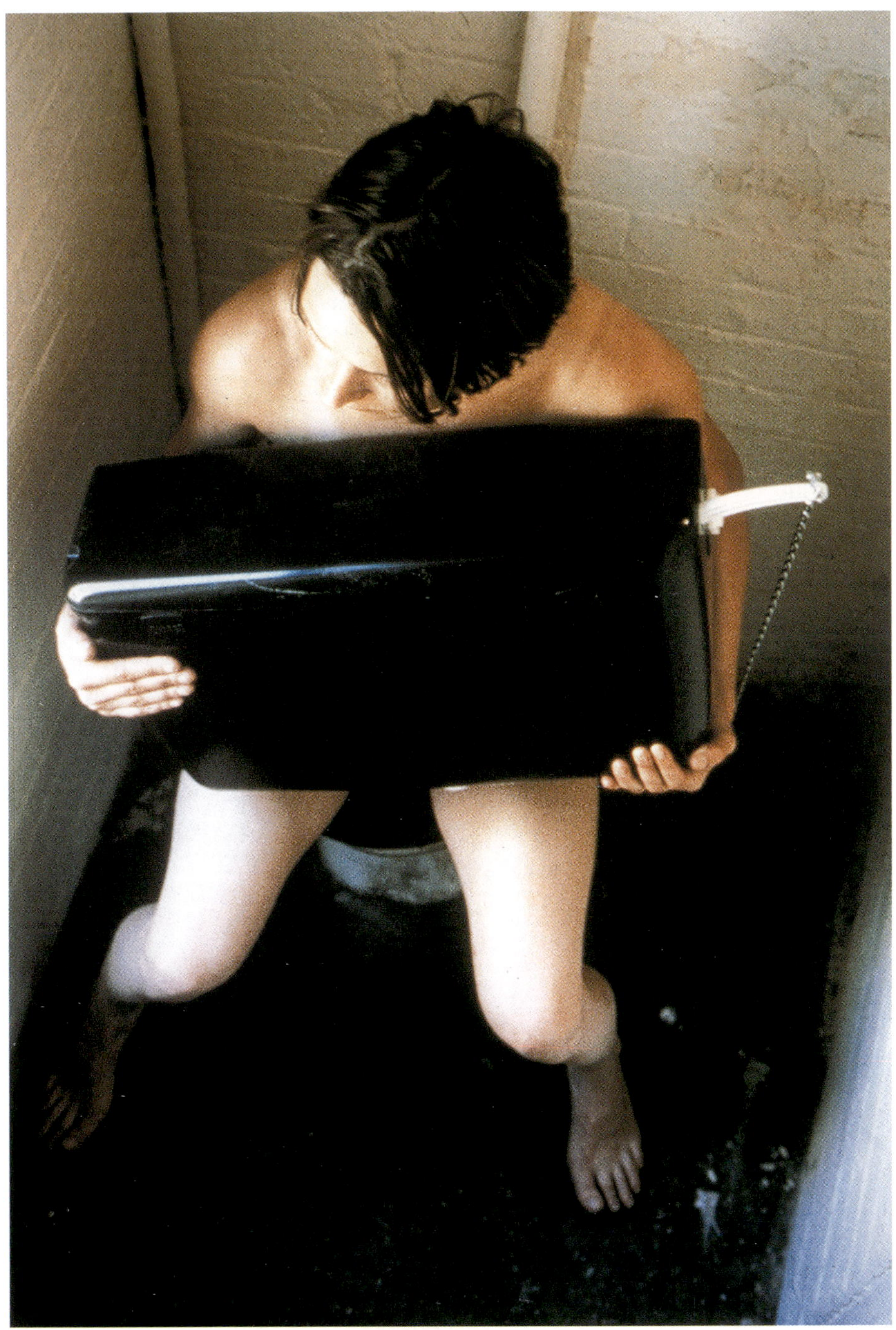

in a private diary. The works are raw and concerned with traumatic events in the artist's life. Most concern young adult experiences, but a suite of very small and simple images look back to Emin's childhood and her early sexual and bodily sensations [plate 113].[25] The frequent representation of herself naked is integral to this fixation on sexuality and intense, private feelings, whether ecstatic or painful. Her work is of a piece with her confessional writings, whether in the form of scribbled sheets reproduced in exhibition catalogues or the more polished newspaper columns and her recent autobiography, *Strangeland.*

Yet her work, for all its apparent artlessness, shows a sophisticated awareness of the 'primitivist' impulse in modern art. The pictures have been compared to earlier artists Emin is known to admire, such as Munch and Schiele, as well as to more recent work like the early etchings of David Hockney (*A Rake's Progress*, 1961–3), which are also faux naïve and autobiographical. This is not to question the 'authenticity' of Emin's work, but simply to suggest that its air of tormented, confessional narrative, and its graphic spontaneity are conceived within the parameters of an available artistic tradition. Equally, the renunciation of refined draughtsmanship and the use of supports such as calico [plate 112], as well as the quilt formats used elsewhere in her work, make knowing reference to the historically marginal status of the female artist. It is as if Emin is consciously reclaiming primitivism for the purposes of articulating a distinctively female persona, one characterised by emotional and sexual frankness, and the opposite of that used by artists like Degas (in his monoprints) or Picasso to subordinate the female body to masculine desire.

Emin has moved freely between fine art techniques and lens-based media, in which she has also appeared naked. In *The Last Thing I Said to You was Don't Leave Me Here II*, we see Emin squatting, with her back to the viewer, inside the beach hut that she had used for holidays in Margate – then appropriated as an art installation [plate 114].[26] The work refers to a tradition of imagery focusing on the female body seen from behind such as Ingres's *Valpincon Bather* or massive oils by Saville (*Trace, Juncture*). The work and its despairing title evoke a state of being stripped back to a psychic condition of extreme alienation and misery. This is the obvious reading, but on reflection the image becomes more ambiguous in tone, and the title delivers a characteristic Emin double-take. Is she in fact celebrating retreat from the world and immersion in solitary, even spiritual contemplation, the beach hut a latter-day hermit's cave? We cannot see her face or what she is doing with her hands, and so we have no access to what is going on in her head. This enigmatic quality suggests an affinity with Francesca Woodman. Emin's title could be a protest to someone (a lover perhaps) who abandoned her. Equally, with a different intonation, it could be saying: I certainly didn't say to you (the viewer) that I don't want to be left here. I just want to be myself. Leave me alone!

A mix of immediacy and allusiveness is encountered again in the work of Sarah Lucas and Jemima Stehli. In one of Lucas's scurrilous self-portraits (*Human Toilet II*), we encounter her naked sitting on the toilet and holding a cistern on her lap, seemingly lost in contemplation [plate 115]. The effect is deliberately anti-feminine, and may make punning reference to the euphemism of '*toilette*' for the process of a woman making herself look good. There may also be a hint of the terminology of female 'plumbing'. This in turn opens up the possibility of an allusion to Duchamp's celebrated *Urinal* ready-made, which was frequently read as a surrogate female body, objectified in the most literal sense.[27]

The work of Jemima Stehli has been said 'to occupy a space somewhere between portraiture and performance'.[28] She is probably best known for her *Strip* series (1999–2000), which also 'blurs the theoretical distinction between object and subject, portrait and self-portrait'.[29] *Strip* comprises several sequences of images in which the shutter-release cable is visibly operated by seated males (described as an art critic, writer etc.), with a sheet of coloured photographer's backdrop paper behind them. In front of them (and so seen by us from the rear) stands the artist herself, who progressively removes her outer clothing and underwear until all she is left wearing is a pair of high-heeled shoes, with all their fetishistic associations.[30] Several types of gaze are brought into play. As viewers we scrutinise the man and the degree of pleasure, feigned indifference or embarrassment with which he studies (or avoids doing so) the stripping female. She, in turn can be assumed, when her posture permits it, to be gazing at him, whilst she is studied from the back by us. The person taking the pictures has no idea what they will look like; paradoxically, it is the naked model who controls the proceedings, both conceptually and practically. Yet her thought processes remain inaccessible, whilst our own are available to introspection (and how much is at stake whether we are male or female?). The project surely makes reference to Marcel Duchamp's *The Bride Stripped Bare by her Bachelors, Even* (1915–23), with a nod perhaps to Hannah Wilke as intermediary. Stehli seems to be reinventing Duchamp's irony and sense of the absurd in the context of a more literally staged imagery. But if Duchamp's Bride is something of a *femme fatale*, a projection of male antipathy, Stehli cuts a more attractive figure in every sense, a post-feminist female artist who evidently experiences no puritanical inhibitions about displaying her own body in the work.

116 Jemima Stehli
Standing Nude 1, 2001/2
Courtesy of the Artist and Lisson Gallery, London

117 Jemima Stehli
Red Turning, 2000
Courtesy of the Artist and Lisson Gallery, London

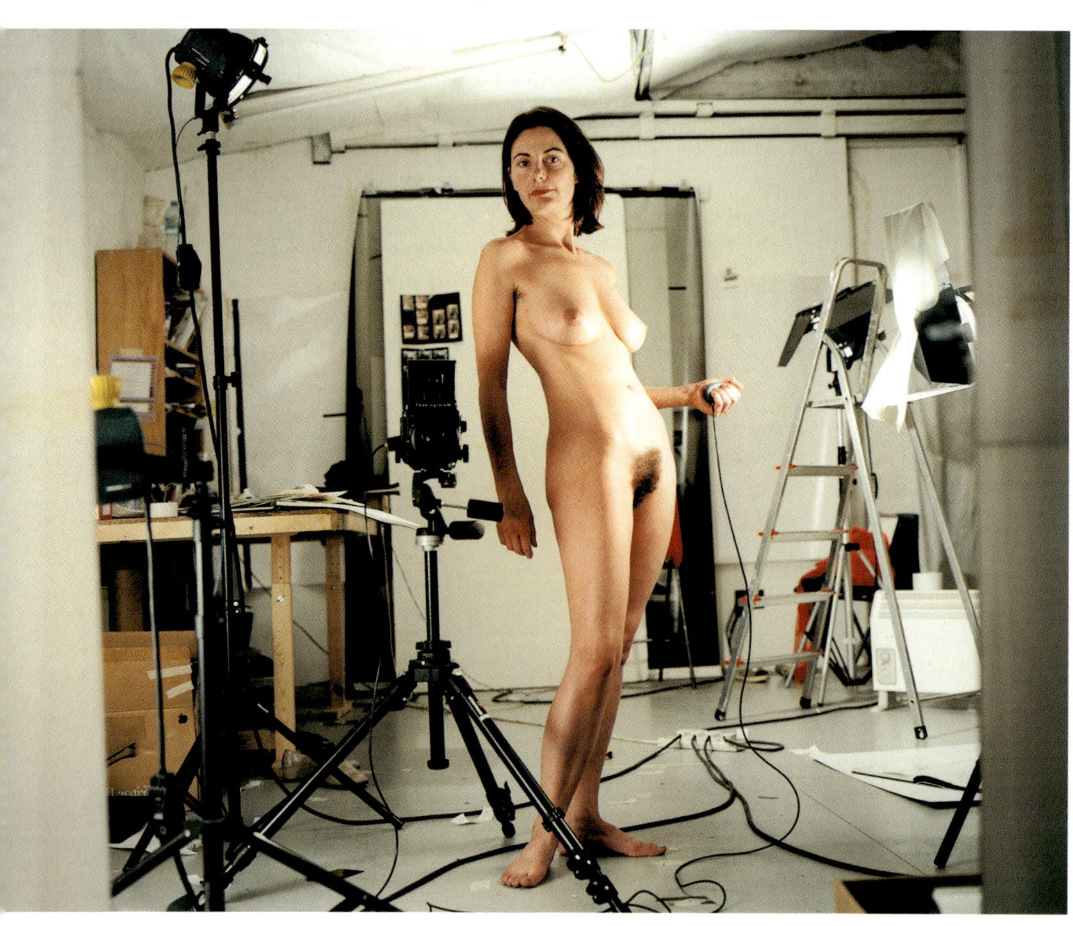

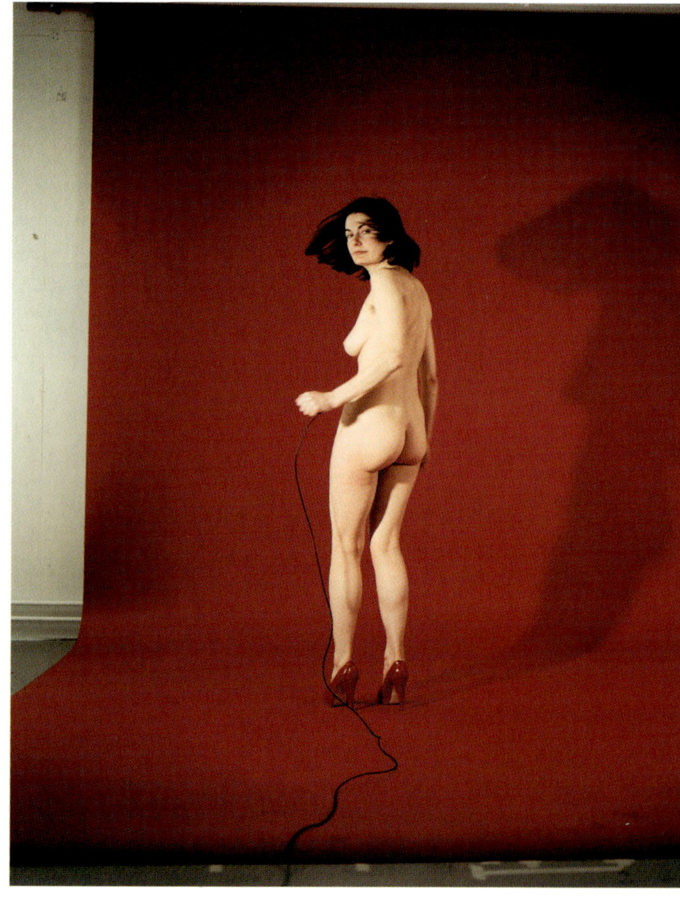

118 Alison Watt
Source III, 1995
Courtesy the Artist and Ingleby Gallery Edinburgh

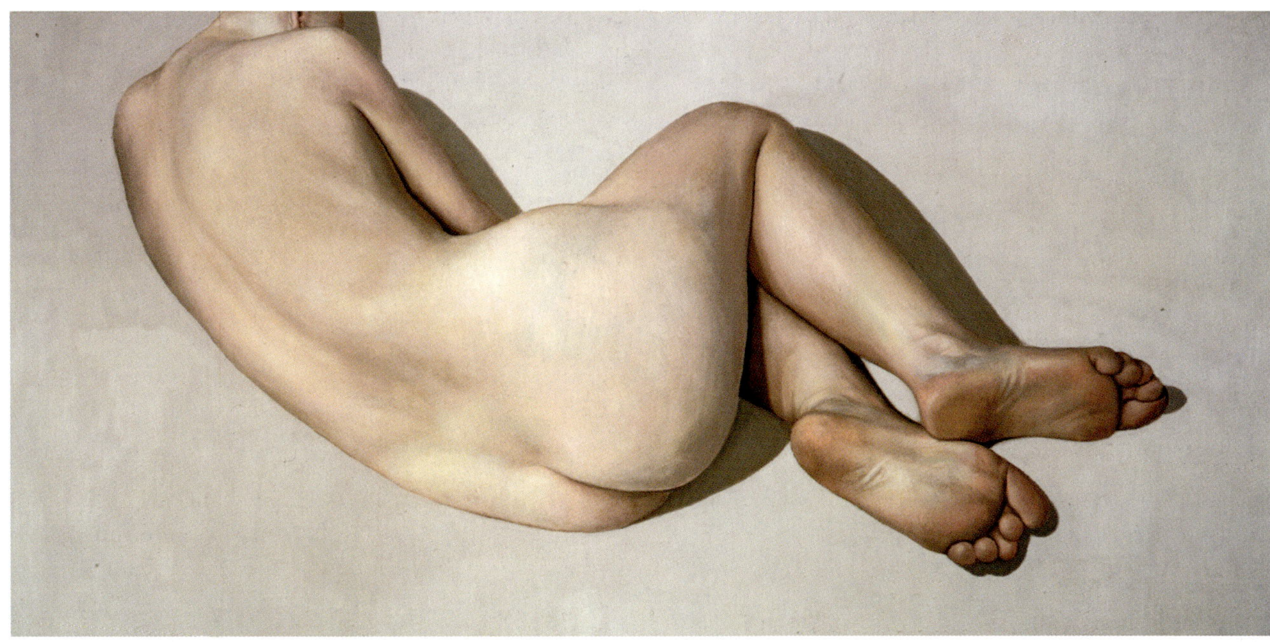

Subsequent larger-scale photographs, such as *Red Turning* and *Standing Nude*, convey an analogous self-awareness and self-assurance [plates 116 and 117]. In each case we encounter the artist, alone in her studio, operating the remote shutter release. In the former, which evokes the paintings of Francis Bacon, she poses theatrically in front of the red studio backdrop and twists round to gaze back towards what then becomes the viewer. We might also notice the blemishes that betray aging, undercutting the theatrical illusion. In *Standing Nude*, we see a reflection in the mirror (whose edges are likewise visible) of the artist surrounded by studio paraphernalia, and directing not just her gaze but also her camera in our direction. As with the work of Joan Semmel, we are invited to imagine ourselves being watched, even though on the face of it it is we who are doing the watching. The picture is hung low to reinforce the continuity between pictorial and real space, and looks straightforward, as if to say: this is who I am, behind the social façade, and this is what I do. Yet it is just as staged in the end as *Red Turning*, and Stehli acknowledges an interest in the encounter with the viewer in Jeff Wall's *Picture for Women* (1979), which itself plays a variation on Manet's *Bar at the Folies-Bergères* (1881–2).[31] Stehli's graceful pose strikes an incongruous note, amongst the clutter of hi-tech studio equipment.

Others have moved into similarly ambiguous territory, alluding to both traditional and contemporary approaches to the body, both self-portraiture and more generic notions of nudity. A particular case in point is Alison Watt's *Source III*, which inaugurated her move away from painting the life model [plate 118]:

I found I was making paintings which were not based on observation alone. Ideas were forming which were not based on what I was seeing. They were also about what I knew about the body and I started to use my own as a point of reference. Source III *is the first painting I made which was, in effect, a hybrid. It was a combination of my own body, what I knew of all the women I had worked with over the years and the strong influence of the French 19th century painting I was looking at … The 'portrait' element of the painting is deliberately ambiguous.*[32]

The approach is in some ways comparable to the early painting of Jenny Saville, but the result utterly different in its disassociation of the body from tactile, sensual associations. Watt's art-historical point of reference is the classicism of Jean-Dominique Ingres. The linear purity and bodily distortions of Watt's painting evokes *Le Grande Odalisque* (1814), and her title alludes directly to Ingres's late painting *La Source* (1859), where, as she remarks, 'what could be an erotic image is strangely sterile'.

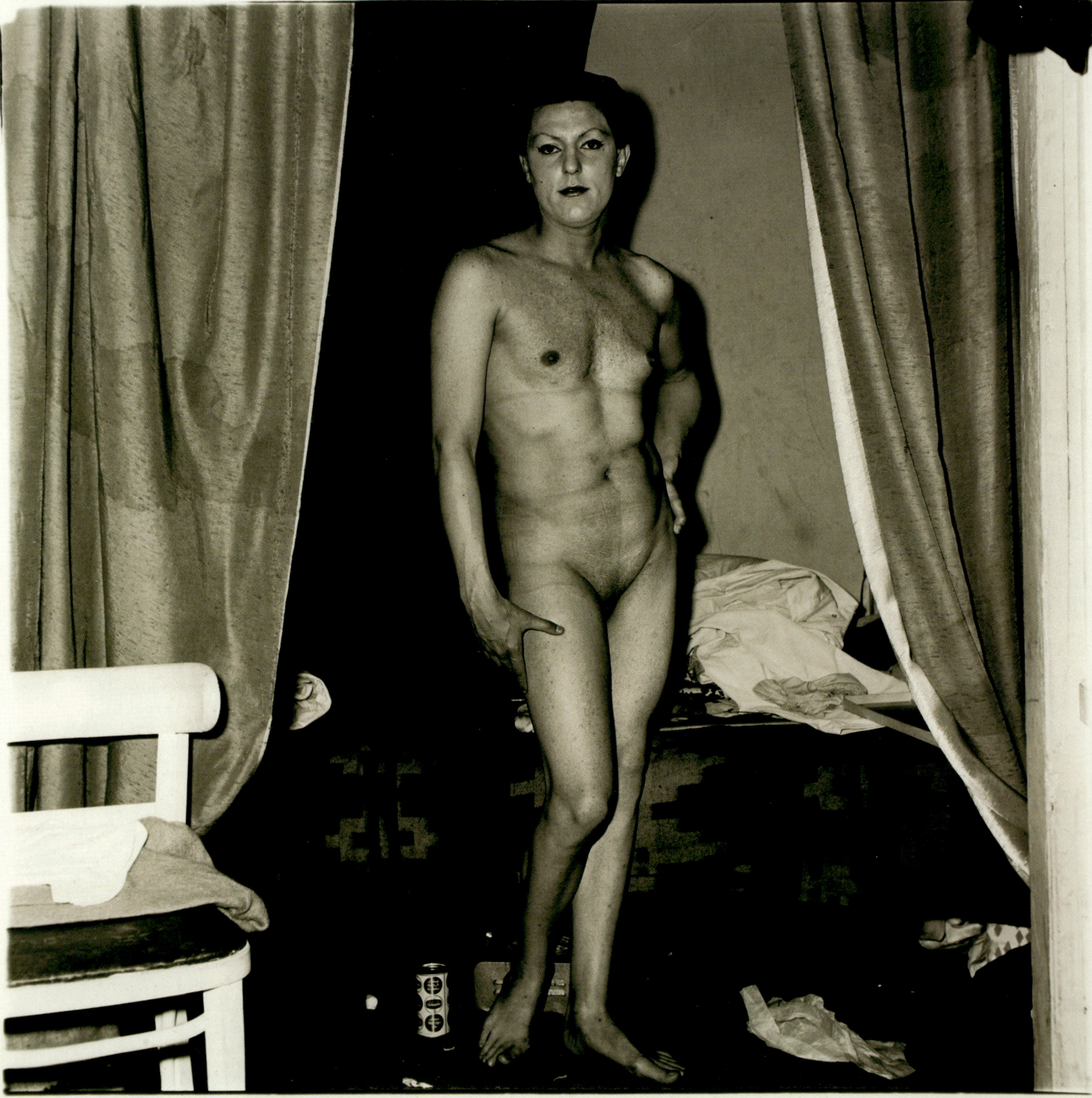

Chapter 8 Brief Encounters

119 Diane Arbus

A naked man being a woman, N.Y.C., 1968

Pompidou Centre, Paris

The work considered so far makes sense in relation to some intimate connection between artist and sitter (who might be one and the same). For the viewer, nakedness is a mark of the tenderness informing an artist's representation of their loved ones and justifies the exposure of their bodies to public scrutiny. But there is another strand in contemporary photography that arises from more fleeting, impersonal transactions between artist and subject. These works incorporate the familiar conventions of the portrait genre, and a portrait dimension is often explicit in the naming of sitters. Yet the images also possess a documentary or anthropological aspect. We are invited to scrutinise people who inhabit places or cultures alien to the typical art gallery spectator. Displays of nakedness may speak to a viewer's sense of universal humanity, but they could equally appeal to voyeuristic sensibilities. As with family imagery (see Chapter 5), much of the work under discussion has generated accusations that sitters are being exploited in the interests of spectacle. One commentator has claimed that 'cultural difference as vicarious thrill is the engine that drives burgeoning forms of self-absorption and voyeurism at play in the American media, entertainment industries, cyberspace, and art alike'.[1] This ambivalence is compounded by the difficulty we have in fathoming artists' motivations, and we are tempted to assume that some metaphorical intention is in play, and to jump to conclusions about meaning and morality.

A key to this version of naked portraiture, as for debates about its underlying ethics, is the work of Diane Arbus.[2] Nakedness, entire or partial, features in some of her most familiar photographs: *The Human Pincushion, Ronald C Harrison, N.J.* (1962), *Muscle man in his dressing room with trophy, Brooklyn, N.Y.C.* (1962), *Stripper with bare breast sitting in her dressing room, Atlantic City, N.J.* (1962), *A naked man being a woman, N.Y.C.* [plate 119], *Girl sitting on her bed with her shirt off, N.Y.C.* (1968), *Superstar at home, N.Y.C.* (1968), and *Mexican dwarf in his hotel room* (1970).[3] Arbus began by acknowledging sitters by name, but usually opted for descriptive titles, perhaps to protect people who had placed their trust in her. Such images went beyond the documentation of individual appearances. The subjects typified her obsessive interest in 'freakishness', which could encompass forms of sexuality or types of physique that ran counter to the norm. Nakedness reinforced the effect, signifying a willingness on the part of the sitter to transgress the perceived conformism of American life. Arbus's project took its cue from August Sander's anthropology of German society in the 1920s, but shifted the emphasis from the social mainstream to deviant subcultures.[4] Yet the iconic simplicity of Sander's imagery continues to resonate in works by Arbus such as *A naked man being a woman.*

Arbus's approach is typified by her nudist camp images. She made the first of several visits in July 1963: 'I had always wanted to go but I sort of didn't dare tell anybody … It was a terrific subject for me.'[5] Of the resulting pictures, *Retired man and his wife at home in a nudist camp one morning, N.J.* has always had a special place in the Arbus canon [plate 120].[6] The viewer's initial response is likely to be wry amusement. The living room is neat and tidy, and the items it contains conform to respectable middle-class taste. The couple return our gaze with cheery friendliness. Their body language is clichéd: he sinks back with masculine assurance into his throne, legs spread outwards and arms extended on either side of a substantial torso; meanwhile, she assumes the characteristic pose of female modesty, legs together and hands on lap, and the inclination of her body and more emphatic smile denote an instinct to engage with the third party present. The fact that they are otherwise completely naked is all that disrupts this conventional vision of domesticity, except that the framed pictures on the wall and TV also show naked people, and the girl floating above his head, like a thought bubble, is by no means as demure as his partner in everyday life. The joke is that people choosing to live in a permanently unclothed state might in all other respects behave and think just like everybody else.

She intended to publish several photos in a magazine, accompanied by her journalistic 'Notes on the Nudist Camp', though this never came to fruition.[7] Arbus wanted to transmit what their lifestyle meant to the nudists themselves. The director of the nudist camp, who met her off the bus, 'explained that it was a clean way to live. He wasn't, he assured me, trying to tell me that the human body was necessarily beautiful but that there was something clean about it.' Others dispelled any preconceptions that nudists were unusually attractive or promiscuous:

As one man put it, no one is a hundred percent perfectly formed … Everyone says sex is not a problem in a nudist camp. As one man said, 'It's what is left to the imagination that is obscene. Here nothing is left to the imagination'. As another man put it, 'Let's face it … most people don't look so good'.

Arbus noted how the continuities with life in mainstream society extended to personal accessories:

Most people are not entirely nude. Some ladies wear beach hats or sunglasses or wedgies and curlers or earrings and pocketbooks. In the cafeteria the teenage waitresses wear organdie demi-aprons. Some men have on only a wristwatch, or shoes and socks with their cigarettes and money tucked into their socks for safekeeping … Nudists aren't purists.[8]

She was struck too by the prevailing cosiness:

Everyone is very hospitable. The chairs and sofas in the parlors often have towels spread over the upholstery for people to sit down on. The pictures on the walls are mostly nudes, the flowers in the vases are mainly plastic, and the magazines on the coffee tables are largely girlie. Often in the evening, friends gather to play cards, drink orange pop, and watch TV together.

It is a good life. You turn one colour all over in the sun and the water feels fine. Everyone leaves their cares behind. It's a little like heaven.

Going off to nudist camps is presented as a latter-day version of the pastoral impulse, escaping the stress of urban life in favour of nature. Arbus acknowledged that such behaviour required courage: 'For many of these people, their presence here is the darkest secret of their lives, unsuspected by relatives, friends, and employers in the outside world, the disclosure of which might bring disgrace'. Yet, however fulfilling it might be, life within the camp is only a little bit like heaven. There are the irritants of intruders and peeping Toms, the problems of dealing with meter readers and the like. Her misgivings bracket the descriptive account. 'There is not much to it', she begins, 'It's like walking into an hallucination without being quite sure whose it is', an apposite gloss on the bizarreness and banality of nudist culture. The most downbeat note comes at the end, echoing the poignant sense of Paradise Lost in A *husband and wife in the woods at a nudist camp, N.J. (1963)*:

Sometimes you begin to wonder. There is an empty pop bottle or rusty bobby pin underfoot, the lake bottom oozes mud in a particularly nasty way … the outhouse smells, the woods look mangy. It is as if way back in the Garden of Eden, after the Fall, Adam and Eve had begged the Lord to forgive them; and God, in his boundless exasperation, had said, 'All right, stay. Stay in the Garden. Get civilised. Procreate. Muck it up'.

And they did.

For Arbus, photographing people involved 'a kind of exactitude, a kind of scrutiny we're not normally subject to … We're nicer to each other than the intervention of the camera is going to make us. It's a little bit cold, a little bit harsh.' Such scrutiny doesn't have to be 'mean', but 'it has to do with not evading facts, not evading what it really looks like'.[9] In their willingness to sit for her, notwithstanding the stigmas attaching to nakedness and the nudist subculture, and in their amiable expressions, we infer that the nudists succumbed to Arbus's charm. She admitted that her capacity to ingratiate herself was 'kind of two-faced'. An underlying detachment permitted Arbus to distil 'something ironic in the world', which she famously called 'the gap between intention and effect':

Everybody has that thing where they need to look one way but they come out looking another way and that's what people observe. You see someone… and essentially what you notice about them is the flaw. It's just extraordinary that we should have been given these peculiarities. And, not content with what we were given, we create a whole other set. Our whole guise is like giving a sign to the world to think of us in a certain way but there's a point between what you want people to know about you and what you can't help people knowing about you …[10]

She then goes on to distance herself from condescension or social satire: 'what I'm trying to describe is that it's impossible to get out of your skin into somebody else's. That somebody else's tragedy is not the same as your own'.[11] This matches the ambivalence in the viewer: 'There are two things that happen. One is recognition and the other is that it's totally peculiar. But there is some sense in which I always identify with them.'[12]

How does that stance operate in *Retired man and his wife*? We take in irony, but also light and composition. The strong sunlight outside is filtered by a net curtain and some kind of blind on the door to the patio.[13] These two areas of luminosity are extended by a shaft of light playing on the man's left shoulder and chest, and a wedge-like shaft that comes through the door and counteracts the diagonal direction of the floorboards and the rug on an axis connecting the seat of the sofa, the television screen and the girlie

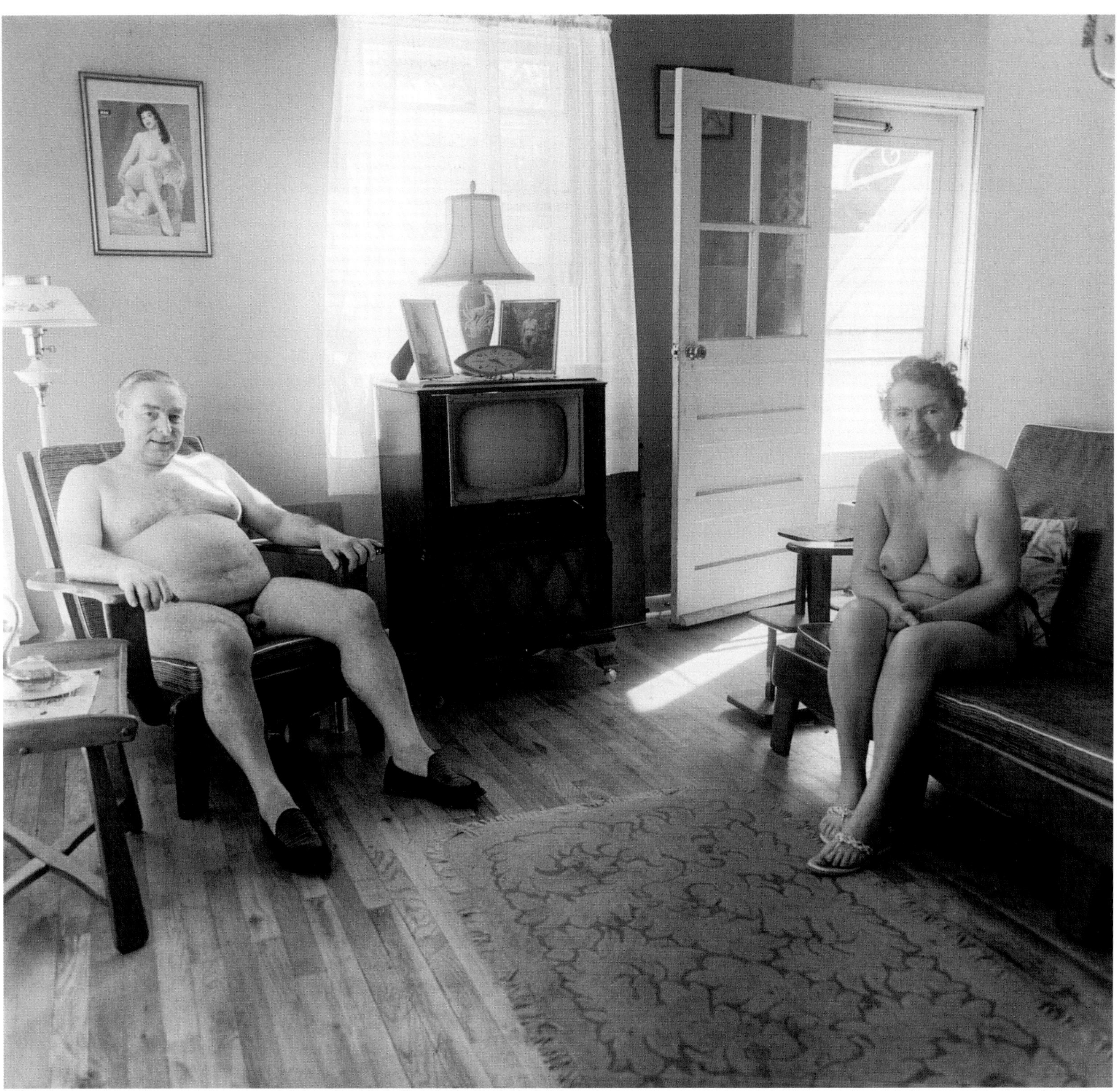

120 Diane Arbus

Retired man and his wife at home in a nudist camp one morning, N.J., 1963

Victoria & Albert Museum, London

picture on the wall. Contemplating a pure square, now the format of much of Arbus's work, induces a subliminal awareness of the transverse diagonals connecting opposite corners. Where these intersect corresponds roughly to the position of the television in the photographic image. But this is also the area of maximum darkness, a combination of the colour of the wood and the *contre-jour* shadow generated by the positioning of the cabinet in front of the window. The television is the fulcrum of the composition, and on top of it the lamp and photographs recapitulate the spatial organisation of the two figures and their furniture supports. The two figures themselves are symmetrically positioned in relation to both the vertical and horizontal edges of the design. The viewing position from which Arbus shot the scene, using a wide-angle lens, means that they are equidistant from us and balanced. The interior recedes at a slight angle, so that the open door provides a secondary light source against which the wife is silhouetted. In the coherence of its organisation, *Retired man and his wife* projects an image of harmonious coupledom, the same state of being that Arbus explored in photographs like *Husband and wife with shoes on in their cabin at a nudist camp, N.J.* (1963), and in *Teenage couple on Hudson St, N.Y.C.* (1963).[14] As an image of naked people, *Retired man and his wife* reflects a natural, uncomplicated way of life. The interior is simple and orderly, as opposed to a visual overload of wealth that cannot compensate for grief – compare, for example, *A widow in her bedroom, N.Y.C.* from the same year.[15] The image combines amused distance with a kind of envy. We are invited to set aside our initial cynicism, and to return the affectionate regard that the two subjects bestow on us. An idealising glow has been cast on these two individuals, on nudism as a way of life, and on the human capacity for acquiring the courage to be oneself, however absurd the result may look from the outside. We find the same qualities in *Stripper with bare breast sitting in her dressing room* (1962), *Seated man in bra and stockings* (1967), *A naked man being a woman* (1968) and *Mexican dwarf in his hotel room* (1970). Nakedness functions not as something erotically charged, but as the expression of an achieved state of being attuned to personal identity and psychological needs. We might extend to these works, as to the nudists, Arbus's commentary for an illustrated feature in November 1961:

These are five singular people who appear like metaphors somewhere further out than we do, beckoned, not driven, invented by belief, author and hero of a real dream by which our own courage and cunning are tried and tested; so that we may wonder all over again what is veritable and inevitable and possible and what it is to become whoever we may be.[16]

In 'In The American West' Avedon turned his camera to focus on the working class, blue collar workers, and out-of-work drifters. In the course of several trips to remote regions, he accumulated images of manual workers or those who had sunk into an economic underclass.[17] These individuals were portrayed in Avedon's characteristically large scale format, in unremitting detail, against his signature plain white backdrop [see plate 19]. The work has been read at one extreme as a bold exercise in social realism, a plea for the sympathy of the afluent majority towards the victims of economic change, and at the other (by Roger Bolton, for example) as a transformation of social victims into picturesque spectacle, or 'universal' tragic types, by a photographer aspiring above all to boost his own artistic reputation.[18]

His intention certainly goes beyond factual documentation. Avedon's symbolic concerns inform the half-length picture of *Ronald Fischer, Beekeeper*, whose body is indeed covered in bees [plate 121]. The staging of the work has recently been described by a collaborator:

A certain calmness came over both the photographer and the subject. Quietly, with hardly a word, Dick worked to heighten the surreal quality of the portrait. Fischer sensed what was required of him without quite understanding all that Dick intended. Over a two-day period, Ronald Fischer was photographed in three sessions, using 121 sheets of film. I think the portrait of the beeman makes it clear that as much as all these photographs may appear to be moments that just occurred, they are finally, in varying degrees, studied works of the imagination.[19]

Another passage reconstructs Avedon's thought processes in selecting the final image for the book:

In the end there were two choices. Each had a different meaning. Dick said, 'In this one (left), he feels the sting of the bees. He feels pain. He accepts suffering – like a Christian martyr. But in the other (right), he removes himself in a Buddhist way. He's oblivious to the stinging. That's the power of the picture for me. It speaks more directly to my understanding of how to endure, of how to prevail.[20]

In reality, we know from the accompanying documentary photographs Fischer was wearing trousers. He looks much more down to earth than anything this description suggests. The pretence of nakedness was essential to the metaphorical suggestion of vulnerability and its transcendence.

Americans such as Avedon, Arbus and Irving Penn had been the touchstones of contemporary photographic expression that Rineke Dijkstra had assimilated at art school in Holland. Like these precursors, she did commercial work for a few years, an experience from which she

121 Richard Avedon
Ronald Fischer, Beekeeper, Davis, California, 9 May, 1981
The Richard Avedon Foundation, New York

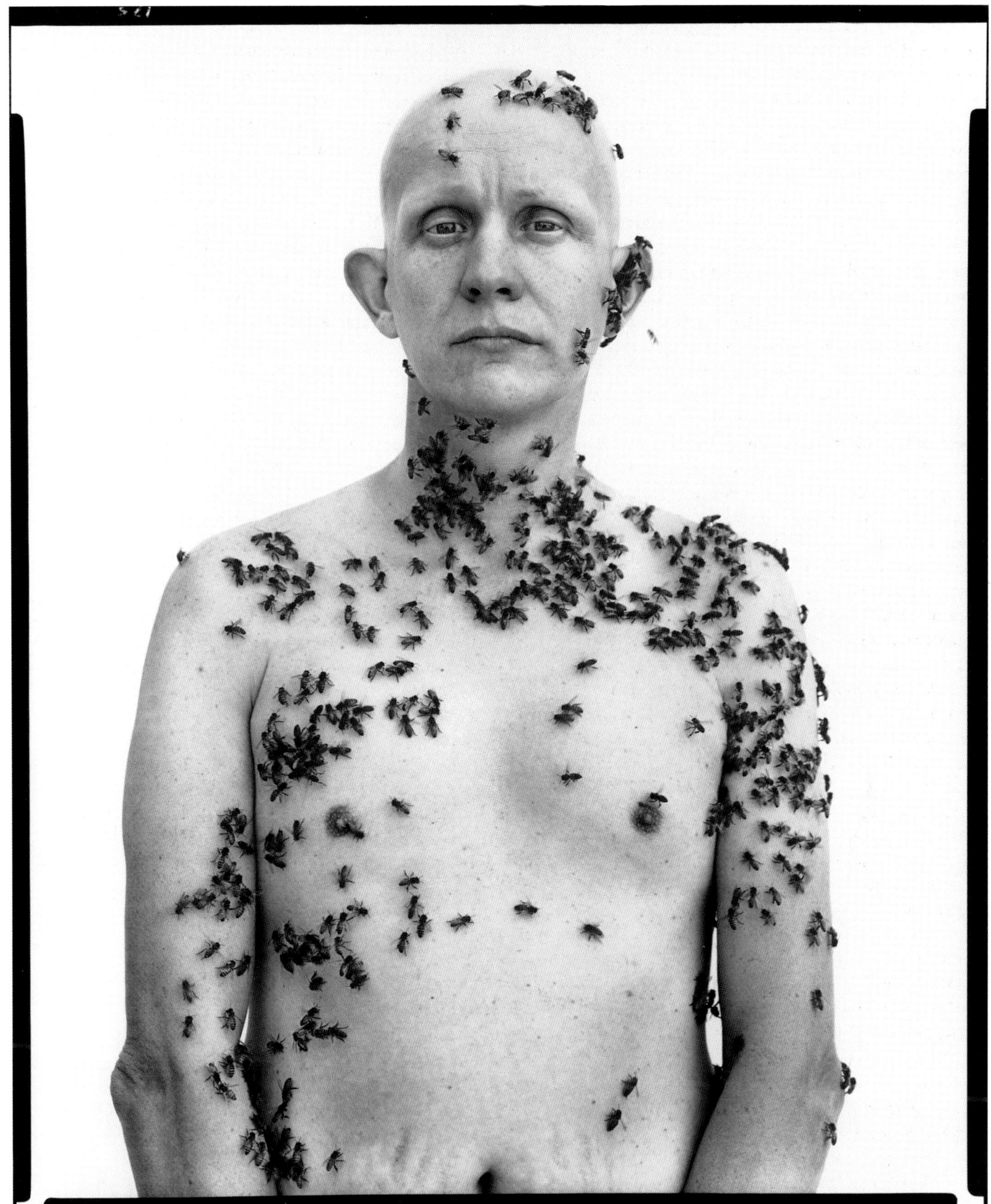

learned 'how to observe and how to grasp what someone is in a very brief moment', but also 'why I wanted to do my own work. The commissioned images were always portraits of a person rather than something more abstract or universal.[21] In her work as an independent artist, the decision about which images to use, from the many photographs taken, reflected her concern to distil 'an essential quality. I am always trying to find the image that has everything in it.'[22] Her engagement with female identity found expression in her exploration of the experience of motherhood. In her *New Mothers* series (1994), Dijkstra presented naked portraits of three young women protectively clutching their babies, printed in colour and almost life-size [plates 122, 123 and 124]. The simple compositions and white backdrops are reminiscent of Avedon. In Dijkstra's pictures, however, the settings serve not just to generate effects of extreme clarity, but also to situate the figures in the institutional environments in which giving birth tends to occur. The contrast between the extreme intimacy of an individual's experience of having a baby, and the impersonal spaces of the high-tech modern hospital is one of the contraries that Dijkstra explores in these works. She remarked: 'after seeing a friend of mine giving birth I realised that it was just completely different from what I expected. It's never uncomplicated – with both the mothers and the bullfighters I think it is this mix of emotions and conflicting feelings that interested me. What I find interesting is to show something very familiar ... but to try to show it differently'.[23]

These ambitions are manifest in her use of the serial format with its common denominators, within which the viewer can discern variations. The triptych form affirms the inevitable thought of Madonna and Child imagery, while the images convey the physical and mental specificity of what it feels like to have a baby. The scale of the photographs sustains the notion of an altarpiece and heightens the sense of human presence. We then encounter a narrative of three women photographed an hour, a day and a week after they have been through the intense experience of

left **122 Rineke Dijkstra**
Julie, Den Haag, Netherlands, 29 February, 1994

right **123 Rineke Dijkstra**
Tecla, Amsterdam, Netherlands, 16 May, 1994

opposite **124 Rineke Dijkstra**
Saskia, Harderwijk, Netherlands, 16 March, 1994

Courtesy of the Artist and Marian Goodman Gallery, New York

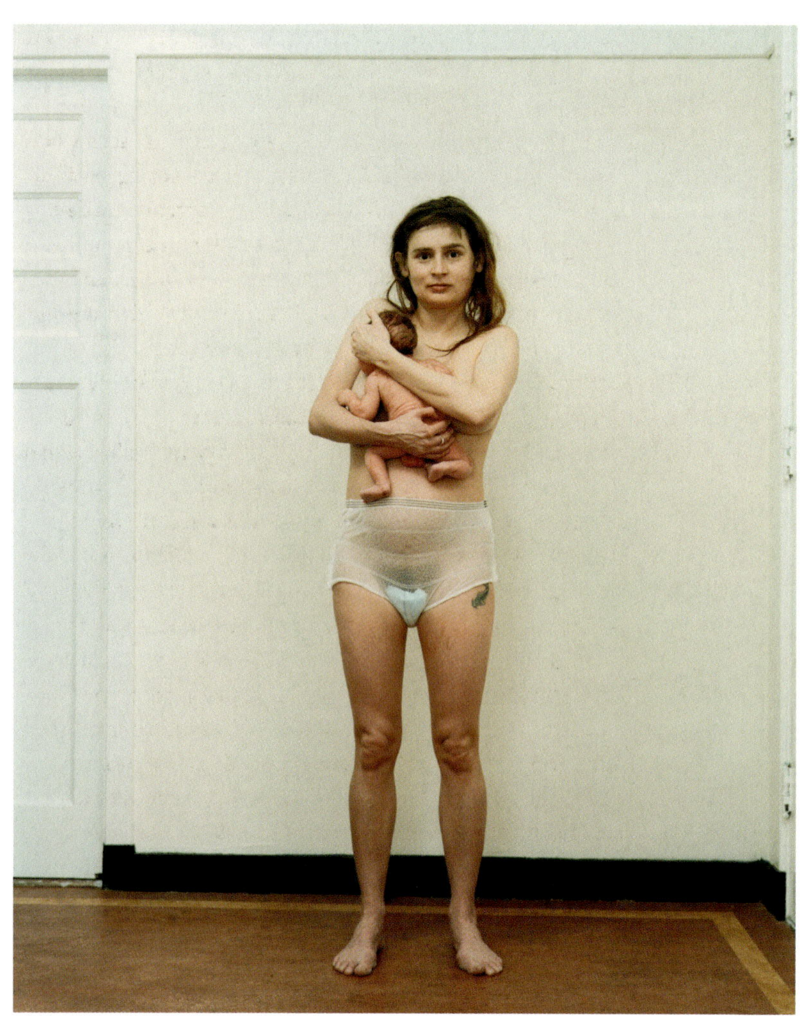

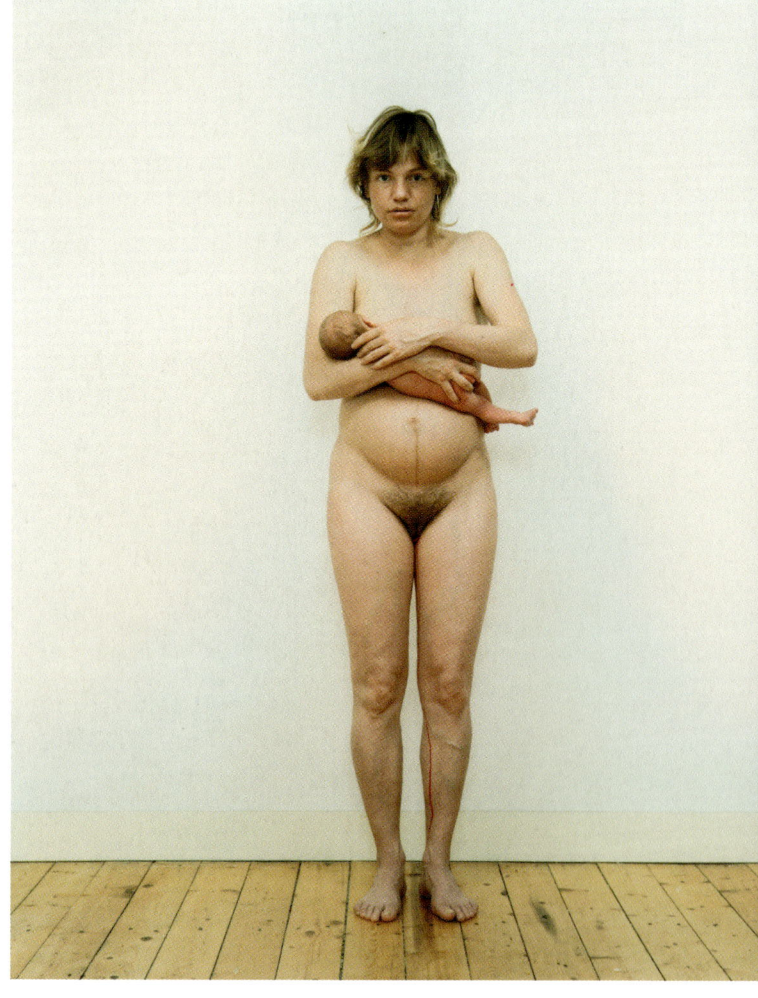

giving birth. The woman called Julie is the most hesitant and vulnerable, as though afraid she might drop her baby. Her excited look is belied by her pallor, untidy hair and by the tension in the muscles around her knees. The institutional pants and sanitary pad heighten our awareness that she has only very recently given birth. Tecla too betrays the physicality of the process, through the drip of blood that runs down the inside of her leg and the scar of her caesarean. She seems more confident holding her suckling baby, but the face communicates exhaustion and anxiety rather than euphoria. Saskia, with her neat, dark hair and exposed breast, returns our gaze almost primly. Her closed legs suggest that she has put the physical process of giving birth behind her, and has attained maternal serenity. Dijkstra has cited her interest in Arbus's idea of 'the gap between intention and effect': 'People think that they present themselves one way, but they cannot help but show something else as well. It's impossible to have *everything* under control. But when I try to photograph somebody, especially with the full body, it always makes them wonder "oh, what am I going to do with my hands etc".'[24]

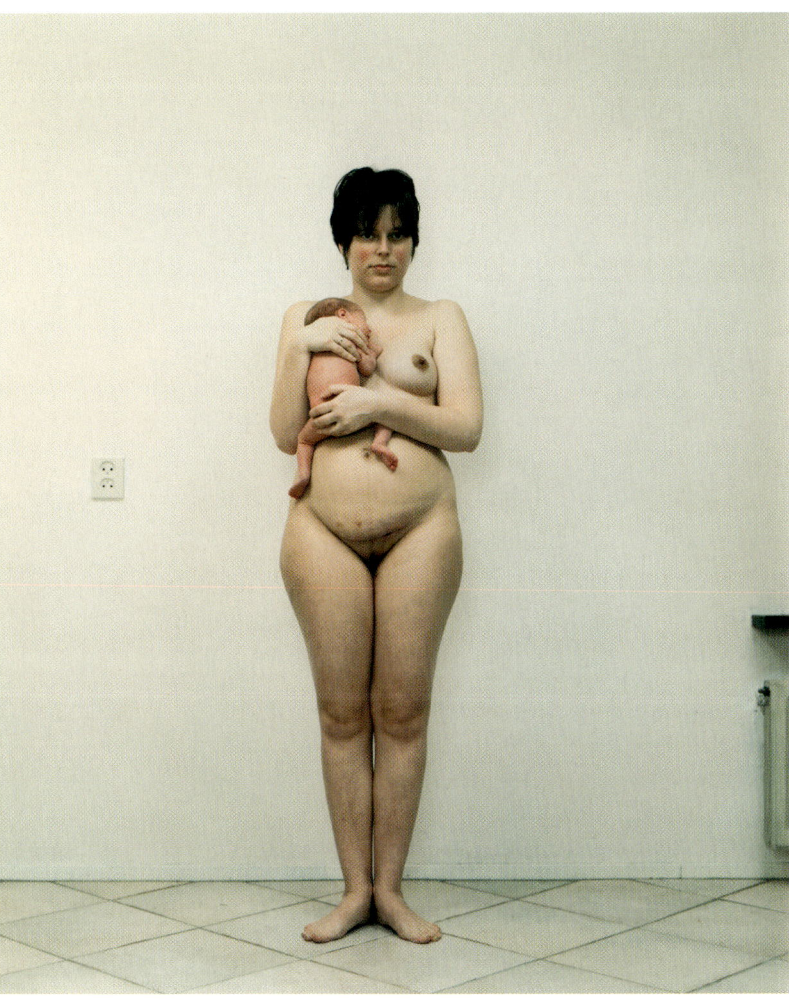

Avedon's *In the American West* provides a useful point of reference when we consider Boris Mikhailov's *Case History*, a sequence of around 500 photographs, made in the late 1990s, that have likewise been exhibited as large-scale prints and assembled into a book [plates 125, 126 and 127].[25] This project too straddles the divide between documentary and portraiture. Where the images come closest to portraiture in format, the sitters are often naked or, more typically, in varied states of undress. They display an array of bodies, complete with sores, growths and tattoos. The grotesque naked portrait could be said to be Mikhailov's singular contribution. Nudity was a longstanding preoccupation, in part because it had been forbidden to artists under the puritanical ethos of the Soviet Union, the system in which he grew up, worked as an engineer, and finally transformed himself into an experimental, dissident photographer. In a culture dominated by the idealising fantasies of Socialist Realism, it seemed important 'to reveal the ugly body, a normal body, not one where a person looks like a beautiful mannequin'. Pictures made at the beach demonstrated that 'the human body had changed. The hero had become fat, obese. He took vacations. He got naked and ceased being merely Soviet, or a social being.'[26] Mikhailov's concern to comprehend humanity in the raw reached its apogee, after the Soviet system had collapsed, with his creation of *Case History*. Here he represented the community of homeless people ('*bomzhes*') in Kharkov, a provincial Ukrainian city, formerly a centre of weapons production, and Mikhailov's home town. The new political freedoms allowed him to begin to divide his time between there and Berlin. Returning after a year abroad, he encountered not the improvements to the quality of life that he was expecting, but rather the onset of 'social disaster and a new social class', whose desperate fate was received with callous indifference.[27] Mikhailov set out to provide a searing account of what life was like for the victims of the transition from Communism to Capitalism, which happened without the safety-nets taken for granted in the West – 'we never saw so many people lying on the ground, hitting the bottom before'.[28]

Despite the fact that Avedon and Mikhailov depicted people ravaged by poverty, violence and disease, the approaches in *Case History* and *In the American West* are very different. On the face of it, the work of Mikhailov heightens Avedon's clinical detachment and his treatment of his sitters as aesthetic and social specimens. Mikhailov's cast of individuals is more animated, and they are characterised over sequences of several images, sometimes alone and sometimes interacting with one another. The homeless are situated in their everyday environments of urban wasteland, or in interior spaces which seem to be the artist's own apartment. The circumstantial detail signals a closer engagement with his sitter's lives than Avedon's neutral backdrops. The sense of raw actuality is intensified by Mikhailov's snapshot-like informality. This marked a departure from the ironic, montage strategies of much of his previous work, as did his turn to colour. He exploited the new availability of Western commercial processing, but subverted its association with the clichés of social ritual and pleasure. In terms of photographic idiom, there is more of an affinity with Nan Goldin, which is not necessarily accidental given Mikhailov's increasing contacts with the international art world.

Case History was a contribution to raising awareness, especially in the West, of the appalling human cost of what tended to be regarded as the defeat of Communism. Nevertheless, Mikhailov too has been accused of exploiting those who modelled for him, in the interests of artistic sensationalism.[29] Critics have reworked the line that Susan Sontag and others had taken on Arbus, namely that such photography, in its unremitting but ultimately picturesque presentation of the horrifying, was working to diminish our capacity for compassion.[30] This was anticipated in Mikhailov's essay for *Case History*. He recorded his impulse to encapsulate a particular moment of 'social oppression and helplessness', which soon led to deaths amongst those he was encountering; 'taking pictures of poverty' he noted, 'was my professional and civic duty'.[31] There were few images to document the millions of deaths in the Ukrainian famine of the 1930s or in the Second World War, but ideological constraints no longer existed to prevent him from recording the tragic events of the present. He described trying to help the people he encountered, and giving them money to pose for him, a financial transaction that mimicked the new social order. Given that 'manipulating with money' was the 'new way of legal relations in all areas of the former USSR', he wanted to demonstrate the fact that 'people can be openly manipulated', and in the making of his work to 'perform the same relations which exist in society'.[32]

With Avedon, individuals are named and defined by their social roles, which gives the works journalistic vividness. Mikhailov avoids giving any verbal accompaniment. This implies that the figures have lost their identity within the social structure. His refusal to particularise also invites the viewer to see his sitters not just as poignant individuals but also as archetypes, a dimension reinforced by the performances of familiar religious or artistic themes that critics have discerned in *Case History*.[33] Certainly, the tragic sensibility manifest in Mikhailov's photographs is rooted in Russian literary traditions. Out of the ruins of Socialist Realism, let alone of a centralised socialist system, *Case History* reinvents an older artistic and literary tradition of social realism. Mikhailov has acknowledged how he found echoes of *The Lower Depths*, Maxim Gorky's 1902 play, in the spectacle of present-day Kharkov. Such continuities are appropriate, given that *Case History* portrays a layer of contemporary society that has in a sense regressed to the condition of the pre-Revolutionary peasantry.

The exposure of the body is the most overtly staged aspect of *Case History*. We regularly encounter individuals, whether old or young, male or female, simply facing the viewer and lifting up dresses or taking down trousers, to expose their breasts, torsos or genitals, in a grotesque parody of striptease or exhibitionism. Underwear is ubiquitous. The artist appears in front of the figures in certain images; he kneels and looks hard as he photographs a girl revealing her torso.[34] In a gesture of identification Mikhailov appears naked in the bath.[35] The images acknowledge that as performers his subjects will do anything for money, but are also complicit in Mikhailov's assertion of their humanity, beneath the façade of social degradation. He stated that his intention in *Case History* was not 'to spy on those whom nobody would like to see', but rather to 'help the model or the situation itself to say – "Here I am"'.[36] The book opens with a short series titled *The Requiem*, devoted to a group of homeless people who had died within two months of the pictures being taken: 'I took the pictures displaying naked people with their things in their hands like people going to gas chambers. They agreed to pose for a so-called historical theme. They agreed that their photos would be published in magazines for others to learn about their lives'.[37] Nakedness, then, encapsulates their suffering and tenuous hold on life, and asserts how far they had been stripped of their dignity. These opening images foreshadow many others in Case History:

After The Requiem, *the idea stuck in my mind to go on taking photos of the naked. Maybe I was driven by the old complex connected with the ban on photographing the naked, which was now connected with the notion of 'nakedness of life itself'. People got undressed, naked and took away the barrier of their dirty, ponging clothes, built between them and others. I was interested in what would happen to a face when a body gets undressed. But sometimes they, simply as people of the 'new' morality, exposed their 'values'. When naked, they stood like people.*[38]

This compassion is paralleled in the very different, sculptural work of Marc Quinn. The genesis of his naked portraiture of the disabled, or people with acute illnesses,

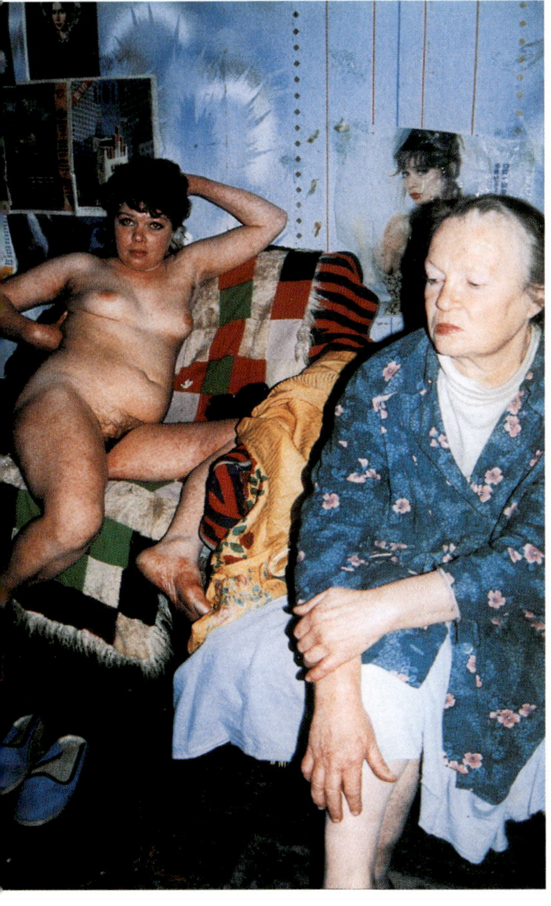
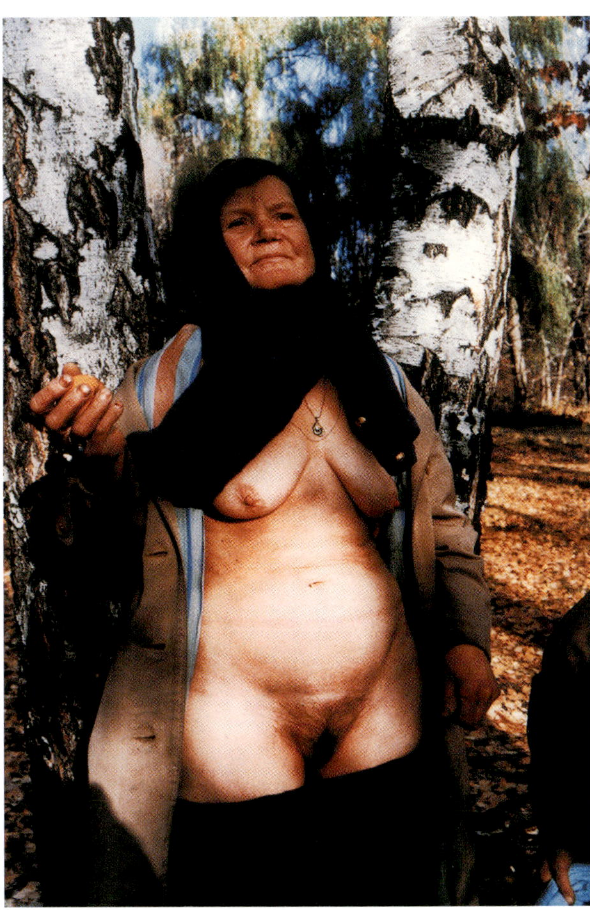
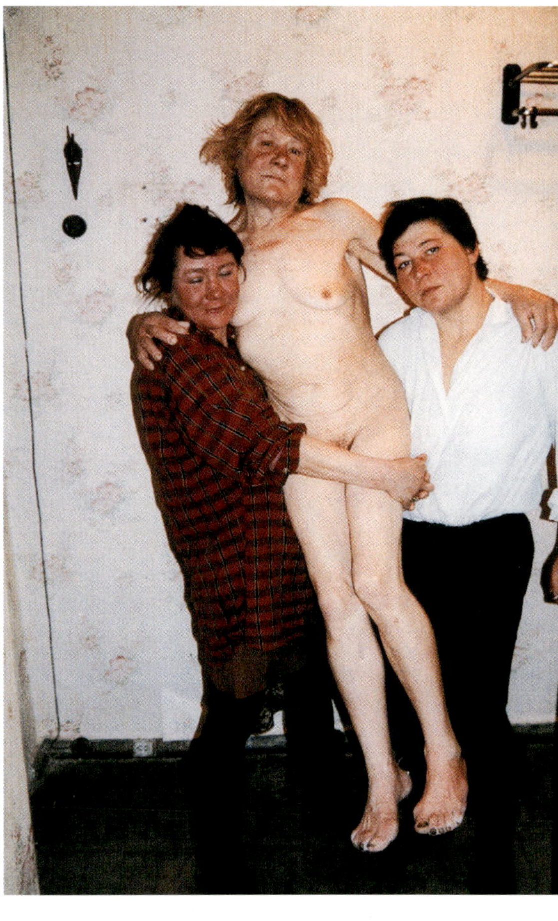

125 Boris Mikhailov
Untitled (from *Case History*), 1998
The Saatchi Gallery, London

126 Boris Mikhailov
Untitled (from *Case History*), 1998
The Saatchi Gallery, London

127 Boris Mikhailov
Untitled (from *Case History*), 1998
The Saatchi Gallery, London

was a visit to the galleries of classical sculpture in the British Museum, and his realisation of a dichotomy in our society. We place the highest cultural and aesthetic value on Greek and Roman statues, which in most cases are missing parts of the body due to the vicissitudes of time, but which are the basis, paradoxically, of the concept of a perfectly-proportioned human body. Despite the missing bits, we have no difficulty in compensating and seeing the *Venus de Milo* as an aesthetic whole. Yet we regard people who are lacking a limb, for whatever reason, as imperfect and ugly, something from which we instinctively recoil. Quinn's response was to produce a series of large-scale sculptures depicting disabled people he approached, such as *Catherine Long*, an art therapist and performance artist, who happens to be lacking her left arm [plate 128]. By using the characteristic white marble and body language of classical statues, Quinn confers on his sitters a heroic status traditionally reserved for the great and the good. We are invited to admire those we might shun in everyday life and at the same time question our prejudice that an 'imperfect' body contains an inadequate being. Quinn's project culminated in the huge, white marble statue of Alison Lapper, when she was eight months pregnant, installed for several months on the empty fourth plinth in Trafalgar Square. The work reinforces the classical aura of its surroundings, and yet undermines the values invested in classicism. As Quinn has remarked:

At first glance it would seem that there are few if any public sculptures of people with disabilities. However, a closer look reveals that Trafalgar Square is one of the few public spaces where one exists: Nelson on top of his column has lost an arm. I think that Alison's portrait reactivates this dormant aspect of Trafalgar Square. Most public sculpture, especially in the Trafalgar Square and Whitehall areas, is triumphant male statuary. Nelson's Column is the epitome of a phallic male monument and I felt that the square needed some femininity … In the past, heroes such as Nelson conquered the outside world. Now it seems to me they conquer their own circumstances and the prejudices of others, and I believe that Alison's portrait will symbolise this … Her pregnancy also makes this a monument to the possibilities of the future.[39]

A variation on the theme is Quinn's subsequent *Chemical Life Support* series, life -size naked portraits of several individuals who keep at bay some chronic illness (such as

HIV or diabetes) by using a particular drug, which is also mixed into the polymer wax from which the sculptures are cast.[40] Here, the bodies look 'normal' and it is only the titles that indicate the fragility of these people's lives, which is only an extension of our collective reliance on obscure, hidden bodily processes, which sustain us for some unpredictable but ultimately fleeting span of life. The ghostly pure white of the sculptures reinforces their pathos.

It is in photographic projects, however, that we more often encounter naked portraiture based on initially casual relations between artist and sitter. The most conventional in conception is *Bailey's Democracy* (2005), a portfolio of naked portraits by the veteran fashion photographer [plates 5 and 63]. The sitters are identified by their full names and their occupation. Many, though by no means all, are models and actors, the kinds of people less worried about exposing their bodies than the rest of us. Bailey let it be known that he was working on this project, and individuals volunteered. They could take up whatever postures or gestures they chose, while Bailey insisted on the uniform format and lighting, and on complete nakedness, including the removal of jewellery and other adornments. He also reserved the right to choose which of the six pictures taken during the ten–minute session would eventually be used. The resulting photographs are black and white, and the backgrounds are a consistent flat white. Apart from the nakedness, they do not depart radically from the conventions of his own work since the 1960s and post-war photographic portraiture generally, with its strong conection to fashion and commercial magazine imagery. The sitters perform for the camera, striking poses, gestures and expressions that often convey a lack of inhibition, and sometimes with a flirtatiousness that matches their nakedness. We also encounter an animal vitality; and the essay in the book is by Desmond Morris, who has been talking for decades about the behavioural affinities between people and animals. *Bailey's Democracy* implies that we are all singular and mortal bodies, before we choose to construct our personal, social or gender identities. For Morris, the project 'forces the viewer … to confront the human form in the most direct and searingly honest way imaginable … What you see here is the stark reality of the human condition.'[41]

In other work, it has to be said, the human reality looks considerably more stark. Katy Grannan's *American Models* (2005) includes a fair proportion of nudes in her compilation of portraits. At first they were usually presented impersonally, but later on titles gave first names and places (mostly small-town New England). The sitters were often people who responded to adverts placed in local newspapers, stating merely that she was a female photographer who wanted to make pictures of people in their homes or chosen surroundings. The majority are young and female, but there are plenty of exceptions. Many are shown in tawdry interiors, while others were photographed in the landscape. Location, body language, characterisation, and costume, or the lack of it, are all decisions negotiated by two strangers, engaged in a brief collaboration from which each derives their own satisfaction. Both the people and the settings often end up looking remote from the glamour and self-assurance of advertisements. The sitters give the impression that their performance is quite an intense and risky experience for them, especially when they are naked. Yet, because they are amateurs at modelling and self-projection, less of their feeling is communicated than we would get in the contrived expressions of the professional role-player. They come across as wooden and inhibited. As Grannan remarked, 'so many portraits work when they are difficult: we believe we're presenting ourselves one way, but the camera always reveals something more vulnerable, despite our best efforts'.[42] We are back in the gap between intention and effect. Grannan's subjects may seem mute and marginal, but, as in Arbus, they challenge us 'to acknowledge the ordinariness of our own lives and how much we're prepared to identify with people who decide, for one reason or another, to take Grannan into their confidence and to reveal themselves to a perfect stranger'.[43] Grannan concedes the inspiration: 'Arbus is one of those artists I think about a lot and am intimately aware of. Her portraits can be very difficult, but there is a tremendous amount of affection, of love, for her subjects: they're never simple.'[44]

There is complexity of a different sort in Philip-Lorca diCorcia's *Lucky Thirteen* series, first exhibited in 2004 [plates 129 and 130]. In these large-scale images of pole-dancers, all are identified by their first (possibly stage) names, and most are posed upside down, in the context of the stage sets and spotlights of their working environment. But silent, static images are very different from the movement and noise associated with such a spectacle. For the gallery audience rather than the girls' usual audience the images might suggest the dramatic chiaroscuro and body language of an artist like Caravaggio. We might detect an echo of the contorted poses of martyred saints in Baroque altarpieces. The images also have tremendous sculptural presence. They read as portraits, evoking an inner life beyond the staged façade of sexual titillation. This concern for the person behind the performance brings to mind works by Arbus such as *Stripper with bare breast sitting in her dressing room, Atlantic City, N.J.* (1962). One critic remarked on diCorcia's departure from the traditional passivity of the nude:

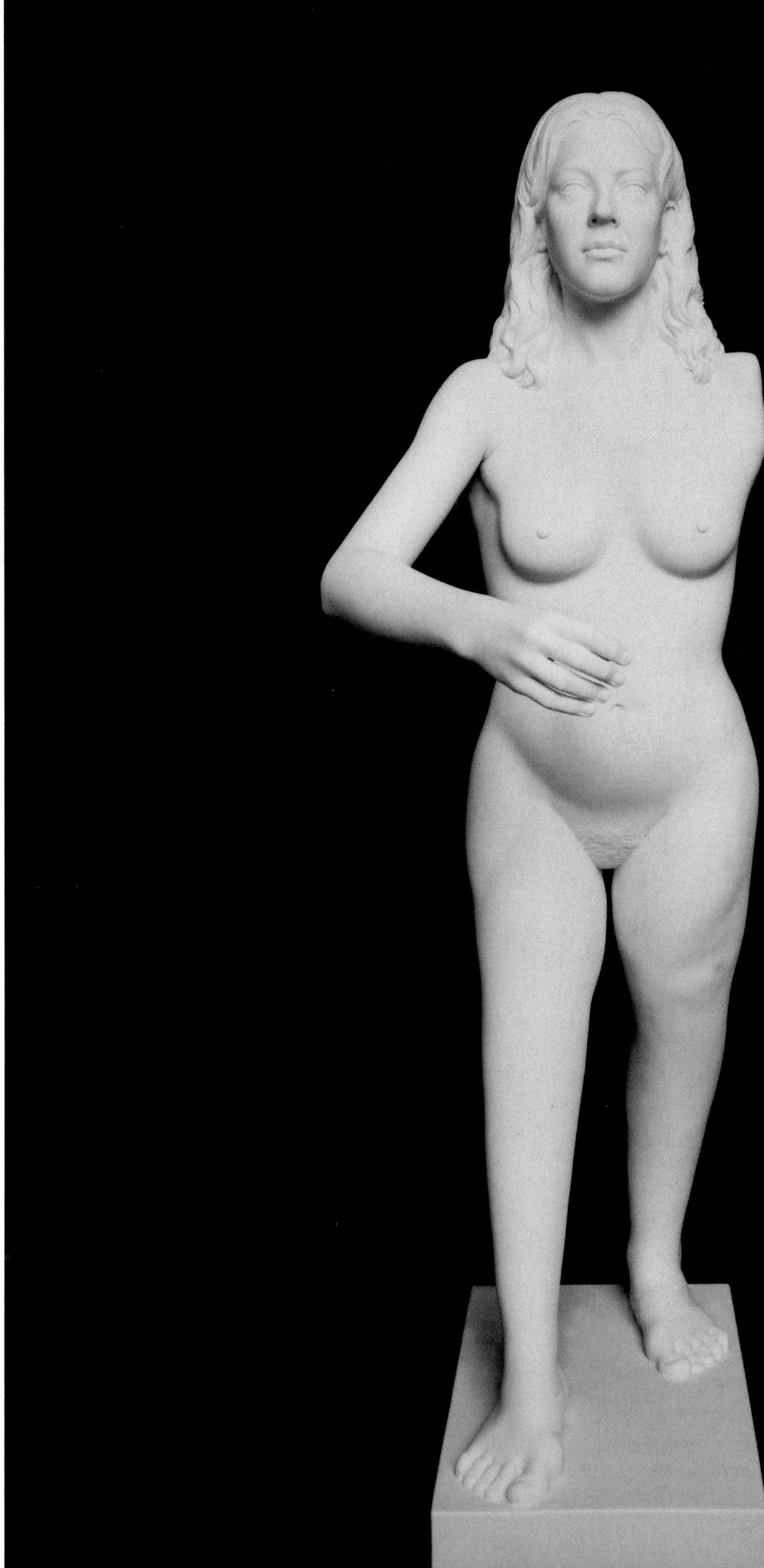

128 Marc Quinn

Catherine Long, 2002

Leamington Spa Art Gallery and Museum (Warwick District Council)

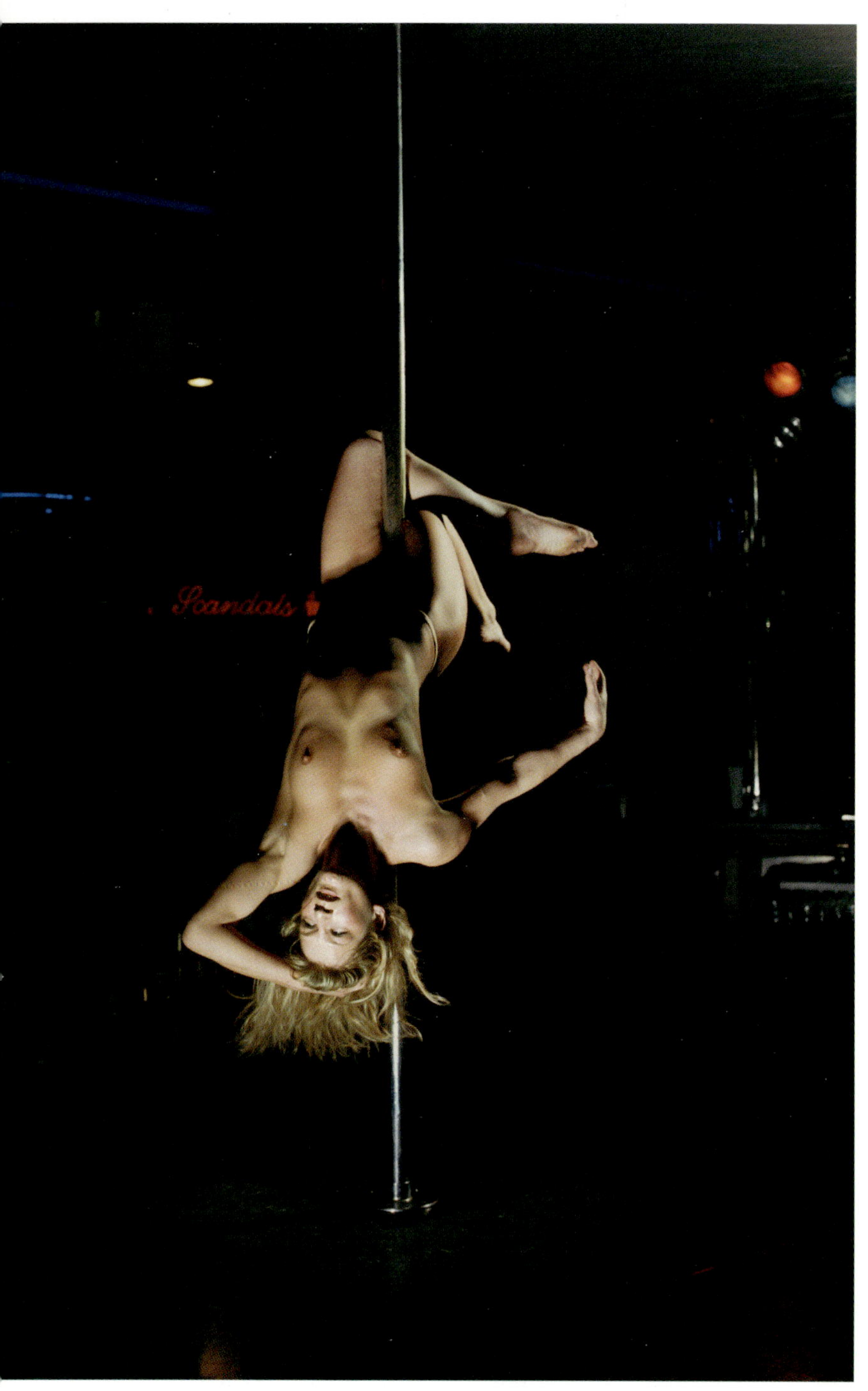

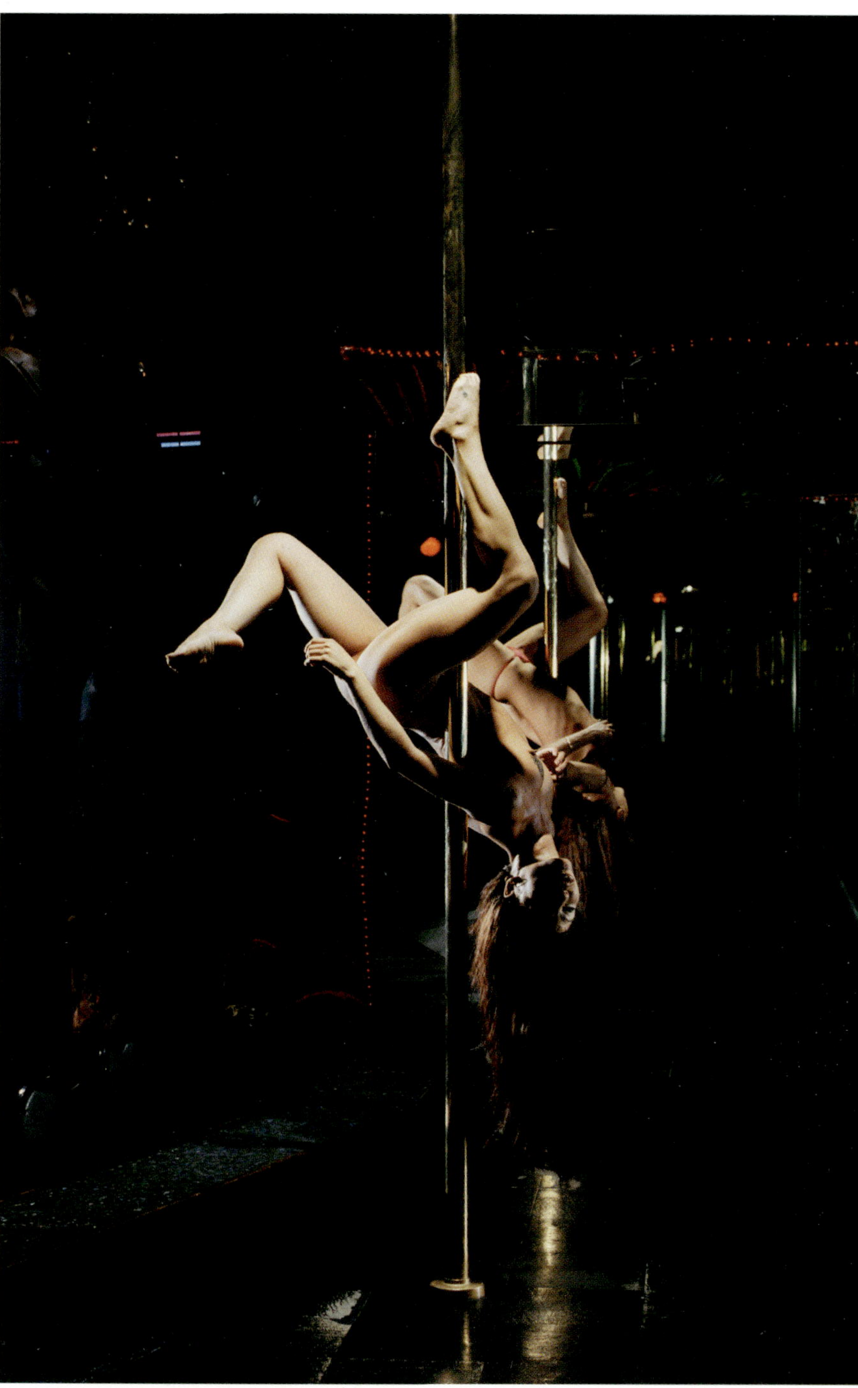

left **129 Philip-Lorca diCorcia** Tennille, 2004

Courtesy the Artist and Pace / MacGill Gallery, New York

right **130 Philip-Lorca diCorcia** Lola, 2004

Courtesy the Artist and Pace / MacGill Gallery, New York

These women are in action, which gives them a sort of power. You have to respect the athleticism of their performance. DiCorcia catches them in incredible poses, holding themselves in the air with one hand on the pole, with two legs wrapped on the pole, with one leg wrapped around the pole, with what looks like nothing ... This light shows dust on the soles of their feet, wrinkles, scars, the sheen of sweat on a dancer's chest, and the way that the pole tugs at the skin of another woman's stomach. It makes them human. It also emphasizes their remarkable physical strength. These women have muscles: *pronounced, tensed, capable muscles, the lines of which are shown up by the black shadows cast in that hard white light. They've arranged their practiced bodies into states of extraordinary grace ... DiCorcia doesn't portray them as desired bodies, or debated bodies, but rather as extraordinary examples of the human body and its potential.*[45]

DiCorcia's interest in humanising bodies that have been reduced to sexual objects finds a parallel in Jean-Luc Moulene's *Les Filles d'Amsterdam* series (2005), large photographs of prostitutes who simply sit and confront the viewer, their genitals fully exposed but with no hint of titillation. In Melanie Manchot's video installation *Security*, a female artist engages with sexually charged male subjects.[46] A line of seven small monitors shows individual bouncers standing impassively outside their clubs in Ibiza. The doors are closed, the daytime sun is shining, and the young men just stand there, fidgeting and looking macho. A second element is a large video projection in which each of the men, now life-size, is shown performing for a few minutes, one after the other, to the accompaniment of traffic noise [plate 131]. To our initial surprise, they take off all their clothes and accoutrements, pose for a time completely naked, then get dressed again and resume their stations. The men give no awareness of an audience; either they were performing for a camera and tripod, which had been set up and left running – or they were behaving as though this were the case. The intimacy and anthropological detachment suggests an affinity with Dijkstra. In her variation on this aesthetic, Manchot offers a wry, disconcerting parody of the familiar routine of the striptease, itself stripped, as it were, of the familiar elements of theatricality and eroticism.

The effect of *Security* is absurd, but also touching. The security men expose (literally and metaphorically) their masculine, or simply human, insecurities. As they perform their task, they manifest varying degrees of awkwardness as they remove clothing and jewellery. They stand there for a while showing their all (or sometimes covering up their genitals in embarrassment). The body beautiful and macho style they have cultivated are revealed as a façade, covering up anxieties about who might see their naked bodies in a public environment and then, bizarrely, on display as a work of art. Given the sculptural beauty of their bodies, and the 'sensitivity' of their behaviour, *Security* could also be interpreted as a female take on the genres of the nude and the striptease.

Security demonstrates that people reveal their inner selves not just through the constructed façade, the common currency of the genre, but also through involuntary gestures and facial expressions which become apparent thanks to the combination of a challenging, unfamiliar task, and the use of a recording medium that incorporates time. Manchot remarks: 'Maybe the portrait can happen more successfully through the accumulation of different layers in the work: a layer of the personal and public protagonist, location and gesture.'[47] She is concerned to explore both 'our expectations of what a portrait can deliver and the limitations and failures that are inherent in images'.[48] Such failings should be borne in mind when we encounter viewers who find a lack of humanity in Arbus and her successors works, where others discern compassion. The contradiction also says something about the limits to psychological communication in portraiture.

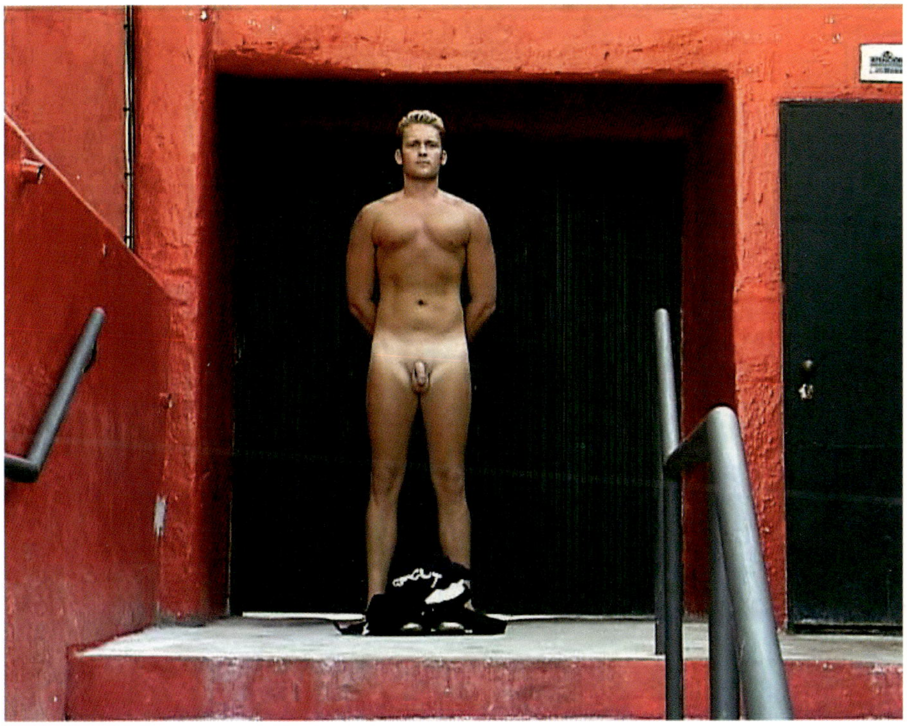

131 Melanie Manchot
Chris, video still from Security, 2006
Fred (London) Ltd and the Artist

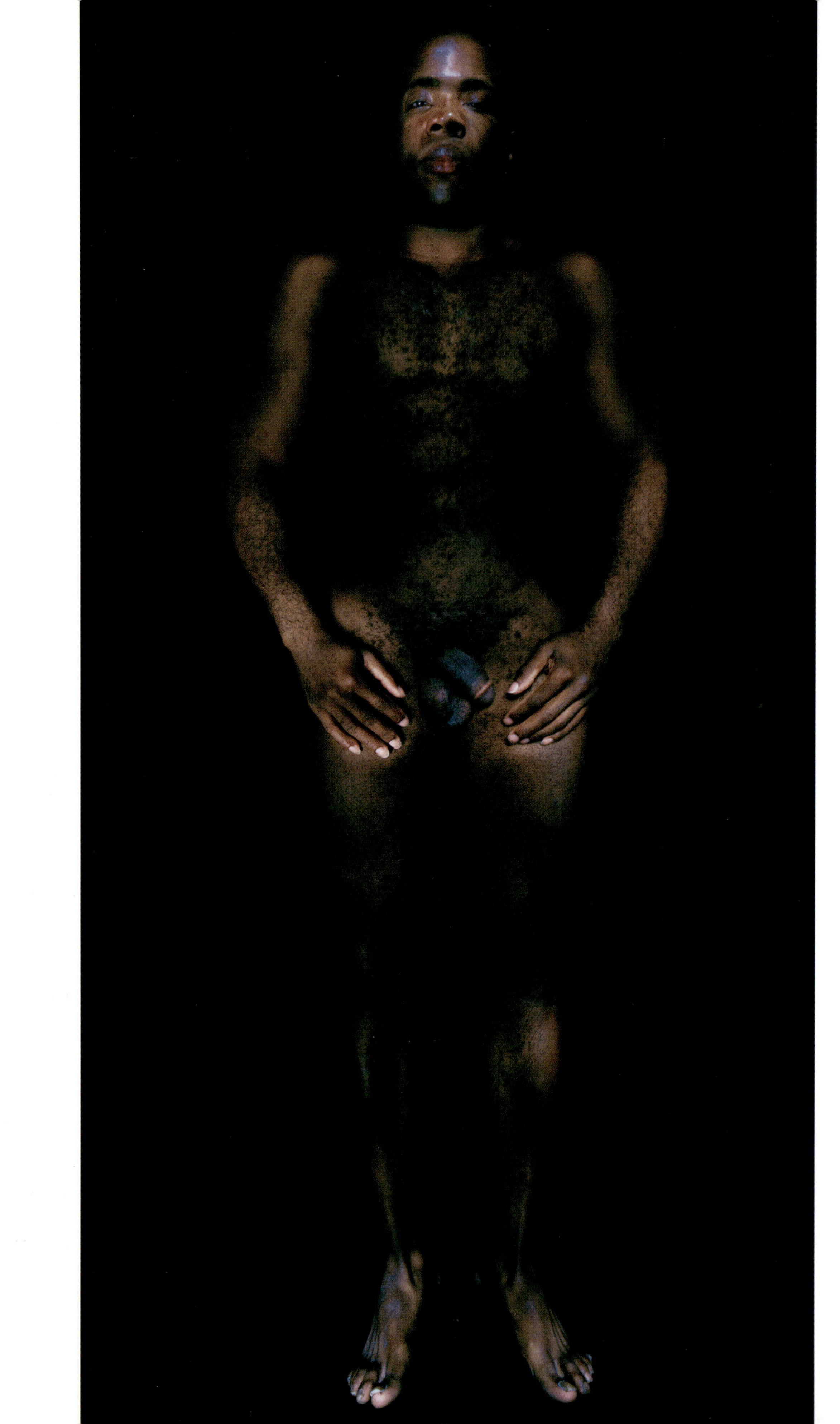

Chapter 9 Time and Motion

132 Gary Schneider
Donald, 2004
Courtesy the Artist

How might a photographic artist work in opposition to the clichés of the portrait genre, and its pretensions to capture something essential about an individual in a single, instantaneous image? Two recent projects using full-length naked figures illustrate very different possibilities. In Gary Schneider's *Nudes*, first exhibited in New York in 2005, the sitters are presented at near life-size emerging from black grounds [plates 132–6]. They are announced simply by their first names. Their images are printed onto textured canvas supports, and Schneider prefers to hang them unglazed, in simple strip frames, as close to the floor as practical. Their effect is a product of the unconventional method by which the pictures were produced. For the viewer, the sitters confront us vertically from the wall plane. But for the artist they were lying flat, looking up at a camera fixed above them whose lens was opened up for approximately an hour. Schneider describes the details of the procedure:

In 1989 I began working in total darkness, using a small flashlight as the sole light source to create a series of close-up portraits of friends' faces. By the end of 2001 I had become so adept at counting light that it became possible to sustain an exposure for the hour or so required to explore an entire human figure. I count out loud – it becomes a chanting meditation for me, and my subject becomes as involved in my performance as I am in theirs. The only task I ask of my subjects is to gaze towards the lens. I take notice if my subject has a fixed stare or is trying to pose. To break the camera face, I have different strategies. I count, make comments, make the subject blink while exposing each eye, and so on.

The information is accumulated sequentially on one sheet of film. Just as a movie unfolds in real time, so I build an image by exposing one part of the person after another with my tiny light. If I add more light, it emphasises the body part; conversely, not enough light and that area never becomes visible. I expose the parts of the body in the same sequence in order to exaggerate the differences between each person's performance. I start with the head, move down the right side of the body, then up the left side. In all the portraits there is an interesting shift in the gaze, from the right eye looking outwards, to the left eye looking inward. This is a result of the long interval between the two eyes.

What happens during the session remains private, an intimate act between me and the subject. There is an enormous amount of information accumulated during the session, both emotional and physical. The accumulation of all this information is impossible to interpret simply or decisively. There are so many variables.[1]

The process sounds ritualistic, and the overall format of the portraits is a constant. In each work, the body possesses a powerful corporeal solidity, and richness of anatomical detail, but at the same time it dissolves into the seemingly arbitrary play of light, almost hovering and without the familiar indications of feet rooting the figure to a ground plane. Many of the details of the body are vividly real, but the transposition from horizontal to vertical produces a disconcerting anatomical distortion, especially in the more ample figures. Schneider denies any expressive intent: 'What can be read as awkwardness or distortion or angularity, which looks like discomfort, is perspective: where my camera is in relation to the body, and because the body is supine.'[2] The impassivity of the sitters, who do not assume clear-cut, readily legible expressions and gestures, is subtly qualified by conscious or involuntary movements, such as a blinking eye, the arousal of a penis, or even in one instance a baby moving within its mother's womb. Signs of life and consciousness, indications of movement and, above all, the intently staring eyes, are countered by implications of mortality in a body that is lying flat (something we soon deduce), which might also suggest a figure in a coffin or on a tombstone, or mortuary slab. Such intimations are also implicit in the pitch black setting in which the figures float. Some viewers have noted an affinity with the images of the body generated by MRI scanning.

Schneider's nudes may seem idiosyncratic in the context

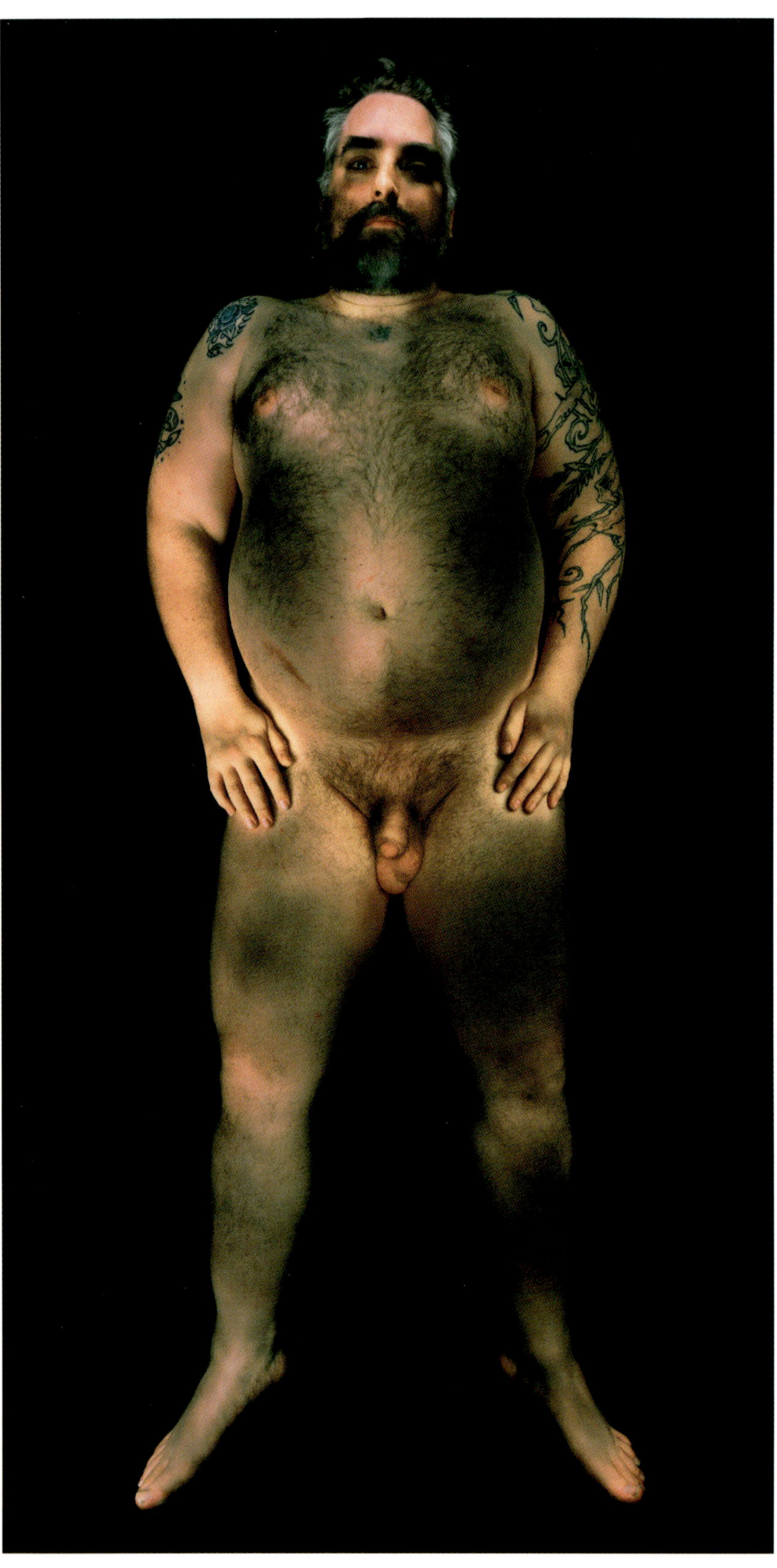

133 Gary Schneider Nayland, 2004

Courtesy the Artist

134 Gary Schneider Terrell, 2004

Courtesy the Artist

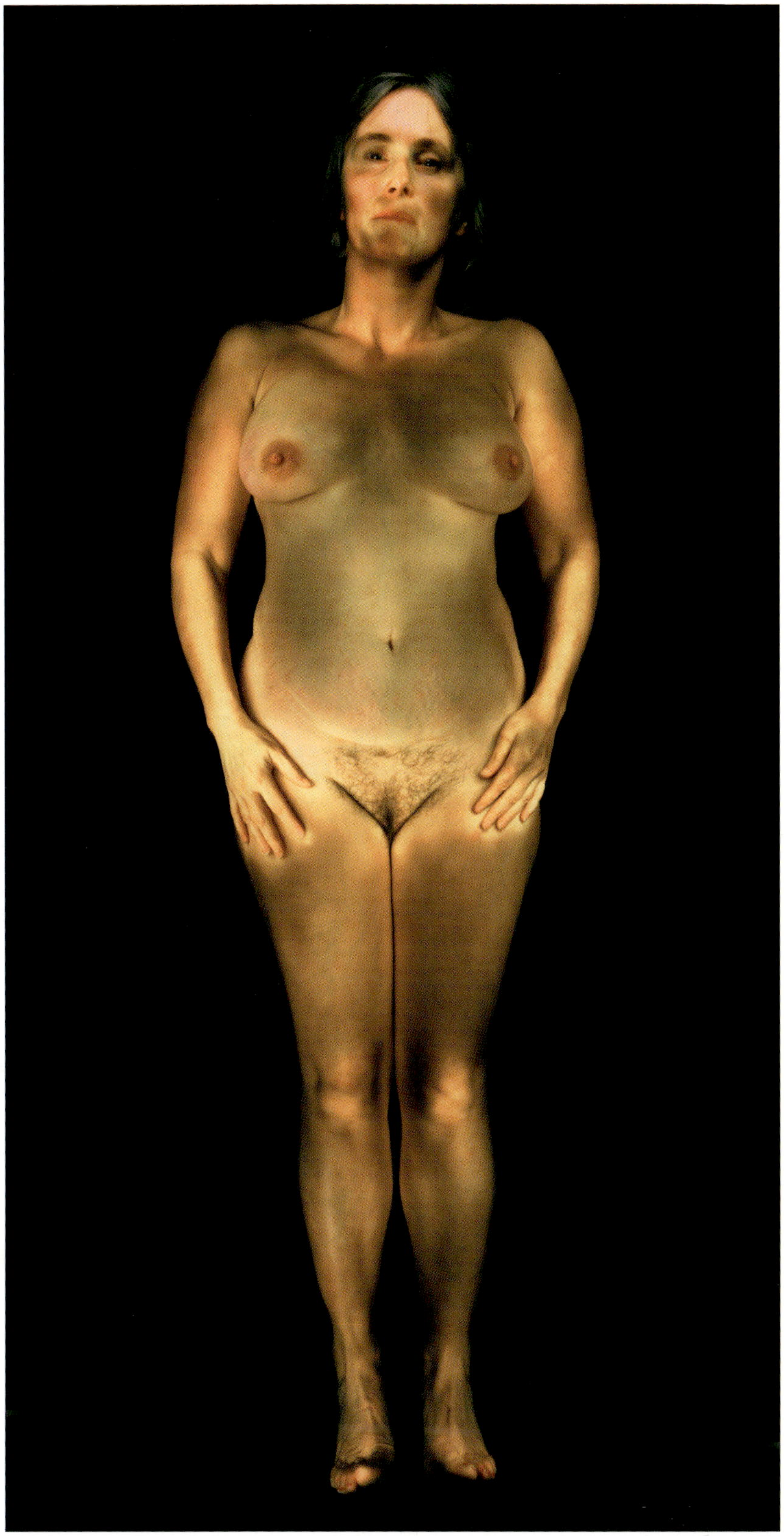

135 Gary Schneider Eve, 2003

Courtesy the Artist

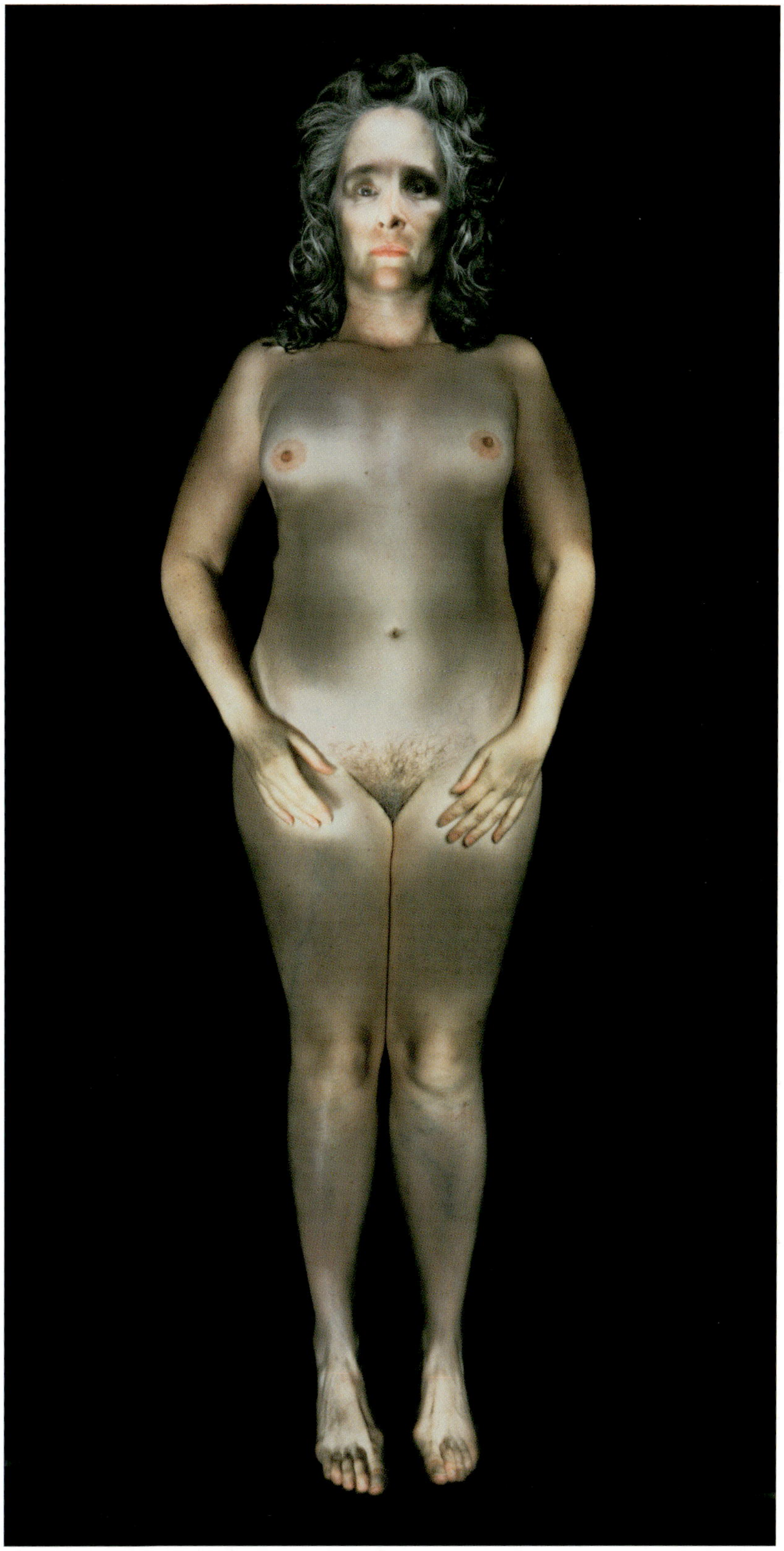

136 Gary Schneider Elena, 2004

Courtesy the Artist

of contemporary photography, but they are not without references to other artists. The performance work of Vito Acconci was a major influence on the work preceding his photography, and remains an element not only in Schneider's emphasis on the naked body as a vehicle, but also in the idea of the portrait sitting as a performance. The exploitation of long exposure times in early photography was another inspiration, and he has remarked that everything he learned 'about what the face would do in a durational portrait' was 'a result of trying to find a new version of making a Julia Margaret Cameron'.[3] Schneider's images have a strongly pictorial presence, thanks to their scale, their rich use of colour and chiaroscuro, and their effects of manipulation, especially in their apparent distortions of anatomy. These pictorial qualities look back to artists like El Greco and Rembrandt, while the passages of blur and movement suggest an affinity with Francis Bacon's portraiture from the 1960s onwards. Schneider's nudes overturn our routine distinction between painting as searching, and photography as instantaneous and superficial.

Schneider seems to be reinventing the representation, however partial or imperfect, of what we might call character. Common denominators of the series only emphasise the strong individuality of the images, a composite of the sitter's distinct physique and presence, and Schneider's manipulations of light in the making process, and his subsequent handling of tone and colour in Adobe Photoshop. We become intensely aware of variations, large and small, across gender, skin colour, age, hairiness, body weight, over and above the specifics of each person's anatomy, body language, and facial expression. In talking to Schneider about particular works, it is clear that one of the things he values about them is their capturing of something profound and fundamental about the particular sitter. The long duration of the exposure and the stripping away of clothes are twin strategies to evade any form of social masquerade. The whole process is geared towards people revealing at least something of themselves, both physically and psychologically. In this sense, the nudes are an extension of an approach to the genre he articulated in relation to the big portrait heads. He wanted, he remarked in 2002, to make images that, in contrast to the prevailing Postmodern ethos of appropriation and ironic detachment, were 'invested with a private authenticity':

I think portraiture is about identity, and how you find identity and what is real, which is hard to talk about these days because there is no such thing as truth or fact. It's an empirical attempt to find something that's real. Because I don't believe that the face can really show us much on the surface of it. We know how to project at the camera, so I found another way to make a portrait that breaks through the camera face.[4]

Schneider acknowledges that the work involves a complex interplay between imposing his own interpretations, and in a more passive way registering 'the secretion of all the expressions they were making during the exposure – what they were thinking, what they were feeling, or what they were projecting. It's all there.'[5] He has commented that the 'central issue' of all his work is 'privacy' and that in making the nudes, 'most if not all of my subjects' experience was relaxed and somewhat sexual. 'It's so intimate. The subject is lying down, made to feel as warm as possible, you're in the dark. You're basically in bed.'[6]

The works provide likenesses of named individuals, a familiar enough concern of portraiture. They articulate each sitter's absolute individuality, at a deeper level than the social façade of clothing and rehearsed expression. Schneider's first name titles imply his own friendship with the sitter, but acknowledge too that this transaction does not normally extend to the spectator in the gallery or someone perusing the book. Whatever affinity we might feel with them, the person in the picture insistently claims a specific identity distinct from, but matching, our own sense of self. Equally, however much the image might appear to suggest specific traits of character, we cannot verify if the work conveys anything significant or truthful about the person, since most of us will have no acquaintance with the sitter, except as the subject of the portrait. The one thing we know for certain about all the sitters is that, for the purpose of collaborating in the creation of their images, they have performed an act of self-exposure.

It would make no sense to create images like these of clothed figures, with their predictable hierarchy of points of focus. But there is more than this to their nakedness. The compelling visual qualities of Schneider's portraits absorb the viewer, and, within that process, the images take on metaphorical meanings. One could read them, for instance, as offering a mirror to a conviction that seems to be widely held in our particular culture (see Chapter 1) that asserts that as individuals, we are most authentically ourselves when we shed the masks of everyday life. The images register a primordial condition of human existence, which is ultimately more real, we might suppose, than the empty rituals and hypocricies of social interaction, or the banalities of work and mass entertainment. Such an idealisation of the authentic private self has of course been current in Western culture since Rousseau and the Romantics, acting as an unspoken assumption in our conception of ourselves.[7] Perhaps we especially value the private and intimate forms of existence that images such as Schneider's evoke when, by contrast, we no longer have confidence in public values and collective forms of progress. An ambition to convey such meanings informs every aspect of the making, realising and presentation of Schneider's images.

Catriona Grant's new project *Leapers* finds meaning in the more conventional momentary aspect that we associate with photography. Yet, the consistent nakedness of the sitters is one signal that something non-traditional is also being attempted [plate 137]. The images dramatise the fact that any portrait arises from some form of collaboration between artist and sitter. Grant takes a more obvious back seat than Schneider and we immediately notice that the men are making certain decisions about how they wish to present themselves. The shutter release cable which they are using is left fully visible (Grant is in the studio, supervising the process, but is not visible to the sitters at the moment of performance). They are projecting themselves to a wholly imaginary audience. This freedom granted to the sitters is an extension of the fact that they initially volunteered to take part in the work, by responding to an advertisement posted by the artist in a local newspaper. None were known to Grant in advance. Their decisions to put themselves forward and to act as they do are open to psychological speculations, in the way that portraits always do invite readings of 'character'.

Grant's role is to set the conceptual and visual parameters of what to some extent becomes an exercise in self-portraiture by her sitters. She chose to limit the project to male subjects, who were over forty. The consistent crimson backdrops remove the imagery from everyday life, with perhaps a reference to the interior of the body. Having talked to the artist and made some trial-run Polaroids, the sitters had to agree to take one shot while they were standing still and looking at the camera, and another while they were jumping, in whatever way suited the individual. The resulting works simply comprise diptychs of the still and leaping images of each subject. The theatrical red backdrops heighten our awareness of visual contrasts, not just between body shapes but also between sharp resolution and blurred passages across the two pictures.

What are Grant's motives? Is she exploring how men project themselves outside an environment of male competitiveness? Is she compiling a set of portraits of individuals, but also presenting for our scrutiny an account of modern masculinity? Is she deliberately turning the tables on the usual formula whereby men make images of naked women, for other men to look at? How might viewing the works be inflected by our own gender, age, physique etc? Nakedness tends to accentuate the differences between individuals that clothes are often designed to conceal. The juxtaposition of the paired images exaggerates this yet further, given the very particular form of body language that the project entails. The sitters could come from any background, but they tend not to be athletes or dancers, with the result that 'the physical effort of the jump precludes the studied performance of self that the standing portrait offers'.[8]

As viewers, we are confronted, as Grant remarks, by 'the disparity (or perhaps the continuity) of seriousness, guardedness or joyfulness in the two portrait images'. The two images are likely to reveal very different aspects of an individual, how they compose themselves, but also how they let go of composure to some degree, in the process of jumping in the air. Both presumably involve an investment of fantasy. Together, the images provide a richer portrayal than one would on its own. But the differences are such that we might equally reflect that individual selves are a complex bundle of personae, layers, and aspects. A proliferation of such contrasting images would take us no nearer to some mythic 'essence' of the sitter, even though nakedness seems to hold out the promise of such revelations.

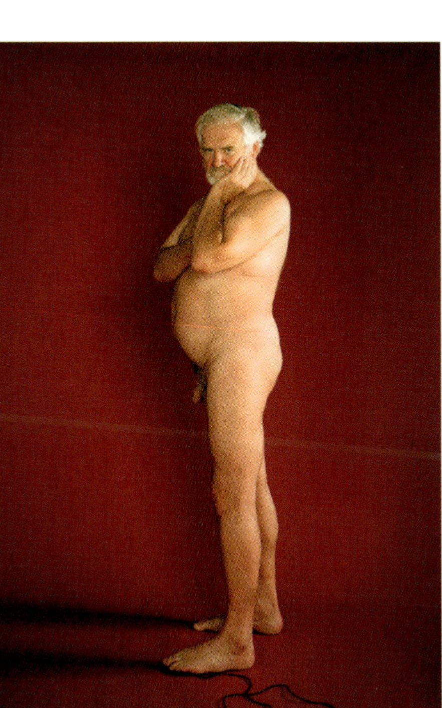

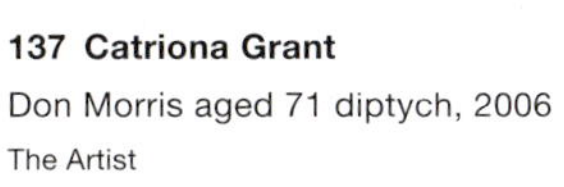

137 Catriona Grant
Don Morris aged 71 diptych, 2006
The Artist

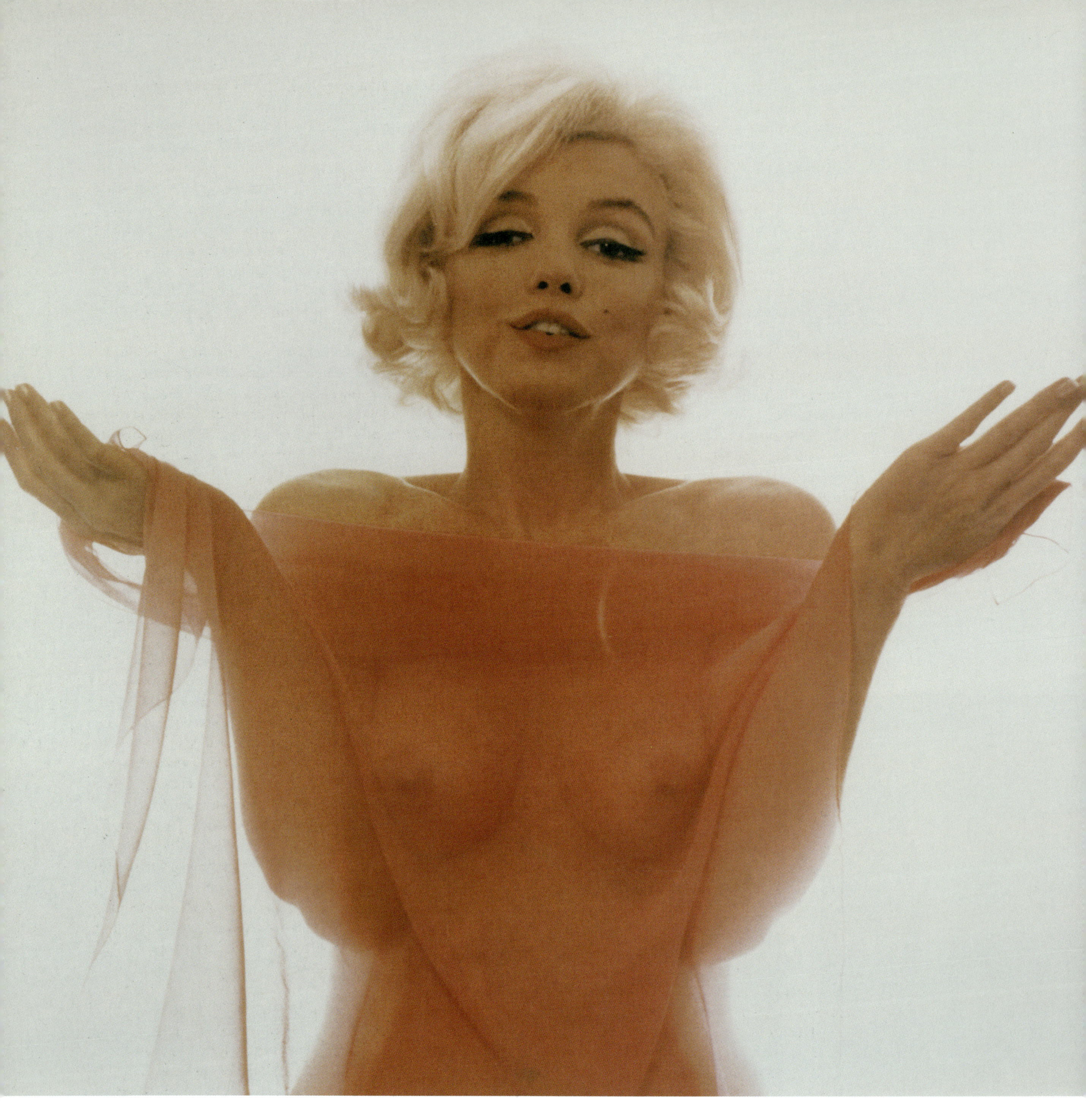

Chapter 10 The Naked Celebrity

138 Bert Stern
Marilyn Monroe, 1962
Fotomuseum, Munich

Portraiture has always been associated with images of the famous, wealthy and powerful. Nudity is one of many rhetorical devices exploited by artists to set such individuals apart from the common herd. Thus, idealising, muscular images of male leaders, distinguished by their military accomplishments, served to assimilate them to the condition of gods. Bronzino's *Portrait of Andrea Doria as Neptune* (1550–5), a tribute to the great Genoese admiral, and Pontormo's *Cosimo I de' Medici as Orpheus* (1538–41) echo the nudity of classical antiquity.[1] Canova's statues of the naked Napoleon include the marble colossus presented to his nemesis the Duke of Wellington by a grateful British nation, still displayed at the Duke's London residence.[2] In recent times we have like images of sporting heroes, such as boxer Sugar Ray Robinson or sprinter Linford Christie [plates 141 and 148]. A parallel strand represented royal mistresses, signifying sexual possession, such as Peter Lely's portrait of Nell Gwynne, painted for Charles II, and Boucher's beguiling *Louise O'Murphy*, the mistress of Louis XV (*c*.1752). Canova contributed another reworking of the classical style in his nude portrait of Pauline Bonaparte (1805–8). Yet such images were the exception rather than the rule. In his *Discourses*, Joshua Reynolds explained the artistic logic to nude portraiture; the sitter's costume would eventually become 'only an amusement for an antiquarian', and by dispensing with it the painter would have full scope to exhibit his artistry, rather than merely reproducing that of the sitter's tailor.[3] In practice, the portraitist was subject to the vanity of his clientele: 'Art is not yet in so high estimation with us, as to obtain so great a sacrifice as the ancients made, especially the Grecians; who suffered themselves to be represented naked, whether they were generals, lawgivers, or kings'.[4]

Much has changed. Inhibitions about nudity have fallen away, and 'generals, lawgivers, or kings', not to mention royal mistresses, have lost their starring role in portraiture. Now we have naked pictures of celebrities of the moment, celebrating their physical beauty and sexual allure. This sometimes infiltrates painting, as in Peter Howson's somewhat grotesque images of the nude Madonna [plate 139]. But generally the vehicle for this association of fame and nudity is photography, produced for endless replication in glossy magazines. The flourishing of these in the 1960s coincided with a sexual revolution heralded by the arrival of the contraceptive pill and the failed prosecution for obscenity of D.H. Lawrence's *Lady Chatterley's Lover*. Thereafter, attitudes were liberated, inhibitions shed, and bodies uncovered; *The Pawnbroker* (1964) and *Blow-up* (1966) were evidently the first commercial films to show, respectively, the female breast and pubic hair. In photography, Marilyn Monroe had appeared naked as early as 1953, when she became the first centrefold in Hugh Hefner's *Playboy* magazine. In June 1962, the famous Bert Stern pictures of Monroe, 2,500 in all, were shot over three days at the Hotel Bel-Air in Los Angeles [plate 138 and 140]. These, too, were remarkably revealing and sexually provocative. They came to be called 'The Last Sitting', because they were taken just six weeks before Monroe died from a drug overdose. The selection published in *Vogue* magazine in June 1962 turned into a memorial, the pictures' sexy vitality becoming intertwined with the sense of pathos and fragility that attached to Monroe.

The transition to a new atmosphere is also registered in the work of Richard Avedon. At the start of the decade, his photographs of Rudolf Nureyev were tasteful images of a cultural icon [front cover]. More iconoclastic was the use of nakedness to signify bohemian freedom and gay sexuality in Avedon's 1963 picture of the two Beat poets Allen Ginsberg and Peter Orlovsky, clasped together in a tender embrace and gazing unashamedly towards the viewer. In the 1969 frieze portrait of the weird and wonderful 'workers' at Andy Warhol's Factory, the naked and the trendily clothed are mingled by Avedon in a distillation of Sixties camp, implied sexual daring combining with the emotional blankness

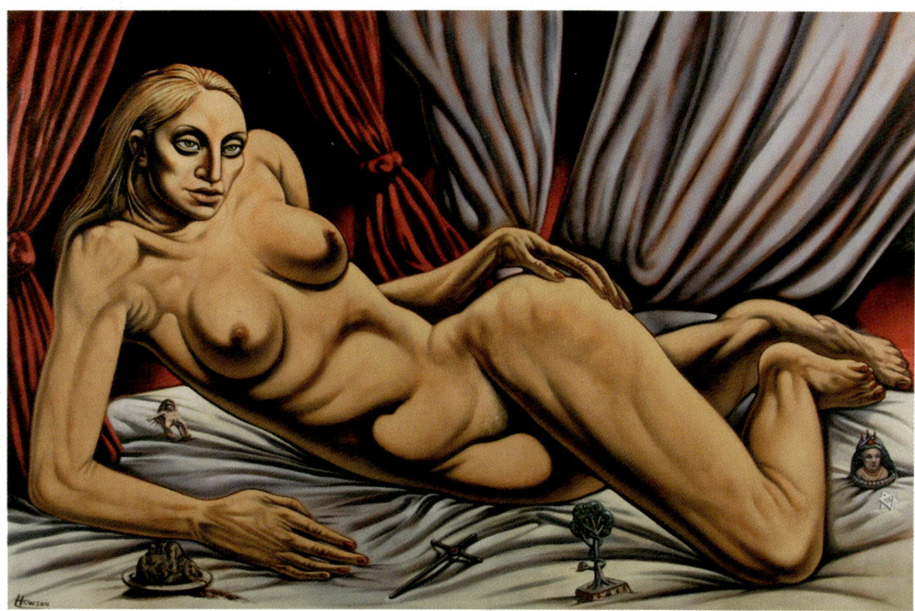

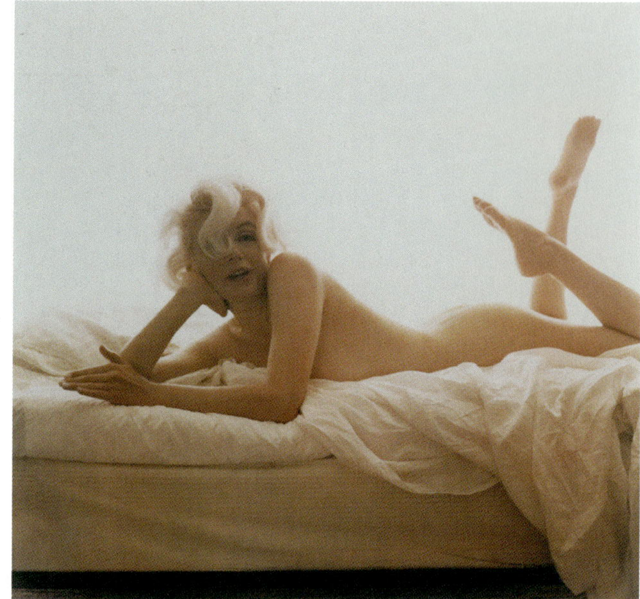

left **139 Peter Howson**
Madonna, 2002
Collection Mr & Mrs Flowers

right **140 Bert Stern**
Marilyn Monroe, 1962
Fotomuseum, Munich

opposite **141 Ernst Haas**
Sugar Ray Robinson Weighing In, 1957
Private Collection, Thomas Koeffer, Zurich

cultivated by Warhol and his acolytes. In subverting the rigid formulae of the group portrait, Avedon implies that the old social order was giving way to a far more anarchic and iconoclastic sensibility, with Warhol as its guiding spirit.

Meanwhile, in May 1963, Lewis Morley created his canonical naked portrait of Christine Keeler [plate 142]. The context was the recent revelations regarding her sexual relationships with the then War Minister, John Profumo, and an attaché in the Soviet Embassy, which led to Profumo's resignation. Plans to tell this sensational story in a film provided the occasion for the photographic session that Morley recalled:

The first two rolls had Christine sitting in various positions on the chair and on the floor, dressed in a small leather jerkin. It was at this point that the film producers who were in attendance demanded she strip for some nude photos. Christine was reluctant to do so, but the producers insisted, saying that it was written in her contract. The situation became rather tense and reached an impasse. I suggested that everyone, including my assistant leave the studio. I turned my back to Christine, telling her to disrobe, sit back to front on the chair. She was now nude, fulfilling the conditions of the contract, but was at the same time hidden.

We repeated some of the poses used on the previous two rolls of film. I rapidly exposed some fresh positions, some angled from the side and a few slightly looking down. I felt that I had shot enough and took a couple of paces back. Looking up I saw what appeared to be a perfect positioning. I released the shutter one more time, in fact, it was the last exposure on the roll of film … It was this pose that became the first published and most used image. The nude session had taken less than five minutes to complete.[5]

The picture quickly gained huge exposure, after being stolen from Morley's studio. In June 1963, it featured in the *Sunday Mirror* and several other tabloid newspapers, accompanying the latest nuggets in the unfolding saga.

The power of the Keeler portrait derives from its fusion of contradictory extremes. It is black and white, with little half-tone, a feature of Morley's work from this time. It registers primarily as an image, but the shapes formed by the thighs, chair back and torso read strongly too in abstract terms. The image has an iconic symmetry, but the slight twist of the upper part of the body and tilt of the arms serve subtly to offset the effect, and, by casting half her face into shadow, to enhance the vampish *femme fatale* persona that Keeler assumes. The photograph possesses the literal modesty that its reluctant sitter demanded, but is all the more erotically suggestive by its concealment of the more obviously sexual parts of her body. The wide open thighs might well be taken to imply a straddled sexual position, with the chair as surrogate partner. The chair back serves at once to conceal, but at the same time provides a magnified, symbolic representation of a patch of pubic hair, with the horizontal hand-hold opening becoming a kind of vertical vagina. The image thus gives off multiple points of reference, from the well-established convention of portrait photography in which the sitter straddles a reversed chair, to the publicity shots and actualities of a strip show revue performed on a spot-lit stage.

The Christine Keeler image served as a prototype for further portrait photographs by Morley. The same chair

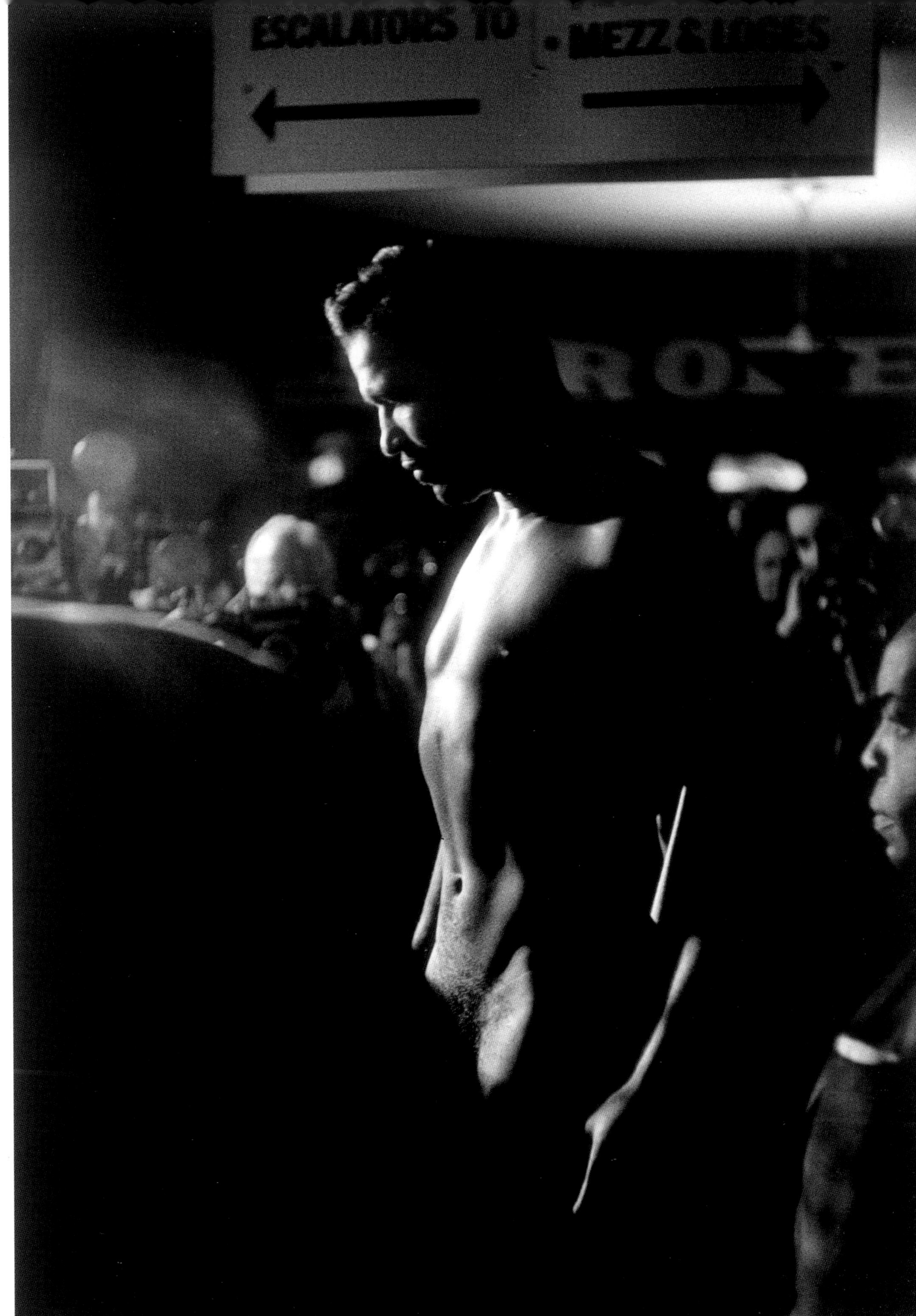
ESCALATORS TO
MEZZ & LOGES

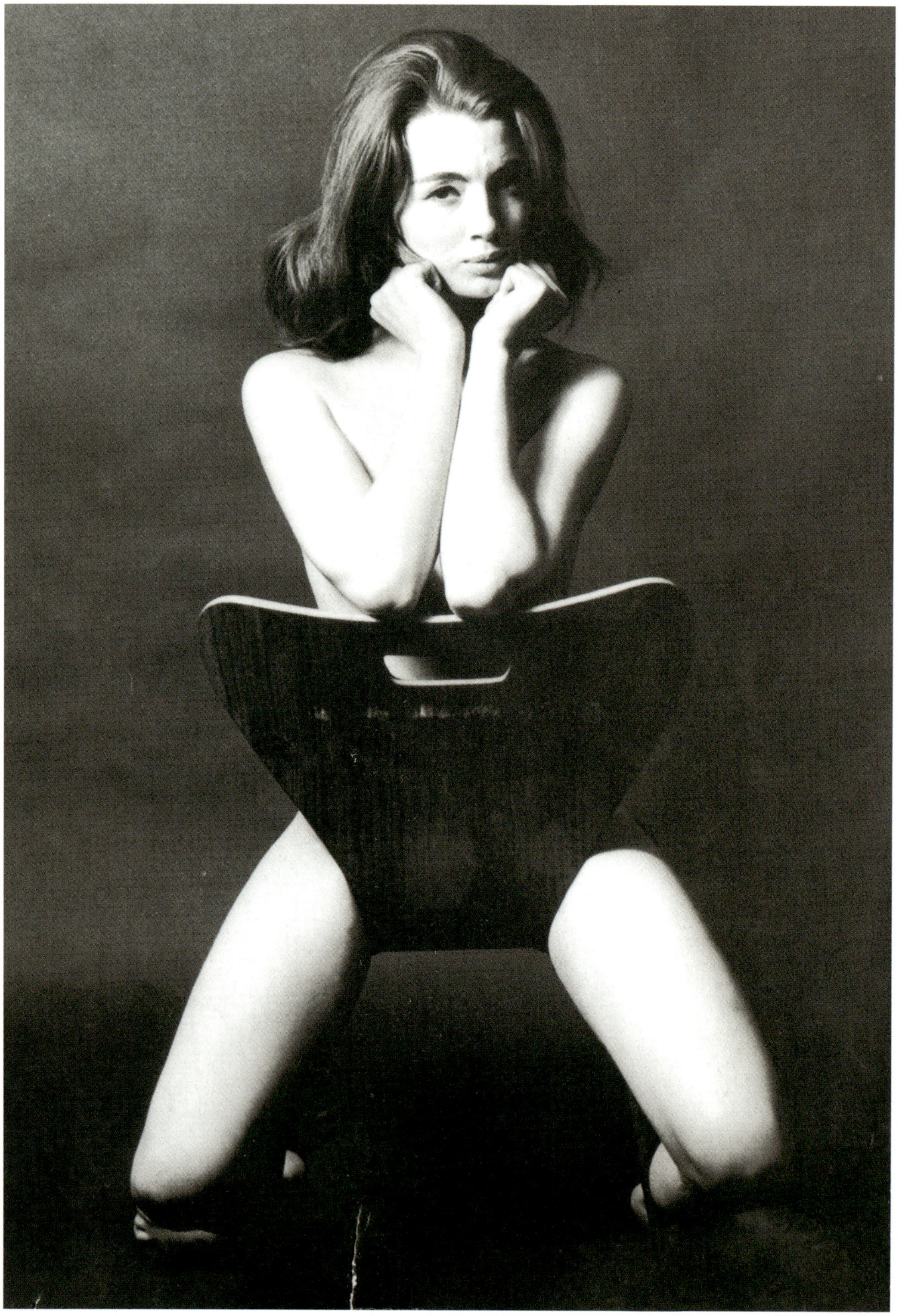

142 Lewis Morley
Christine Keeler, 1963
National Portrait Gallery, London

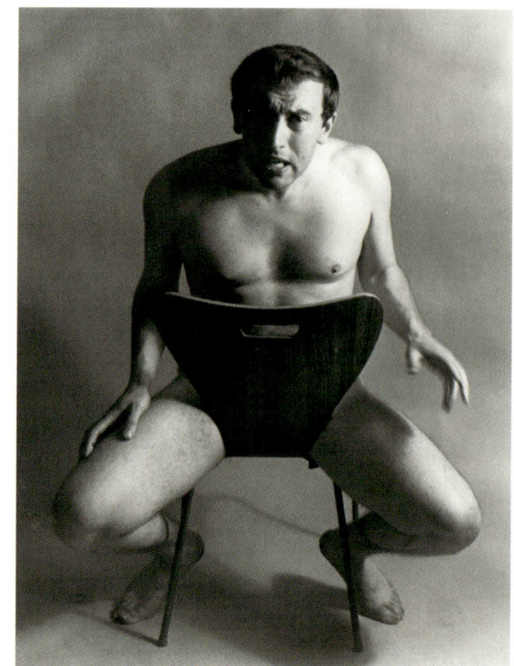

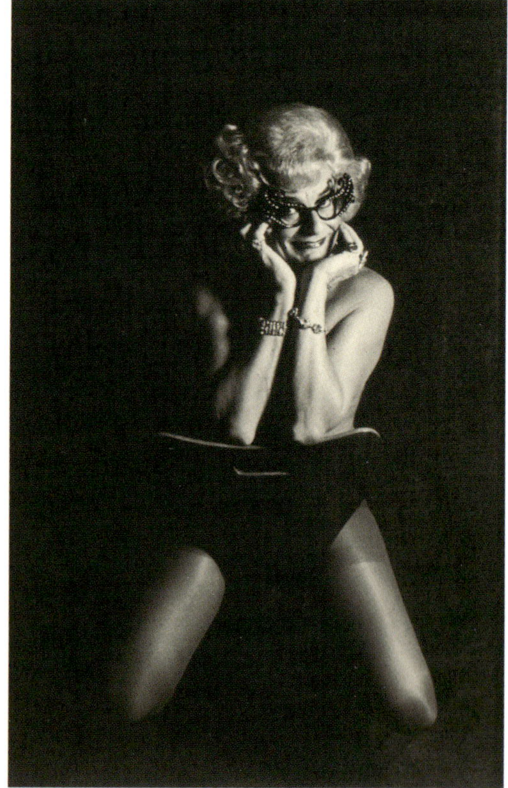

143 Lewis Morley
Sir David Frost, 1963
National Portrait Gallery, London

144 Lewis Morley
Barry Humphries as Dame Edna Everage, 1982
National Portrait Gallery, London

was occupied by David Frost, who cuts a male, animated, altogether less sexy figure than his predecessor [plate 143]. The echo associates Frost with the irreverent, anti-establishment mood that had been given such a boost by the Prufomo saga, and characterises him as a fearless seeker after the naked truth. The format was redeployed again in 1965 for one of Morley's portraits of the writer Joe Orton, whose overt homosexual identity was expressed in plays such as *Entertaining Mr Sloane* (1964). Orton's 'mock-serious body building' staged him as a 'muscle-man' to Christine's 'pin-up'.[6] A final variation on the Keeler format was devoted to Dame Edna Everage, whose alter-ego Barry Humphries was himself a product, like Morley, of the satire subculture in 1960s London [plate 144].

The sexual liberation of the period comes across in the work of other up-and-coming photographers, such as David Bailey. The influence of Avedon is apparent in the portrait idiom and the book format of Bailey's *Goodbye Baby and Amen: A Saraband for the Sixties* (1969). The picture of Sharon Tate and Roman Polanski reads as a heterosexual version of the Ginsberg and Orlovsky image. Bailey's portrait of Jane Birkin, actress and model, coincided with the appearance of her infamous hit single *Je t'aime* and epitomised the skinny physique so admired in the 1960s

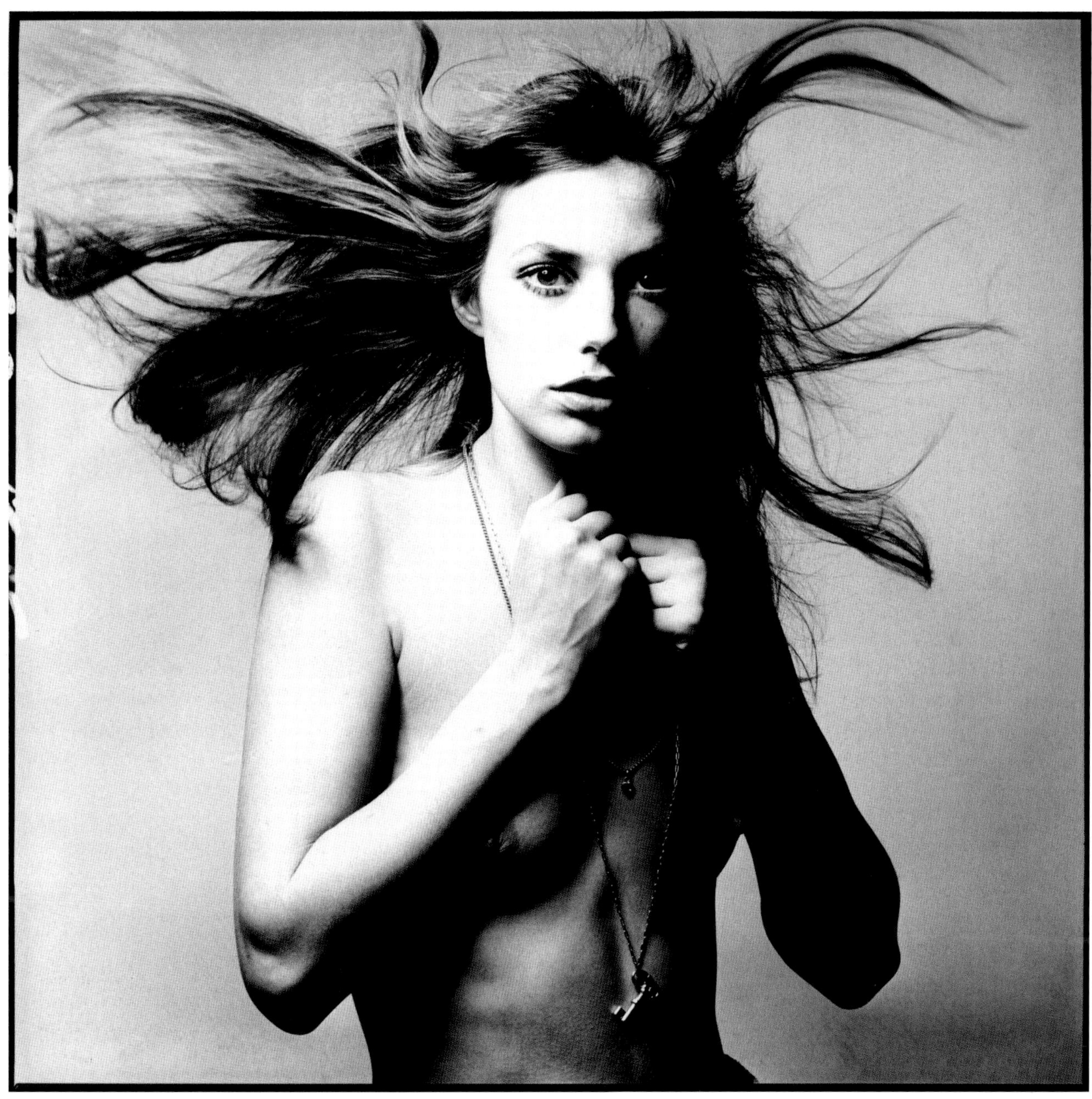

145 David Bailey
Jane Birkin, 1969
National Portrait Gallery, London

[plate 145]. From the simplicities of Morley and Bailey, it is a jump to the almost absurd vulgarity of Helmut Newton's portrait of actress Charlotte Rampling (1973). The image is one of Newton's earliest forays into a genre that would loom large in his subsequent production. His background in fashion photography is a crucial determinant of his almost fetishistic approach in the Rampling portrait. Newton evokes the sophistication and self-assurance associated with Rampling's screen persona. The image is unashamedly staged, hinting at some filmic scenario – a narrative of debauchery in a setting of aristocratic indulgence. We may fantasise that our entry to the room has prompted this beautiful girl to put down her glass of wine, in anticipation of sensual pleasures. The twist of her body, silhouetting breast and nipple, uncannily inverts the figure of the goddess in Titian's *Diana and Actaeon*, who turns away from the intruder's gaze to reach for a garment. In Newton's picture the setting reads as an extension of the sexuality implicit in Rampling's naked body. Her pale, lithe form floats against the surrounding darkness. She forms the still centre of a riot of visually animated fixtures, the patterned carpet and net curtain, the shiny barley-sugar components of the furniture, the blazing, ornate chandelier, and, above all, the gilt mirror frame, whose organic curves echo the mane of hair framing Rampling's sensual gaze.

Over the past thirty years, nudity has increasingly seemed a good career move: 'artful nakedness has become almost *de rigueur* for film stars, models and elite sportsmen and women'.[7] The ubiquity of such imagery is one, up-market symptom of a climate in which almost anything goes, on television, in pop videos, films, and on the web. Back in the early 1980s, Tom Wolfe was moved to remark: 'We happen to live in an era of skinny topless celebrities. When a camera appears, it's all you can do to get them to keep their clothes on their bony X-ray bodies… Why are so many celebrities willing, even desperate to take their shirts off for the photographer?'[8] The answer seemed to have something to do with the influence of rock music, the Rolling Stones in particular. Annie Leibovitz made some remarkable pictures of Mick Jagger and his fellow wild men, but the canonical rock image is her photograph of John Lennon and Yoko Ono, taken in December 1980 for the cover of an issue of *Rolling Stone* magazine that tragically turned into a memorial, as Lennon was shot dead outside his New York apartment building a few hours after the session with Leibovitz [plate 146]. The picture captured their mutual devotion, with Lennon clinging naked and foetus-like to the more impassive but serene figure of his wife.

Images of glamorous young actresses and models descend from the traditional iconography of the idealised female nude, and it is usually asserted that such figures are portrayed nude rather than naked. Lord Snowdon's portrayal of Emma Thompson, in the style of the Velázquez *Rokeby Venus*, is a case in point.[9] But Leibovitz is the photographer most identified with the celebration of the body both famous and beautiful. Nudity is suggested and cunningly avoided in a sequence of pictures where the celebrity is covered in roses (*Bette Midler*, 1991), mud (*Lauren Hutton*, 1991), and a bathtub of milk (*Whoopi Goldberg*, 1994). Leibovitz's other iconic magazine cover is the heavily pregnant Demi Moore, who graced *Vanity Fair* in August 1991. This has been described as 'a watershed moment in the representation of female sexuality and motherhood', though when the issue first appeared Moore's body was veiled by a sheet of brown paper inside the plastic bag, to protect sensitive shoppers.[10] With hindsight, it is stylisation rather than realism that characterises the image, a product of the artful lighting and the contrived elegance of the sitter's expression, hair, jewellery and posture. A recent Leibovitz *Vanity Fair* cover (February 2006) showed two successful and glamorous film stars, Keira Knightley and Scarlett Johansson, both nude, accompanied by the clothed figure of guest editor and celebrated fashion designer Tom Ford. The knowing viewer will spot the allusion to Manet's *Le Déjeuner sur l'Herbe*, while Johansson reprises the alluring pose of Boucher's *Louise O'Murphy*.

The numerous nude pictures by David La Chapelle of the likes of Pamela Anderson, Naomi Campbell and many an actress and singer provide a late, mannered variant on this form of celebrity imagery. Photographer, sitter and viewer unite in recognising that fantasy, camp and self-promotion are central to the genre. We all understand that celebrities provide springboards for our yearnings. Their imagery allows us to fantasise about being that person, looking and dressing like that, living that glamorous lifestyle in those beautiful places. Hollywood and its equivalents function as latter day variants on the myth of Arcadia. There is a subtle double message. The pictures acknowledge that the individual is ultimately mere flesh and blood, one of us, beneath the signature façade. But, the implication also is that those achieving a certain level of fame and glamour are set apart from the rest of us by a willingness to expose their naked bodies to an audience of millions, providing the image is stylish and flattering. They are a new aristocracy, socially elevated by tasteful artistic presentation. The fantasy that the famous live by different, more sexually liberated, codes of behaviour and morality becomes an assumption they share with their adoring public.

146 Annie Leibovitz
John Lennon and Yoko Ono, 1980
Scottish National Portrait Gallery, Edinburgh

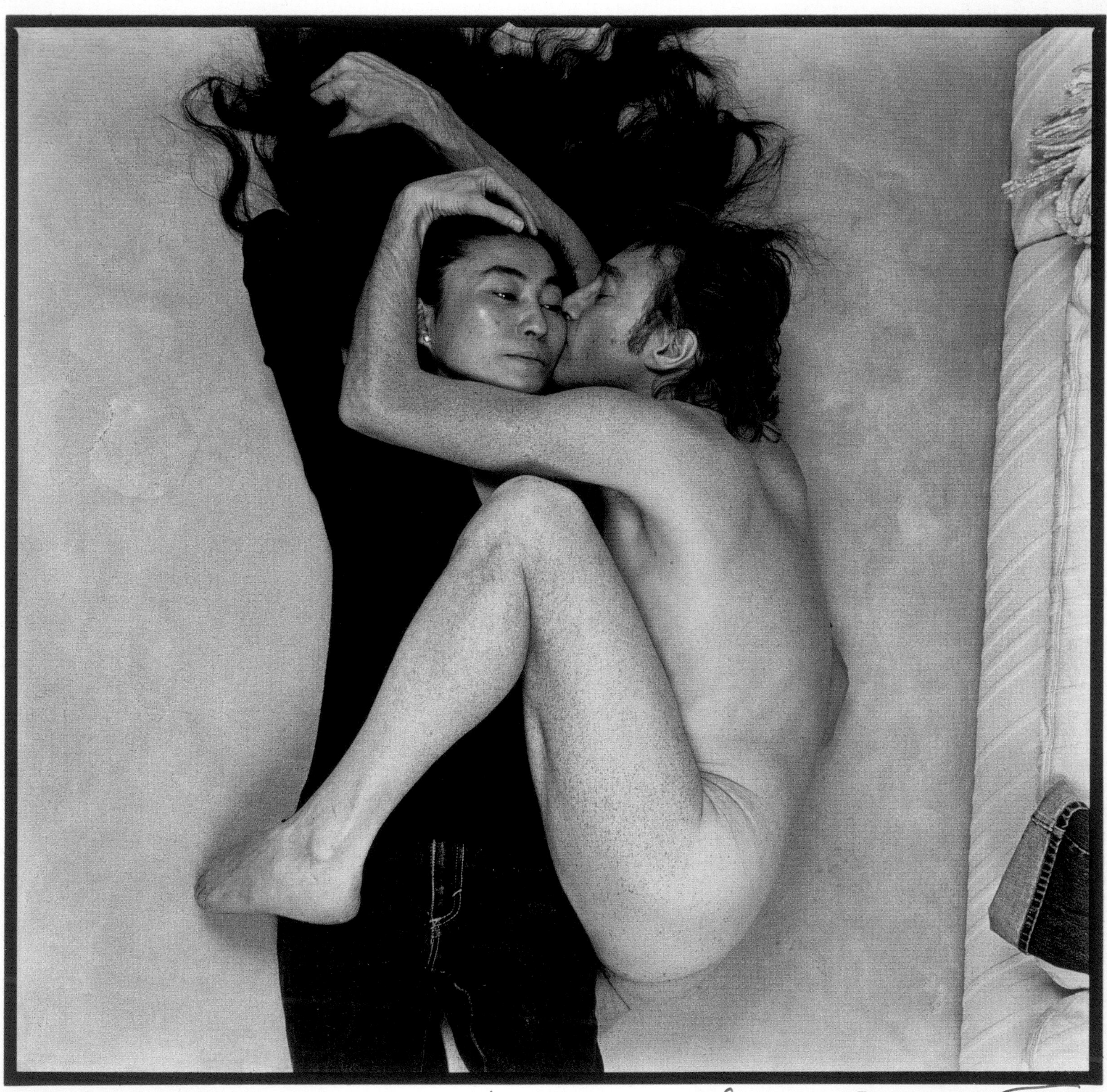

john lennon and yoko ono   new york 1980   ap9

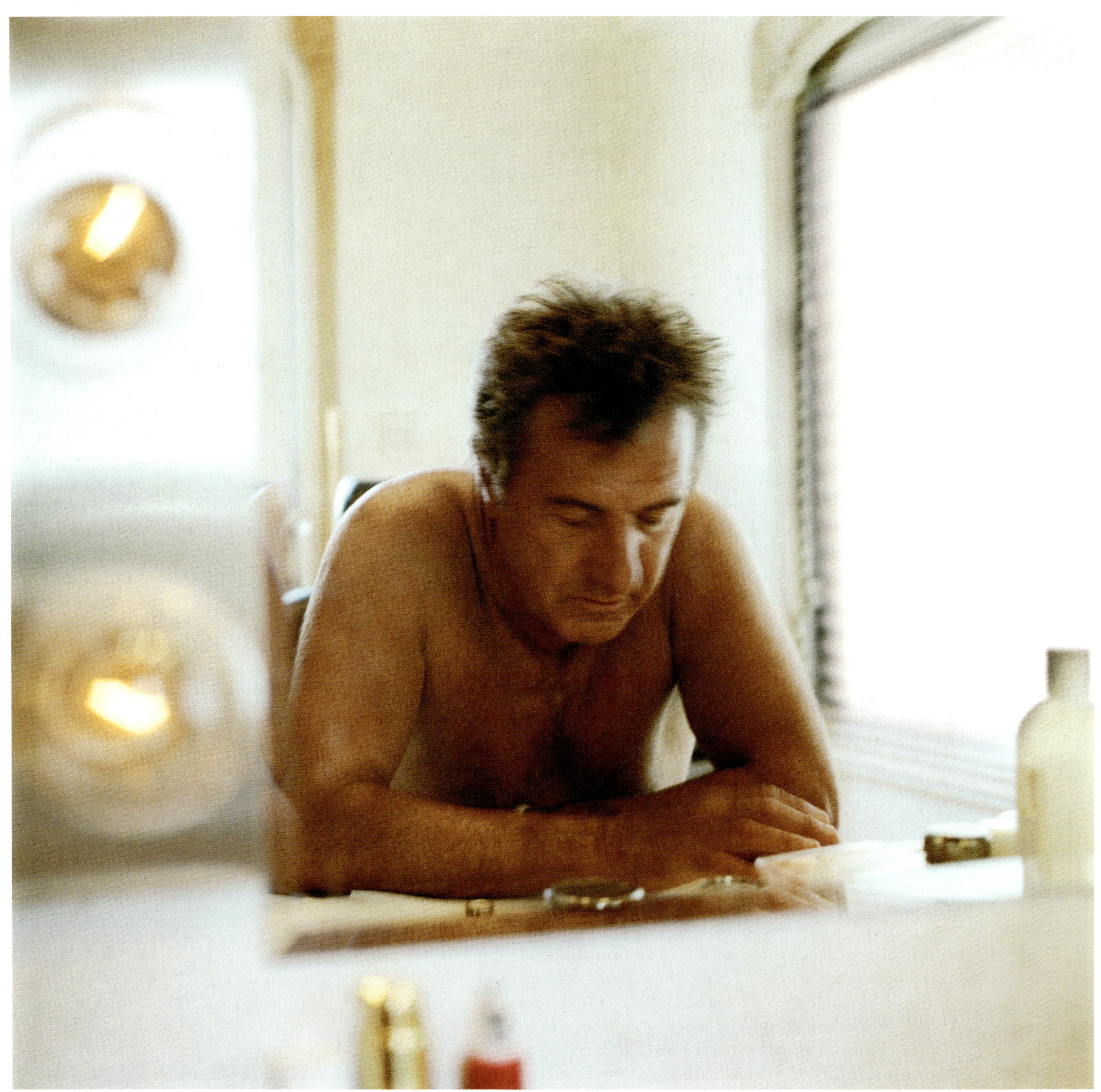

147 Sam Taylor-Wood

Dustin Hoffman (from the Crying Men series), 2004

The Artist (White Cube, London)

By now, sitting for the likes of Leibovitz or La Chapelle has become a badge of honour. The fame of photographer and sitter have become mutually sustaining. Magazine journalism is merely a take-off point for the careers celebrity images can enjoy. Later on, we are likely to encounter them in glossy books or catalogues devoted to Newton, Avedon or Bailey, or as fine prints in blue-chip commercial galleries or prestigious art museums. The latest example is the big touring show and enormous, expensive book devoted to Leibovitz's work since 1990, where her celebrity work is controversially interspersed with private, intimate imagery such as the pictures, sometimes naked, that she took of her partner Susan Sontag in the last years of her life.[11]

Even ardent feminists are willing to play the game. When Germaine Greer posed nude, not for the first time, for a project about famous Australians, she showed off a fine body for her time of life, against a suitably, perhaps ironically, feminine backdrop, but kept her distance from vulgarity by her joky expression, and by leaving in shot the glasses that she has also removed, signifying her age and intellectual credentials. A younger American successor, Periel Achenbrand (best known for the slogan 'The only bush I trust is my own') volunteered to appear naked on the cover of a book of political essays: 'I think there is liberation in standing there naked and having a message … It's not a case of being outrageous just for the sake of it. But I do want people to pay attention.'[12]

The psychological function of celebrity imagery is explored in the work of Sam Taylor-Wood, notably the *Crying Men* series and the video portrait of the sleeping David Beckham, her response to a commission from the National Portrait Gallery to portray one of the most celebrated living Englishmen. Robert Downey Jr and Dustin Hoffman are the only *Crying Men* to qualify as naked portraits, while David too is naked to the waist, where the sheet intervenes. Beckham is unconscious of his occasional twitches, whereas the actors are weeping because Taylor-Wood asked them to. But this is a point of connection. Neither with Beckham nor Hoffman do we really know what is going on in their heads, what the former is dreaming about, or what the latter is thinking about in order to simulate an effect of profound sadness. We are confronted by an image of Hoffman sitting in his dressing room, 'vulnerable and desolate', lowering or closing his eyes to avoid seeing himself in the mirror where we view his reflection [plate 147].[13] Downey is more obviously performing, and 'doesn't let grief interfere with sensual self-display'.[14] Nevertheless, throughout the series, as with the dramas or movies where we usually encounter such figures, we may allow ourselves to be moved by their representations of deep feeling, even while we recognise that it is all wholly contrived. Actors function as gateways for our own feelings, and we value the experience of identifying with them as cathartic. This might apply to Taylor-Wood, whose battles with cancer are well-known.

The sitters are all men. Much has been written about the 'male gaze' and the ways in which it is pandered to in female roles in film, and, by extension, in still imagery. Perhaps on one level Taylor-Wood is concerned with addressing a distinctively female gaze. *David* removes the man from his familiar action-packed context, and focuses on his physical beauty and also his vulnerability, from the perspective of someone who might be lying beside his naked form in bed. The title establishes a double-edged reference to Michelangelo's *David* and both can be seen as gorgeous hunks and expressions of the sexual preferences of the artist, beneath the veneer of an official commission. But the juxtaposition also highlights how hero-worship, with its connotations of moral improvement, has given way to the shallowness of celebrity-worship, just as the permanence of marble has been replaced by the transience of film. The *Crying Men* series presents for our contemplation a stereotype of vulnerability, and a willingness to express feelings that are supposed to be attractive to many women. Linda Nochlin at any rate acknowledged what was involved in her aesthetic response: 'They're so sexy when they're sad, these beautiful men. Their tears make them still more alluring.'[15]

It is a suitable point on which to end. Portraits of naked people might seem transparent and revealing, more natural and honest than representations of figures using clothes to manipulate our responses. A photograph of a naked man *pretending* to be sad, for whom we might feel desire rather than sympathy, suggests that naked portraits are potentially a good deal more complex.

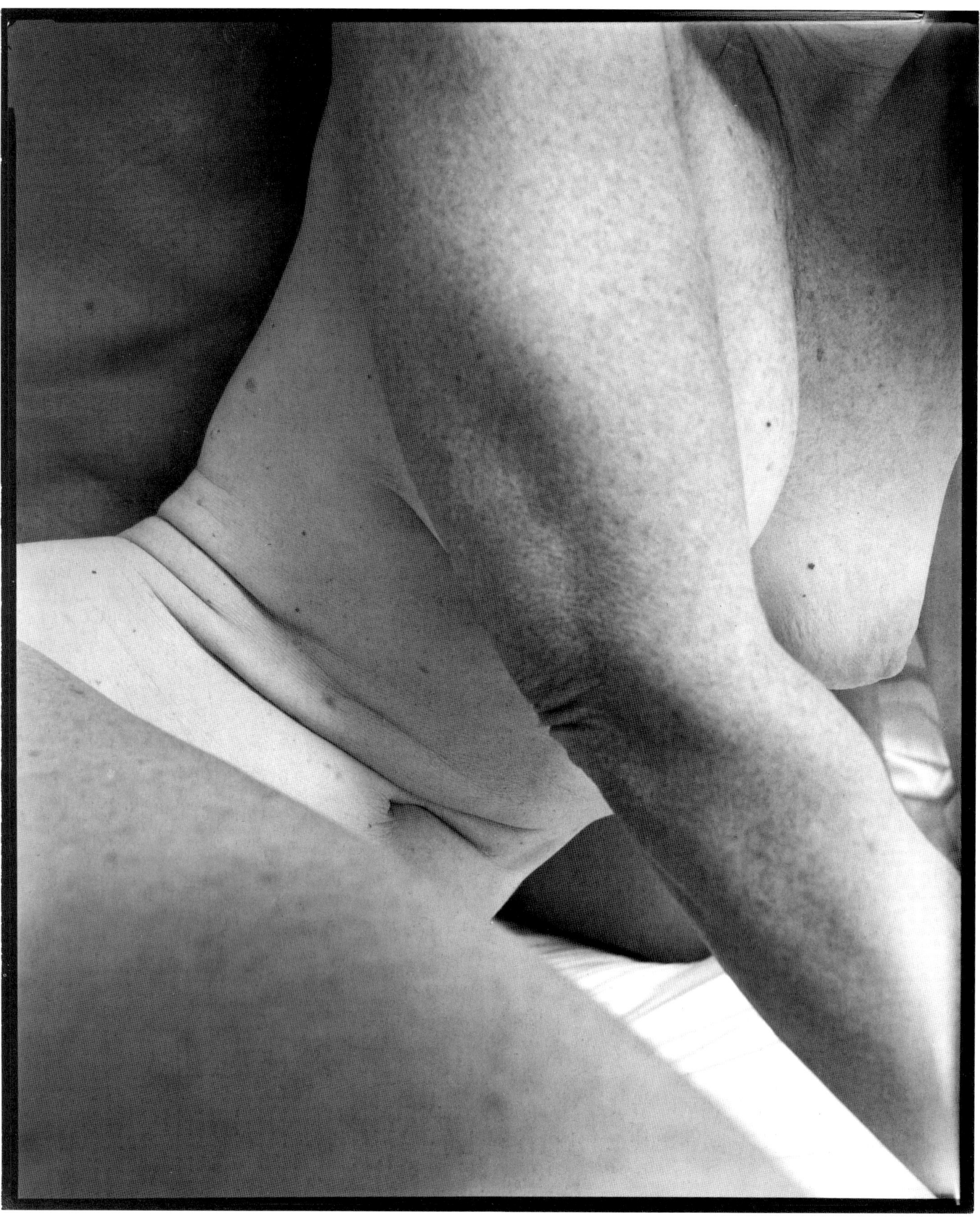

Exhibition Checklist

148 Nicholas Nixon
Bebe and I, 1997
Courtesy Yossi Milo Gallery, New York

All dimensions are given in centimetres, height × width

Arbus, Diane American, 1923–1971

Retired man and his wife at home in a nudist camp one morning, N.J., 1963
Silver gelatin print · 78.7 × 57.7
Victoria & Albert Museum, London
Plate 120

A husband and his wife in the woods at a nudist camp, N.J., 1963
Silver gelatin print · 37.4 × 37.4
Pompidou Centre, Paris
Edinburgh only

Nudist lady with swan sunglasses, 1965
Silver gelatin print · 38 × 37.4
Pompidou Centre, Paris
Edinburgh only

A naked man being a woman, N.Y.C., 1968
Silver gelatin print · 37.9 × 37.5
Pompidou Centre, Paris
Edinburgh only · Plate 119

Girl sitting in her bed with her shirt off, N.Y.C., 1968
Silver gelatin print · 36.8 × 37.3
Pompidou Centre, Paris
Edinburgh only

Arikha, Avigdor French, b.1929

Nude Self-portrait from Back, 1986
Oil on canvas · 65 × 45.5
The Artist
Plate 87

Avedon, Richard American, 1923–2004

Rudolf Nureyev, Dancer, 25 July 1961, Paris, 1962
Silver gelatin print · 61 × 50.8
The Richard Avedon Foundation, New York
Cover illustration

Allen Ginsberg and Peter Orlovsky, poets, New York City, 30 December 1963, 1963
Silver gelatin print · 61 × 50.8
The Richard Avedon Foundation, New York

Andy Warhol and Members of The Factory, New York City, 30 October 1969, 1969
Silver gelatin print · 20.3 × 76.2
The Richard Avedon Foundation, New York

Hansel Nicholas Burum, Coal Miner, 1985
Silver gelatin print · 143 × 114.5
Collection Fotomuseum,Winterthur, Permanent loan from Andreas Reinhart
Plate 19

Bacon, Francis British, 1909–1992

Study from the Human Body, 1991
Oil on canvas · 198 × 147.5
The Estate of Francis Bacon, courtesy Faggionato Fine Arts, London and Tony Shafrazi Gallery, New York
Plate 14

Bailey, David British, b.1938

Jane Birkin, 1969
Bromide print · 40.9 × 40.7
National Portrait Gallery, London
Plate 145

Belinda Selby, 2002
Digital silver gelatin print · 128 × 104
David Bailey (Camera Eye Ltd)
Plate 5

Denise and Andrew Ward, Actress and Writer, 2002
Digital silver gelatin print · 128 × 104
David Bailey (Camera Eye Ltd)
Plate 63

Balthus French, 1908–2001

Le Lever (Getting up),1955
Oil on canvas · 161 × 130.4
Scottish National Gallery of Modern Art, Edinburgh
Edinburgh only · Plate 21

Bamgboye, Odalebe Nigerian / British, b.1963

The Lighthouse, 1989
Colour transparency in light box
128 × 104.5 × 20
Private Collection, Thomas Koerfer, Zurich
Plate 149

Bell, Vanessa British, 1879–1961

David Garnett, 1915
Oil and gouache on cardboard
76.4 × 52.6
National Portrait Gallery, London
Plate 16

Bomberg, David British, 1890–1957

Lilian, 1932
Oil on canvas · 76.2 × 55.9
Tate, London
Plate 44

Bonnard, Pierre French, 1867–1947

Nude Woman in Black Stockings, *c.*1900
Oil on wood · 59 × 43
Private Collection on loan to Sheffield Galleries and Museum Trust
Plate 46

Bathing Woman, Seen from the Back, *c.*1919
Oil on canvas · 44.1 × 34.6
Tate, bequeathed by the Hon. Mrs A.E. Pleydell-Bouverie through the Friends of the Tate Gallery, 1968
Plate 47

Borland, Polly Australian, b.1959

Germaine Greer, 1999
C-type colour print · 39.6 × 49.5
National Portrait Gallery, London

Bratby, John British, 1928–1992

Jean and Still Life in Front of a Window, 1954
Oil on board · 122 × 108
Southampton City Art Gallery
Plate 51

Brown, Don British, b.1962

Yoko VIII (naked), 2002
Acrylic composite and acrylic paint
117 × 30 × 30
The Artist (via Sadie Coles)

Callahan, Harry American, 1912–1999

Eleanor,1947
Silver gelatin print · 25.2 × 20.2
Pompidou Centre, Paris
Edinburgh only

Eleanor, Chicago, 1949
Silver gelatin print · 20 × 25
Pompidou Centre, Paris
Edinburgh only · Plate 150

Eleanor, Chicago, 1949
Silver gelatin print · 15.4 × 14
Pompidou Centre, Paris
Edinburgh only · Plate 49

Carline, Hilda British, 1889–1950

Stanley Spencer, 1931
Pencil on paper · 50.8 × 35.2
Scottish National Gallery of Modern Art, Edinburgh
Plate 42

Carucci, Elinor Israeli / American, b.1971

PMS,1997
C-type print · 50.8 × 60.9
Courtesy Edwynn Houk Gallery, New York
Plate 74

My Mother and I, 2000
C-type print · 40.6 × 50.8
Courtesy Edwynn Houk Gallery, New York
Plate 83

Mom Takes a Bath, 2001
C-type print · 40.6 × 50.8
Courtesy Edwynn Houk Gallery, New York

Chadwick, Helen British, 1953–1996

Ego Geometria Sum:
The Labours I–X, 1983

I: The Incubator – Birth
II: The Font – age 3 months
III: The Pram – 10 months
IV: The Boat – age 2 years
V: The Wigwam – 6¾ years
VII: The Piano – age 9 years
VIII: The Horse – age 11 years
IX: High School – age 13 years
X: The Statue – age 30 years
10 photographs · each 29 × 29 · made with the assistance of Mark Pilkington
Eric Franck
Illustrated (except no.X) Plate 105

Vanitas II, 1986
Cibachrome print · 50.9 × 51
National Portrait Gallery, London
Plate 107

Clemente, Francesco Italian, b.1952

Self-portrait with Skull, 2002
Oil on canvas · 76.8 × 153
Private Collection, Thomas Koerfer, Zurich
Plate 90

Coplans, John British / American, 1920–2003

Self-portrait (Back with Arms Above), 1984
Photograph · 121.3 × 93.5
Tate, presented by the American Fund for the Tate Gallery, courtesy Marsha Plotnitsky, 2000
Plate 85

Self-portrait (Torso, Front), 1984
Photograph · 115.6 × 81.7
Tate, presented by the American Fund for the Tate Gallery, courtesy Marsha Plotnitsky, 2000

Self-portrait (Hands Spread on Knees), 1985
Photograph · 96.8 × 110.8
Tate, presented by the American Fund for the Tate Gallery, courtesy Marsha Plotnitsky, 2000

Self-portrait: Reclining Figure, Two Panels, 1996
Photograph · 84 × 191 each
Scottish National Gallery of Modern Art, Edinburgh
Plate 93

Currie, Ken British, b.1960

Unfamiliar Reflection, 2006
Oil on canvas · 198.5 × 137.5
The Artist
Plate 91

diCorcia, Philip-Lorca American, b.1951

Lola, 2004
Fuji crystal archive print · 182.9 × 121.9
Courtesy the Artist and Pace/MacGill Gallery, New York
Plate 130

Tennille, 2004
Fuji crystal archive print · 182.9 × 121.9
Courtesy the Artist and Pace/MacGill Gallery, New York
Plate 129

Dijkstra, Rineke Dutch, b.1959

Julie, Den Haag, Netherlands, 29 February, 1994, 1994
C-type print · 62 × 52
Courtesy of the artist and Marian Goodman Gallery, New York
Plate 123

Tecla, Amsterdam, Netherlands, 16 May, 1994, 1994
C-type print · 62 × 52
Courtesy of the artist and Marian Goodman Gallery, New York
Plate 122

Saskia, Harderwijk, Netherlands, 16 March, 1994, 1994
C-type print · 62 × 52
Courtesy of the artist and Marian Goodman Gallery, New York
Plate 124

Emin, Tracey British, b.1963

Carry Myself (from Family Suite), 1994
Monoprint on paper · 11.6 × 10.6
Scottish National Gallery of Modern Art, Edinburgh

Me at 10 (from Family Suite), 1994
Monoprint on paper · 11.6 × 10.6
Scottish National Gallery of Modern Art, Edinburgh
Plate 113

Blood Thing at 10 (from Family Suite), 1994
Monoprint on paper · 11.6 × 10.6
Scottish National Gallery of Modern Art, Edinburgh

Just Remember How It Was, 1998
Monoprint on calico with stitching
34.2 × 41 (irregular)
Scottish National Gallery of Modern Art, Edinburgh
Plate 112

The Last Thing I Said to You was Don't Leave Me Here II, 2000
Ink-jet print on paper · 80.5 × 109.5
Tate, presented by Anne-Katrin Meier zu Sieker, 2002
Plate 114

Freud, Lucian British, b.1922

Small Naked Portrait, 1974
Oil on canvas · 22.2 × 20
The Ashmolean Museum, Oxford
Plate 23

Naked Girl with Egg, 1980–1
Oil on canvas · 75 × 60.5
British Council
Plate 24

Two Men, 1987–8
Oil on canvas · 106.70 × 75
Scottish National Gallery of Modern Art, Edinburgh
Plate 70

Furuya, Seiichi Japanese / Austrian, b.1950

Portrait of Christine Furuya, Graz, 1979
Silver gelatin print · 37.1 × 25
Collection Fotomuseum, Winterthur, Gift Seiichi Furuya

Portrait of Christine Furuya, Vienna, 1982
Silver gelatin print · 37.1 × 25
Collection Fotomuseum, Winterthur, Gift Seiichi Furuya

Portrait of Christine Furuya, Vienna, 1982
Silver gelatin print · 37.1 × 25
Collection Fotomuseum, Winterthur, Gift Seiichi Furuya
Plate 61

Gearon, Tierney American, b.1963

Untitled (from The Mother Project), 2001
C-type print · 50.8 × 60.9
Courtesy of Yossi Milo, New York

Untitled (from The Mother Project), 2003
C-type print · 50.8 × 60.9
Courtesy of Yossi Milo, New York
Plate 77

Gilbert & George British b.1943 and b.1942

In the Piss, 1997
Photo-piece of nine panels · 226 × 190
National Portrait Gallery, London
Plate 75

Goldin, Nan American, b.1953

David and Bruce after Sex, Provincetown, 1975
Cibachrome · 101.6 × 76.2
Private Collection, London
Plate 71

Self-portrait on my Bed, New York City, 1983
C-print · 76.2 × 101.6
Collection Fotomuseum, Winterthur

Self-portrait in Kimono with Brian, 1983
C-print
76.2 × 101.6
Collection Fotomuseum, Winterthur, Gift of Andreas Reinhart
Plate 73

Patrick and Teri on their Wedding Night, New York City, 1987
C-print · 61 × 51
Collection Fotomuseum, Winterthur
Plate 72

Siobhan in the Shower, 1991
Silver dye bleach print · 121.9 × 91.4
Whitney Museum of American Art, New York

Siobhan in the Woods, Provincetown, 1991
C-print · 51 × 61
Collection Fotomuseum, Winterthur
Plate 57

Siobhan in my Bathtub, Berlin, 1992
C-print · 51 × 61
Collection Fotomuseum, Winterthur
Plate 58

Gowin, Emmet American, b.1941

Edith, Danville, Virginia, 1967
Toned silver gelatin print · 25.4 × 20.3
Courtesy Pace/MacGill Gallery, New York
Plate 54

Edith, Danville, Virginia, 1973
Toned silver gelatin print · 25.4 × 20.3
Courtesy Pace/MacGill Gallery, New York

Edith, Newtown, Pennsylvania, 1974
Toned silver gelatin print · 25.4 × 20.3
Courtesy Pace/MacGill Gallery, New York
Plate 56

Edith, Danville, Virginia, 1980
Toned silver gelatin print · 25.4 × 20.3
Courtesy Pace/MacGill Gallery, New York

Edith, Danville, Virginia, 1983
Toned silver gelatin print · 25.4 × 20.3
Courtesy Pace/MacGill Gallery, New York

Edith, 1986
Toned silver gelatin print · 25.4 × 20.3
Courtesy Pace/MacGill Gallery, New York
Plate 55

Edith in Panama, 2005
Unique gold-toned salt print · 35.7 × 25.8
Courtesy Pace/MacGill Gallery, New York

Grannan, Katy American, b.1969

Allan, b.1951, 2004
Archival pigment print · 71.91 × 90.17
Private Collection, Thomas Koerfer, Zurich

Michele, b.1977, 2004
Archival pigment print · 71.91 × 90.17
Private Collection, Thomas Koerfer, Zurich

Grant, Catriona British, b.1964

Don Morris aged 71 diptych, 2006
Photograph · 76 × 112
The Artist (Edinburgh)
Supported by Edinburgh College of Art
Plate 137

Jim Groark aged 44 diptych, 2006
Photograph · 76 × 112
The Artist (Edinburgh)
Supported by Edinburgh College of Art

Grant, Duncan British, 1885–1978

David Garnett, 1915
Oil on canvas · 61 × 53.3
Private Collection, London
Edinburgh only · Plate 15

Gunn-Cairns, Joyce British, b.1948

Self-portrait, Deposition, 1998
Oil on board · 121.9 × 78.7
The Artist
Plate 109

Haas, Ernst Austrian, 1921–1986

Sugar Ray Robinson Weighing In, 1957
Silver gelatin print · 50.8 × 40.6
Private Collection, Thomas Koerfer, Zurich
Plate 141

Hilton, Roger British, 1911–1975

Dancing Woman, 1963
Oil on canvas · 152.5 × 127
Scottish National Gallery of Modern Art, Edinburgh
Edinburgh only · Plate 22

Hockney, David British, b.1937

The Beginning, 1966
Etching · 57 × 39.5
Scottish National Gallery of Modern Art, Edinburgh
Plate 69

Peter, 1969
Etching · 92.5 × 71
Goldmark Gallery, Rutland

Howson, Peter British, b.1958

Madonna, 2002
Oil on canvas · 122 × 183
Collection Mr & Mrs Flowers
Plate 139

Hujar, Peter American, 1934–1987

TC, 1976
Silver gelatin print · 40.6 × 50.8
Courtesy Gary Schneider and John Erdman

Gary, 1982
Silver gelatin print · 40.6 × 50.8
Courtesy Gary Schneider and John Erdman
Plate 12

Jones, Lucy British, b.1955

Asleep, Seeing or Dead, 2000
Oil on canvas · 218.5 × 157
The Artist, Courtesy Flowers
Plate 110

Remove your Gaze, 2001
Oil and acrylic on canvas · 183 × 121.5
The Artist, Courtesy Flowers

Kokoschka, Oskar Austrian, 1886–1980

Self-portrait, Poster for *Der Sturm*, 1910
Colour lithograph · 70.7 × 47.3
Victoria & Albert Museum, London
Plate 33

Kossoff, Leon British, b.1926

Fidelma No.1, 1978
Oil on canvas · 93 × 61
James Hyman Fine Art, London
Plate 9

Summer in the Studio, Pilar and Jacinto II, 1997
Oil on board · 147 × 135
Annely Juda Fine Art, London
Plate 68

Leibovitz, Annie American, b.1949

John Lennon and Yoko Ono, 1980
Colour photograph · 30.5 × 31
Scottish National Portrait Gallery, Edinburgh
Plate 146

Lucas, Sarah British, b.1962

Self-portraits 1990–1998 (Human Toilet II, 1997)
Iris print · 80 × 60
Scottish National Gallery of Modern Art, Edinburgh
Plate 115

Man Ray American, 1890–1976

Lee Miller Triptych, early 1930s
Vintage silver gelatin prints · 11.5 × 8 each
Private Collection, Thomas Koerfer, Zurich
Plate 48

Manchot, Melanie German / British, b.1966

Mrs Manchot: Hands on Hips, 1996
Silver gelatin and mixed media on canvas 140 × 110
Fred (London) Ltd and the Artist
Plate 82

Liminal Portrait – with Mountains I, 1999–2000
C-type print · 130 × 135
Fred (London) Ltd and the Artist
Plate 84

The Fontainebleau Series: Emma and Charlie 1, 2001
C-Type print · 100 × 125
Fred (London) Ltd and the Artist
Plate 76

Mapplethorpe, Robert American, 1946–1989

Patti Smith, 1976
Silver gelatin print · 50.8 × 40.6
Private Collection
Plate 13

Bob Love, 1979
Silver gelatin print · 35 × 35.2
Victoria & Albert Museum, London
Plate 10

Self-portrait in Drag, 1980
Silver gelatin print · 35.7 × 35.6
Pompidou Centre, Paris
Edinburgh only · Plate 17

Self-portrait with Cigarette, 1980
Silver gelatin print · 35.7 × 35.6
Pompidou Centre, Paris
Edinburgh only · Plate 18

McCartney, Linda American, 1941–1998

Mary McCartney, Sir Paul McCartney, 1969
Platinum print · 35.6 × 51.4
National Portrait Gallery, London

Medley, Robert British, 1905–1994

Self-portrait after Watteau's Gilles, *c.*1985
Oil on canvas · 101.5 × 88.5
Private Collection, courtesy James Hyman Fine Art, London
Plate 89

Mikhailov, Boris Ukrainian, b.1938

Untitled (from Case History), 1998
Colour photograph · 66 × 95
Saatchi Gallery

Untitled (from Case History), 1998
Colour photograph · 18.5 × 27
Saatchi Gallery

Untitled (from Case History), 1998
Colour photograph · 18.5 × 27
Saatchi Gallery

Untitled (from Case History), 1998
Colour photograph · 18.5 × 27
Saatchi Gallery

Untitled (from Case History), 1998
Colour photograph · 66 × 95
Saatchi Gallery

Modersohn-Becker, Paula German, 1876–1907

Self-portrait on her Sixth Wedding Anniversary, 1906
Oil on board · 101.8 × 70.2
Kunstsammlungen Boettcherstrasse / Paula Modersohn-Becker Museum, Bremen
Edinburgh only · Plate 25

Morley, Lewis British, b.1925

Christine Keeler, 1963
Vintage silver gelatin print · 50.8 × 41.3
National Portrait Gallery, London
Plate 142

Sir David Frost, 1963
Resin print · 39.2 × 30.1
National Portrait Gallery, London
Plate 143

Anthony Fry and Family, 1964
Bromide fibre print · 33.3 × 49
National Portrait Gallery, London

Barry Humphries as Dame Edna Everage, 1982
Bromide fibre print · 34.4 × 21.1
National Portrait Gallery, London
Plate 144

Morrison, Alastair British, b.1957

Linford Christie, 1996
Bromide print · 48.4 × 40.6
National Portrait Gallery, London
Plate 1

Neel, Alice American, 1900–1984

Ethel Ashton, 1930
Oil on canvas · 61 × 55.9
Tate, lent by the American fund for the Tate Gallery, courtesy of Hartley and Richard Neel, the artist's sons, fractional and promised gift, 2001

John Perreault, 1972
Oil on canvas · 96.5 × 161.2
Whitney Museum of American Art, New York
Plate 8

Andrew, 1978
Oil on canvas
76.1.x 61.5
Tate, London
Plate 78

Self-portrait, 1980
Oil on canvas · 54 × 40
National Portrait Gallery, Smithsonian Institute
Plate 98

Newton, Helmut German / French, 1920–2004

Charlotte Tessa Rampling,1973
Bromide print · 46.2 × 31.3
National Portrait Gallery, London

Nixon, Nicholas American, b.1947

Bebe and I, 1997
Silver gelatin print · 25.4 × 20.3
Courtesy Yossi Milo Gallery, New York
Plate 148

KH and SW, Jamaica Plain, 2001
Silver gelatin print · 25.4 × 20.3
Courtesy Yossi Milo Gallery, New York

Paolozzi, Eduardo British, 1924–2005

Self-portrait of the Artist with a Strange Machine, 1987
Bronze · 149.8 high
Scottish National Gallery of Modern Art, Edinburgh

Quinn, Marc British, b.1964

Template for my Future Plastic Surgery, 1992
Four-colour screenprint with varnish
86 × 68
Scottish National Gallery of Modern Art, Edinburgh
Plate 20

Catherine Long, 2002
Macedonian white marble · 159 × 50 × 74
Leamington Spa Art Gallery and Museum (Warwick District Council)
Plate 128

Richter, Gerhard German, b.1932

I.G.,1993
Oil on canvas · 82.2 × 92.2
Contemporary Art Collection Fundacion 'la Caixa', Barcelona
Plate 53

Rodin, Auguste French, 1840–1917

Eve,1902
Bronze · 75h.
Glasgow City Council (Museums)

Saville, Jenny British, b.1970

Closed Contact No 4, 1995–6
C-type print · 181.6 × 181.6 · made with Glen Luchford
Aberdeen Art Gallery and Museums Collections
Plate 111

Schiele, Egon Austrian, 1890–1918

Erwin Dominik Osen with Crossed Arms, 1910
Black crayon, watercolour and gouache on paper · 44.7 × 31.5
Leopold Museum, Vienna
Edinburgh only · Plate 7

Erwin Dominik Osen with Fingertips Touching, 1910
Black crayon and gouache on paper
38.3 × 30.3
Leopold Museum, Vienna
Edinburgh only · Plate 3

Self-portrait in Grey with Open Mouth, 1910
Gouache and black crayon on paper
44.2 × 30.3
Leopold Museum, Vienna
Edinburgh only · Plate 35

Nude Self-portrait with Hand on Genitals, 1911
Pencil on paper · 47.7 × 30.8
Leopold Museum, Vienna
Edinburgh only

Nude Self-portrait Crouching, 1912
Pencil on paper · 47.3 × 29.8
Leopold Museum, Vienna
Edinburgh only · Plate 34

Schneider, Gary American, b.1954

Eve, 2003
Pigmented ink on canvas · 221 × 106
Courtesy the Artist
Plate 135

Donald, 2004
Pigmented ink on canvas · 221 × 106
Courtesy the Artist
Plate 132

Nayland, 2004
Pigmented ink on canvas · 221 × 106
Courtesy the Artist
Plate 133

Terrell, 2004
Pigmented ink on canvas · 221 × 106
Courtesy the Artist
Plate 134

Trevor, 2004
Pigmented ink on canvas · 221 × 106
Courtesy the Artist

Elena, 2004
Pigmented ink on canvas · 221 × 106
Courtesy the Artist
Plate 136

Semmel, Joan American, b.1932

Out of Darkness, 1977
Oil on canvas · 124.5 × 170.2
The Artist
Plate 2

With Stripes, 2003
Oil on canvas · 172.7 × 147.3
The Artist
Plate 96

Spence, Jo British, 1934–1992

Narratives of Dis-ease: Expunged, 1989
Colour photograph · 96 × 65
Glasgow City Council (Museums)
Plate 103

Narratives of Dis-ease: Included, 1989
Colour photograph · 96 × 65
Glasgow City Council (Museums)
Plate 104

Narratives of Dis-ease: Exiled, 1989
Colour photograph · 96 × 65
Glasgow City Council (Museums)
Plate 102

Spencer, Stanley British, 1891–1959

Hilda Spencer, 1931
Pencil on paper · 50.8 × 35.2
Scottish National Gallery of Modern Art, Edinburgh
Plate 41

Nude (Portrait of Patricia Preece), 1935
Oil on canvas · 76.2 × 50.8
Ferens Art Gallery, Hull Museums and Art Gallery
Plate 43

Stehli, Jemima British, b.1961

Red Turning, 2000
C-type print · 217 × 179
Courtesy of the Artist and Lisson Gallery, London
Plate 117

Standing Nude I, 2001/2
C-type print · 188 × 238
Courtesy of the Artist and Lisson Gallery, London
Plate 116

Stern, Bert American, b.1929

Marilyn Monroe, 1962
Photograph · 48.5 × 47
Fotomuseum, Munich
Plate 138

Marilyn Monroe, 1962
Photograph · 48.5 × 47
Fotomuseum, Munich
Plate 140

Stieglitz, Alfred American, 1864–1946

A Portrait Torso (Georgia O'Keefe), 1918
Palladium print · 24.5 × 20
Victoria & Albert Museum, London
Plate 36

Georgia O'Keefe, 1918
Palladium print · 24.7 × 19.5
Victoria & Albert Museum, London
Plate 38

Georgia O'Keefe, 1918/19
Palladium print · 23.2 × 18.5
Thomas Koerfer, Zurich

Georgia O'Keefe, 1918/19
Palladium print · 23.4 × 18.9
Victoria & Albert Museum, London
Plate 39

Georgia O'Keefe, 1931
Palladium print · 11.6 × 23.8
Victoria & Albert Museum, London

Taylor-Wood, Sam British, b.1967

Robert Downey Jr, 2002
C-type print · 131.7 × 172.7
The Artist (White Cube, London)

Dustin Hoffman, 2004
C-type print · 87.4 × 87.4
The Artist (White Cube, London)
Plate 147

Tillmans, Wolfgang German, b.1968

Arnd, Nude, Sitting, 1991
C-type print · 18 × 11.5
Victoria & Albert Museum, London
Plate 11

Lutz and Alexandra Sitting in the Tree, 1992
C-type print · 18 × 11.5
Victoria & Albert Museum, London
Plate 62

Tynan, Steven British, b.1960

Untitled, 1997
Polaroid · 21.3 × 27.6
The Artist
Plate 94

Untitled, 1998
Polaroid · 27.6 × 21.3
The Artist

Untitled, 2000
Polaroid · 27.6 × 21.3
The Artist
Plate 95

Untitled, 2001
Polaroid · 21.3 × 27.6
The Artist

Untitled, 2004
Polaroid · 21.3 × 27.6
The Artist

Untitled, 2005
Polaroid · 21.3 × 27.6
The Artist

Walton, Cecile British, 1891–1956

Romance, 1920
Oil on canvas · 100.6 × 150.9
Scottish National Portrait Gallery, Edinburgh
Plate 97

Watt, Alison British, b.1965

Source III, 1995
Oil on canvas · 91.4 × 182.8
Courtesy the Artist and Ingleby Gallery, Edinburgh
Plate 118

Weston, Edward American, 1886–1958

Neil, taken 1922, printed 1960s/70s
Photograph · 57.5 × 42.3
Victoria & Albert Museum, London
Plate 81

Wilke, Hannah American, 1940–1993

Super-T-Art, 1974
Photographs (20) · 25.4 × 20.3 each
Courtesy Ronald Feldman Fine Art, New York
Plate 99

Williams, David British, b.1952

Triptych: Williams Family Portrait, 1999
Silver gelatin print · 64 × 53.5
The Artist
Supported by Edinburgh College of Art
Plate 80

My Son Samuel, Kos, Greece, 1998
C-type print · 45.7 × 45.7
The Artist
Supported by Edinburgh College of Art
Plate 79

Wood, Christopher British, 1901–1930

Nude Boy in a Bedroom, 1930
Oil on hardboard laid on plywood
53.8 × 65
Scottish National Gallery of Modern Art, Edinburgh
Plate 40

Woodman, Francesca American, 1958–1981

Self-portrait with Lily, 1972–5
Vintage silver gelatin print · 15.5 × 15.5
Thomas Koerfer, Zurich

Self-Deceit, 1977–8
Silver gelatin print · 8.5 × 8.8
Scottish National Gallery of Modern Art, Edinburgh
Edinburgh only · Plate 101

Self-Deceit 1 (Roma), 1977–8
Silver gelatin print · 9.2 × 9.2
Scottish National Gallery of Modern Art, Edinburgh
Edinburgh only

Self-Deceit 4, 1977–8
Silver gelatin print · 9.8 × 9.8
Scottish National Gallery of Modern Art, Edinburgh
Edinburgh only · Plate 100

Self-Deceit 5, 1977–8
Silver gelatin print · 9.2 × 9.2
Scottish National Gallery of Modern Art, Edinburgh
Edinburgh only

Self-Deceit 6,1977–8
Silver gelatin print · 8.5 × 8.5
Scottish National Gallery of Modern Art, Edinburgh
Edinburgh only

Wright, Alexa British

'I' no. 3, 1999
Digitally manipulated photograph
75 × 100
The Artist
Plate 108

'I' no. 7, 1999
Digitally manipulated photograph
100 × 75
The Artist

Yeo, Jonathan British, b.1970

Being Geri Halliwell (Ivan Massow diptych), 2000–2
Oil on canvas · 95 × 80 each
Ivan Massow
Plate 6

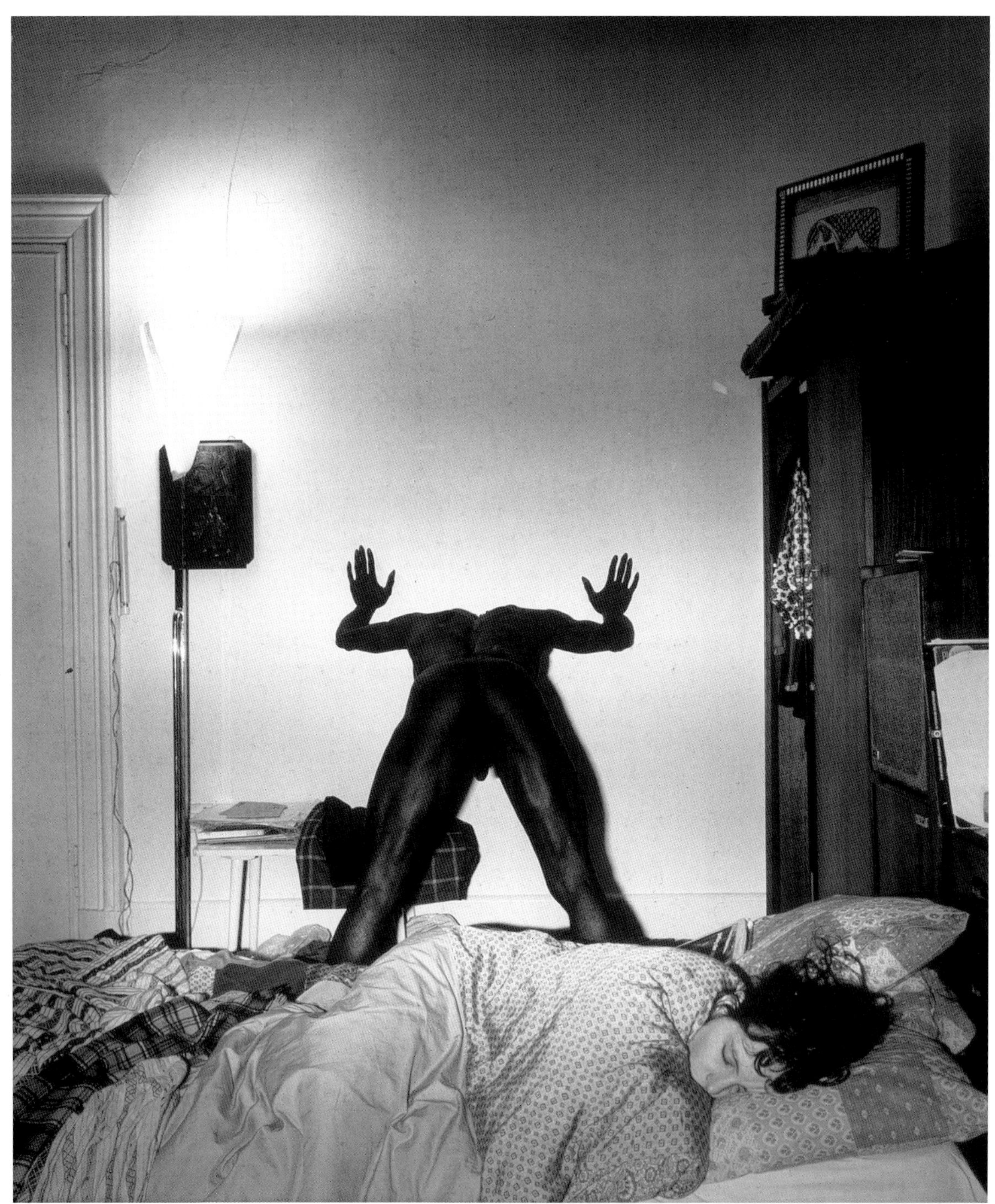

149 Odalebe Bamgboye

The Lighthouse, 1989

Private Collection, Thomas Koeffer,
Zurich

Bibliography

AMSTERDAM 2004
Rineke Dijkstra: Portraits, Stedelijk Museum, Amsterdam, 2004

AUERBACH 2005
Lucian Freud Portraits, DVD, Jake Auerbach Films Ltd, London, 2005

BAILEY 2005
David Bailey, *Bailey's Democracy*, London, 2005

BARCAN 2004
Ruth Barcan, *Nudity: A Cultural Anatomy*, Oxford and New York, 2004

BARCELONA 2006
J. Ribalta, *Jo Spence: Beyond the Perfect Image, Photography, Subjectivity, Antagonism*, Museu d'Art Contemporani de Barcelona, Barcelona, 2006

BERGER 1972
John Berger, *Ways of Seeing*, London, 1972

BERNARD AND BIRDSALL 1996
Bruce Bernard and Derek Birdsall (eds.), *Lucian Freud*, London, 1996

BROUDE 1994
Norma Broude and Mary D. Garrard (eds.), *The Power of Feminist Art: the American Movement of the 1970s, History and Impact*, London, 1994

CARDIFF 2003
K. Newton and C. Rolph (eds.), *Masquerade: Women's Contemporary Portrait Photography*, Ffotogallery, Cardiff, 2003

CARUCCI 2003
Elinor Carucci, *Closer*, New York, 2003

CLARK 1956
Kenneth Clark, *The Nude: A Study of Ideal Art*, London, 1956

COPLANS 2002
John Coplans, *A Body*, New York, 2002

EWING 1994
William E. Ewing, *The Body: Photoworks of the Human Form*, London, 1994

FREEDMAN AND LUARD 2006
Carl Freedman and Honey Luard, *Tracey Emin*, New York, 2006

FREUD 1962
Sigmund Freud, *Two Short Accounts of Psychoanalysis*, Harmondsworth, 1962

GOLDIN 1986
Nan Goldin, *The Ballad of Sexual Dependency*, London, 1986

GRANNAN 2005
Katy Grannan, *Model American*, London and New York, 2005

GUIGNON 2004
Charles Guignon, *On Being Authentic*, London, 2004

HOLLANDER 1975
Anne Hollander, *Seeing through Clothes*, London, 1975

KALLIR 1998
Jane Kallir, *Egon Schiele: The Complete Works. Expanded Edition*, New York, 1998

KARABELNIK 2004
Marianne Karabelnik (ed.), *Stripped Bare: The Body Revealed in Contemporary Art*, London, 2004

KELLY 1979
Jain Kelly (ed.), *Nude:Theory*, New York, 1979

KIRBY 2006
John Kirby *et al.*, *Lucy Jones: Looking at Self*, London, 2006

LEIBOVITZ 2006
Annie Leibovitz, *A Photographer's Life: 1990–2005*, London, 2006

LONDON 1978
Frank Auerbach, Arts Council of Great Britain, London, 1978

LONDON 1998
Sarah Whitfield and John Elderfield, *Bonnard*, Tate Gallery, London, 1998

LONDON 2001
Timothy Hyman and Patrick Wright (eds.), *Stanley Spencer*, Tate, London, 2001

LONDON 2002
William Feaver, *Lucian Freud*, Tate, London, 2002

LONDON 2003
Diane Arbus: Revelations, San Francisco Museum of Modern Art, London, 2003

LONDON 2004
Mark Sladen (ed.), *Helen Chadwick*, Barbican Art Gallery, London, 2004

LONDON 2006
Alexander Sturgis *et al.*, *Rebels and Martyrs. The Image of the Artist in the Nineteenth Century*, National Gallery, London, 2006

LONDON 2006 (2)
Iris Müler-Westermann, *Munch by Himself*, Royal Academy of Arts, London, 2006

MANN 1991
Sally Mann, *Immediate Family*, New York, 1991

McNAIR 2002
Brian McNair, *Striptease Culture: Sex, Media and the Democratization of Desire*, London, 2002

MERCK AND TOWNSEND 2002
Mandy Merck and Chris Townsend (eds.), *The Art of Tracey Emin*, London, 2002

MIKHAILOV 1999
Boris Mikhailov, *Case History*, Zurich, Berlin and New York, 1999

NEAD 1992
Lynda Nead, *The Female Nude. Art, Obscenity and Sexuality*, London, 1992

NEW YORK 1992
Germano Celant, *Robert Mapplethorpe*, Solomon R Guggenheim Museum, New York, 1992

NEW YORK 1996
Nan Goldin, *I'll be Your Mirror*, Whitney Museum of American Art, New York, 1996

NEW YORK 2000
A Temkin (ed.), *Alice Neel*, Whitney Museum of American Art, New York, 2000

NIXON 2003
Carlos Gollonet (ed.), *Nicholas Nixon*, Madrid, 2003

OLLMAN 1999
Arthur Ollman, *The Model Wife*, Boston, 1999

PHILADELPHIA 1990
Emmet Gowin: Photographs, Philadelphia Museum of Art, Philadelphia, 1990

SAVILLE 2005
Jenny Saville, New York, 2005

SCHNEIDER 2005
Gary Schneider: Nudes, New York, 2005

SMEE 2005
Sebastian Smee, *Lucian Freud 1996–2005*, London, 2005

SPENCE 1995
Jo Spence, *Cultural Sniping: The Art of Transgression*, London and New York, 1995

STEINER 2001
Wendy Steiner, *The Trouble with Beauty*, London, 2001

STIEGLITZ 1978
Georgia O'Keefe. A Portrait by Alfred Stieglitz, Washington, 1978

TAYLOR 1989
Charles Taylor, *Sources of the Self: The Making of Modern Identity*, Cambridge, 1989

TOWNSEND 1998
Chris Townsend, *Vile Bodies: Photography and the Crisis of Looking*, London, 1998

TOWNSEND 2006
Chris Townsend, *Francesca Woodman*, London and New York, 2006

VIENNA 2006
Klaus Albrecht-Schröder, *Egon Schiele: Eros and Passion*, Albertina, Vienna, 2006

VIOLETTE AND OBRIST 1997
Robert Violette and Hans-Ulrich Obrist (eds.), *The Words of Gilbert & George: With Portraits of the Artists from 1968 to 1997*, London, 1997

WARR 2000
Tracey Warr (ed.), *The Artist's Body*, London 2000

WASHINGTON 1996
Sarah Greenough, *Harry Callahan*, National Gallery of Art, Washington, 1996

WASHINGTON 1999
Sarah Greenough and Juan Hamilton, *Alfred Stieglitz: Photographs and Writings*, National Gallery of Art, Washington / Bullfinch Press, 1999

WASHINGTON 2002
Sarah Greenough, *Alfred Stieglitz: The Key Set: The Alfred Stieglitz Collection of Photographs*, Washington, 2002

ZELDIN 1994
Theodore Zeldin, *An Intimate History of Humanity*, London, 1994

ZURICH 1994
Urs Stahel and Hripsimé Visser (eds.), *Peter Hujar: A Retrospective*, Zurich, Berlin and New York, 1994

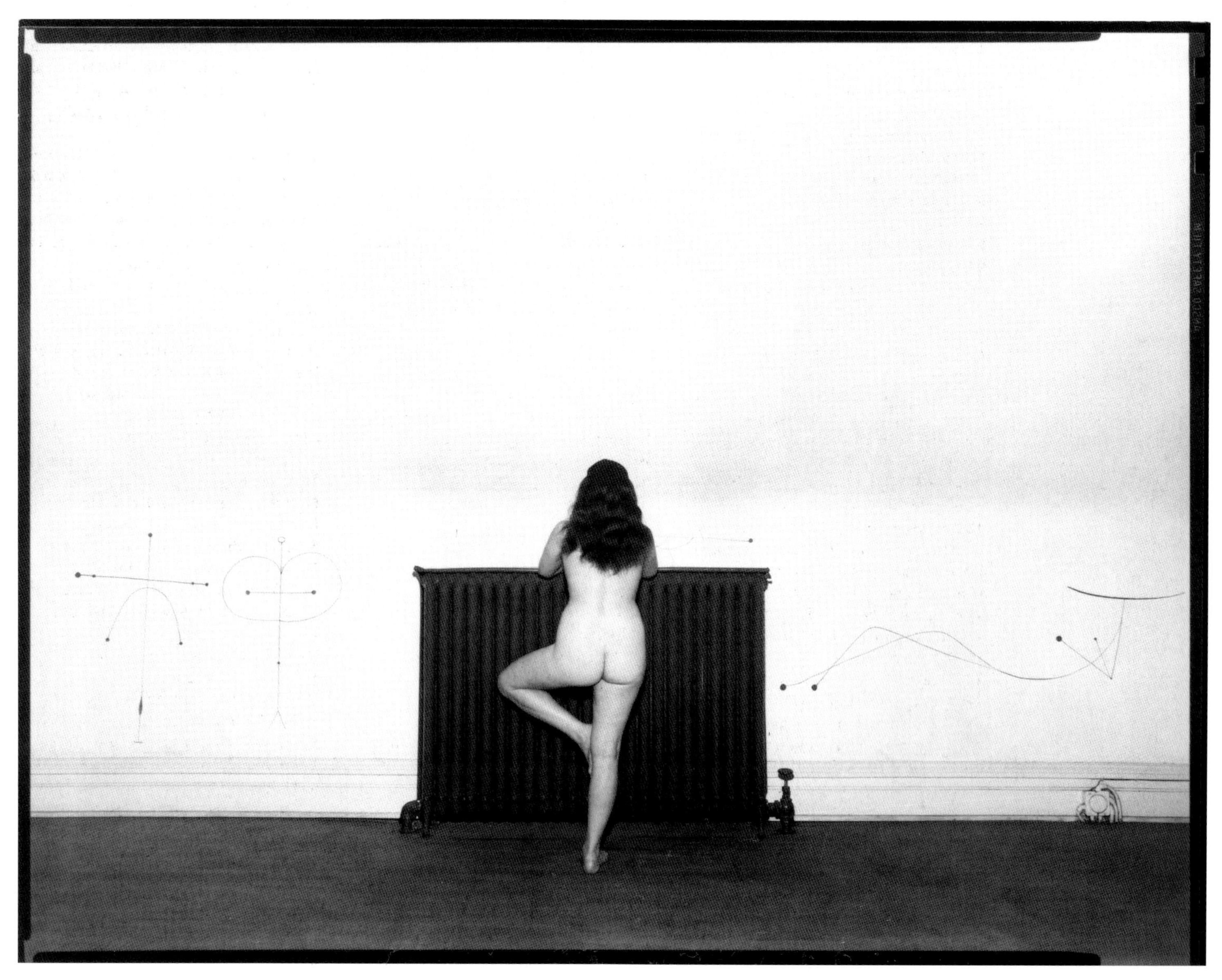

Notes and References

Chapter 1

1 See Erwin Panofsky, 'Iconography and Iconology: An Introduction to the Study of Renaissance Art', *Meaning in the Visual Arts*, Harmondsworth, 1970, pp.51–67.
2 David Sylvester, *London Recordings*, London, 2003, pp.50–1.
3 'Melanie Manchot interviewed by Toyoko Ito, http://www.fogless.net/artreview/030825_rm_mm/manchotE.htm.
4 The most comprehensive survey remains Clark 1956.
5 Anthony Bond and Joanna Woodall (eds.), *Self Portrait: Renaissance to Contemporary*, exh. cat., National Portrait Gallery, London and Art Gallery of New South Wales, Sydney, 2005.
6 Hollander 1975, p.84.
7 Ewing 1994, p.9.
8 Karabelnik 2004.
9 On Massow's career and portraits see 'Aspects of Me', *The Guardian Weekend*, 26 April 2003, pp.24–8.
10 Estate of Larry Rivers, New York; a characteristic Klein is *Arman*, Centre Pompidou, Paris (all are dated to 1962, though only the Arman relief was cast in bronze and painted with Klein's trademark ultramarine before his death that year).
11 http://johnperreault.com/_wsn/page15.html.
12 Paul Moorhouse, '"The eye sees more than the heart knows": The Work of Leon Kossoff', *Leon Kossoff*, exh. cat., Tate Gallery, London, 1996, p.24.
13 Richard Marshall, 'Mapplethorpe's Vision', *Richard Mapplethorpe*, London, 1988, p.156.
14 Kobena Mercer, 'Looking for Trouble', *Transition*, no.51, 1991, pp.184–97. Melody Davis critiques Mapplethorpe's work in similar terms by comparison with the more empathetic work of George Dureau, who may indeed have influenced the former's turn to black models (*The Male Nude in Contemporary Photography*, Philadelphia, 1991, chapter 2).
15 Ibid., p.99.
16 Zurich 1994.
17 Scottish National Gallery of Modern Art, Edinburgh.
18 See Penelope Curtis *et al.*, *Return to Life. A New Look at the Portrait Bust*, exh. cat., Henry Moore Institute, Leeds, 2000.
19 See Richard Shone, *The Art of Bloomsbury: Roger Fry, Vanessa Bell and Duncan Grant*, exh. cat., Tate Gallery, London, 1999, pp.105–7.
20 Nicholas Fox Weber, *Balthus. A Biography*, London, 1999, pp.456–7; *Companion Guide to the Scottish National Gallery of Modern Art*, Edinburgh, 1999, p.138.
21 See Stamislas Klossowski de Rola, *Balthus*, London, 1996, plates 58–9.
22 Gemäldegalerie, Berlin. Precursors for such imagery include *Nu aux bras levés* (1951) and *La Chambre* (1952–4).
23 *Companion Guide to the Scottish National Gallery of Modern Art*, p.170. *Oi, yoi, yoi* was the title given to the first version (Tate).
24 'A conversation with Frank Auerbach', in London 1978, p.16.
25 Mary Beard and John Henderson, *Classical Art, From Greece to Rome*, Oxford, 2001, p.205.
26 McNair 2002, p.ix.
27 http://johnperreault.com/_wsn/page15.html.
28 Malcolm Bradbury, *The History Man*, London, 1977, p.73.
29 Zeldin 1994.
30 Susan Bright, *Art Photography Now*, London, 2005, p.21.
31 Taylor 1989.
32 Ibid., p.456.
33 Ibid., p.457.
34 Ibid., p.460.
35 Guignon 2004, p.80 ff.
36 Ibid.
37 Clark 1956.
38 Berger 1972, p.54.
39 Brendan Prendeville, *Realism in Twentieth-Century Painting*, London, p.50.
40 Arthur Danto, 'Lucien [*sic*] Freud', *The Madonna of the Future*, New York, 2000, pp.30 and 34.
41 Ibid., p.33.
42 Violette and Obrist 1997, p.250. The point is reiterated in another 1995 interview (ibid., p.199).
43 'Di wasn't a great beauty' (interview with Lynn Barber), *The Independent on Sunday*, London, 20 November 2005.
44 Balthus claimed to have 'taken care' of Freud when the latter was spending time in Paris, presumably in the late 1940s (Fox Weber, p.118, see note 20).
45 For reproductions, see Bernard and Birdsall 1996; London 2002; Smee 2005.
46 Robert Hughes, *Lucian Freud Paintings*, London, 1987, p.21.
47 Ibid., p.20.
48 Kallir 1998, no.306.
49 Prendeville, pp.186–7 (see note 39).
50 One might note an affinity between Freud's settings and the bare rooms, with flaking plaster and boards, that Francesca Woodman was using around 1980 as the setting for posed naked bodies, mainly her own.
51 Quoted in John Russell, 'Introduction', *Lucian Freud*, exh. cat., The Arts Council of Great Britain, London, 1974, pp.23–7. The sitters may become close friends in the process of being painted, although in recent years they might also be handsomely paid for their time and trouble.
52 Cited (from conversations with the artist 1995–6) in William Feaver, 'Lucian Freud', *Lucian Freud: Paintings and Etchings*, exh. cat., Abbot Hall Art Gallery, Kendal, 1996, p.10.
53 Shearer West, *Portraiture*, Oxford, 2004, p.38.
54 Smee 2005, p.7.
55 William Feaver, 'Lucian Freud: Life into Art', in London 2002, p.39.
56 'Seeing through the Skin', *The Guardian*, London, 18 May 2002.
57 'Lucian Freud's working practices revealed', *The Art Newspaper*, no.176, January 2007.
58 Auerbach 2005.
59 London 2002, p.10.
60 'Seeing through the Skin' (see note 56).
61 London 2002, p.40.
62 Desmond Morris, *The Naked Ape*, London, 1967.
63 Hughes, p.18 (see note 46).

Chapter 2

1 *Rodin*, exh. cat., Royal Academy of Arts, London, 2006, p.224.
2 I am grateful to Richard Thomson for informing me about this episode, which is widely noted in the Rodin literature.
3 Private Collection. My account is

150 Harry Callahan
Eleanor, Chicago, 1949
Pompidou Centre, Paris

indebted to Belinda Thomson's seminar presentation on the picture in June 2003 (History of Art Department, Edinburgh).
4 See Jill Lloyd, *German Expressionism: Primitivism and Modernity*, New Haven and London, 1991, chapter 3.
5 *Katalog zur Ausstellung der K.G. "Brücke" in Galerie Arnold, Dresden, Schlosstrasse, September 1910*, exh. cat., no.25 (with Haeckel woodcut of the picture opposite).
6 The debt to Munch is noted in Jill Lloyd, 'Kirchner's Metaphysical Studio Paintings', in Jill Lloyd and Magdalena Moeller (eds.), *Ernst Ludwig Kirchner: The Dresden and Berlin Years*, exh. cat., Royal Academy of Arts, London, 2003, p.18.
7 Freud, 1962, p.70.
8 London, 2006 (2), pp.75 and 108 (note 11).
9 Ibid., pp.73–4.
10 Elizabeth Cowling, *Picasso: Style and Meaning*, London, 2002, p.144.
11 Reproduced in Marilyn McCully (ed.), *Picasso: The Early Years 1892–1906*, exh. cat., National Gallery of Art, Washington, 1997, pp.344–5.
12 Reproduced ibid., pp.340 and 346.
13 Tim Hilton, 'Introduction', *Picasso's Picassos*, exh. cat., Hayward Gallery, London, 1981, p.32.
14 Carol Duncan, 'Virility and Domination in Early Twentieth-Century Vanguard Painting', *Artforum*, December, 1973, pp.30–9.
15 London 2006, p.180.
16 Leopold Museum, Vienna. Illustrated in London 2006, p.161.
17 Gemma Blackshaw, 'The Jewish Christ: Problems of Self-presentation and Socio-Cultural Assimilation in Richard Gerstl's Self-Portraiture', *Oxford Art Journal*, vol.29, no.1, 2006, p.28.
18 Ibid., p.46.
19 London 2006, pp.162–3.
20 Kallir 1998, p.60.
21 Ibid., p.294.
22 Ibid., nos.174, 175, 191, 192, 275, 326 and 328.
23 Ibid., p.647.
24 Vienna 2006, p.17.
25 Cited in Vienna 2006, p.17.
26 Kirk Varnedoe, *Vienna 1900: Art, Architecture & Design*, exh. cat., Museum of Modern Art, New York, 1986, p.174.
27 Such readings are summarised in Vienna 2006, pp.33–9.
28 See Freud's 'Formulations regarding the Two Principles in Mental Functioning' (1911), cited in Hal Foster *et al.*, *Art since 1900*, London and New York, 2004, p.20.
29 Andrew Bennett, *The Author*, London and New York, 2005, p.70.
30 Ibid., p.71.

Chapter 3

1 Harry Callahan, untitled essay, in Kelly 1979, p.30.
2 See *Yoko. Don Brown*, exh. cat., Sadie Coles, London, 2005.
3 Berger 1972, pp.57–8.
4 Kunsthistorisches Museum, Vienna. The picture was a visual love letter; it stayed in the family home, and Rubens bequeathed it to the sitter on the condition that she did not have to reimburse the other heirs for a share of its value.
5 See the discussion in Julia Lloyd-Williams *et al.*, *Rembrandt's Women*, exh. cat., National Galleries of Scotland, Edinburgh, 2001, p.182.
6 For a recent discussion of the likely identity of the models see Volker Manuth, '"As stark naked as one could possibly be painted…": the reputation of the nude female model in the age of Rembrandt', ibid., pp.47–53.
7 Stielgitz 1978, n.p.
8 Washington 2002, vol.1, p.xxxvi.
9 Ibid., vol.1, nos.635–8 and 750–71.
10 For the 1917 nudes, and the likelihood that they are self-portraits, see Barbara Buhler Lynes, *Georgia O'Keefe: Catalogue Raisonné*, New Haven and London, 1999, vol.1, pp.106–13.
11 Stieglitz 1978, n.p.
12 Washington 1999, p.201.
13 Letter to Sadakichi Hartmann, 27 April 1919, Washington 1999, p.205.
14 Stielgitz 1978, n.p.
15 Cited in Anne Wagner, *Three Artists (Three Women) : Modernism and the Art of Hesse, Krasner, and O'Keeffe*, Berkeley and London, 1996, p.81.
16 Ibid., p.91.
17 Ibid., p.37.
18 Washington 2002, vol.1, p.xxxv.
19 Sarah Greenhough, 'Alfred Stieglitz, Facilitator, Financier, and Father, Presents Seven Americans', *Modern Art and America: Alfred Stieglitz and his New York Galleries*, exh. cat., National Gallery of Art, Washington, 2000, pp.281–3.
20 Lynes, pp.112–3 (see note 10).
21 See Francis Rose, *A Saying Life*, London, 1961, p.151.
22 Richard Ingelby, *Christopher Wood. An English Painter*, London, 1995, p.246.
23 Cited in *Stanley Spencer RA*, exh. cat., Royal Academy, London, 1980, p.141.
24 London 2001, p.146.
25 Richard Cork, *David Bomberg*, New Haven and London, 1987, p.193.
26 Ibid., p.194.
27 The fullest account of the works is Robert Rosenblum, 'Picasso's Blonde Muse: The Reign of Marie-Thérèse Walter', in William Rubin (ed.), *Picasso and Portraiture: Representation and Transformation*, exh. cat., Museum of Modern Art, New York, 1996, pp.336–83.
28 Picasso's *Girl in front of a Mirror* and Bonnard's *The Bathroom*, both pictures from 1932, were tellingly juxtaposed in the recent hang of the permanent collection at the Museum of Modern Art, New York.
29 The section that follows draws upon Sarah Whitfield, 'Fragments of an Identical World', in London 1998, pp.9–32.
30 Christopher Green, *Art in France 1900–1940*, New Haven and London, *c.* 2000, p.168.
31 David Sylvester, 'Bonnard', *About Modern Art*, London, 2002, p.140 ('slightly revised' version of a 1966 text that pioneered an emphasis on the role of Marthe in Bonnard's work).
32 Cited in Whitfield, p.27 (see note 29).
33 Whitfield, p.28 (ibid.).
34 Sylvester, p.138 (see note 31).
35 Man Ray, 'The Age of Light', and André Breton, 'The Visages of the Woman', *Photographs by Man Ray, 105 works, 1920–1934*, New York, 1979 (reprint of 1934 original), n.p.
36 See Jennifer Mundy (ed.), *Surrealism: Desire Unbound*, exh. cat., Tate Gallery, London, 2001, pp.224–5.
37 Jane Livingstone, 'Man Ray and Surrealist Photography', in *L'Amour Fou*, exh. cat., Hayward Gallery, London, 1986, p.123.
38 This cluster of works is usefully discussed in Dawn Ades, *Dalí: A Centenary Retrospective*, exh. cat., London, 2005, nos.206, 207 and 213. See too Fiona Bradley, 'Gala Dalí: The Eternal Feminine', Dawn Ades and Fiona Bradley, *Salvador Dalí: A Mythology*, London, 1999, pp.54–77.
39 Cited in Ian Gibson, *The Shameful Life of Salvador Dalí*, London, 1997, p.441. On the iconographic programme, see Bradley, pp.68–9 (see note 38).
40 Ibid., p.76.
41 Eleanor Callahan, untitled essay, in Kelly 1979, p.36.
42 Callahan, untitled essay, ibid., p.30.
43 Reproduced in Ollman 1999, p.101.
44 Washington 1996, p.50.
45 Ibid.
46 The importance of the Annette pictures in his development is indicated in Christian Klemm *et al.*, *Alberto Giacometti*, exh. cat., Museum of Modern Art, New York, 2001, p.206. There are versions in the Hirshchorn Museum, Washington, and the Staatsgalerie, Stuttgart.
47 See James Hyman, *The Battle for Realism*, New Haven and London, 2001.
48 'A Conversation with Frank Auerbach', London 1978, p.14.
49 Auerbach 2005.
50 Hans-Ulrich Obrist (ed.), *Gerhard Richter. The Daily Practice of Painting. Writings and Interviews 1962–1993*, London, 1995, p.57.
51 Ibid., pp.224–5.
52 See Marco Livingstone, *David Hockney*, London, 1981, pp.96–101.
53 Cited in Ollman 1999, p.121.
54 Gowin 1990, n.p.
55 Goldin 1986, p.6.
56 'On Acceptance: A Conversation', Goldin 1996, p.454.
57 Ibid., p.454.
58 Jonathon Weinberg, *Fantastic Tales: the Photography of Nan Goldin*, London, 2005, p.19.
59 Elisabeth Sussman, 'In/Of Her Time: Nan Goldin's Photographs', Goldin 1996, p.39.
60 Ibid.
61 Richard Calvocoressi and Martin Hammer, *Francis Bacon: Portraits and Heads*, exh. cat., National Galleries of Scotland, Edinburgh, 2005, pl.26.
62 See Martin Hammer, 'Clearing away the Screens', in *Francis Bacon: Portraits and Heads*, pp.23–4.
63 Cited in Monika Faber, 'Portrait', in Seiichi Furuya, *Portrait. Christine Furuya-Gössler 1978–1985*, Fotohof, 2000, p.124.
64 Ibid., p.125.

Chapter 4

1 Frank Kermode, *Lawrence*, London, 1973, p.22.
2 Reproduced in *1900*, exh. cat., Royal Academy, London, 2000, p.16.
3 Sarah Whitfield, 'Fragments of an Identical World', London, 1998, p.16.
4 Ibid.
5 Cited in London 2006 (2), p.97.
6 Ibid., pp.97–103.
7 Cited in Frank Whitford, *Oskar Kokoschka: A Life*, London, 1986, p.91.
8 Patrick Werkner, 'Gestures in Oskar Kokoschka's Early Portraits', Tobias Natter (ed.), *Oskar Kokoschka: Early Portraits from Vienna and Berlin 1909–14*, exh. cat., Hamburger Kunsthalle / Neue Galerie, New York, 2002, p.35.
9 Carl Schorske, *Fin-de-Siècle Vienna: Politics and Culture*, Cambridge, 1980, p.342.
10 See Renée Price (ed.), *Egon Schiele: the Ronald S. Lauder and Serge Sabarsky Collections*, exh. cat., Neue Galerie, New York, 2005, p.188.
11 Adrian Glew, *Stanley Spencer: Letters and Writings*, London, 2001, pp.162 and 189.
12 Ibid., p.182.

13 Ibid., p.190.
14 Ibid., p.243.
15 Cited in Kitty Hauser, *Stanley Spencer*, London, 2001, p.51.
16 Glew, p.168 (see note 11). The succeeding imagery about underwear correlates with *Nude (Patricia Preece, or Girl Resting)* of 1936.
17 Ibid., p.178.
18 Ibid., p.174.
19 The combination of realism, albeit with stylised treatment of objects and space, and an imagery of the untravelled fantasy world of young children, in Spencers such as *The Nursery, or Childhood Stockings* (1936) recalls an artist like Max Ernst. In *Christmas*, from the same year, the hallucinatory clarity and homespun sense of metamorphosis, especially in the patchwork elephant, recall Salvador Dalí. The Spencers are reproduced in London 2001, pp.190–1.
20 Figueres, Fundació Gala-Salvador Dalí. Reproduced in Dawn Ades, *Dalí: A Centenary Retrospective*, exh. cat., London, 2005, p.176.
21 Alex. Reid & Lefevre Gallery, *Salvador Dali*, June-July 1936, cat. no.11. Within Surrealism, the juxtaposition of desired female flesh and meat subsequently found its most extreme and outrageous expression in André Masson's *Gradiva* of 1939.
22 For Spencer's subsequent, overtly sexual work, London 2001, pp.158–75.
23 D.H. Lawrence, *Pornography and So On*, London, 1936, pp.26, 28, and 102.
24 The picture is reproduced alongside Nemser's commentary on its making in New York 2000, p.69.
25 http://homepage.mac.com/jsemmel/PhotoAlbum2.html.
26 Andrew Brighton, 'Introduction', *David Hockney Prints 1954–77*, The Midland Group/Scottish Arts Council, 1977, n.p.
27 The former group includes *Annie and Alice* (1975), and *Pluto and the Bateman Sisters* (1995–6); the later *Large Interior W9* (1973), *Naked Man with his Friend* (1978–80), and *Painter and Model* (1986–7).
28 Information from Scottish National Gallery of Modern Art curatorial files.
29 For this and the following quotations, see Goldin 1986, pp.7–8.
30 See Karabelnik 2004.
31 Nixon 2003.
32 Thomas Koerfer, 'As if in a Mirror. The influence of the cinema on the depiction of the body in contemporary art', in Karabelnik 2004, pp.91–2.
33 Carlo McCormick, 'talking pictures' (interview with Tillmans), http://www.artnet.com/magazine_pre2000/features/mccormick/mccormick11-25-98.asp.
34 Violette and Obrist 1997, p.290.
35 Ibid., p.250.
36 Ibid., p.229.
37 School of Fontainebleau, *Gabrielle D'Estrées and One of Her Sisters*, early sixteenth century, Louvre, Paris. A detail of this prototype featured on the cover of Theodore Zeldin's *An Intimate History of Humanity*, London, 1995 (paperback edition).

Chapter 5

1 Freud 1962, p.71.
2 See Arthur Danto, *Playing with the Edge*, Berkeley, Los Angeles and London, 1996, pp.59–69.
3 Nixon 2003, p.86.
4 Carlos Gollonet, 'Foreword', ibid., p.10.
5 Ibid., p.15.
6 Mann 1991, n.p.
7 Joanna Bourke, *Fear: A Cultural History*, London, 2005, p.327.
8 Janet Malcolm, 'The Family of Mann', *Diana & Nikon*, New York, 1997, p.173.
9 Mann 1991, n.p.
10 Townsend 1998, p.16.
11 Matt Seaton, 'The myth of childhood innocence', *The Guardian*, London, Special Report: Child Protection, Tuesday 13 March, 2001. See also Sarah Edge and Gail Baylis, 'Photographing Children: the Works of Tierney Gearon and Sally Mann', *Visual Culture in Britain* (Manchester), vol.5, issue no.1, summer 2005, pp.75–90.
12 Seaton (see note 11).
13 Polly Toynbee, 'The Voyeurs have won', ibid.
14 Cited in London 2002, p.35.
15 Ibid.
16 Cited in Townsend 1998, p.103.
17 Ibid., p.102.
18 Cited in Val Williams, 'Melanie Manchot', *look at you loving me. Bilder meiner Mutter von 1995–1998*, Basel, 1998, n.p.
19 See London 2004 and Helen Chadwick, *Enfleshings*, New York, 1989, pp.74–83.
20 'Introduction', Carucci 2003, p.11.
21 Ibid., p.9.
22 Ibid., p.10.
23 The works were first shown at the Yossi Milo Gallery, New York, October-November 2006.

Chapter 6

1 London 2001, p.200.
2 Duncan Thomson, *Arikha*, London, 1994, p.141.
3 'The Artist out of Cage', *The Observer Review*, no.10496, 6 December 1992, pp.45–6.
4 Thomson, p.222 (see note 2).
5 Andrew Graham-Dixon, 'Portrait of the tyrant as an old man', *The Independent*, London, 14 September 1993, p.22.
6 Arthur Danto, 'Lucien [*sic*] Freud', *The Madonna of the Future*, New York, 2000, pp.37–8.
7 Linda Nochlin, 'Flesh for Phantasy', *Art Forum*, March 1994, p.58.
8 Max Kozloff, 'The Self-portrait: the Conflict between Self-representation and Self-exposure', in *Missing Link, The Image of Man in Contemporary Photography* (ed.) Christoph Doswald, Zurich, New York, 2000, p.51.
9 See Warr 2000.
10 Willoughby Sharp, 'Body Works ...' (1970), reprinted in Warr 2000, p.231.
11 This is W.J.T. Mitchell's reading in 'Wall Labels: Word, Image, and Object in the Work of Robert Morris', in *Robert Morris: The Mind/Body Problem*, exh. cat., Solomon R. Guggenheim Museum, New York, 1994, pp.72–3.
12 See Amelia Jones, *Body Art: Performing the Subject*, Minneapolis / London, 1998, pp.215–20.
13 On Koons see David Hopkins, *Dada's Boys*, exh. cat., Fruitmarket Gallery, Edinburgh, 2006, pp.39–45.
14 Ibid.
15 Marla Prather, *Unrepentant Ego: The Self-portraits of Lucas Samaras*, exh. cat., Whitney Museum of American Art, New York, 2003.
16 Ibid., pp.210–20.
17 *A Self-portrait: John Coplans 1984–97*, exh. cat., P.S.I. Contemporary Art Centre, New York, 1997, p.138.
18 Stuart Morgan (ed.), *Provocations: Writings by John Coplans*, London, p.227.
19 David Anfam, *Abstract Expressionism*, London, 1990, p.156.
20 *A Self-portrait*, p.138 (see note 17).
21 Coplans 2002, p.7.
22 Ibid.
23 Boris Mikhailov with Alla Efimova, 'Feeling Around', in Diane Neumaier (ed.), *Beyond Memory: Soviet Nonconformist Photography and Photo-Related Works of Art*, exh. cat., The Jane Voorhees Zimmerli Art Museum / Rutgers University Press, 2004, p.273.
24 Steven Tynan, *Underpants*, Cornwall, 2001; Steven Tynan, *Astronaut*, Cornwall, 2003.

Chapter 7

1 Berger 1972, chapters 2 and 3. Lisa Tickner's phrase 'The Old Master / *Playboy* tradition' appeared in 'The Body Politic: Female Sexuality and Women Artists since 1970', her controversial 1978 article in *Art History*, as cited in Nead 1992, p.64.
2 Nead 1992, p.60.
3 Boston Women's Health Book Collective, *Our Bodies, Ourselves*, New York, 1973.
4 Nead 1992, p.61.
5 Frances Fowle, 'Cecile Walton's *Romance*', *Women's Art Journal*, fall 2002 / winter 2003, p.10.
6 Ibid., p.13.
7 See Joanna Frueh, 'The Body through Women's Eyes', Broude 1994, pp.190–207.
8 Cited in Nead 1992, p.67.
9 See Chris Townsend, 'Scattered in Time and Space', Woodman 2006, pp.28–37 ('Woodman and Surrealism').
10 Townsend, 'Scattered in Time and Space', ibid., p.60.
11 Betsy Berne, 'To Tell the Truth', Woodman 2006, ibid., p.247.
12 The richest attempt to contextualise her work is now Townsend, 'Scattered in Time and Space', ibid.
13 Jo Spence, 'Identity and Cultural Production', Spence 1995, p.134.
14 Ibid., pp.134–5.
15 Ibid., p.135.
16 Nead 1992, p.81.
17 'A Mirror to Yourself: Helen Chadwick interviewed by Tom Evans (June 1986)', reprinted in David Brittain (ed.), *Creative Camera: 30 Years of Writing*, Manchester, 1999, p.149.
18 Cited by Eva Martischnig in ' *My Personal Museum': Ego Geometria Sum from the Helen Chadwick archive*, exh. cat., Henry Moore Institute, Leeds, 2004.
19 London 2004, pp.36 and 18.
20 'Daughters of Eve' (Joyce Gunn-Cairns interviewed by Julie Lawson), in Joyce Gunn-Cairns, *Daughters of Eve*, exh. cat., Highland Council, 2004, pp.1–2.
21 Cited in Frank Whitford, 'Totally Lucy Jones', in Kirby 2006, p.90.
22 Susie Orbach, *Fat is a Feminist Issue*, London, 1979.
23 Reprinted Saville 2005.
24 The comparison was made, to Saville's detriment, in Alison Rowley, 'On Viewing Three Paintings by Jenny Saville: Rethinking a Feminist Practice of Painting', in Griselda Pollock, *Generations and Geographies in the Visual Arts*, London, 1996, pp.88–109. On the Glasgow showing, see Spence, 'Identity and Cultural Production' in Spence 1995, p.134.
25 Collection Scottish National Gallery of Modern Art, Edinburgh.
26 Illustrated Neal Brown, *Tracey Emin*, London, p.97 (subsequently destroyed in the Momart fire 2003).

27 For a general account of Lucas's Dadaist roots, see David Hopkins, *Dada's Boys*, exh. cat., Fruitmarket Gallery, Edinburgh, 2006, pp.58–61.
28 Jane Fletcher, 'Sweet Liberties: Narratives of Resistance and Desire', *Masquerade*, 2003, p.49.
29 Ibid., p.50.
30 See David Burrows (ed.), *Jemima Stehli*, Birmingham 2002; Fletcher, p.50 (see note 28).
31 Conversation with the author, November 2006.
32 Communication with the author, March 2007.

Chapter 8

1 Jan Avigdos, 'Some other place than here', Grannan 2005, n.p.
2 The reading of Arbus's work as voyeuristic was famously launched in Susan Sontag, *On Photography*, New York and London, 1977.
3 Reproduced in London 2003, pp.34–5, 66, 98, 231, 235, 260 and 286.
4 On Arbus's interest in Sanders, see London 2003, pp.56–7, 148 and 162; Anthony W. Lee and John Pultz, *Diane Arbus : Family Albums*, New Haven and London, 2003, pp.43–50. From the same period and culture as Sander, Christian Schad's painting *Agosta, the Pigeon-Chested Man, and Rasha, the Black Dove* (1929) foreshadows Arbus's fascination with fairground performers, and life at the margins (on loan to Tate, London).
5 London 2003, p.167.
6 A print, along with another nudist camp picture, was one of seven acquired in 1964 by the Museum of Modern Art, New York, her first works to enter a museum collection. She later included the work in her 1970–1 portfolio of ten photographs, six of which, including *Retired man and his wife*, were reproduced in *Artforum* magazine in May 1971, a couple of months before Arbus died.
7 Facsimile of 1966 typescript in Doon Arbus and Marvin Israel (eds.), *Diane Arbus: Magazine Work*, New York, 1984, pp.68–9.
8 The obvious equivalent is *A young waitress at a nudist camp, N.J.* (1963), reproduced in London 2003, p.72.
9 *Diane Arbus: An Aperture Monograph*, New York, 1972, pp.2–3.
10 Ibid., pp.1–2.
11 Ibid., p.2.
12 Ibid., p.1.
13 Compare *Lady in a rooming house parlor, Albion, N.Y.* (1963), London 2003, p.106.
14 Ibid., pp.102 and 167.
15 Ibid., p.44.
16 Ibid., p.159. 'The Full Circle' appeared in *Harper's Bazaar*.
17 Richard Avedon, *In the American West*, London, 1985.
18 Richard Bolton, 'In the American East: Richard Avedon Incorporated', in Richard Bolton (ed.), *The Contest of Meaning: Critical Histories of Photography*, Cambridge, Mass., 1989, pp.261–83.
19 Laura Wilson, *Avedon at Work in the American West*, Austin, 2003, p.47.
20 Ibid., p.47.
21 'Interview', in *Rineke Dijkstra. Portraits.* 1991, pp.74–5.
22 Ibid., p.79.
23 Ibid., pp.79–80.
24 Ibid., p.76.
25 Mikhailov 1999.
26 Boris Mikhailov and Alla Efimova, 'Feeling Around' (interview), Diane Neumaier (ed.), *Beyond Memory. Soviet Nonconformist Photography and Photo-Related Works of Art*, exh. cat., Jane Vorhees Zimmerli Art Museum and Rutgers University Press, 2004, p.268.
27 Ibid., p.275.
28 Ibid., p.275.
29 Inka Schube, 'Working Images: The Theatre of Bodies in Boris Mikhailov's Work', in Urs Stahel (ed.), *Boris Mikhailov: A Retrospective*, exh. cat., Fotomuseum, Winterthur, pp.156–7.
30 See Mark Durden, 'Degraded Realities: Boris Mikhailov's Case Histories', *Portfolio* 33, 2001, pp.54–5.
31 Mikhailov 1999, p.6.
32 Ibid., p.9.
33 Anne von der Heiden, 'Consumatum Est: "Case History" by Boris Mikhailov', in Stahel, pp.170–1 (see note 29).
34 Mikhailov 1999, pp.421 and 434.
35 Ibid., p.128.
36 Ibid., p.9.
37 Ibid., pp.6–7.
38 Ibid., p.9.
39 www.marcquinn.com.
40 Exhibited White Cube Gallery, London, March – April 2005.
41 Desmond Morris, 'Introduction', in Bailey 2005, n.p.
42 Cited in Melissa Denes. 'Our Little Secret', *The Guardian Weekend*, 5 November 2005, p.37.
43 Avigdos, 'Some other place than here', n.p.
44 Denes, p.38 (see note 42).
45 http://www.culturecatch.com/art/philip-lorca_dicorcia.
46 Exhibited at Fred, London, March-May 2006.
47 Melanie Manchot, 'An Elongated Moment: A Conversation between Melanie Manchot and John Slyce', *Moscow Girls*, exh. cat., Haus am Waldsee, Berlin, 2006, n.p.
48 Ibid.

Chapter 9

1 Schneider 2005, n.p. (end page).
2 'Counting light. Photographs by Gary Schneider' (interview by Lynne Tillman), *Aperture*, New York, p.39.
3 'Gary Schneider in Conversation', in Deborah Martin Kao, *Gary Schneider Portraits*, New Haven and London, 2004, pp.108–9.
4 Ibid., p.107.
5 Ibid., p.113.
6 'Counting light', pp.34 and 38 (see note 2).
7 See Guignon 2004.
8 Artist's statement, as provided to the author, January 2007.

Chapter 10

1 On the classical precedents, see Christopher Hallett, *The Roman Nude: Heroic Portrait Statuary 200 BC – 300 AD*, Oxford, 2005.
2 Apsley House, London.
3 Sir Joshua Reynolds, *Discourses on Art*, New Haven and London, 1975, p.128.
4 Ibid.
5 http://www.vam.ac.uk/collections/photography/past_exhns/seeing/modern_icon/.
6 David Alan Mellor, 'Scandalous Bodies', *Art & the 60s: This was Tomorrow*, exh. cat., Tate, London, 2004, p.78.
7 Barcan 2004, p.242.
8 Tom Wolfe, 'Introduction', *Annie Leibovitz Photographs*, New York, 1983, n.p.
9 *Photographs by Lord Snowdon*, exh. cat., National Portrait Gallery, London, 2000, p.213.
10 Lisa O'Malley, 'Does my Bump Look Like This: Visualising the Pregnant Body', *Advertising and Society Review*, 2006 (http://muse.jhu.edu/journals/asr/v007/7.3omalley.html). See also Imogen Tyler, 'Skin-Tight: Celebrity, Pregnancy, and Subjectivity', Sara Ahmed and Jackie Stacey (eds.), *Thinking Through the Skin*, New York, 2001, pp.69–85.
11 Leibovitz 2006.
12 'Who are you calling a feminist', *Observer Woman*, April 2006 (no. 4), p.30.
13 Linda Nochlin, 'When the Stars Weep', Sam Taylor-Wood, *Crying Men*, London, 2004, n.p.
14 Ibid.
15 Ibid.

Copyright Credits

1 © Alistair Morrison; **2, 96** © Joan Semmel 1977; **4** © ADAGP, Paris and DACS, London 2007; **5, 63, 145** © The Artist (London); **6** © Jonathan Yeo; **8, 78, 98** © the Estate of the Artist; **9, 68, 98** © Estate of Alice Neel, 1980; **10, 17, 18** © Robert Mappelthorpe Foundation. Used with Permission; **11** Courtesy Maureen Paley, London; **12** © The Peter Hujar Archive, courtesy Matthew Marks Gallery, New York; **14, 59, 60** © Estate of Francis Bacon / DACS 2007; **15** © Estate of Duncan Grant / Licensed by DACS 2007; **16** © Estate of Vanessa Bell, Courtesy Henrietta Garnett; **19, 121** © 2007 The Richard Avedon Foundation; **21** © ADAGP, Paris and DACS, London 2007; **22** © Estate of Roger Hilton / DACS 2007; **23, 24, 70, 88** © Lucian Freud; **25** © Paula Moderson-Becker Museum Bremen; **28** © Ingleborg & Dr Wolfgang Henze-Ketterer, Wichtrach / Bern; **30** © Munch Museum / Munch - Ellingson Group, BONO, Oslo / DACS, London 2007; **31, 45** © Succession Picasso / DACS 2007; **33, 65** © DACS 2007; **36** © ARS, NY and DACS, London 2007; **38, 39** © Georgia O'Keefe Museum / DACS 2007; **40** © the artist's estate; **41, 43, 67** © Estate of Stanley Spencer / DACS 2007; **42** © Estate of Hilda Carline / DACS 2007; **44** © The Artist's Family; **46, 47, 64, 86** © ADAGP, Paris and DACS, London 2007; **48** © Man Ray Trust / ADAGP, Paris and DACS, London 2007.; **49, 150** Copyright The Estate of Harry M. Callahan Courtesy Pace / MacGill Gallery New York; **50** © ADAGP, Paris and DACS, London 2007; **51** © Southampton City Art Gallery, Hampshire, UK / The Bridgeman Art Library; **52** © David Hockney; **53** © Gerhard Richter; **54–6** © Emmet and Edith Gowin; **57, 58, 71–3** Courtesy Nan Goldin and Matthew Marks Gallery, New York; **61** © Seiichi Furuya; **62** Courtesy Maureen Paley, London; **66** © Christian Schad Stiftung Aschaffenburg / VG Bild-Kunst, Bonn and DACS, London 2007; **67** © Estate of Stanley Spencer / DACS 2007; **69** © David Hockney; **74, 83** © Elinor Carucci Courtesy Edwynn Houk Gallery, New York; **75** © Gilbert & George; **76, 82, 84, 131** © The Artist courtesy of Fred (London) Ltd.; **77** © Tierney Gearon, Courtesy Yossi Milo Gallery, NYC; **79, 80** © David Williams; **81** © **1981** Center for Creative Photography, Arizona Board of Regents; **85, 93** The John Coplans Trust; **87** © Avigdor Arikha; **89** © the Artist's Estate, Courtesy of James Hyman Fine Art, London; **90** © Francesco Clemente; **91** © Ken Currie; **92** © ARS, NY and DACS, London 2007; **93** The John Coplans Trust; **94, 95** © Steven Tynan; **97** © The family of the artist; **99** © DACS, London / VAGA, New York 2007; **100, 101** © George and Betty Woodman; **102–4** Jo Spence in Collaboration with Dr Tim Sheard, Copyright Jo Spence Memorial Archive London; **105–7** The Helen Chadwick Estate; **108** © Alexa Wright; **109** © Joyce Gunn-Cairns; **110** © Lucy Jones, Courtesy Flowers; **111** Image courtesy of Gagosian Gallery. © Jenny Saville and Glen Luchford.; **112–14** © The Artist, courtesy Jay Jopling / White Cube (London); **115** Copyright the Artist; courtesy Sadie Coles HQ, London; **116, 117** © The Artist, courtesy Lisson Gallery, London; **118** © the artist; **119, 120** © the Estate of Diane Arbus; **122–4** © the Artist; **125–7** © Boris Mikhailov, 2007; **128** Courtesy Jay Jopling / White Cube (London); **129, 130** © Philip-Lorca deCorcia; **132–6** © Courtesy the artist; **137** © Catriona Grant; **138, 140** © 1962 Bert Stern; **139** © Peter Howson, Collection Mr & Mrs Matthew Flowers; **142–4** © Lewis Morley Archive / National Portrait Gallery, London; **146** © Annie Leibovitz (Contact PressImages), courtesy of the artist; **147** © courtesy the artist and Jay Jopling / White Cube, London; **148** © Nicholas Nixon, Courtesy Yossi Milo Gallery, NYC; cover © 2007 The Richard Avedon Foundation.

Photo Credits

4 RMN © Jacques Faujour; **8** © Geoffrey Clements Photography; **9** © Miki Slingsby Fine Art Photography; **22, 26, 37, 41, 42, 69, 91, 93, 100, 101, 109, 112, 113, 115, 146** © Antonia Reeve Photography; **24** © British Council, London, UK / The Bridgeman Art Library; **27** © Private Collection / Giraudon / The Bridgeman Art Library; **29** © Oto Palan; **30** © Munch Museum (Andersen / de Jong); **31** RMN © Rene-Gabriel Ojeda; **43** R & R Summer 1991; **44, 47** © John Webb; **46** © Sheffield Galleries and Museums Trust, UK / The Bridgeman Art Library; **49** RMN © Adam Rzepka; **51** © Southampton City Art Gallery, Hampshire, UK / The Bridgeman Art Library; **64** RMN © Gerard Blot; **65** © 2007 Museum of Fine Arts, Boston; **67** © Fitzwilliam Museum, University of Cambridge, UK / The Bridgeman Art Library; **86** RMN © Jacques Faujour; **97** © Jack Mackenzie AIC Photography; **121** Photograph Richard Avedon. Courtesy The Richard Avedon Foundation; **128** Photo: Attilio Maranzano

Every effort has been made to contact the copyright holders of the material in this book. If any rights have been omitted, the publisher offers their apologies and will rectify this in any following edition following notification.

Index

Page numbers in **bold** refer to images; names in *italics* indicate people appearing solely as sitters

aging 79, 83, 84, 101
Agnew, Lady, of Lochnaw **32**
Arbus, Diane **108**, **111**; 109–12
Arikha, Avigdor **84**; 83
Avedon, Richard **21**, **113**; 17, 19, 112–14, 116, 129–30

babies 75–9
Bacon, Francis **19**, **59**, **60**; 17, 59–60
Bailey, David **13**, **64**; 12, 24, 118, 133
Balthus **22**; 18, 20, 22
Bamgboye, Odalebe **144**; 71
Beckham, David 12, 137
Bell, Vanessa **20**; 18
Birkin, Jane **133**; 133
Bomberg, David **47**; 45, 47
Bomberg, Lilian **47**; 45, 47
Bonnard, Pierre **48**, **49**, **65**, **84**; 18, 47–50, 63, 65, 83
Boursin, Marthe 48–50
Bowery, Leigh 26, 28
Bratby, John **53**; 54
Brown, Don 41
Burchill, Brian **70**; 56, 59, 71
bust portraits 18, 83, 89

Callahan, Eleanor **51**, **146**; 52
Callahan, Harry **51**, **146**; 52
Carline, Hilda **45**; 44
Carucci, Elinor **71**, **80**; 71, 81
celebrities 129–37
Chadwick, Helen **98**, **99**, **100**; 81, 98–100
children 75–9
Christie, Linford **6**; 129
Clemente, Francesco **86**; 86
Cook, Angus **69**; 68
Coplans, John **82**, **89**; 14, 89, 90–1
Corinth, Lovis **33**; 32, 33
Currie, Ken **87**; 86

Dalí, Gala 50–2
Dalí, Salvador 50–2, 67
diCorcia, Philip-Lorca **120**; 118, 121
Dijkstra, Rineke **114–15**; 12, 114–15
disabled people 12, 101, 102, 117
Downey, Robert, jr 137
Dürer, Albrecht 35
Dyer, George 59–60

Emin, Tracey **104**; 12, 102, 105
Everage, Dame Edna **132**; 133

family 75–81
feminism 91, 93, 94, 96, 100
Fischer, Ronald **113**; 112
Freud, Lucian **25**, **27**, **69**, **84**; 11, 12, 26–9, 54, 68, 79, 83–4
Freud, Sigmund 32, 38, 39, 41, 63, 67, 75
Frost, Sir David **132**; 133
Furuya, Seiichi **61**; 60
Furuya, Christine née Gössler **61**; 60

Garnett, David **20**; 18
Gauguin, Paul **32**; 31
gay sexuality 17, 44, 55, 68, 88–9, 129
Gearon, Tierney **74**; 77, 79, 81
Gerstl, Richard **34**; 34
Giacometti, Alberto **52**; 54
Giacometti, Annette **52**; 54
Gilbert & George **72**; 24, 71–3, 89
Goldin, Nan **58**, **70**; 56, 59, 68, 71
Gowin, Emmet **57**; 56
Grannan, Katy 12, 118
Grant, Catriona **127**; 127
Grant, Duncan **20**; 18
Greer, Germaine 137
Gunn-Cairns, Joyce **101**; 100–1

Haas, Ernst **131**
Harris, Lyle Ashton 89
Heckel, Erich 31
Hilton, Roger **22**; 20, 22
Hockney, David **54**, **68**; 54, 55–6, 68, 89
Hoffman, Dustin **136**; 137
homosexuality 16, 17, 44, 55, 68, 88–9, 129
Howson, Peter **130**; 129
Hujar, Peter **18**; 17
Humphries, Barry **132**; 133

interiority 23–4

Jones, Lucy **101**; 100–1

Kahlo, Frida 93
Keeler, Christine **132**; 130
Kirchner, Ernst Ludwig **32**; 31
Klein, Yves **12**; 12
Klimt, Gustav 35
Kokoschka, Oskar **35**, **65**; 35, 65
Koons, Jeff 89
Kossoff, Leon **16**, **68**; 16, 68

La Chapelle, David 134
Lacy, Peter 59
Lapper, Alison 12, 117–18
Lawrence, D.H. 63, 67
Leibovitz, Annie **135**; 134, 137
Lennon, John **135**; 134
Liddell, Siobhan **58**, **70**; 56, 59
Long, Catherine **119**; 117
Love, Bob **17**; 17
Lucas, Sarah **105**; 102, 106
Luchford, Glen 102

Madonna **130**
Mahler, Alma 65
Man Ray **50**; 18, 50
Manchot, Melanie **73**, **79**, **81**; 73, 79–81, 121
Mann, Sally 75–7
Mapplethorpe, Robert **17**, **18**, **21**; 17, 18, 75, 89
Massow, Ivan **14**; 14
Medley, Robert **85**; 83
Mikhailov, Boris **117**; 91, 115–17
Miller, Lee **50**
Modersohn-Becker, Paula **30**; 33, 34, 93
Monroe, Marilyn **128**, **130**; 129
Moore, Demi 134
Morley, Lewis 130, 132–3
Morris, Edith **57**; 56
Morris, Robert **88**; 88
Moulene, Jean-Luc 121
Munch, Edvard **33**; 31, 32–3, 63, 65

naked portraiture 11–12
  viewer's response to 11, 14, 18, 23, 73, 109
nakedness versus nudity 22, 24
Neel, Alice **16**, **76**, **95**; 16, 67, 75, 93–4
Newton, Helmut 134
Nixon, Nicholas **138**; 71, 75–6

O'Keefe, Georgia **40**, **43**; 41–4
older people 79–81, 83, 84
Ono, Yoko **135**; 134
Osen, Erwin Van **10**, **15**; 16

Paul, Celia **27**; 28, 54
Perreault, John **16**; 16
Picasso, Pablo **35**, **48**; 18, 33–4, 47
portraiture
definition 11, 12, 14, 20, 22
double 63–73
serial 97–100, 101, 106, 114–15, 118
  see also naked portraiture; self-portraiture
Preece, Patricia **46**, **66**; 44–5, 66–7

Quinn, Marc **21**, **119**; 12, 18, 117

Rampling, Charlotte 134
Rembrandt **42**; 41
Richter, Gerhard **55**; 54–5
Rivers, Larry 14
Robinson, Sugar Ray **131**; 129
Rodin, Auguste 31, 63
Rubens, Peter Paul 41, 43

Samaras, Lucas 89
Sargent, John Singer **32**; 31
Saville, Jenny **103**; 12, 102
Schad, Christian **66**; 65–6
Schiele, Egon **10**, **15**, **36–7**; 12, 16, 26, 35–9, 65
Schlesinger, Peter **54**; 55–6
Schneider, Gary **122**, **124–5**; 123–7
Selby, Belinda **13**
self-portraiture 12, 18, 32–3, 34–5, 38–9
  female 93–107
  male 83–91
surrogate 52
Semmel, Joan **8**, **92**; 67–8, 94
sexuality 26, 32, 41, 47–8, 75
Smith, Patti **18**; 17
Snowdon, Lord 134
Spence, Jo **98**; 97–8
Spencer, Stanley **45**, **46**, **66**; 44–5, 66–7, 83
Stehli, Jemima **106**; 106–7
Stern, Bert **128**, **130**; 129
Stieglitz, Alfred **40**, **43**; 14, 41–4
Surrealism 50, 67, 96

Taylor-Wood, Sam **136**; 11–12, 137
Tilley, Sue 26, 28
Tillmans, Wolfgang **17**, **62**; 12, 17, 71
Tison, Frédérique 18, 20
Tynan, Steven **90**; 91

Walter, Marie-Thérèse 18, 47
Walton, Cecile **94**; 93
Ward, Denise and Andrew **64**
Watt, Alison **107**; 107
Weston, Edward **78**; 75
Wilke, Hannah **96**; 94
Williams, David **76**, **77**; 75
Wood, Christopher **44**; 44
Woodman, Francesca **97**; 12, 96
Wright, Alexa **100**; 101–2
Wynn-Evans, Cerith **69**; 68

Yeo, Jonathan **14**

Zych, Anthony 17